Fathers and Anglicans

To the memory of Tom and Eliza Middleton, my late parents, who handed on to me the *paradosis*

Fathers and Anglicans

The Limits of Orthodoxy

Arthur Middleton

Gracewing.

First published in 2001

Gracewing
2 Southern Avenue, Leominster
Herefordshire HR6 0QF

ISBN 0 85244 450 8

Front Cover:
The drawings of John Keble and of John Henry Newman, by George Richmond, are repro-duced by courtesy of the National Portrait Gallery, London. The painting of Daniel Waterland is reproduced by kind permission of the Master and Fellows of Magdalene College, Cambridge.

Typesetting by Action Publishing Technology Ltd., Gloucester, GL1 5SR

Printed by MPG Books Ltd., Bodmin PL31 1EG

Contents

Acknowledgements

The author expresses his thanks to the staff of the University and Cathedral Libraries in Durham and to the staff of the Bodleian Library in Oxford for their kindness and help in enabling the author to find the various resources necessary to this research. He also thanks St Chad's College Durham for the use of its resources. The author is immensely grateful to the Very Reverend Dr George Dragas, Archpriest and Proto-Presbyter of the Greek Orthodox Church at Holy Cross Greek School of Theology in Boston, Massachusetts, for his inspiration and guidance over many years. He also thanks numerous friends and audiences to whom he has spoken over the years as this work has been in preparation. The author is most grateful to Jill Pinnock for reading the manuscript and for her editorial comments, suggestions and corrections. He also thanks Gracewing for their support, especially Jo Ashworth for her encouragement and assistance.

Foreword

In a world where the economy is global and where communication flows through a worldwide web, Christians are searching with renewed urgency for a way in which they can fulfill Jesus Christ's desire for a united universal church.

Christian unity of the kind envisaged by Jesus Christ in the Gospel of St John is much more than a merger of ecclesiastical institutions, although it is naïve to suppose that it will be achieved without an appropriate institutional framework. We are invited to grow into the full stature of Christ in a culture of mutual love. As we seek to love our Christian neighbours and those who have gone before us in obedience to the gospel, love of our own church and her own insights into the living reality of Christ in every age is a vital ingredient in becoming mature in love. Jesus Christ invites us to a marriage in the coming Great Church not a reversion into some undifferentiated primal soup. Partners to a marriage need to bring self-understanding and the self-respect which is the basis for the confidence needed to make a gift of ourselves to the other.

It seems to me that Anglican self-understanding and self-respect is at a low ebb. We experience our share of a general cultural confusion and babel. Without some clarity, however, we shall not be able to contribute our best to the global Christian unity which is to come.

Fathers and Anglicans helps us to re-appropriate a vital part of the Anglican approach to the living reality of Christ. This book deals with the very great significance attached by classical Anglican divines to developing a 'patristic mind' which is neither afraid to reason nor ashamed to adore

We rightly place an emphasis on the need to proclaim Christian truth 'afresh' in each generation but it sometimes seems as if we have forgotten that if we are confined to our own point in space and time then our understanding of the gospel will be very provincial.

To make a rich response to the future we must develop a rich memory which enables us to detect what is merely passing fashion and puts us in touch with 'the dearest freshness deep down things'.

Memory and mission belong together. If there is simply consciousness of the exigencies of the passing moment, then even if there is some acquaintance with the isolated New Testament moment, it is doubtful whether our analysis of the contemporary situation will be very profound or our understanding of the witness of the New Testament really adequate. There will be too much temptation to read the Scriptures in the light of a somewhat superficial grasp of contemporary issues.

That is not to say that we need to import a load of learned lumber from the patristic muniment room or freight our sermons with copious citations from Theodore of Mopsuestia. Rather we need to recognise afresh the significance for the classical Anglican tradition of developing the 'patristic mind' which does not confuse witness to tradition with an arid traditionalism.

When we immerse ourselves in tradition we enter the living stream which unites the Church of all the ages and in which Christ is really present to his beloved. Traditionalism by contrast witnesses to the exhaustion of tradition and lacks the courage to go beyond repetition of previous formulations.

The theologians of the undivided Church of the first five centuries were faithful to scripture and showed a marked reluctance to go beyond its language to attempt definition in areas where there was little biblical guidance. Their approach to scripture was exegetical, historical and mystical rather than systematic. The Bible is itself witness to the living tradition of God's communication with human beings and is not to be reduced to any system of philosophical or ethical abstractions. But in seeking to illuminate the sacred text, the theologians of the Early Church were not content simply to repeat old formulations in the very different cultural circumstances in which they found themselves. To have developed a patristic approach is to have acquired through prayer and study of the Bible a capacity to discern the signs of the times and the freedom to use or discard the categories of contemporary discourse in the service of the gospel.

A good example is to be found in the work of the Cappadocian Fathers who discerned that Arianism was the most profound threat to New Testament understandings of Christ and to the Christ they encountered in prayer. In the struggle for orthodoxy they enlisted some resources from contemporary culture and in particular they selectively employed some of the highly developed categories of Neo-Platonic thought.

The appeal to the 'patristic mind' and a preference for their theological approach is characteristic of the English Reformation. Cranmer in the Preface to the First Book of Common Prayer, published 450 years ago, appeals to the authority of the 'auncient fathers' as a guide in liturgical matters. Queen Elizabeth I, in her letter to the Roman Catholic Princes of Europe, amplified the point 'that there was no new faith propagated in England, no new religion set up but that which was commanded by Our Saviour, practised by the Primitive Church and approved by the Fathers of the best antiquity'.

The questions which confronted the sixteenth century are not the ones which are most urgent for us. They were called to reflect on the later mediaeval developments of the papal monarchy and to consider the direction of scholastic theology and the domination of Aristotle in philosophy. In the comparatively short period of the crusades and Western European cultural isolation there had been some developments, which needed correction in the light of Scripture and church tradition, eastern and western. Many of the particular points at issue in the sixteenth century have been settled. The whole western church has a vernacular liturgy and since Vatican II a new vision of the whole people of God. The temporal power of the Pope has been reduced but the spiritual and evangelistic potential of the office has been demonstrated. There are still some questions that linger, such as the issue of whether clerical celibacy is obligatory. The Holy Paphnutius at the Council of Nicaea successfully argued that it was not obligatory but a special vocation, but this position still has to win universal acceptance.

Our questions are very different. How do we interpret the spiritual vitality of other faiths? How do we cope with the prevalent despair about the possibility of establishing any public truth in the sphere of faith and morals? As we seek the light of the gospel on these challenges the experience of the theologians of the undivided Church struggling to communicate the gospel in a pagan culture is fresh and relevant.

We are indebted to Fr Middleton for tracing the story of how Anglicans since the Reformation have sought to develop the 'patristic mind'. His book is a contribution to a loving understanding of why a twentieth-century seer like T. S. Eliot could find in Anglicanism 'a way of living and thinking the Christian tradition which had taken humanism and criticism into itself without being destroyed by them'.

More than that, however, this book gives us vignettes of attractive Christian lives like that of Lancelot Andrewes of whom the Church historian Thomas Fuller wrote, 'the fathers are not more faithfully cited in his books than lively copied out in his countenance and carriage'. The large number of our contemporaries who are serious in their spiritual search but sceptical about the possibility of there being resources to assist them in the Christian tradition can be converted by such lives. The most crucial patristic insight is that progress in theology is not made on the basis of mere erudition and intellect but in proportion to the spiritual development of the theologian. As Cranmer said, quoting Nazianzen, 'the fear of God must be the first beginning and as it were an ABC of an introduction to all them that shall enter to the very sure and most fruitful knowledge of Holy Scriptures'.

+ Richard Londin

Introduction

When I stand at the chancel step and face east to say the Nicene Creed in St Nicholas's Boldon, I gaze at two Byzantine mosaics, one of St Nicholas and the other of St George, on each side of the East window depicting Van Eyck's *Adoration of the Lamb*. It is a typical thirteenth century English chancel, built by Benedictine monks from Wearmouth and Jarrow. As we turn eastward and say those words proclaiming the Nicene faith, '*God of God, Light of Light, Very God of Very God, Begotten not made, Being of one substance with the Father. By whom all things were made. Who for us men and for our salvation came down from heaven; And was incarnate by the Holy Ghost of the Virgin Mary, And was made man*', one senses a convergence and harmony in these words and imagery of the Christian East and West. The architecture and history of continuous worship initiated by the Anglo-Saxons, continued by the Benedictines, with their roots in Cassian and the Desert Fathers, the mosaics and the Russian icons above the chantry altar, are not out of place and there is no clash of traditions. These associations from East and West do not represent an eccentric accommodation of Anglicanism to Eastern Orthodoxy, but illustrate how the many associations of Orthodox Christianity can live together and not look out of place.

Catholicity and Apostolicity

The scene before me as I celebrate the daily Liturgy of Eucharist and Office focuses in a tangible way a conviction that has guided my spiritual pilgrimage over twenty years. That conviction is that it is imperative for the Christian East and West to rediscover the fundamental synthesis of perspective that characterized the ancient, undivided Church, for which Lancelot Andrewes prayed.

This must be a crucial priority, not a pious hope, and a fundamental requirement if we are to be faithful to the Gospel. This vision is no idiosyncracy but is endemic to Anglicanism, and has been since the Reformation, because Protestantism in Anglicanism (unlike Anabaptism) was a quest for catholicity. For the Reformers, as for the Fathers, catholicity was a theological and historical concept before it was a geographical and statistical one. The essence of such catholicity lies in faithfulness to the gospel word and sacramental usage given to the Church by Christ through the apostles from the beginning, so that catholicity is a matter of apostolicity and apostolicity primarily a matter of doctrine. The Reformers are concerned with the restoration of catholic doctrine and institution, the re-establishment of biblical faith, which they were convinced had been preserved in the Fathers, who had, on the whole, been faithful expositors of it. Thus the catholic integrity of Anglicanism is patristic rather than papal. As E. Charles Miller Jr points out,

> The particular character of the Anglican settlement – with its interplay between Scripture, tradition, and reason, together with its constant, if sometimes clumsy, will, to profess only the faith of the undivided Church – has fostered a proximity with Orthodoxy which cannot be ignored. The history of Anglican thought abounds with examples of those who have seen in the East an uninterrupted expression of this same synthesis which became the peculiar gift of Anglicanism.[1]

H. A. Hodges and a western Orthodoxy

Forty years ago the philosopher and theologian H. A. Hodges wrote his essay on *Anglicanism and Orthodoxy* and expressed the conviction that Anglicanism is uniquely called to be the embodiment of Orthodoxy in the West. This was no naïve call for Anglicans to start wearing chimney-pot hats and grow beards. It was a daring cry for a judicious and explicit expression of an indigenous *Orthodoxy* in terms of the life and thought of western peoples,

> ... coming with all their western background, their western habits and traditions, into the circle of the Orthodox Faith. Then we should have an Orthodoxy which was really western because its memory was western – a memory of the Christian history of the West, not as the West now remembers it, but purged and set in perspective by the Orthodox Faith.[2]

He sees this enriching *Eastern Orthodoxy,* setting it free from its merely ethnic and parochial character by giving it a more universal and catholic perspective. It will be a matter not of reconstituting the western experience in a new and alien cosmetic, but of learning to possess the western inheritance in a new way, by discerning 'the vein of error in what we have hitherto found convincing, and to possess the whole in thankfulness and penitence'.[3] For Hodges this embodying of a western Orthodoxy is the vocation of Anglicanism. For me this is essential, if to make a theology means to make more and more truly one's own, by experience, the mystery of the relation of God to Man that has been traditionally lived by the Church. This is what we find in the theology of the Anglican divine Lancelot Andrewes. The Eastern Orthodox theologian Nicholas Lossky said that the originality of Andrewes consisted, not so much in innovation, as in enabling the whole era to grasp the genuine essence of the Christian message. This is consistent with how Hodges sees the possibility of embodying this western Orthodoxy. It requires a vigorous decision 'not to become identified with any special form of doctrine over and above that of the whole undivided Church, and not to let the Papal autocracy be replaced by an oligarchy of Biblical theologians and preachers of the Word.'[4] Anglicanism's concern is for a balanced synthesis between Scripture, tradition, and reason, a discovery of which for Hodges would be 'western Orthodoxy at last made visible'.[5]

For many Anglicans this balanced synthesis is not part of their experience. In the history of Anglicanism numerous divines have encountered in themselves the convergence of East and West, put succinctly by Lancelot Andrewes in his *Private Devotions* where he prays 'for the whole Church Catholic, Eastern, Western, our own'. Some have their doubts about the interaction of two streams of tradition that for centuries have developed in such seemingly different ways. The criticism often made is that Orthodoxy has not had to deal with the particular issues that have shaped and challenged western Christianity. While this evaluation may be correct, Miller points out that

> ... this gives the Orthodox a unique and potentially invaluable perspective on our western situation. Precisely because they speak objectively, from without, they may be able to offer evaluations and insights after which we in the West could only grope. To think that their vibrant tradition, shaped, as we must suppose, by the prompting of the Holy Spirit, is of little or no

use to the life and thought of western Christianity is an affront
to the Gospel dictum that 'they may all be one' (John 17: 11).[6]

The Crockford's Preface

The hysteria surrounding Gareth Bennett's *Crockford's Preface* in
1987 caused many to miss its most important point. In a section
entitled '*A Theology in Retreat*', he pinpointed the crisis within
Anglicanism as being fundamentally theological and stemming
from a deliberate rejection of this balanced synthesis.

> ... the most significant change is the decline of a distinctive
> Anglican theological method. In a magisterial study of the great
> divines of the seventeenth century: H. R. McAdoo (*The Spirit of
> Anglicanism*) identified this as giving attention to Scripture,
> Tradition and Reason to establish doctrine. The context of such
> theological study was the corporate life of the Church and the
> end was to deepen its spirituality and forward its mission. Such a
> view of theology still appears in official Anglican reports and in
> archiepiscopal addresses. But the last real exponent of classical
> Anglican divinity was Archbishop Michael Ramsey whose many
> scholarly studies represent a last stand before the citadel fell to
> the repeated assaults of a younger generation of academics. The
> essential characteristic of the new theologians lies in their
> unease in combining the role of theologian and churchman,
> and their wish to study both Scripture and the patristic age
> without reference to the apologetic patterns of later Christianity
> ... Such a distancing of the modern Church from what had been
> regarded as its prescriptive sources clearly has serious conse-
> quences for Anglican ecclesiology, and this has been helpfully
> set out in Mr J. L. Houlden's book *Connections* (1986). Here he
> quite specifically rejects the notion of 'living in a tradition'. It
> would seem that modern man must live amid the ruins of past
> doctrinal and ecclesiastical systems, looking to the Scriptures
> only for themes and apprehensions which may inform his indi-
> vidual exploration of the mystery of God.[7]

Schmemann and *a return to the Fathers*

In 1961 Alexander Schmemann wrote an article entitled 'Theology
and Eucharist'. His concern was to expound a way in which

Orthodox theology could overcome its inner weakness and deficiencies by *a return to the Fathers*. He did not mean a mere repetition
of what the Fathers had said, nor the transforming of them into a
purely 'formal and infallible authority, and theology into a patristic scholasticism'. That would be 'a betrayal of the very spirit of
patristic theology'. He explains that a *return to the Fathers* means
above all 'the recovery of their spirit, of the secret inspiration
which made them true witnesses of the Church'.[8] It is not merely a
return to texts, abstract tradition, formulas and propositions. The
Russian Orthodox theologian Georges Florovsky is making the
same point when he says that our contemporary appeal to the
Fathers is much more than a historical reference to the past, but is
an appeal to the *mind of the Fathers*, and to follow them means to
acquire their mind. We return to the Fathers

> when we recover and make ours the experience of the Church
> not as mere 'Institution, doctrine or system' ... but as the all-
> embracing, all-assuming and all-transforming *life*, the passage
> into the reality of redemption and transfiguration. This experi-
> ence ... is centred in the Eucharist, the Sacrament of the
> Church, the very manifestation and self-revelation of the
> Church. The Eucharist, whether it is expressly referred to or
> not, is the organic source and necessary ' term of reference' of
> theology. If theology is bearing witness to the faith and life of
> the Church, to the Church as salvation and new life in Christ, it
> bears witness primarily to the experience of the Church mani-
> fested, communicated and actualized in the Eucharist. It is in
> the Eucharist that the Church ceases to be 'institution, doctrine,
> system' and becomes Life, Vision, Salvation; it is in the Eucharist
> that the Word of God is fulfilled and the human mind made
> capable of expressing the mind of Christ. Here then is the
> source of theology, of *words about God*, 'the event' which trans-
> forms our human speculation into a message of Divine Truth.[9]

Bennett and Schmemann agree

In principle Bennett and Schmemann agree on the need to return
to prescriptive sources, and in seeing the corporate worship of the
Church as the context of Christian thinking, the source of theology, where theology and experience, intellect and intuition,
thinking and praying are kept together. Anglicanism has always
sought to keep them together from Reformers and Carolines to

the Oxford Fathers, Butler, Maurice, Temple, and one could cite
many other names. Their concern was for an ideal of theology that
was not divorced from prayer and liturgy, for a way of life and
worship informed and structured by theological vision. We have a
patristic theology when we rediscover the eucharistic character of
the Church's life, in which we experience the Church as 'the
passage into the reality of redemption and transfiguration', a
patristic perspective in which the Eucharist generates the Church's
life and informs all aspects of her life. As the theology of
Athanasius cannot be understood apart from the liturgy of Bishop
Serapion, so the theology of the Reformers and Carolines must
find its origin and explanation in the Book of Common Prayer.
Such an approach is not alien to Anglicans, for the *appeal to the
Fathers* has been a seminal feature of the Anglican theological tradition since the sixteenth century. Similarly the appeal for a more
eucharistic theology in the broadest sense chimes in with the
Anglican insistence upon the interaction of theology and worship.
The rediscovery of the Eucharist within Anglicanism as a consequence of the Catholic Revival and the Liturgical Movement, has
been inspired by *a return to the Fathers*. This offers us a unique
opportunity to recover in a balanced synthesis these dynamics of
our tradition, a truly vibrant Christianity that is patristic in spirit
and orthodox in belief and practice.

Here are the seeds of a *western Orthodoxy* as envisaged by
Hodges. Anglicanism is unique in Christendom in having the
potential that could embody such an orthodoxy of faith and practice within a western context. Here we would find important
insights for understanding aspects of our Anglican tradition that
have been forgotten or misunderstood, in the same way that the
Oxford Fathers enabled us to recover forgotten aspects of our
tradition.

The Fathers in Anglicanism

An examination of Anglican roots will demonstrate that the
Anglican study of the Fathers was primarily in relation to controversies that Anglicanism had to face in the aftermath of the
Reformation and the struggle for Anglican identity, rather than for
their own sake. Throughout these controversies it is the Fathers
who speak, not only in the defence of Anglicanism, but in defence
of themselves and a proper *use* of their writings. In this sense there
is a kinship with the Fathers and the search for Anglican identity,

in that it was the controversies of their own times that gave birth to their writings.

The thesis of this book examines these roots and divides into four parts. The first part, *The Fathers in the English Reformation*, examines the way in which the Reformers used the Fathers chiefly as a means of proving what had and what had not been primitive doctrine and practice and as a valuable authority secondary to the Bible. The Reformers used the Fathers in two ways: negatively, to prove the absence of Roman doctrines, and positively, to promote a right interpretation of Scripture and indicate a Scriptural way of life for the Church. This is shown in relation to two Reformers, Thomas Cranmer and John Jewel, and then in relation to Anglican foundation documents.

The second part, *Fathers and Carolines*, demonstrates how the Anglican divines of the seventeenth century, building on the scriptural and patristic foundation laid by the Reformers, go farther and use the thought and piety of the Fathers within the structure of their own theological vision. Their theology finds its centre in the Incarnation, a kinship shared with the Nicene Fathers, and characterized by a vision of the Church that embraces East and West, a consequence of their immersion in Greek and Latin divinity. Again it is a theological vision that is wrought in controversy, in relation to Puritanism and Calvinism on the one side, and to Roman Catholicism on the other.

Part Three, *Objections and Responses*, examines the Anglican response to objections brought against the appeal to the Fathers. Anglican patristic theologians in this group do not fall neatly into the category of Reformer, Caroline or Tractarian and are not so well known, even though they did make their contribution to the Anglican appeal to antiquity. In their time they faced the anti-patristic bias of those who argued against the relevancy of any appeal to the Fathers and those movements of thought that sought to demolish classical Christian doctrine in Creed and Council.

It is the presence and voice of the Fathers at the heart of Anglicanism that gives to the Church of England what Dr Jebb, the Bishop of Limerick described as '*The Peculiar Character of the Church of England*'. Part Four, *Rediscovering the Fathers*, examines the use of the appeal to antiquity in *Fathers and Tractarians*, and demonstrates how the leaders of the Oxford Movement made a plea for new possibilities in the use of this Anglican appeal. It also considers how the Tractarians may provide a starting point for rediscovering the Fathers today that will lead the way forward to the reintegration of the One, Holy, Catholic and Apostolic Church.

Notes

1.   E. C. Miller Jr. *Toward a Fuller Vision* (Morehouse Barlow, Wilton, CT, 1984), p. 2.
2.   H. A. Hodges, *Anglicanism and Orthodoxy* (SCM, 1957), p. 52.
3.   *Ibid.* p. 52.
4.   *Ibid.* p. 53.
5.   *Ibid.* p. 56.
6.   Miller, *ibid.* p. 4.
7.   G. Bennett, *Preface to Crockford's Clerical Directory* 1987–88 (CIO).
8.   A. Schmemann, *Liturgy and Tradition, Theological Reflections of Alexander Schmemann* (SVS Press, 1990), ed. Thomas Fisch, p. 84.
9.   *Ibid.* pp. 84–85.

Part One:

Fathers and Reformers

1

An Ecclesiastical Mind

Oxford and Patristic Studies

The number of participants in their variety of nationality and ecclesiastical denomination is always impressive to one regularly attending the International Conference on Patristic Studies in Oxford. It confirms what Henri Irenée-Marrou said at the First International Conference in 1951, that there exists an extraordinary vitality in patristic studies. Speaking of the international scene, what he said has particular relevance for the convening of such a conference in Oxford ever since and is therefore significant.

Oxford has always been a centre for patristic studies, and though the lamp may have dimmed or brightened from one time to another it never went out. When William Warham became Archbishop of Canterbury in 1503, Oxford University became the centre of a remarkable revival of ancient literature which greatly assisted decisions upon ecclesiastical affairs demanding reform. The movement which began in Italy through researches among pagan classics soon led to studies in the original works of the early Latin Fathers of the Church, and after the fall of Constantinople in 1453 which brought many Greek scholars westward, in the writings of the Greek Christian Fathers also. Warham was a great patron of what came to be known as the *New Learning*, which was transplanted from its cradle in Italy to its new home in Oxford. Arthur C. Lane describes the influence of John Colet, the future Dean of St Paul's, on the young Thomas More and Erasmus; convinced of the need for church reform, he told scholars to 'Keep to the Bible and the Apostles' Creed, and let divines, if they like, dispute about the rest'.[1] Long before the Reformation in England, Colet was influencing the English mind with Jerome's exegesis of the New Testament and Dionysius's 'Celestial Hierarchy', and was sowing seeds for a revival of interest in the New Testament and the

Fathers, particularly the Greek Fathers. These mutual influences between Colet, More and Erasmus and the Oxford Humanists initiated a Christian Renaissance that brought a new life and vitality to scriptural studies. The Bible was neither infallible nor cut off from the interpretation of the Fathers of the Church, making for what Fr George Tavard calls 'the coinherence of the Church and Scripture', so that the Bible did not have an authority independent of the Church. This principle, fundamental to the English Reformation, is traceable to Erasmus, who, knowing the contemporary church needed correction, was not prepared to separate himself from it or repudiate ancient Catholic Order. The basis of reform could be neither *Scriptura Sola* nor *Ecclesia Sola*, but rather the Scriptures giving insight to the Church and the Church through the great Fathers giving meaning to the Scriptures. Such reformation followed the genius of patristic rather than Protestant exegesis. From that time the watchword of English Reformers was Scripture and the primitive Fathers *versus* medieval tradition.

During the Oxford Movement in the nineteenth century there was a revival of patristic studies, which gave impetus to the pursuit of such study as a basic subject in the theological syllabuses and research programmes of theological faculties in English universities. It is not surprising that there have always been Anglican divines, parish priests as well as academics, whose theology was formed by the mind of the Fathers, and who were ready to vindicate the patristic dimension as essential to Anglican divinity. This patristic orientation is present in the Anglican reformers of the sixteenth century who made the appeal to the Fathers a foundation stone of their divinity, building their theology on patristic dogma, belief and practice. This appeal to antiquity continued as part of Anglican theological method and has always been present in the historical development of Anglican theology, though there have been variations in the precise nature of this appeal in different ages and for different people.

The Ecclesiastical Mind

The fundamental thesis of this book is that Anglican theological method has from its beginning – if it had a beginning at the Reformation and was not merely an inheritance – always included as integral a concern for church history and the 'proper' historical setting or context of the Bible: that is, the living apostolic community, the catholic Church of the Fathers, which ensures authoritatively, normatively, and critically, the historic continuity of the apostolic community and her apostolic faith and praxis. This ecclesial dimension, the patristic and catholic *ekklesiastikon phronēma*, was appropriated by Anglicanism and made the basis of Christian living, the context of Christian thinking. Ecclesiastical understanding does not attempt to add anything to Scripture, but to ascertain and to disclose fully the true meaning of Scripture. As Hanson put it, 'The life of Christianity depends upon the Church dancing with the Bible, and the Bible with the Church. The Church may indeed be lost without the Bible, but the Bible without the Church is dead, a collection of ancient documents and no more'.[2] The Jesuit theologian Fr George Tavard claimed that, in making Scripture the self-evident basis of Anglicanism but along-side Tradition as mutually inclusive, a consistency with the patristic spirit is maintained.

> The Anglican Church ... tried to maintain the Catholic notion of perfect union between Church and Scripture. The statement of Johann Gropper, that the Church's authority is not distinct from that of Scripture, but rather that they are one, corresponds to the Anglican view of the Early Church, as it corresponds to the catholic conception of the Church at all times.[3]

Tavard pointed out that most theologians of the Counter-Reformation separated Scripture and Tradition, at different times making one or the other a partial source of faith. He added that 'In both cases the theology of the catholic eras, patristic and medieval, was better represented by the Anglican view than by many Catholic writers in the Counter-Reformation period.'[4]

This ecclesial context of Anglican divinity understands the Church as bearing witness to the truth not merely from written documents, but from its own living, unceasing experience, from its catholic fullness. This has its roots in continuity with the primitive church, where the mind of Christ and the mind of the Church are mutually interrelated. It is in this person and in this mind that the historic tradition has its power and beginning and where the mind of the Church is established. This is what constitutes that 'tradition of truth' in which, as Florovsky reminds us 'the apostolic teaching is not so much an unchangeable example to be repeated or imitated as an eternally living and inexhaustible source of life and inspiration. Tradition is the constant abiding Spirit, not only the memory of words'. It is, therefore, a charismatic not a historical principle, but together with Scripture contains the truth of divine revelation, a truth that lives in the Church.

This experience of the Church has not been exhausted either in Scripture or Tradition; it is only reflected in them. Therefore only within the Church does Scripture live and become vivified, only within the Church is it revealed as a whole and not broken up into separate texts, commandments and aphorisms. This means that Scripture has been *given* in tradition, but not in the sense that it can be understood only according to the dictates of tradition, or that it is the written record of historical tradition or oral teaching. Scripture needs to be explained. It is revealed in theology. This is possible only through the medium of the living experience of the Church.[5]

This is the *ekklesiastikon phronēma*, and it has been one of the outstanding characteristics of the English church in all the principal periods of its life, and is what distinguished it from Continental Protestantism.

The Fathers and Anglican Theology

In 1961 Michael Ramsey was writing, 'The ancient Fathers were important to our Reformers because they stood near to the Holy Scriptures in time, and were witnesses to what the Church had believed before it had begun to deviate from Scriptural truth'.[6] He delineates three groups of Anglican theologians in three crucial epochs of modern Anglican history who made particular use of the Fathers. These were the English Reformers, the Anglican Divines of the seventeenth century, and the Tractarians in the nineteenth century. The Bishop's article, to some extent, has been an inspiration behind this book in its attempt to delineate the patristic mind in Anglican divinity. The inclusion of three centuries needs some qualification because it has been necessary to be selective. These three crucial epochs have received detailed treatment in this book: in *Part One: Fathers and Reformers, Part Two: Fathers and Carolines,* and *Part Four: Rediscovering the Fathers. Part Three: Objections and Responses,* examines the Anglican response to different kinds of objection brought against the Fathers, which Bishop Ramsey did not consider. It is in relation to this particular theme that certain Anglican theologians of the seventeenth, eighteenth and nineteenth centuries were included, as they respond to *Direct Objections* to the Fathers in such people as John Daillé, in the Ignatian Controversy, and John Barbeyrac. Then came the *Indirect Objections* in the rise of a new Arianism, its associations with Socinianism and its English expression in Unitarianism, its advocates using the Fathers to support their attacks on orthodoxy while others wanted to reject the appeal to antiquity altogether. Here, rather than in *Part Two: Fathers and Carolines*, the major contribution of the Caroline divine George Bull is included, because Bull's work was a response to misrepresentations of the orthodoxy of the Fathers. He prepared the way for the continuation of that work in his heir and successor Daniel Waterland. During this period less well-known divines were found defending the Anglican appeal to the Fathers in their Bampton Lectures. George Croft in 1786 applauds Joseph Bingham for vindicating Anglican doctrine and discipline from 'the practice of the primitive churches',[7] and answers some of Gibbon's criticisms of the Fathers in chapters 15 and 16 of *The Decline and Fall of the Roman Empire*. Henry Kett, in his lectures in 1790, addresses himself to *A Representation of the Conduct and Opinions of the Primitive Christians with Remarks on Certain Assertions of Mr. Gibbon and Dr. Priestley,* and in 1813 John Collinson delivered his Bampton Lectures on *A Key to the Writings of the Principal Fathers of the Christian Church (during the first three centuries)*, dealing in his first lecture with objections and responses to the appeal to antiquity. It is not surprising that a consciousness of the value of the Fathers began to emerge in England at the beginning of the nineteenth century.

> The number of books concerned with the teaching of the Fathers which appeared in the first half of the 19th century shows how great was the interest felt in them and the anxiety of English Churchmen at that period to claim unity of principle with them. Wigan Harvey's three-volume *Ecclesiae Anglicanae Vindex Catholicus* (Cambridge, 1841) is an example. Cary's *Testimonies of the Fathers of the first four centuries* (Oxford, 1835) is another. Cave's three volumes of the *Lives of the Fathers* were reprinted by Cary at Oxford in 1840.[8]

J. J. Blunt, the Lady Margaret Professor of Divinity in Cambridge in 1840, published 'an Introductory Lecture' that he had delivered to introduce a course of lectures on the early Fathers. He gave these lectures in 1840 and 1843 on *The Right Use of the Early Fathers.*[9] His purpose was to protect the Fathers from misrepresentation and misconstruction and that he might 'call the attention of Churchmen to a principle that ruled the Reformers in their revision of our Church, and succeeding divines in defence of her'. This task he set himself in his lectures on *The Right Use of the Early Fathers,* defending the value of the Fathers against the criticisms of the French Protestant theologian Daillé, the Dutchman lawyer Barbeyrac, the English historian Gibbon, Socinianism and the meaning of Scripture in Calvinism, influences that he maintained had depreciated their study in England. With the dominating influence of Tractarianism's concern to reintegrate the place of the Fathers in English theology, it was often forgotten that before and outside that movement there were others equally concerned. Bishop Kaye of Lincoln (1783–1853) when he was Regius Professor at Cambridge was the first to recall theological students to the study of the Fathers.

Notes

1. Arthur C. Lane, *Illustrated Notes on English Church History* (SPCK, London, 1904), p. 271.
2. R. P. C. Hanson, *The Bible as A Norm of Faith: An Inaugural Lecture as Lightfoot Professor of Divinity* (University of Durham : Titus Wilson & Son, Kendal, 1963), p. 11.
3. George Tavard, *Holy Writ or Holy Church* (Burns Oates, London, 1959), p. 245.
4. *Ibid.*
5. Georges Florovsky, *Bible, Church, Tradition: An Eastern Orthodox View* (Nordland, Massachusetts, 1972), pp. 47–8.
6. A. M. Ramsey, 'The Ancient Fathers and Modern Anglican Theology', in *Sobornost*, Series 4: no. 6 (Winter – Spring 1962), pp. 289–94.
7. George Croft, Sermon I, 'The Use and Abuse of Reason', *Vindication of the Church of England against the Objections of the Principal Sects* (Clarendon Press, Oxford, 1786), p. 2.
8. W. J. Sparrow-Simpson, 'The Study of the Fathers', in *The Priest as Student*, ed. H. S. Box (SPCK, London, 1939), p. 97.
9. J. J. Blunt, *An Introduction to a Course of Lectures on the Early Fathers* (Cambridge University Press, Cambridge, 1840); *On the Right Use of the Early Fathers* (John Murray, London, 1857).

2

Fathers and Reform in Thomas Cranmer and John Jewel

The patristic argument in the Reformers

The English Reformation made biblical truth an important criterion for faith, order, and life, but alongside the Church Fathers who were seen as guides to the right interpretation of Holy Scripture. For the English Reformers Scripture is the supreme standard of faith, but the Fathers represent the tradition of the Church by which Scripture has been interpreted correctly. The late Professor Greenslade makes the general point that,

> ... however tenacious their hold upon the principle *Sola Scriptura* the Reformers argued extensively from the Ancient Fathers of the Church who are named in the full title of the Chair which I have the honour to hold; and the particular point, ... that the full range of patristic literature was only gradually becoming known in the sixteenth century, that books were not always easy to procure, that many problems of text and authenticity had yet to be settled (or even to be raised); so that, in examining the influence of the Fathers upon the Reformers or the Anglican appeal to the Fathers, the historian should take account of many matters which he may sometimes be tempted to leave to the spiritual interests of the librarian and bibliographer.[1]

Some made little use of them but nobody would doubt their value and authority, though they regarded them as secondary to the Bible. Such was their importance that, Greenslade[2] makes some important points about the patristic argument in the Reformers which can be summarized in the following way. First, although no Anglican Reformer would reject the significance, value and weight of the Fathers' testimony, and some would regard the patristic

appeal as unnecessary, the authority of the Fathers is always
secondary to Scripture. Secondly, the appeal was largely to the
Church of the first five centuries, and though Jewel speaks of six
hundred years, the designation of 'primitive church' normally
meant five hundred years, as at the Westminster Conference of
1559. There are quotations from sixth-century authors, from Bede,
John of Damascus and even the much later St Bernard, who
breathes the spirit of the Fathers rather than the scholastics, so that
in some quarters he is regarded as the last of the Fathers. Thirdly,
the particular context of the English Reformation, namely, the
dispute with the Church of Rome, determined to a large extent the
nature of the Anglican appeal to antiquity, so that the appeal to the
Fathers relates to the particular theological and ecclesiastical
points of controversy between the two churches. This results in the
Reformers using the Fathers in two ways, first, negatively, to prove
the absence of Roman doctrines and practices from the primitive
church, secondly, positively, to promote the right interpretation of
Scripture and demonstrate a Scriptural way of life for the Church;
therefore, as Greenslade states, 'they have *auctoritas,* weight, they
are to be esteemed'. So their authority is limited because they are
biblical, meaning that rather than merely quoting the Bible they
breathe the spirit of the Bible, not that of philosophy, subordinat-
ing their own teaching to Scripture. The primary concern is to
grasp the 'Scriptural mind' that results when one bends one's
thought to the mental habits of the biblical language and relearns
the idiom of the Bible. This 'Scriptural mind' is what the Fathers
have grasped. This is important in relation to the reaction against
scholastic philosophy that was seen to be too dependent upon
Aristotle and in which philosophical concepts were used to interpret the Bible. The way of the Fathers is exegetical and historical,
not systematic.

   Greenslade cites John Jewel as representing this twofold use of
the appeal to antiquity, negative in that they are not witnesses to
later erroneous innovations, and positive in that they are of greater
value than later developments. Hence, fourthly, the patristic
appeal was normally focused upon the biblical character of the
patristic witness, meaning 'biblical' in both the literal and the
conceptual sense. Often the biblical criterion is exalted above the
patristic, though as a rule it remained the presupposition to the
development of the latter. However, the dividing line between the
Bible and the Fathers was not always clear. Fifthly, the appeal to the
Fathers was hampered by a number of inevitabilities, the most
important of which was the non-availability of patristic texts, the

simultaneous publication of genuine and spurious patristic literature without distinctions, and the limited historical knowledge of
the patristic period. With the publication of texts in the sixteenth
century, patristic studies blossomed and developed, and so it was
natural for the Anglican appeal to the Fathers in theological argument and discourse to keep pace with this development. Sixthly, it
is crucial to discern the fact that at this stage the Fathers were not
studied for their own sake, but for the sake of providing important
evidences in the Anglican disputes with Rome. Thus the quotations
from the Fathers are easily borrowed from author to author and
especially from collections of *Patristic Testimonia* (an ancient
custom) arranged under theological headings, such as the *Unio
Dissidentium* of Hermann Bodius published in 1527. These important points about the patristic argument in the English Reformers
will be discussed in relation to Thomas Cranmer and John Jewel.

Thomas Cranmer 1489–1556

Patristic learning

Thomas Cranmer succeeded William Warham to become
Archbishop of Canterbury in 1533, some claiming that it was
almost by accident, and others, that God moves in mysterious ways.
He was not a personally ambitious man and placed a low priority
on such honours, so that he came unwillingly to a bishopric. He
was a student of a very thorough kind, 'seldom reading without
pen in hand' and leaving extensive notebooks which to this day
illustrate his extensive research and careful observation. A
Cambridge man, Cranmer had been a Fellow of Jesus College as
early as 1510 and was a scholar of no ordinary attainments who was
exceptionally well versed in the learning of his day.

> Foxe speaks of Cranmer in his days at Cambridge rubbing away
> the old rustiness of Scholasticism as on a whetstone, and it can
> be safely assumed that an interest in the Fathers was part of his
> general attachment to the new learning from the beginning.
> From what is known of the contents and utilisation of his library,
> one would have to gather that this interest matured into an
> exceptional dedication with Cranmer pursuing – perhaps from
> as early as the 1520s – an avid and up-to-date collector of patris-
> tic editions that appeared.[3]

Canon Smyth claimed that Cranmer was

... a notable Patristic scholar: but, as Dr. Bromiley has pointed out in his new book, *Thomas Cranmer, Theologian* – which is, I believe, the first serious and dispassionate study of him regarded simply as a theologian – in Cranmer's approach to all doctrinal questions, he proceeds by the three-fold rule of Scripture, the Fathers, and reason, in that order.[4]

Smyth described him as anticipating the defence of the Anglican position in the seventeenth century by Richard Hooker in his reply to the Puritan attack. Colin Dunlop pointed out that under God's Providence Cranmer infused into the One, Catholic Church of Christ, certain neglected graces. Though they were not new, what resulted was the formation a new alignment of ecclesiastical polity, neither solely Catholic nor solely Protestant, that came to be called Anglicanism.

In that great valley of decision in which the Church found itself at the Reformation, Thomas Cranmer as Archbishop of Canterbury, felt unable to guide the destinies of the Church of England along the well-worn road of Papal and Medieval Latin Christendom, nor yet to lead it into the new pastures of Luther or Calvin. Instead he set himself to find traces of that lost thoroughfare which has been called the *Via Media*, but which to Cranmer was 'the godly and decent order of the ancient Fathers'.[5]

Attention was drawn to Cranmer's interest in the Fathers in the nineteenth century edition of *Cranmer's Works* published by the Parker Society, where there is the first elucidation of his patristic sources. Greenslade cautions against 'exaggerating the erudition' that looks impressive in the works of the Reformers but raises complex questions about their use of the Fathers. This was a time of patristic revival, Scripture and the Fathers being the double-edged component of the 'new learning' associated with Colet, More and Erasmus, referred to in the first chapter. In consequence printed editions of texts began to emerge, making the Fathers more accessible to scholars and contributing to a better standardization of texts and more accurate citations. Methods of study were transformed as the need to memorize chunks of texts became less urgent, since printed works provided a more reliable source of theological reflection and scriptural commentary. The whole horizon of Greek and Latin patristic literature widened with fresh translations more fully indexed, providing the sixteenth-century scholar with an invaluable resource and a growing understanding of key aspects of early Christian thinking. Not unnaturally, in the wake of something new, enthusiasm often clouded accuracy and editors made mistakes so that some texts were faulty and others incomplete. Despite these scholarly limitations the impact of this 'new learning' on those concerned to recall the church to the following of the Fathers was enormous.

Cranmer was part of this enthusiasm. Hence, his own personal collection of patristic texts was continually brought up-to-date as they became available, but as Walsh[6] claims, Cranmer's library was more up-to-date than Burbridge had thought. Greenslade[7] points out that Peter Martyr assisted Cranmer in forming the excellent but still far from complete collection of patristic texts that he possessed and read in the 1550s. The range of Cranmer's learning can be assessed from examining the list of his remaining books made by Edward Burbridge at the end of the last century and printed in Bernard Quaritch's *Contributions towards a Dictionary of English Book-Collectors,* Part I (London, 1892).[8] Among these books is an almost complete set of the available writings of the Latin and Greek Fathers, several of them in various editions, as well as works of the Schoolmen, contemporary writers, and liturgy. It testifies to an immense and highly diversified erudition. Cranmer's annotations prove that he was well acquainted with these books, especially, as Burbridge points out, in his copies of Eusebius and Epiphanius. Walsh claims that his library reflected the dislikes of the reformers for certain Fathers. These included the Cappadocians, some Alexandrians and Greeks, excepting Eusebius of Caesarea, Chrysostom and Epiphanius, in editions produced in the 1540s; but it also indicates the archbishop's retarded and fragmentary interest in eastern patristic writing, and the functional bias of the library. Nevertheless, these texts had alerted him to their exciting possibilities, so that, when he visited his cathedral church in 1550, he made it an article of enquiry 'whether there be a library within this church and in the same St. Augustine's works, Basil, Gregory Nazianzen, Hierome, Ambrose, Chrysostom, Cyprian, Theophylact.'

The advent of new technology gave to these sixteenth-century scholars new and more powerful tools to assist them. To progress from scripting to printing, from auditory to visual methods of communication, was bound to have a significant effect on the scholarship of the day. It meant words could be studied in their context, the system of citation could be more uniform and accurate, and the range of writings spanning the early centuries could be studied in their historical context. Such transformation might be compared with the advent of the word-processor today and the new possibilities this technology has given to scholars.

In his manuscript *Commonplace Books* there is similar evidence of his patristic learning. The most important of these went missing and Archbishop Parker found it to be in the possession of Dr Nevison, Canon of Canterbury, from whom it was recovered. This unpublished work, which is now in the British Museum, was written in the hand of secretaries and put together in different epochs of Cranmer's life.

> It contains an immense number of extracts from – Clement of Rome and Ignatius; from Irenaeus and Tertullian, Origen and Cyprian; Lactantius, Hilary, Ambrose, Paulinus of Nola, Augustine, Fulgentius, Jerome, Vincent of Lerins, Cassian, Prudentius, Gelasius, Leo, Sulpicius Severus, Gregory the Great and Bede; from Eusebius, Epiphanius, Athanasius, Basil, Gregory of Nazianzus, Chrysostom, Cyril of Alexandria, Socrates and Sozomen, Theophilus of Alexandria, Denys the Areopagite, John Damsacene, Nicephorus Chartophylax; from Rabanus and Haymo, Aldhelm, Bruno, Bernard, Anselm ...[9]

The list continues through the Schoolmen and contemporary writers. Gregory of Nyssa is not mentioned though Cranmer possessed at least one of his works, and similarly, though Clement of Alexandria, Didymus, Cyril of Jerusalem, Isidore of Seville and Amalarius are not mentioned, he possessed MSS of some of their writings. An annotated copy of his *Nazianzus MS* is in the Durham Cathedral library.

The *Defence*

The evangelical, Dr J. I. Packer, claims that it would be true to Cranmer's own mind to say that he was burned for being a catholic so that for him as for all the Reformers, Protestantism (unlike Anabaptism) was precisely a quest for catholicism,

> ... that is for solidarity with the catholic church that Jesus founded ... a conscious attempt to restore to the Church of the West the catholicity that it had so long lost. To the Reformers, as to the Fathers, catholicity was a theological and historical concept before it was a geographical or statistical one; they saw the essence of catholicity as lying in faithfulness to the gospel word and sacramental usage given to the church by Christ through the apostles in the beginning. Thus catholicity was to

them in the first instance a matter of apostolicity, and apostolicity was in the first instance a matter of doctrine.[10]

His concern as a reformer in the restoration of catholic doctrine and institution was for the re-establishment of biblical faith, which, he was convinced, had been preserved in the Fathers who had, on the whole, been faithful expositors of it. Hence the full title of his work on the Eucharist defines an approach in which Bible and Fathers stand together; *A defence of the True and Catholic Doctrine of the Sacrament... grounded and stablished upon God's holy Word, and approved by the consent of the most ancient Doctors of the Church.* In the *Defence* the appeal to the Fathers falls into a category of theological arguments that Cranmer claims 'prevail not against God's Word, yet when they be joined with God's Word, they be of great moment to confirm any truth'. Packer states that Cranmer,

> ... having studied Scripture in its 'literal' (i.e. natural, grammatical, intended) sense, letting one text comment on another and relating each author's statements to his overall scope, as the humanists taught all the Reformers to do, and having studied patristic theology by the same method, he had come to see that what the Fathers said coincided for substance with what the Scriptures said on each point dealt with. Thus he was able to appeal to both Scripture and the Fathers in the same breath, and to profess his entire solidarity with 'the most ancient doctors'.[11]

This is not quite the case as demonstrated in his approach to the Fathers where Cranmer was not always concerned to take note of the context of his patristic texts. Packer states that the *Defence* was no mere piece of polemics, but reflected the verdict of a scholar that in the Fathers we find an exposition of the essence of biblical catholicism. Therefore they deserve the recognition traditionally paid them as authoritative guides in doctrine, thus illustrating the positive side to the patristic argument. On the negative side his purpose was to demonstrate how un-catholic the teaching had been since the twelfth century in twisting not only the Scriptures but also the Fathers. In his *Appeal at His Degradation* it was to the spirit of his theological method that he could appeal in defence of his doctrine:

> And touching my doctrine of the sacrament, and other my doctrine, of what kind soever it be, I protest that it was never my mind to write, speak, or understand anything contrary to the most holy Word of God, or else against the holy catholic church

of Christ; but purely and simply to imitate and teach those things only, which I had learned of the sacred scripture, and of the holy catholic church of Christ from the beginning, and also according to the position of the most holy and learned fathers and martyrs of the church.[12]

Walsh[13] highlights the fact that Cranmer, in the *Defence,* scarcely uses the words Father and Doctor, referring to these early Christian writers as *authors.* It was a distinctive term in the schools where author (*auctor*) has as its correlative 'authority' (*auctoritas*), which referred to a citation taken from the writer's work. 'Thus the archbishop can speak in the treatise of "authorities wrested from the intent and mind of the authors", or refer to "all the authorities of St Augustine".' The word *auctor* does not mean simply a writer, but is used in the specific sense of a person with an established right to be heard in the discussion of a particular question. The views of such a person were held to be 'authentic', or normative, 'a synonym for *auctoritates* being *authentica,* meaning judgements that carried more weight than "glosses", or "sentences" or *dicta magistralia'* In scholastic discussions the *auctoritates* are always treated respectfully or reverently, whereas the 'glosses' or 'sentences' or *dicta magistralia* could be dismissed without scruple. A chronological significance was attached to *auctoritates,* contrasting it with *moderni,* commentators whose views carried less weight.

It would be naïve to assume that the methods of the schools did not continue to have some influence on the Reformers. In the *Defence,* Walsh sees in Cranmer something of this influence in his readiness to trade 'authorities' with authority-mongers. This was only sleight because it was Cranmer's style to invest an old term with a new meaning.

He probably wanted it clearly seen that his authorities were decidedly not the normal run of Schoolmen. He was appealing beyond them to more substantial and authoritative witnesses. And he was, in a sense, accepting their testimony as normative but in his own way, and according to the reformed understanding of the primacy of God's Word over any human judgement. Cranmer's 'authorities' are of weight only in so far as they conform to the proper interpretation of the scriptures. Given that conformity they have an authority. When that is lacking they have none. Possibly this is why the archbishop rather shunned references to 'Father' and 'Doctors', to whom traditionally a certain Church-sanctioned authority was attributed (pères de l'Église) – something the reformers would not accept.[14]

Despite references to later authors Cranmer's primary aim is an appeal to what he terms the 'old authors' in his concern to set them against the 'school authors' of later years whom he viewed as suspect.

The methodology

Cranmer's method of working was to collect into notebooks useful quotations that would be of use in future publications. To this end he also used secretaries to collect such quotations for his requirements, to which he added his own annotations and cross-references to other commonplace books not yet identified. Behind the *Defence* there was a draft of notes entitled 'De re Sacramentaria' (*c.* 1547) preserved at Corpus Christi College, Cambridge, in which Walsh claims it is possible to identify citations and headings that resemble the second, third and fourth sections of Cranmer's *Defence;* he cites Strype's[15] claim that it represented the archbishop's 'meditations and conclusions' when he became preoccupied with the sacramental controversy, and Jenkyns's[16] recognition of it as a likely source of the scriptural and patristic documentation of the *Defence,* a point recognized by the more recent research of Dr Brooks[17] who like Strype sees it as a document evolving over a period of time. Walsh finds this last point unlikely, because the hand seems uniform throughout and the numbering format would have prevented subsequent inclusions, and the reference to material which Peter Martyr made available confirms it, because he did not arrive until that time. In a careful comparison of the 'Sacramentaria' with the *Defence,* Dr Walsh has demonstrated how Cranmer used his knowledge of the Fathers, and that 'there can be no doubt at all that it provided him with the basis for the patristic documentation of the *Defence*'. Popular *catenae* were accessed, Gratian's *Decretum* (twelfth century) being a well-used source, and where there were errors in the extracts Cranmer was able to correct them from more up-to-date printed editions of patristic texts. The *Unio Dissidentium* (1520s) was another source of patristic texts used by Cranmer. Its eucharistic stance was that of continental Protestantism which became congenial to Cranmer in 1550 and his selected citations appear in their same order in his published text.

There was nothing especially original in his research: why should there be? The job of dragooning the Fathers into supporting the spiritual presence view of the eucharist had mostly been done already by the *Unio* and by Johannes Oecolampadius of Basel. Peter Martyr added other important witnesses in his innovative use of Chrysostom and Theodoret, and indeed Cranmer had no hesitation in incorporating passages from the writings of Martyr himself in his text. This was a book designed for polemical use, not to show off an archbishop's cleverness.[18]

The 'Sacramentaria' demonstrates Cranmer's working methods and the nature of the material available to him from which he built his arguments from the Fathers. The mention of forty authors indicates a wider selection than was the case. While there is mention of post-patristic authors such as Bede, Rabanus Maurus, Ratramnus and even some medieval writers, his primary concern is with what he defined as the 'old authors' whom he regarded as more reliable than the scholastic authors of later years.

> The battle here was for the sanction of Christian antiquity, as the archbishop's assorted challenges to his opponents throughout the *Defence* pointedly show (pp. 140–1, 143–4). It was the voice of 'the primitive or catholic Church' – not that of 'the malignant and papistical Church of Rome' – which Cranmer claimed he wanted to be heard. (p. 121–2). And the best of his 'good' and 'approved' authors were those 'which were nearest unto Christ's time, and therefore might best know the truth' (p. 88) – that is, the figures we would normally know as the Church Fathers.[19]

Nevertheless, his choice is selective, preferring a few: Cyprian is most favoured in the second and third centuries with Origen, Irenaeus and Tertullian prominent and John Chrysostom dominant from the later Fathers. His sparse citations from the Greeks, apart from John Damascene, Eusebius of Emesa, Epiphanius, Hesychius of Jerusalem and the Antiochene Theodoret of Cyrrhus, popularized in these English eucharistic debates by Peter Martyr, leaves the late Latin Fathers, Jerome, Ambrose and Augustine as the predominant sources of his original collection. Popes Gelasius, Julius I, Leo and Gregory are mentioned alongside Fulgentius of Ruspe, Vigilius of Thapsus and briefly, Pseudo-Denys and the Council of Nicaea. The omissions are due, no doubt, to this being a preliminary notebook and a limited area of theological study on which there may not have been anything of significance in what the omitted authors had to say, and its deficiencies would be rectified by Cranmer's annotations and final work.

Walsh[20] points out that the collection indicates that the use of *catenae* of patristic references known in the schools and used in the eucharistic debates were being increased only marginally through fresh editions of patristic texts. New material, especially from the second and third centuries and the East, had hardly begun to emerge. Cranmer himself seemed to rely on older sources, particularly Gratian's *Decree*, 'whole blocks of texts' from it being in the manuscript. There is evidence of newer patristic texts being used by this time in the corrections of doubtful attributions; in particular, a citation wrongfully attributed to Augustine,[21] is correctly attributed to Ambrose after consultation with the Basle (1527) edition of his works. Another source from which he collected quotations for his manuscript was Hermann Bodius's *Unio dissidentium*, a collection of patristic texts on central theological themes that included the eucharist and influenced the view of the sacrament adopted by Cranmer and other Reformers. Bodius, whose actual identity is still disputed, preferred the more recent humanist texts rather than dependence on medieval *catenae*, and in his collection texts from Augustine were predominant but texts from Jerome, Chrysostom and Origen were also included. Cranmer copied two large chunks of these texts from Bodius into his manuscript, retaining the same order and inserting them into the *Defence*. Walsh identifies in Book Four citations from Augustine and one from Origen, 'a succession of patristic passages extending over several pages, which all stem from the *Unio*'. Some of Bodius's collection of texts were used by Oecolampadius in his *Dialogue* (1530) whose primary concern was the eucharistic controversy.

> ... citations from it were included in the largest of the commonplace books associated with Cranmer which, almost certainly, was assembled before the one we are considering here. The use of the *Dialogue* in the Cambridge manuscript looks certain, but it was restricted. There are echoes in the collection of important passages from Oecolampadius – notably a citation from Augustine's *De doctrina christiana*, which Cranmer used in the *Defence*. But the most obvious borrowing is from Athanasius and, as it happens this is the only passage of his included in the manuscript. [Walsh's note: Cf. *Defence*, p. 202 with Oecolampadius, *Dialogus*, n. 1, 1530, sig. F. viii ^{v}; also *Defence*, pp. 197–8 (= ms. 102, pp. 161–2 with *Dialogus*, sigs E. vi ^{v} – vii ^{v}].[22]

Cranmer was only working in tune with the methods of his time in using such citations but there were also notable additions from Peter Martyr that the archbishop adopted as his own. This need not shock, because Cranmer was educated in an oral culture where

the conventions and etiquette were different from those of a printing culture. There is evidence in the manuscript collection that
Cranmer was beginning to move from the one to the other when
reliance upon *catenae* became less restrictive as they were able to
point the scholar to search for these citations in new editions of the
original patristic texts that were emerging. Where required, such
citations could be corrected or enlarged. Walsh claims that in the
citations from Gratian there are signs that Cranmer was doing this,
but it is less certain with Bodius and Oecolampadius. Nevertheless,
from the manuscript collection as a whole it can be seen that new
editions of patristic texts were being used, but the approach is
verbal rather than contextual with the title of the work mentioned
but not page-numbers and editions. Walsh[23] states that there is also
indirect evidence for the use of new texts, citing Cyprian in the
commonplace collection as coming from Erasmus's edition,
exhibiting Cranmer's meticulous handling and discounting the
accusation that he handled the Fathers unfairly in the *Defence.*

Nevertheless, Walsh sees little evidence that the range of patristic citations had been broadened from a familiarity with the new
editions. Despite Cranmer's desire to command a much larger
resource of patristic passages from the newer humanist texts
becoming available, his method was to stay with the anthologies
and use the researches of others. His use of patristic citation
continued to be primarily verbal rather than contextual, his
purpose being to gather ammunition rather than instruction,
tearing passages from their context.

> The flowing argument of the *Defence* is really composed of a
> series of definite, carefully delineated assertions, in support of
> which the patristic testimony is introduced. The effect of this was
> to constrain some of the statements of the Fathers, and some-
> times to force them where they were never originally intended
> to go. The crisp brilliance of Cranmer's cumulative arguments
> can easily blind us to the challenging interpretations of patristic
> statements that he was often proposing.[24]

The *Confutation*

In 1558 Cranmer's *A Confutation of Unwritten Verities*[25] quickly
followed the publication of Justus Jonas's translation of Osiander's
catechism. Apologists for the Church of Rome were claiming the
authority of 'Unwritten Verities' for their teachings, a device
forged by Bishop Stokesley of London. There is some doubt about

Cranmer's responsibility for the entire authorship, and Jenkyns, the editor of the 1833 edition of the *Remains*, holds this view, but Bromiley in his work *Thomas Cranmer* disagrees. It has already been demonstrated that he was an avid and methodical collector of authorities on all the ecclesiastical questions of his day. The treatise contains various extracts from his *Commonplace Books* in which he gathered a collection of authorities, biblical, patristic, and Schoolmen, on various subjects. The purpose is to prove from the Holy Scriptures, and from the ancient Fathers, that the Word of God contains all things necessary to salvation, and to point out that neither patristic writings themselves, nor general Councils, nor the oracles of angels, nor apparitions from the dead, nor customs of churches, are sufficient of themselves to establish doctrines, or maintain a new Article of Faith. It stands alongside the Sixth Article. In the *Confutation*, which has an introduction and concluding chapter added posthumously by 'E. P.', the editor, we find an illustration of the theological method he defended at his *Appeal.* There is a demonstration of Scriptural authority in the form of twenty-four texts to establish true and wholesome doctrine containing all things needful for salvation, which is followed by a multitude of quotations, mainly patristic, to confirm that neither Fathers nor Councils, nor anything else can establish articles of faith apart from Scripture. It illustrates his method, the establishing of that coincidence between biblical doctrine and patristic doctrine, thereby in a positive way using the Fathers to identify what the catholic faith is, and negatively to illustrate where Rome is seen to be in error.

An English Bible

One great practical reform that Cranmer longed to promote, though he was not the first English churchman to desire it, was the circulation of the Bible in English. The inspiration for this general diffusion of the Bible for 'vulgar people' in the 'vulgar tongue', came from his reading of the Fathers, and from the fact that the Anglo-Saxons had translated the Bible and read it in what was their 'vulgar tongue'. Bede is a prime example, who in the hours before he died was busy translating St John's Gospel into the vernacular. To this end Cranmer's liturgical revision was concerned to embody such biblical material in its lections. It is to the Fathers he appeals to justify an English Bible, in the face of petty quibbling objections from bishops. In 1539 Cranmer wrote a *Prologue* or *Preface*, which was published in April 1540 and prefixed to the *Great Bible,*

appointed to be read in churches that year. In it he replied with a
long and spirited translation from St John Chrysostom's sermon
'*De Lazaro*', on the benefits 'lay and vulgar people' will derive from
reading the Scriptures. He himself intended to claim nothing
more than what was 'said and written by the noble doctor and most
moral divine'. Chrysostom's concern is, that those who listen to his
sermons should read their bibles at home between these sermons
and memorize what he has preached on such texts as they read;
'and also that they might have their minds the more ready and
better prepared to receive and perceive that which he should say
from thenceforth in his sermons'.[26]

> All these things have been written for us for our edification and
> amendment, which be born towards the latter end of the world.
> The reading of Scriptures is a great and strong bulwark against
> sin; the ignorance of the same is the greater ruin and destruc-
> tion of them that will not know it. That is the thing that bringeth
> in heresy; that is that it causeth all corrupt and perverse living;
> that is that bringeth all things out of good order.[27]

As Chrysostom is invoked to reprove those who refused to read the
Bible, St Gregory Nazianzen is brought in to reprove another sort
of offender.

> It appeareth that in his time there were some (as I fear me there
> have been also now at these days a great number) which were
> idle babblers and talkers of the Scripture out of season and all
> good order, and without any increase of virtue, or example of
> good living. To them he writeth all his first book, *De Theologia*.

Cranmer then proceeds to give a vigorous summary of what
Gregory wrote. Gregory states that it is not fit for every man to
dispute the high questions of divinity and 'dangerous for the
unclean to touch that thing that is most clean; like as the sore eye
taketh harm by looking at the sun'. Contention and debate about
Scriptures does most hurt to ourselves and to the cause we have
furthered.

> I say not this to dissuade men from the knowledge of God, and
> reading or studying of the Scripture. For, I say, that it is as neces-
> sary for the life of a man's soul, as for the body to breathe. And
> if it were possible so to live, I would think it good for a man to
> spend all his days in that, and to do no other thing. I commend
> the law which biddeth to meditate and study the scriptures
> always, both night and day, and sermons and preachings to be

made both morning, noon and eventide ... I forbid not to read but I forbid to reason. Neither forbid I to reason so far as is good and godly.[28]

He quotes from another of Gregory's works:

the fear of God must be the first beginning, and as it were an A.B.C., of an introduction to all them that shall enter to the very sure and most fruitful knowledge of holy scriptures. Where, as is the fear of God, there is the keeping of the commandments, there is the cleansing of the flesh, which flesh is a cloud before the soul's eye, and suffereth it not purely to see the beam of the heavenly light. Where, as is the cleansing of the flesh, there is the illumination of the Holy Ghost, the end of all our desires, and the very light whereby the verity of the scriptures is seen and perceived.[29]

Here he uses the Fathers in a positive way to commend a translation of the Bible into the 'vulgar tongue', but indirectly there is implicit in his argument a negative use that is concerned to undermine the reasoning and quibbling of those opposed to it. Anglicans can be thankful that through the influence of the teaching of the Fathers an English Bible is authorized and their liturgy packed with biblical material that is read and heard throughout a continuous cycle.

The Ten Articles

In 1536 the *Ten Articles*, what might be termed the antecedents of the *Thirty-Nine Articles*, were prepared to give expression to what the English church meant by her claim of not having varied in any point from the true Catholic faith since the breach with Rome. These represent Cranmer's doctrinal position at the time, the true basis of our Catholic Reformation and what he terms the great rediscovery of the time.[30] Divided into two parts, the first part contains Articles of faith commanded by God and necessary for salvation. In practical terms it means acceptance of the canonical Scriptures, and the three Creeds, Apostles', Nicaean and Athanasian, as the rule of faith, along with the decisions of the first four Councils as the foundations of the Church of England, Holy Baptism, the sacrament of Penance, as a necessity for all who have committed mortal sin after Baptism, and the real presence in the Eucharist, though not in the definition of transubstantiation. Justification is also included. The second contains 'such things as have been of a long continuance for a decent order and honest policy prudently instituted and used in the churches of our realm, although they be not expressly commanded by God, nor necessary to our salvation.'[31] Such matters were honour to the saints, the use of images, rites and ceremonies, and prayers for the departed.

In 1537 these were extended into *The Institution of a Christian Man,* that came to be called *The Bishops' Book:* it contained an explanation of the Creed, the Seven Sacraments, the Ten Commandments, the Lord's Prayer and the Hail Mary. Justification was understood as due entirely to the merits of Christ, but involving an obligation to good works afterwards. Purgatory was repudiated and prayer for departed souls was declared laudable: praying for the dead is laudable because it is a charitable deed commended in the Book of Maccabees and in numerous ancient doctors and has been a practice in the Church from the beginning. Doctrinally, this work occupied the same position as the *Ten Articles* upon which it was founded. In 1543 this was further revised into *The Necessary Doctrine and Erudition of a Christian Man* (also called *The King's Book*). It was submitted to Convocation and approved and published with a commendatory preface by the King. It contained a long exposition of the Eucharist, in which the word 'transubstantiation' was avoided but the doctrine of conversion into the substance of the body and blood of Christ was taught,

> Seeing it is the very body of our Saviour Christ, which is united and knit to His Godhead in one Person, and by reason thereof hath the very virtue and substance of life in it, it must needs consequently by the most holy and blessed participation of the same give and communicate life also to them that worthily receive it.[32]

Eucharistic doctrine

In his *Catechismus,* published in 1548, Cranmer, while not denying that the consecrated Sacrament is the body and blood of Christ, and that the body and blood are to be received by the 'bodily mouth', does not assert anything more than that they are received by the communicants. By 1550, Cranmer's doctrine of the Eucharist is fast diverging from that of Stephen Gardiner, the Bishop of Winchester, a dispute which in the 1550s demonstrates Cranmer's theological method in which the Fathers are placed next to or along with the Bible. In his *Defence* the title page expresses the principle of the English Reformation, that it is to

Holy Scripture that we must look for the ground of doctrine, while the testimony of the early church is given a valued place in confirmation of the inferences drawn from Scripture. Furthermore what is maintained is that this is the catholic doctrine. In the Preface to his *Answer to Gardiner,* he writes:

> Where I used to speak sometimes (as the old authors do) that Christ is in the Sacraments, I mean the same as they did understand the matter; that is to say, not of Christ's carnal presence in the outward Sacrament but sometimes of His Sacramental presence. And sometimes by this word Sacrament I mean the whole ministration and receiving of the Sacraments either of Baptism or of the Lord's Supper; and so the old writers many times do say that Christ and the Holy Ghost be present in the Sacraments, not meaning by that manner of speech that Christ and the Holy Ghost be present in the water, bread, or wine, which be only the outward visible Sacraments, but that in the due ministration of the Sacraments according to Christ's ordinance and institution Christ and His Holy Spirit be truly and indeed present by their mighty and sanctifying power, virtue, and grace, in all them that worthily receive the same.[33]

Dugmore pointed out that on this subject Cranmer was steeped in patristic thought:

> Not only had Cranmer recovered from his reading of the 'ancient doctors' the primitive notion that in the Eucharist Christ mingles himself with the bodies of believers (so, Gregory of Nyssa) in order that by union with that which is immortal man also may participate in incorruption. He was, also, trying to explain the term 'corporally' in its true Cyrilian sense of σωματικῶς, as against the Western medieval notion of *'corporaliter'*, i.e. the notion of a material presence of Christ's body in the Host on the altar. Thus he says, Cyril 'neither saith that Christ dwelleth corporally in the bread, nor that he dwelleth in us corporally only at such times as we receive the sacrament ... which dwelling is neither corporal nor local, but an heavenly, spiritual and supernatural dwelling', i.e. 'the natural property of his body, which is life and immortality'. It is in this context, and in this context alone, that Cranmer can say: 'the Son of God, taking unto him our human nature, and making us partakers of his divine nature, giving unto us immortality and everlasting life, doth so dwell naturally and corporally in us, and maketh us to dwell naturally and corporally in him.' This was his reply to

Gardiner who likewise appealed to Cyril and Hilary in support of the doctrine that Christ's flesh is corporally and naturally contained under the form of bread, i.e. *corporaliter*, in the Western medieval sense of the term. In a letter written to Somerset in May 1547, Gardiner had described Anne Askew as 'blasphemously denying the presence of Christes natural body'. In other letters, addressed to Cranmer during the summer of 1547, he had quoted Zwingli against Luther that the 'doctrine, *Solafides justificat,* is a foundation and principle to deny the presence of Christ's natural body really in the Sacrament' and maintained that 'whoever has admitted the doctrine of "only faith" in justification is compelled to reject the Sacrament of the Eucharist in the way we profess it.' Evidently the way in which Gardiner professed it was that, after consecration, the natural body and blood of Christ are present *corporaliter*. We must beware, however, of imputing to Gardiner a gross belief in a carnal presence. We have seen that Ambrose, from whom the realist tradition stems, and even Paschasius, insisted upon the spiritual nature of the 'natural' body present in the sacrament.[34]

He also wrote a Latin letter to Vadianus, a Swiss opponent of the Real Presence, pointing out that it was one thing to refute 'papistical and sophistical errors', but he had wished that he had stopped at those limits,

> ... and had not trampled down the wheat with the tares. I do not think any fair reader will be convinced that the ancient authors are on your side in this controversy. If this is an error, it is one commended to us by the Fathers and by the Apostolic men themselves; and what good man could not listen to such a statement, not to speak of believing it ?[35]

He exhorts men to unite with him in propagating 'the one pure evangelical doctrine, which is in accordance with the primitive church'.

Others were of the same opinion, including Bishop Tunstall, who told his nephew Bernard Gilpin that Innocent III had been 'greatly overseen' in pressing transubstantiation upon the Church.[36] Redmayne, the first Master of Trinity, who certainly never rejected the Real Presence, said on his deathbed in 1551 that he had studied the matter for twelve years, and found that some of the Fathers had written plainly contrary to transubstantiation, and that in others it was not taught nor maintained.[37] It is clear from what Cranmer wrote later, 'that not long before I wrote the said

Catechism, I was in error of the real Presence, as I was many years past in divers other errors, as of transubstantiation',[38] that Cranmer makes a distinction between a doctrine of the Real Presence and explaining it in terms of transubstantiation. Cranmer had begun to feel that it was possible to believe in the Real Presence without holding either transubstantiation or the Lutheran doctrine of consubstantiation. Mason goes on to point out that it was from this high ground, on the one hand a belief in the Real Presence and on the other a rejection of transubstantiation, that Cranmer was dragged down by Nicholas Ridley, Bishop of London. Ridley had been influenced by reading Bertram Ratramnus, and his work subsequently influenced Cranmer. Ratramnus (AD 868) questioned the implicit transubstantiation in the Benedictine Radbertus's (AD 785–860) work *De Corpore et Sanguine Domini* (831), claiming a more spiritual conception of the Real Presence than Radbertus's more carnal. Ratramnus's work was condemned in AD 1050 and put on the Index in 1559, to be removed in 1900. Pusey takes this book as representing the views of Ridley and Cranmer. Cranmer wrote that Ridley 'did confer with me, and by sundry persuasions and authorities of doctors, drew me quite from my opinion'.[39]

> By an intermediate position between any kind of assertion of the reception of the actual body and blood of Christ and any merely figurative view, he maintained the opinion which had sometimes been described as Virtualism, namely, that the faithful communicant sacramentally receives those effects of Christ's life and death which would be conveyed if there were a beneficial reception of His actual body and blood.[40]

It was this opinion that he embodied in his *Defence of the True Catholic doctrine of the Sacrament,* described as 'grounded and established upon God's Holy Word, and approved by the consent of the most ancient doctors of the Church'. He found no difficulty in exposing the doctrine of transubstantiation, but it was not so easy for him to be constructive. It immediately brought a reply from Stephen Gardiner, the Bishop of Winchester, who defended transubstantiation, and in 1551 elicited Cranmer's rejoinder. Cranmer's triumph was to dispose of the attempt to identify the teaching of the English Reformers in this matter as Zwinglian. In his biography A. J. Mason points out that this was a contest between experts, and in order rightly to judge Cranmer's doctrine on the subject it is necessary to realize how degraded and materialistic was the general opinion of the Mass at the time.

[Cranmer] would not in honesty give less than their fullest force
to those expressions in Scripture and in the Fathers which
seemed to treat the mystery as nothing but a virtual presence
and a commemorative token. It was an interpretation as one-
sided as that which Cranmer had discarded. But his
readjustment of belief never made him irreverent towards the
sacred ordinance, nor was he conscious of any departure from
loyalty to the teaching of the primitive Church.[41]

Both men were united in their desire to defend the catholic
doctrine of the Real Presence, but they differed in their understanding of the nature of that Presence in the definition of
transubstantiation, Cranmer repudiating it and Gardiner seeing it
as essential to a particular understanding of the Eucharistic
Presence. It was natural, therefore, that they should both appeal to
Scripture with equal devotion, but in comparing and contrasting
them, Tavard[42] points out that Gardiner

would not read Scripture against the common consent of the
Church at any period of her history. Cranmer would find a
wonderful agreement between the Church and Scripture in the
first five or six centuries, over against the subsequent Church,
poisoned, as he thought, by the Bishops of Rome.

Cranmer's conviction was that the faith of the early centuries was
nearer to the scriptural source of doctrine, and so he used the
Fathers negatively to eliminate defining the Real Presence in terms
of transubstantiation, making the point that this doctrinal definition had strayed from how the Fathers had understood the
Eucharistic Presence. Then he uses the Fathers positively to
support his doctrine of the Real Presence. In Gardiner this use of
Scripture and the Fathers is reversed, positively to support transubstantiation and negatively to dismiss Cranmer's viewpoint, but
his appeal is also to the consensus of the Roman Church at that
time. Tavard accuses Cranmer of reading the Bible and the Fathers
through the spectacles of the Continental Reformers, but is forget-
ting that his own spectacles are a particular Roman point of view
he shares with the Anglican Gardiner and so is not wholly objective
himself.

The martyr's cause

Whatever others may have said, Cranmer claimed to the end, and
his appeal testifies to this, that he never meant to teach anything

contrary to the Word of God or to the Holy Catholic Church of Christ. His aim was to teach the doctrine which was held by the most holy learned Fathers and martyrs of the Church. He said that the real meaning of the accusation brought against him was that he did not allow the modern doctrine of the Sacrament. This was because he would not consent to words unauthorized by Scripture and unknown to the ancient Fathers, the innovations invented by men to overthrow the old and pure religion. His use of the patristic argument in its negative and positive applications has already been demonstrated, and other examples will be given from his contributions to The Book of Homilies in a later chapter. As the architect of Anglican liturgical reconstruction the same underlying principles are present. There is no iconoclastic fury and no intention of unnecessary change, but a determined aim to restore the liturgy to the tone and spirit of the earlier centuries, the centuries of the Four Ecumenical Councils. Some would have extended the catholic period to include the Sixth or Seventh Councils, except for the use of images sanctioned by the latter. Negatively and positively the patristic argument is used to remove all expressions representing doctrines unknown to earlier ages and at variance with primitive teaching, and in the spirit of the primitive church the 'vulgar tongue' replaces Latin. Cranmer was a conservative reformer, and differed from those whose appeal was to *Sola Scriptura:* he took his stand on the Bible as interpreted by antiquity.

To estimate Cranmer justly is difficult because he lacked the moral courage for dealing with the Tudor monarchs and was prone to changing his views when pressure was put upon him. Nevertheless, despite his weaknesses – and there are many – Cranmer is at his best in an age of bitter controversy when reforming the formularies of the church in that mediating and temperate spirit which breathes through the English Articles. It also finds expression in his genius for language and liturgy in the Prayer Book. Though influenced by Continental reformers, his primary aim was to preserve the continuity of the Church of England, and this gave to the English Reformation largeness and capacity. He anticipated Richard Hooker's argument that the sufficiency of Scripture was necessary for what pertained to salvation, but for the ordering of the Church it gave no complete guidance, so that respect should be had to tradition, 'the mind and purpose of the old Fathers', and to 'sound reason'. In resting its defence on the fundamental principles of Catholic Christianity, the supreme authority of the Bible and sound learning, what emerged in the Church of England was Anglicanism that could never be labelled

Cranmerianism in the same sense that Luther and Calvin gave birth to Lutheranism and Calvinism. It was the presence on English soil of the primitive church of antiquity.

John Jewel 1522–1571

Archbishop Parker, in the reign of Queen Elizabeth I, never lost sight of the importance of asserting before the whole Church the true and Catholic character of the Church of England. The position of Anglicanism, a word not used in the sixteenth century, is described often, somewhat unfairly, as a *via media,* a sort of compromise that equally removes it from Roman Catholicism and popular Protestantism. Anglicanism is founded not upon any compromise but upon a distinct principle, and this principle is the retention of everything scriptural and primitive, and the rejection of everything medieval which was inconsistent with primitive Christianity. The Archbishop's concern was that the Church of England required a clear enunciation of these principles upon which it was grounded in order to prevent it drifting away from its moorings. Parker himself was sufficiently equipped to do this, though his own humble estimate of himself and the burdens of his office may be reasons for his disinclination. This important work was assigned to John Jewel.

An assessment

'John Jewel was an Anglican, after Archbishop Parker the most important of the first generation of Elizabethan churchmen, the heir of the Christian humanists, of Cranmer, and the progenitor of Richard Hooker.'[43] With the persecution and death of Cranmer, Latimer and Ridley, John Jewel was one of the exiles driven from his native land. Sometime Fellow of Corpus Christi College, Oxford, he had a reputation as a student for rising at four in the morning and working continuously until ten at night. At an early period of his life he began to study St Augustine, and in after years followed this by an acquaintance with the whole range of patristic literature. During his exile in Strasbourg and Zurich as the guest of Peter Martyr it was his practice every afternoon to read aloud to his host the works of the ancient Fathers, and here it was that he built up the stores of learning which he employed afterwards with such effect.

When Queen Mary died in 1558 he returned to England, and as

Bishop of Salisbury from 1559–71 he became the defender and apologist of the Church of England, first as an outspoken critic of the Elizabethan settlement of religion and later against all those who were critical of it. J. C. Sladden describes the impression made upon one by a straightforward unaided reading of Jewel's works.

> Such a reader quickly becomes aware of the reformer's immense erudition, nowhere greater than in the patristic field. Even allowing for the environment of similar learning, and the help Jewel may have had from like-minded colleagues, his knowledge appears colossal and his power of selection and arrangement usually most effective. Further perusal discloses a tendency towards a regular method of presentation in dealing with the several points of doctrine, use and discipline which he takes up. At its best the author carries all before him in an almost devastating way, although he never loses control and does not often stray beyond the bounds of courtesy. His typical way is to leap off from a Scriptural spring-board and dive into the Fathers of the first six centuries, emerging triumphant after a shorter or longer sojourn and (whenever possible) not without reference to some later writer of the Roman obedience whom he can claim to be on his side.

He adds in a footnote,

> He can be almost violent on occasion, as when he accuses Harding and his fellow-Romanists of 'infinite follies and errors' wherein they have forsaken the fellowship of the most holy Fathers; and 'as Eudoxius said to the heretic about Eutyches ... Ye have removed yourselves both from all priestly communion, and also from the presence of Christ'. (*Defence*, p. 56). Jewel rarely goes as far as this.[44]

The Challenge Sermon

It all began with his famous sermon at Paul's Cross on 26 November 1559. The contention of what has come to be regarded as a 'remarkable discourse' was that the Church of England, in the points on which she differed from the Roman Church, had Christian antiquity on her side. It avoided theological speculations and its method was historical. Twenty-seven propositions were laid down, most of them relating to the Eucharist and the Roman usages in the celebration of the Mass. In arguing against private Masses and non-communicating attendance he not only quotes

Callixtus, a former Bishop of Rome, in support of his argument, but also St Chrysostom on the *Epistle to the Ephesians* and St Gregory in his *Dialogues,* citing their support in the exhorting of the people to receive Holy Communion.[45] Then he points out to the Roman Church that in their practice,

> ... they stand this day against so many old fathers, so many doctors, so many examples of the primitive church, so manifest and so plain words of the holy scriptures; and yet have they herein not one father, not one doctor, not one allowed example of the primitive church to make for them.[46]

Then came the famous oft-quoted statement:

> If any learned man of all our adversaries, or if all the learned men that be alive, be able to bring one sufficient sentence out of any old catholic Doctor, or Father, or out of any old General Council, or out of the Holy Scriptures of God, [that is relating to the proving of the twenty-seven propositions], I am content to yield unto him and subscribe.[47]

So he became the representative of English reform,

> but committed only to such assertions of catholic truth as could be justified by reference to the double standard of the Scriptures and the doctrine of the primitive Church, as expressed by authoritative councils and the consent of the Fathers.[48]

Frere continues:

> Thus the contest was a contest of methods quite as much as results. It was only to be expected that the exact application of the Anglican method could not take place all at once, and that, so far as results went, its earlier conclusions must needs be somewhat provisional: further enquiry and exacter scholarship were sure hereafter to modify them in detail. But meanwhile Jewel pledged himself and others to obtain the best results that they could, and before all things to maintain the supremacy of their method as against the papal method. It was a fortunate circumstance that such a scholar as Jewel was available for the task.

The title-page of the 'Challenge Sermon'[49] bears two mottoes which highlight the central thought – the appeal to antiquity. The first is a sentence from Tertullian: *Praejudicatum est adversus omnes haereses: id est verum quodcunque primum; id est adulterum quodcunque posterius;* This is a prejudice against all heresies : that that thinge is true, whatsoever was first : that is corrupt, whatsoever came after'.

The second is a clause from the Nicene Canon, Σ Εθη ἀρχαῖα κρατείτω: 'let the ancient customs prevail or be maintained', and is found in Canon VI. This canon was formulated with particular reference to the Church of Alexandria, which had been troubled by the irregular proceedings of Meletius. It was to confirm the ancient privileges of the bishops of that see which he had invaded, while the latter part of it applies to all metropolitans and confirms all their ancient privileges. This general principle of the appeal to antiquity, and (to be consistent with Tertullian's dictum) to the earliest antiquity, has been absorbed into the system of Anglican divinity. There is no deviation in Jewel from Scripture as the ultimate standard of doctrine, while the Fathers help in guiding us to the sense of Scripture. The challenge was issued on three other occasions, the following Lent after his consecration, once at Court and again at Paul's Cross.

Henry Cole's response

Henry Cole, who had been Dean of St Paul's in Queen Mary's time, and a papist participant in the Westminster Disputation, was first to pick up the gauntlet thrown down by Jewel in the second preaching. This produced a correspondence, in which Cole attempted to put Jewel on the defensive by challenging him to prove the points made in his sermon. Jewel retained his initiative as accuser, insisting that the imprisoned Cole prove the existence of private Masses, communion in one kind, the liturgy 'in a strange tongue', the Pope as head of the universal Church, transubstantiation, the people forbidden to pray or read the Scriptures in their mother tongue, and various articles in the early church, from Scripture, the Councils, and the writings of the Fathers.[50] Cole responded,

> If it be as you say, all is said that can be then you and I should do well to weigh the reasons of both sides ... Let you and me weigh your men's reasons and ours by the fathers' weights and balances, and see who reasoneth most like St. Augustine, St. Basil, St. Cyprian, Tertullian, Irenaeus, and Dionysius, the councils and other such weights fit for that purpose. Thus we see there is yet good cause, why men should soberly learn from one another.[51]

Jewel has been described as grossly unfair to Cole, 'who upheld the opinions of John Gerson on the superiority of a general council to the pope'. Cole 'found it impossible to argue with the Bishop of Salisbury, who entrenched himself in what he called the primitive

church and refused to accept anything that he could not find
there'.[52] It was the static conception of Jewel that destroyed any
development or unfolding of the doctrines Cole had pointed out,
and Jewel was forced to modify later his limitation of the first six
hundred years. Cole, not being free to debate, was not the right
person to challenge Jewel, and frustrating though it was for both of
them, the publication of the correspondence added to Jewel's
reputation as an apologist for the Church of England.

The *Apologia* and *Defence*

It was the response of Thomas Harding, a man of considerable
learning and much ability, formerly Professor of Hebrew at
Oxford, then at Louvain, which produced from Jewel his *Apologia*
and *Defence*. It was called ' the first methodical statement of the
position of the Church of England against the Church of Rome,
and the groundwork of all subsequent controversy'.[53] J. E. Booty
points out that this statement by Mandell Creighton is borne out
by the literature of the *Admonition Controversy*. He quotes John
Whitgift: 'It were needless labour to make any particular recital of
those points of doctrine which the Church of England at this day
doth hold and maintain; for they be at large set out in sundry
English books, and especially in the *Apology for the Church of
England,* and the *Defence* of the same'.[54] These works were not
considered private and personal writings, but were recognized as
official documents of the English Church and State. The
Convocation of 1563, according to Bishop Burnet, wanted to have
Jewel's *Apologia* joined to the Articles, and Archbishop Parker
wanted all cathedrals and collegiate churches and private houses
to have copies.[55] Booty also points out that diocesan articles,
injunctions and parish account books provide further evidence
that the *Apologia* and the *Defence* were treated as official and necessary, together with the Bible, the Book of Common Prayer and the
Homilies. Bishop Barnes of Durham in 1577 issued injunctions
that the *Defence of the Apology* is a requirement in every church in
the diocese and elsewhere, as 'commended by public authority'.[56]
Jewel was also involved in the production of the Thirty-Nine
Articles[57] and the Second Book of the Homilies.[58]
    This classic in the literature of English theology, *Apologia
Ecclesiae Anglicanae*, appeared in 1562 and is described by the
author as 'a little book in the Latin tongue ... containing the whole
sum of the catholic faith, now professed and freely preached in
England'. It was translated into English, Italian, Spanish, French,

German, Greek, and Welsh. Its importance was recognized by the English Church, and the Council of Trent is said to have appointed two learned prelates to furnish a reply, which never appeared. Jewel was the chief author rather than the sole author, receiving 'notes, counsels, and devises' of many, as Harding put it, and while in the 1567 and 1570 editions of the *Defence* Jewel wrote as if he were the sole author of the original work, he implied that it was representative of the convictions of the entire English church, the product of her long history and recent reformation. Jewel's concern was that the *Apologia* be an expression of the mind of the English church rather than the views of certain persons within it. Its concern is not to upset or destroy, but to recover and reconstitute the true Church and to rejoin the Christians of the sixteenth century to the pure church of the first few centuries.

The first part of the *Apologia* claims that if the Church of England

> ... do but shew it plain, that God's holy gospel, the ancient bishops, and the primitive church do make on our side, and that we have not without just cause left these men, and rather have returned to the apostles and old catholic fathers; ... and if they themselves which fly our doctrine, and would be called Catholics, shall manifestly see how all those titles of antiquity, whereof they boast so much, are quite shaken out of their hands, and that there is more pith in this our cause than they thought for.[59]

The second part sets out the essential faith of the Church of England, following the lines of the Nicene Creed on the subjects of the Trinity and Incarnation, the rites and ceremonies briefly reviewed in turn. In the third part, charges of sectarianism and antinomian tendencies are rebutted and from here we quote:

> Were Origen, Ambrose, Augustine, Chrysostom, Gelasius, Theodoret, forsakers of the catholic faith? Was so notable a consent of so many ancient bishops and learned men nothing else but a conspiracy of heretics? or is that now condemned in us which was then commended in them? or is the thing now, by alteration only of men's affection, suddenly become schismatic, which in them was counted catholic? or shall that which in times past was true, now by and by, because it liketh not these men, be judged false?[60]

The fourth part attacks the abuses of the Church of Rome, while the fifth part weighs many of its customs in the balance of antiquity

and finds them wanting. The final section deals with the question
of supremacy, with crown, pope, and council, asserting the Church
of England's independence from the Bishop of Rome, who has no
more authority over her than the Patriarch of Antioch or the
Patriarch of Alexandria. The canonical Scriptures are the ultimate
test of all ecclesiastical doctrines. Frere[61] describes it in literary
terms alone as a 'masterpiece of terseness and cogency' in fifty
pages of close argument, designed to show that no charge of heresy
can be brought against the English church, because the necessary
changes are within its competence and consistent with a catholic
position. The method of Jewel is to 'shew it plain that God's holy
gospel, the ancient bishops and the primitive Church do make on
our side, and that have not without just cause left these men, or
rather have returned to the apostles and old catholic Fathers'.

Among a number of inferior responses from the Roman side,
the able Harding's *Answer* (1564) to the sermon, and *Confutation*
(1565) in response to the *Apologia,* are pre-eminent. Jewel
answered the *Confutation* in his *Defence of the Apology* (1567).
Harding responded with *A Detection of Sundry Foul Errors uttered by
M. Juell,* to which the bishop responded with an enlarged edition
of his *Defence.* Frere points out that the controversy was swollen
beyond all bounds, and the terse, pointed statements of the
Apologia were in danger of being lost in the thousand pages of
these men's controversial writings. The *Defence* is a work that
displays great powers of argument, an extraordinary wealth of
patristic learning, and carries a perplexing bibliography that is
discussed by Dr Jelf in the Preface to his edition of Jewel.[62] Yet both
men for all their learning did at times miss the sense of the authors
whom they cited, and at times the authorities they cite will not
sustain the weight of the argument constructed upon them. They
were also ensnared into quoting as genuine works which, in the
light of more information and keener criticism, have since been
questioned, discredited, or set aside as spurious. For example,
Jewel refuses to acknowledge the *Apostolical Constitutions* to be a
work of St Clement of Rome as Harding had claimed. His reason
must now be abandoned, that a Bishop of Rome would write his
books in Latin not Greek. He argues for the authenticity of the
medieval legend of 'Pope Joan', in vogue before the Reformation
and not questioned until Luther. There is no excuse for Harding
accepting as genuine the *Donation of Constantine,* it had been amply
exposed as a forgery.

Jewel's Use of the Fathers

Both Southgate[63] and Booty[64] acknowledge that Jewel has no cut-and-dried thesis on the authority of the early Fathers for doctrine. The authority of the primitive church is limited; its test is the authority of Scripture and, as Sladden[65] points out, 'Cyprian and others are cited as showing that genuine "tradition" is that which is built upon authentically apostolic (i.e. Scriptural) foundations', and while Augustine is shown to rely on Scripture alone in dealing with Arians, Tertullian, Hilary and Augustine are quoted to reveal a healthy economy in Christian truth. In other words the Fathers served as an aid toward the understanding of Scripture, though Bromiley thinks that Jewel exalted the authority of the Fathers more than this, and pointed the way forward to the use made of them by Hooker and the Caroline divines.[66] Southgate views Jewel as considering that the Fathers were a 'primary authority in the interpretation of scriptures'.[67] Booty claims Jewel did not go that far, but limited the authority of the Fathers to whatever assistance they might give in attempting to understand a difficult passage.[68] He claims that while Jewel may use the Fathers to prove that private Masses were not the practice of the early church, he may not always use them in the same way as to matters of doctrine, or with regard to those things about which Scripture had something definite and important to say.

Booty concludes that to read Jewel's works is to discover that when he found an authority that seemed at odds with his convictions, he belittled that authority, demonstrating it to be in error. Hence, Jewel was not an altogether rational man, according to Booty, even when respecting reason and using it, but an emotionally-committed man. Southgate[69] claims that Jewel's conception of the interpretative authority of the patristic writings was neither rigid nor absolute. Interpreting the Scriptures was their primary function that meant studying patristic interpretations against the background of the scriptural passages interpreted. Any accepted conclusion had then to be subjected to reasonable demonstration and proof. Following Augustine, Jewel maintained that no teaching is received because of those who held it, but because such proponents are 'able to persuade' the student 'either by canonical writers or else by some likely reason'.[70]

> Throughout the whole discourse of this Apology, in the defence of the catholic truth of our religion, next unto God's holy word, [we] have used no proof or authority so much as the expositions and judgements of the holy fathers. We ... give God thanks in

their behalf, for that it hath pleased him to provide so worthy instruments for his church.[71]

Southgate claims that Jewel consistently and skilfully applied these principles in his own handling of the patristic exegesis, giving the method he advocated the all-important support of example. None of the Fathers were systematic thinkers and their writings in variety and quantity were not therefore definitive works, and so they were free from the limitations that prevented the conciliar decrees from having a similar usefulness in scriptural interpretation. Jewel had not only a sound knowledge of the literature and its historical background but also an unusual fund of common sense, and though he was criticized for his habit of piling up quantities of patristic citations, as Southgate points out,

> When numerous passages were cited from different works of an author, when additional passages were cited to the same effect, almost in the same words, from other fathers, both Greek and Latin, the reader could not but agree that Jewel had managed to come very close to the original patristic meaning; that he was not forcing the patristic words into a sixteenth-century mould.[72]

From the canon of Scripture to that of faith and order, the doctrine of the Church of England 'be cases not of wit, but of faith; not of eloquence but of truth; not invented or devised by us, but from the apostles and holy fathers and founders of the Church by long succession brought unto us ... we claim to be "the keepers not the masters" ... Touching the substance of our religion we believe that the ancient catholic fathers believed ...'[73] When Harding in the confutation of the *Apology* made the accusation that in doing away with the control of the church over doctrine and the interpretation of the Bible, the reformers would fall prey to individualism, Jewel rejected this criticism. In no way had the Church of England been reduced to relying upon wit and individual inspiration. Indeed the Church of England claimed the authority of an older tradition, that of the Fathers, a tradition objective and substantial that led neither to Rome nor to anarchy. So he turned Harding's argument on himself, insisting that it was Rome, not the Church of England, that had substituted the judgement of men for the patristic tradition. In embracing the Fathers as witnesses of God's truth the Church of England 'alleges against you the manifest and undoubted and agreeable judgements of the more learned holy fathers, and thereby, as by approved and faithful witnesses, we disclose the infinite follies of your doctrine.'[74]

As for Cranmer before him, for Jewel the Fathers were not the fountainhead of original doctrine but the interpreters of that fountainhead which was Holy Scripture. Hence of itself their teaching could not be authoritative because it was patristic because their primary function is the interpretation of the Scriptures, so that whatever they wrote must be interpreted in the light of the scriptural passages interpreted. He would not accept a teaching on the ground of one writer only, unless the teaching was consistent with other canonical writers or for some likely reason. Similarly, in his interpretative method in handling patristic texts and their historical background, of which his knowledge was as extensive as it was profound, any patristic teaching to be regarded as valid authority must be consistent with a general agreement among the Fathers, not merely an individual opinion. This was the reason for the plethora of patristic citations in his works, because whatever question he put to the Fathers he always sought a unanimous agreement and knew that this could never be based on the slightness of one citation. This was entirely consistent with the method of the Fathers themselves who would never expect any teaching to be accepted on their individual authority but only after due consultation with their fellow bishops. His concern as a scholar was to examine these texts in their original form and contexts, rather than at a distance in lists of collected quotations on particular theological themes, as Cranmer had done. He was sceptical about such lists of quotations lifted from their context.

As a scholar, Jewel was concerned not merely with whether the work was genuine but also with historical criticism, so that the historical context, the circumstances surrounding the composition of the work, had to be studied in relation to the author's life and the wider context of all his writings. This enabled disputed passages to be seen in comparison with others, providing a clearer context of more immediate understanding. As a corollary to this, the Fathers must be certain in their conclusions. Finally, of necessity, any particular teaching must be regarded as essential to Christian doctrine, not a matter of choice, regardless of their agreement and certainty. Like the Fathers, Jewel himself was a preacher and a controversialist, and was not always consistently objective himself. Therefore he could appreciate that their words were not always to be taken with complete literalness, because 'In the sway of disputation' they used 'oftentimes to enlarge their talk above the common cause of truth', when as pastors their concern was to enlighten their hearers with wisdom. Southgate points out that Jewel's procedure is consistent with the generally-accepted methods of modern scholarship, even though it was as rare in his own day as it is today.

> ... when allowance is made for the limitations of historical study in the sixteenth century, Jewel's conclusions do not appear to differ markedly from those of the moderate Roman Catholic scholars like Duchesne. Without question Jewel himself was honestly convinced of the rightness of his own conclusions; he believed patristic authority to be valid authority; on patristic evidence he judged the Church of Rome guilty of denying its early heritage. That he could prove this in open controversy with an able opponent backed by the full resources of Louvain must in itself have been singularly convincing to him. Not once in all his writings was he forced either to avoid a challenge or to admit that the teachings of the fathers went against him. It was a heartening achievement.[75]

None of the contestants escaped the appearance at one time or another of fitting the authorities to preconceived notions. From the markings in Jewel's books the suggestion is that as he read them he was looking for passages which would add weight to his preconceived arguments. Nevertheless, Greenslade quotes an eloquent passage to exemplify the attitude of the Reformers to the Fathers:

> But what say we of the Fathers, Augustine, Ambrose, Hierome, Cyprian, etc. What shall we think of them, or what account may we make of them ? They be interpreters of the word of God. They were learned men and learned Fathers; the instruments of the mercy of God and vessels full of grace. We despise them not, we read them, we reverence them and give thanks unto God for them. They were witnesses unto the truth, they were worthy pillars and ornaments in the church of God. Yet may they not be compared with the word of God. We may not build upon them: we may not make them the foundation and warrant of our conscience; we may not put our trust in them. Our trust is in the name of the Lord ... They are our fathers, but not fathers unto God; they are the stars, fair and beautiful and bright; yet they are not the sun; they bear witness of the light, they are not the light. Christ is the sun of righteousness, Christ is the Light which lighteneth every man that cometh into this world. His word is the word of truth.[76]

Greenslade comments: 'In this spirit, grateful, respectful, but cautious, many of the earlier English Reformers were building a stronghold from which Hooker and others could defend the

Church of England when the battle shifted to another front against the biblicist Puritans of the next generations.' J. J. Blunt,[77] Lady Margaret Professor of Divinity at Cambridge in 1839, wrote that Jewel was 'a man, indeed, of matchless learning, which he nevertheless wields, ponderous as it is, like a plaything; of a most polished wit; a style whether Latin or English, the most pure or expressive, such as argues a precision in the character of his ideas, and a lucid order in the arrangement of them, quite his own'. Southgate claims that Jewel's

> chief concern therefore was to provide an interpretative authority without accepting either the solution of an authoritative church or the opposite extreme of complete dependence upon special revelation ... He endeavoured to find an authority which was objective and whose meaning was demonstrable to reason. This authority for interpretation he found in the early church, particularly in the writings of the Fathers ... he stands alone in the completeness of his authoritative method. His writings constitute the first thoroughgoing attempt to prove to the world the Catholicity of English Doctrine, to demonstrate that the teachings of the English Church at no point departed from the Church of the apostles and the fathers.[78]

Hooker, who was under Jewel's patronage in his early years described Jewel as 'the worthiest divine that Christendom hath bred for some hundreds of years',[79] and 'certainly no private doctor of the Church of England have so nearly attained the authoritative position of symbolical books'.[80]

Notes

1. S. L. Greenslade, *The English Reformers and the Fathers of the Church, An Inaugural Lecture as Regius Professor of Ecclesiastical History* (Clarendon Press, Oxford, 1960), p. 3.
2. Greenslade, pp. 4ff.
3. K. J. Walsh, *The Acts and Monuments of John Foxe* (London, 1843–9), vol. viii, p. 4, cited by K. J. Walsh, in 'Cranmer and the Fathers, especially in the *Defence*', *Journal of Religious History* 11 (1980), p. 234.
4. C. Smyth, 'Thomas Cranmer and the Church of England', in *Thomas Cranmer*, with new Preface by A. C. Capey (Brynmill Press, Doncaster, 1989), p. 13.
5. C. Dunlop, 'The First Great Figure in Anglicanism', *ibid.* p. 18.
6. K. J. Walsh, *ibid.* p. 235
7. Greenslade, *ibid.* p. 11.
8. Thomas Cranmer, 'Cranmer's Library', *Works*, vol. ii, sect. X, ed. G.

E. Duffield (Courtenay Reformation Classics, Appleford, 1964),
p. 341.

9.   A. J. Mason, *Thomas Cranmer* (Methuen, London, 1898), p. 85;
Thomas Cranmer, *Works*, vol. ii (Parker Society, Cambridge, 1846,
Johnson Reprint), ed. Rev. John Edmund Cox, p. 161.

10. J. I. Packer, 'The Introduction', *The Work of Thomas Cranmer*
(Courtenay Library of Reformation Classics 2, Sutton Courtenay
Press, Appleford, 1964), ed. G. E. Duffield, pp. xi–xii.

11. *Ibid.* p. xii.

12. Cranmer, *Works*, vol. ii, p. 227.

13. Walsh, *ibid.* p. 237.

14. *Ibid.* p. 238.

15. J. Strype, *Memorials of Thomas Cranmer* (Oxford 1848-54), vol. ii. pp.
335–7; cited by Walsh, *ibid.* p. 239.

16. H. Jenkyns, *The Remains of Thomas Cranmer,* vol. I (Oxford, 1833),
pp. lxxvii; vol. ii. p. 291; cited by Walsh, *ibid.* p. 239.

17. P. Brooks, *Thomas Cranmer's Doctrine of the Eucharist* (London, 1965),
pp. 41–3; cited by Walsh, *ibid.* p. 239.

18. D. MacCulloch, *Thomas Cranmer* (Yale University Press, New Haven
and London 1996), p. 468.

19. Walsh, *ibid.* 238.

20. *Ibid.* p. 242.

21. *Ibid.* p. 243.

22. *Ibid.* p. 244.

23. *Ibid.* p. 245.

24. *Ibid.* p. 247.

25. Cranmer, *Works*, vol. ii, pp. 1–67.

26. *Ibid.* pp. 118ff.

27. *Ibid.* p. 121, citing John Chrysostom, *De Lazaro.*

28. *Ibid.* p. 122, citing Gregory Nazianzen, *Orat.* xxvii., *Theol. I. Adver.
Eunomian.*

29. *Ibid.* p. 124, citing Gregory Nazianzen, *Id. Orat.,* xxxix.

30. Mason, p. 98, citing H. Jenkyns, *The Remains of Thomas Cranmer*
(Oxford 1833), vol. i, p. 216.

31. *Ibid.*

32. *A Necessary Doctrine and Erudition for Any Christian Man, or The King's
Book* (SPCK, London, 1932, published for the Church Historical
Society), being a photographic reprint of Bishop Charles Lloyd's
edition of *Formularies of Faith Put Forth by Authority during the Reign of
Henry VIII* (Oxford, 1825), p. 213 to the end, p. 55.

33. Cranmer, 'On the Lord's Supper', *Works* (Parker Society,
Cambridge, 1844), p. 3.

34. C. W. Dugmore, *The Mass and the English Reformers* (London, 1958),
pp. 184–5

35. Mason, p. 125, citing Jenkyns, vol. i, p. 193.

36. *Ibid.* p. 127, citing Bernard Gilpin, *Gilpin's Gilpin,* (London, 1752),
p. 170.

37. *Ibid.* citing Foxe, *Acts and Monuments* (London, 1641), vol. vi, pp. 267ff.

38. *Ibid.* citing Jenkyns, vol. iii, p. 13.

39. *Ibid.* citing Jenkyns, vol. iv, p. 97.

40. Darwell Stone, *A History of the Doctrine of the Holy Eucharist* vol. ii (Longmans & Co, London, 1909), p. 128.

41. Mason, p. 136.

42. George Tavard, *The Quest for Catholicity* (William Clowes & Sons, London and Beccles, 1963), p. 8.

43. W. M. Southgate, *John Jewel and the Problem of Doctrinal Authority* (Harvard University Press, 1962), p. x.

44. J. C. Sladdon, *The Appeal to the Fathers in John Jewel, Bishop of Salisbury, 1560–1571.* (Texte u.Untersuchungen Studia Patristica vol. ix, p. 594; Akademie – Verlac – Berlin, 1966).

45. John Jewel, *Works,* vol. i (Parker Society, Cambridge, 1845), pp. 19, 20.

46. *Ibid.*

47. *Ibid.* p. 20.

48. W. H. Frere, *A History of the English Church in the Reigns of Elizabeth and James I. 1558–1625* (Macmillan & Co, London, 1904), p. 86.

49. Jewel, *Works,* The First Portion, 1560 Edition (Parker Society, Cambridge, 1845).

50. Jewel, *Works,* vol. i (Parker Society, Cambridge, 1845), p. 28.

51. *Ibid.* p. 30.

52. J. E. Booty, *John Jewel as Apologist of the Church of England* (SPCK, London, 1963), p. 34, citing J. M. Veech, *Dr. Nicholas Sanders* (Louvain, 1935), p. 76, cf. E. J. MacDermott, 'The Life of Thomas Stapleton' (Unpublished Dissertation, University of London, 1950).

53. Mandell Creighton, 'John Jewel', *Dictionary of National Biography,* vol. xxix, p. 378.

54. Booty, p. 3, citing John Whitgift, *Works,* vol. i (Parker Society, Cambridge, 1852); cf. Hooker's *Laws of Ecclesiastical Polity* (London, 1907), p. 260 ; Lancelot Andrewes, *Opuscula Quaedam Posthuma,* (*LACT,* Oxford, 1852), p. 90.

55. *Ibid,* p. 6, citing Gilbert Burnet, *The History of the Reformation of the Church of England,* ed. Nicholas Pocock (Oxford, 1865), vol. iii, p. 516.

56. *Ibid.* p. 7, citing W. M. Kennedy, *Elizabethan Episcopal Administration* (London, 1924), vol. ii, p. 79.

57. *Ibid.* p. 290, citing J. Jewel, *Works,* vol. iv (Parker Society, Cambridge 1845–50), p. xviii. E. T. Green, *The Thirty-Nine Articles and the Age of the Reformation* (London, 1896).

58. John Griffiths, ed. *The Two Books of the Homilies* (Clarendon Press, Oxford, 1859; SPCK, London, 1908), p. xxxiv.

59. Jewel, *Works,* The Third Portion, p. 56.

60. *Ibid.* p. 67.

61. Frere, p. 91.

62. Jewel, *Works,* The Third Portion, p. xxvii.
63. Southgate, ch. 11.
64. Booty, ch. 6.
65. Sladden, p. 596.
66. G. W. Bromiley, *John Jewel, 1522–72, the Apologist of the Church of England* (CBR Press, London, 1948), p. 29.
67. Southgate, pp. 178–9.
68. Booty, p. 137.
69. Southgate, pp. 179ff.
70. Jewel, *Works,* vol. iii, 'Defence', p. 227.
71. Jewel, *Works,* vol. iii, 'Defence', p. 225
72. Southgate, *ibid,* p. 175.
73. Jewel, *Works,* vol. ii, 'Reply', p. 810.
74. Jewel, *Works,* vol. iii, p. 229.
75. Southgate, *ibid,* pp. 182–3
76. Greenslade, p. 8.
77. J. J. Blunt, *The Reformation in England* (H. Virtue & Co, no date), p. 305.
78. Southgate, pp. 119–20.
79. Richard Hooker, 'The Laws of Ecclesiastical Polity', Bk. II, ch. vi, 4, in *The Works of that Learned and Judicious Divine, Mr Richard Hooker: with an account of his Life and Death by Isaac Walton* (OUP, Oxford, 1880), vol. i, p. 254.
80. John Dowden, *Outlines of the History of the Theological Literature of the Church of England from The Reformation to the End of the Eighteenth Century, The Bishop Paddock Lectures,* 1896–7 (SPCK, London, 1897), p. 29.

3

Fathers and Formularies

The desire of his contemporaries to place Jewel's *Apologia* along-side the Formularies of the Church of England, its foundation documents, is testimony to the great esteem in which the Church of England has always held the Fathers. Their value was twofold, as witnesses to the content of the primitive faith and as a guide to the right interpretation of Holy Scripture. Scripture was the supreme standard of faith and the Fathers represented the tradition of the Church by which Scripture was rightly interpreted, The Vincentian Canon was the test of genuine tradition, what has been believed everywhere, always, and by all. Those foundation documents, The Canons, the Thirty-Nine Articles, the Homilies, the Book of Common Prayer, and the Ordinal, reinforce the importance of the place of the Fathers in Anglican divinity.

The Canons of 1571

An attempt to reform Canon Law resulted in the Canons of 1571. In the ten sections there is a memorable Canon on preaching that embodied the spirit of the Reformers. It states explicitly that preachers shall 'see to it that they teach nothing in the way of a sermon, which they would have religiously held and believed by the people, save what is agreeable to the teaching of the Old or New Testament, and what the catholic fathers and ancient bishops have collected from this self-same doctrine.' It goes on to stress that such preachers are to uphold the authority of Articles, Prayer Book, and Ordinal; 'Whoever does otherwise, and perplexes the people with contrary doctrine, shall be excommunicated.'[1] In an official Anglican document is the expressed intention of the English church to promote the study of the Fathers among its clergy. Here is expressed the true Catholicism of the Church of

England. The limits of toleration in variations of doctrine within
the Church of England are, first of all, that which can be proved by
Holy Scripture, and secondly, that which the Catholic Fathers and
ancient Bishops have collected out of that Scripture. That is the
fundamental theological principle of our Reformers in requiring
from clergy and laity in their submission to doctrine, nothing more
and nothing less than could be proved from Scripture and which
had been collected from the Scriptures by the Catholic Fathers. As
part of the Catholic Church, the Church of England bound herself
to the teachings and decisions of the Primitive Catholic Church,
and this placed upon it an oecumenical responsibility not to depart
from the faith and order of the One, Holy, Catholic and Apostolic
Church. Hence we are bound by the Creeds which have received
the sanction of Councils, and must refrain from putting upon
them any sense not intended by their authors. While she may have
authority to decree rites and ceremonies, she has no authority to
depart from the faith and order of that Apostolic tradition. It is an
appeal, not to a particular individual theologian, but to the mind
of the Church, the *ecclesiastical mind*. This is, in itself, consistent
with the method of the Fathers whose definitions of doctrine were
never based on the mind of an individual or mere group, but must
be expressive of the mind of the whole Church. For the word
catholic, from the Greek word καθολικός, originates from two
words, κατά and ὅλος[2] which in their root meaning define the
inner wholeness rather than mere communion, and certainly far
more than empirical communion. They describe the inner essence
rather than the external manifestation. Even when the word
embraces in itself the notion of universality, it certainly is not an
empirical universality, but an ideal one, the communion of ideas
not facts. Εκκλησία Καθολική never meant the 'world-wide
Church', but 'the orthodoxy of the Church', the truth of the 'Great
Church' as contrasted with the spirit of sectarian separation and
particularism.[3] It is the idea of integrity and purity that is being
expressed. It embraces the world rather than the world embracing
it, and then transforms and transfigures the world rather than the
world changing and adjusting it to the world's relativism. To live in
the καθολική is to live in life which is salvation, the life that the
Church is, the divine life of the Blessed Trinity, the catholic
process of *theosis*, deification, which is saving life.

Bishop Cosin was to commend this Canon as 'the Golden Rule
of the Church of England'.[4] On this same Canon, Bishop
Beveridge preached:

So wisely hath our Church provided against novelties; insomuch that had this one rule been duly observed as it ought, there would have been no such thing as heresy or schism amongst us; but we should have all continued firm both to the doctrine and discipline of the Universal Church, and so should have 'held fast the form of sound words' according to the apostle's counsel.[5]

The Canons of 1603

The Canons of 1603 root their authority for certain doctrine and practice in the ancient Fathers. Thus Canon XXXI reads, 'Forasmuch as the ancient Fathers of the Church, led by the example of the Apostles, appointed, &c., we following their holy and religious example, do constitute and decree, &c'. Canon XXXII reads, 'According to the judgement of the ancient Fathers, and the practice of the primitive Church, We do ordain, &c'. Canon XXXIII states, 'It hath been long since provided by many decrees of the ancient Fathers, &c'. Canon LX begins, 'Forasmuch as it hath been a solemn, ancient, and laudable custom in the Church of God, continued from the Apostles' time, That, &c'. These Canons appeal to patristic authority for the observance of special seasons of ordination, for refusing to ordain a man both deacon and priest on the same day; for ordaining no man either deacon or priest without assigning to him some special sphere wherein his function might be exercised. Canon XXX states that the use of the sign of the Cross is retained as being consonant to the Word of God, and the Judgement of all the ancient Fathers.

The Thirty-Nine Articles

Within the contemporary disputes of reform the Thirty-Nine Articles provided an agreed body of teaching in the Church of England, but not a complete conspectus of religious teaching, and are no more a final exposition of Anglican teaching than the Elizabethan Prayer Book is Anglicanism's final word on liturgy. Unlike the Catholic Creeds, which have permanent and universal value, the value of the Articles is temporary, being concerned with disputes particular to this country in a former age. Nevertheless, in his famous *Tract XC* Newman could maintain 'our Articles ... the offspring of an uncatholic age, are through God's good providence, to say the least, not uncatholic, and may be subscribed to by those who aim at being catholic in heart and doctrine'. Owen

Chadwick comments that the novelty of Newman's handling of the Articles lay, not so much in an attempt 'to extract the maximum breadth from the language,' but in his handling of them in 'a Catholic direction.' He goes on to point out that, for the Oxford men, 'Their tradition had long sought to draw its divinity from the wells of antiquity, and assumed that the Articles of the sixteenth century would be found to be in agreement with the divinity thence drawn.'[6] The appeal to the Articles is to that which is much wider than its own particular age or place; it is to the faith of the universal Church of Christ contained in the Holy Scriptures as interpreted by the Church from the beginning.

Alexander Forbes (1817–75), the Bishop of Brechin, in writing on the interpretation of the Articles[7] stated that 'They must be read with the gloss of antecedent faith and preconceived notion.' 'At the time of their enforcement', he claims 'that they must have been read with the deep consciousness of the old traditional Christianity ... which had obtained in England since the days of St. Augustine of Canterbury, which had animated the faith of Lanfranc and of St. Anselm ...' Forbes points out that there is no other way to account for the rise of the Caroline school.

> There is nothing in Bishop Andrewes' works to shew that his views were those of a counter-Reformation, as we find later in the time of Laud. Educated in such a religion as I have attempted to describe, he applied his learning to develope his position, and the reverence in which he was held in the next generation, as well as during his lifetime, shews that his views had the strength and consistency of a hereditary position.

The Church of England holds neither more nor less than that, 'the Faith once delivered to the saints'. J. J. Blunt said of the Articles,

> ... though not formed expressly out of ancient models, they are to a very great degree consistent with ancient patristical precedent, and have been shown to correspond in the main, both in sentiment and phraseology, with the writings of the Primitive Church, both by Bishop Beveridge in his notes on his *Exposition of the Articles*; by Welchman; more recently and more fully by Mr Harvey (*Ecclesiae Anglicanae Vindex Catholicus.* Cambridge 1841); and still more recently by Mr. Browne (*An Exposition of the Thirty-Nine-Articles*, Edw. Harold Browne, 1850). Nor, indeed, does the language itself of the Articles fail, occasionally at least, to point to this fact; sufficiently often, at any rate, to show that their compilers were not under the impression which now prevails

among so many, that those writings are but dangerous edge-tools.[8]

(i) The Faith of the Undivided Church

In the spirit of this appeal to antiquity, Articles 1–5 and 8 assume without question the truth of the Catholic Creeds, affirming the doctrines of the Trinity and the Incarnation in the language of the ancient ecumenical councils, which can be nothing less than an affirmation of the authority of these councils and their definitions, which 'may be proved by most certain warrants of holy Scripture'. The spirit of the first five Articles is not restatement but the protecting of the familiar truths of the Faith, with the eighth Article expressing the conviction that the Church is to teach and the Bible to prove. The aim is apologetic, the preserving of the ancient faith from innovation by the Anabaptists on one side and the Roman church on the other. The doctrines of the Incarnation and Trinity are safeguarded, while the Creeds, like the Bible, are documents of the Faith rather than the Faith itself and so can never be isolated from the life of the Church.

(ii) Scripture and Tradition

Chillingworth's statement 'the Bible and the Bible only is the religion of Protestants' in the use that some have made of it, is not only inadequate in fairly representing what he meant originally, but misrepresents the place of the Bible in Anglican thinking, as the earlier quotation from Tavard concerning the Anglican understanding of the relationship between Scripture and Tradition demonstrates. It is the purpose of Articles 6, 20 and 21 to make this plain. While Article 6 says that 'Holy Scripture containeth all things necessary to salvation', and that nothing is to be believed as an article of faith that cannot be proved thereby, Article 20 states, 'The Church hath ... authority in Controversies of Faith ... yet it is not lawful for the Church to ordain anything that is contrary to God's Word written ...'. The Bible is to be expounded by the Church, which is not to stray outside Scriptural limits, which therefore means to teach the Creeds, 'for they may be proved by the most certain warrants of Holy Scripture'.

The Church's doctrinal authority rests in the Bible and the Creeds as expounded by the Church. In company with the early Fathers the Church of England denies the existence of any dogmatic tradition independent of the Bible, whereas in medieval

times the Roman church tended to put 'Tradition' on an equal
standing with Scripture as another source of doctrine. Article 21
which is really aimed at the Council of Trent may seem somewhat
negative, but its concern is to underline that only general consent
can give weight to dogmatic decisions, and the more general the
consent, the greater the authority with which they must be
regarded. The decisions of the first four General Councils are
unquestionably accepted in the Church of England, and, less
certainly the fifth, sixth, and seventh, though

> In fact, the fifth and sixth councils gave definitions on the
> refinements of Christology which the Anglicans of the sixteenth
> and seventeenth century happily accepted. Their handling of
> the seventh council condemning iconoclasm needs special treat-
> ment.[9]

This patristic spirit that is found in these Articles is such that
Bishop Forbes can state,

> ... it will be observed, that many of the sentences are almost in
> the very words of approved Church doctors and schoolmen. Not
> to mention the references to St. Jerome in the Sixth, and to the
> Pseudo-Augustine in the Twenty-ninth Articles, we shall find
> that many of the Articles enunciate truth in authoritative
> language. The seventeenth Article is a concise summary of St.
> Augustine's teaching, and the end of that on free-will is in his
> own words, and the corroboration of grave divines may be
> adduced for some of the most startling of the propositions.[10]

This same concern to remind the Church of England of the patris-
tic roots of her foundation documents is embodied in the revised
Canons and specifically stated in Canon A5, 'Of the Doctrine of the
Church of England'. This states,

> The doctrine of the Church of England is grounded in the Holy
> Scriptures, and in such teachings of the ancient Fathers and
> Councils of the Church as are agreeable to the said Scriptures.
> In particular such doctrine is to be found in the Thirty-Nine
> Articles of Religion, the Book of Common Prayer, and the
> Ordinal.

(iii) The Canon of Scripture

Article 6 is also expressing that the Church of England understands by Holy Scripture, only those canonical books of the Old

and New Testaments, 'of whose authority was never any doubt in the Church'. Such is the principle of St Vincent of Lerins: 'we hold that which has been believed everywhere, always and by all men'. With the Apocrypha, which finds a place in the Church's lectionaries, she follows the teaching of St Jerome and Rufinus, who put them on a lower level of canonicity, regarding them as having ecclesiastical, but not full dogmatic, authority.

(iv) Anglicanism and the primitive faith

Similarly in the Articles concerning the Church, Ministry, and Sacraments, there is that same concern to model the primitive church. This is found in the acceptance of infants for Baptism and the understanding of its regenerative effects, as well as a belief in the Real Presence in the Eucharist and an apostolic order of ministry. Such doctrine and practice is consistent with primitive Christianity. Edmund Welchman's work, *Exposition of the Thirty-Nine Articles* in Scripture and the Fathers (1790), sets out to make this point concerning the Articles. A similar work by William Beveridge (1638–1708), Bishop of St Asaph, *Discourse on the XXXIX Articles* (which in its full and correct form did not appear until 1843), is an able defence of the 'doctrine of the Church of England as consonant to Scripture, reason, and the Fathers'. In the nineteenth century Cary's *Testimonies of the Fathers* (1835), is concerned to expound the Articles from the writings of the Fathers. There are thirty-six Fathers from the first four centuries he lists as authorities quoted, among others. In the Preface he acknowledges borrowing from Cranmer, Beveridge, Tomline, Wall, and the massive patristic researches of Bingham's *Christian Antiquities*. Not only has he consulted Welchman, but relied heavily on Dr Burton, Regius Professor of Divinity at Oxford, particularly for the first five Articles that are from Burton's two volumes of *Testimonies*, whose scholarly concerns in this matter were similar. He is concerned to remind the clergy of his time of the important principle that characterizes the Church of England, and distinguishes her from every other reformed communion, 'her marked and avowed adherence to the Catholic faith as received in the primitive and purest ages of Christianity'. Therefore his purpose is to invite his fellow clergy to the storehouses of divine knowledge in the Fathers. There they will find the Church's interpretation of Scripture, following 'that path so plainly pointed out to us by the authoritative records of our own Church...' His purpose is to establish the authority of the Fathers by illustrating how fundamental and basic they are to the doctrine

enshrined in the Articles. A quotation from Bishop Michael
Ramsey might well sum up these thoughts. Writing of the existence
of Episcopacy in the English Church he says,

> ... its existence declared the truth that the Church in England
> was not a new foundation nor a local realisation of the invisible
> Church, but the expression on English soil of the one historical
> and continuous visible Church of God. It meant that, in spite of
> the pressure of Erastianism and even the frequent acceptance of
> Erastianism by the church's leaders, the English Church was
> reminded by its own shape and structure that it was not merely
> an English institution but the utterance in England of the
> Universal Church.
>
> This fact about the Anglican Church coloured the thought of
> the Caroline divines. Their theology was anti-papal, but was
> opposed also to the new scholasticism of the Reformers. It
> appealed to the Bible as the test of doctrine and also to the
> fathers and to the continuous tradition of Church life, *semper et
> ubique et ab omnibus,* both in West and East alike. The study of
> Greek theology gave to the churchmanship of these
> seventeenth century divines a breadth which reached beyond
> the West and its controversies; and their idea of the Church is
> summed up by Bishop Lancelot Andrewes when, in his *Preces
> Privatae,* he prays 'for the whole Church Catholic Eastern,
> Western, our own.'[11]

The Carolines would never have seen such a vision if it were not
already there in an embryonic understanding in the Church of
England's Formularies.

The Homilies

(i) The First Book of the Homilies

This first book of homilies, twelve in number, was printed and
ordered by royal authority in 1542, obtaining the authority of
Convocation in 1547 during Edward VI's reign. Ridley[12] points out
that they do not appear to have been approved by any Commission
of bishops and divines. Opinions expressed in them may be
assumed to be those of Cranmer, who for the first time in his life
was able to issue a theological statement exactly as he desired it in
his pastoral concern for sound teaching in the vernacular. The
intention was to produce a second book, to which reference is

made in the 1552 Prayer-Book, where a rubric authorizes the reading of one of the homilies if a sermon is not preached. However, the death of the King frustrated the design. They were 'appointed by the King's majesty to be declared and read by all parsons, vicars, and curates every Sunday in their churches at High Mass'. During Mary's reign this was exchanged for other homilies, projected both in Royal Articles, 1554, and in Synod, 1555, but never achieved.

(ii) The Second Book of the Homilies

A second book of homilies appeared during the reign of Elizabeth and was approved in Convocation along with the Thirty-Nine Articles in 1553; it was probably completed by 1563, but did not appear in its final form until 1571. It is commended, along with the former book, in Article 35, which orders them to be read in churches . . . diligently and distinctly. The object of this Article is to commend the doctrine contained in the Books of Homilies, and secure the reading of them in the parish churches. The reason for the order lies in the fact that there was resentment to the Homilies, and many of the old-fashioned clergy reacting to their doctrinal content read them unintelligently. The nature of assent demanded to the Homilies is that required of documents of general authority and so they do not stand on equal authority with the Articles and Prayer Book.

They came into existence to meet a temporary need. Preachers were scarce and, as Kidd points out,[13] they were either incapable of preaching owing to the decay of learning in the Universities which followed the destruction of the monasteries, or they were intemperate because those who could preach were partisan. Hence the need to put Homilies composed by prominent divines into the hands of the clergy. Peter Toon[14] thinks that Cranmer may have been inspired by his knowledge of Luther's collection of sermons for reading in parish churches. But Wheatly[15] claims,

> . . . that this is not at all contrary to the practice of the ancient Church, is evident from the testimony of Sixtus Sinensis, who, in the fourth book of his Library, saith, 'that our countryman Alcuinus collected and reduced into order, by the command of Charles the Great, the homilies of the most famous doctors of the Church upon the Gospels, which were read in churches all the year round.

They numbered two hundred and nine. In *Theophilus Anglicanus*

(1886), Bishop Wordsworth of Lincoln posed the question about the whereabouts of the Faith of the English Church before the Articles were drawn up. His answer stated that such Faith is found in the Holy Scriptures, as interpreted by the Church from the beginning, and the Three Creeds. He goes on to say '... she appeals to Ancient Authors, Ancient Canons, Fathers, and Decrees of the Church in her Ordinal, Homilies, and Canons. She is ready to be judged by the earliest and best ages of the Church.' As a specimen, Wordsworth quotes from the 'Homily against Peril of Idolatry',

> It shall be declared that this truth and doctrine ... was believed and taught of the old holy Fathers, and most ancient learned Doctors, and received in the old Primitive Church, which was most uncorrupt and pure; and this declaration shall be made out of the said holy Doctors' own writings, and out of the ancient Histories Ecclesiastical to the same belonging.[16]

A single volume containing the two books of Homilies was published in 1843, edited by John Griffiths and republished in 1908. It is introduced by the Elizabethan Preface. The first book of twelve homilies was written mainly by Cranmer, Bonner, and Bonner's chaplain. The second book is mainly the work of John Jewel, but Parker and Grindal contributed to it. The Preface expresses the royal concern that the people of England should have the Word of God preached to them so that they may be guided by it into the ways of true doctrine, godliness and virtue, and safeguarded from erroneous doctrines, superstition and idolatry. So the clergy are charged to read these homilies on Sundays and Holy-days when there is no sermon.

(iii) Selected References from the First Book

The first book contains twelve homilies. The first, (Cranmer) 'Concerning the Reading of Holy Scripture' quotes John Chrysostom and Fulgentius[17] on salvation in relation to what is contained in Holy Scripture. In the second part of the sermon Chrysostom is used in a lengthy quotation to remind the hearer that God does not leave without help those who wish to understand the Scriptures; and St Augustine's encouragement to persevere in reading until the meaning is made known is quoted. The second Cranmer sermon on 'The Salvation of Mankind' quotes from Hilary, Basil and Ambrose and then cites in support of his argument on justification by faith, Origen, Chrysostom, Cyprian,

Augustine, Prosper, Oecumenius, Photius, and Bernard.[18] 'And after this wise to be justified, only by this true and lively faith in Christ, speaketh all the old and ancient authors, both Greeks and Latins.' His concern is to prove that he does not subscribe to Solifidianism. In view of Article 11 on Justification which refers to this homily, there is a measure of authority about it, as there is about all these homilies because of Article 35, which commends the doctrine contained in the Books of the Homilies and is concerned to secure their being read in churches. In Cranmer's third homily on 'Good Works Annexed to Faith' he makes wide use of St Augustine's exposition of the Psalms, quotes St Ambrose (*De Vocatione Gentium,* Lib. i cap. 3.) and then weaves in a quotation from a Chrysostom sermon on faith.[19] Ridley points out that Cranmer's three homilies, 'Salvation', 'Of True, Lively and Christian Faith', and 'Of Good Works Annexed unto Faith', form a continuous statement of the doctrine of Justification. Here Cranmer uses the Fathers, Hilary and Ambrose, to declare that 'faith alone justifieth' and that 'he which believeth in Christ should be saved without works, by faith alone', adding that forgiveness of sins is a free gift of faith without works. However, he is quick to qualify what kind of faith he means, that the faith necessary for salvation must be 'a true and lively faith', which manifested itself in good living and good works. A person living in ungodliness while professing belief in Christ, in the words of Scripture, cannot claim to have faith. However, in exceptional circumstances like the thief on the Cross, a person can be saved by true faith alone without works. Quoting the Fathers, he agrees with Augustine that if a Jew or pagan clothed the naked and fed the poor, he would receive no heavenly reward for this. Added to his argument is the statement of Chrysostom:[20] 'I can show a man that by faith without works lived and came to heaven; but without faith never man had life.'[21]

(iv) Selected References from the Second Book

The second book comprises twenty-one homilies. The second homily, 'On the Peril of Idolatry', resorts to Jerome and Tertullian for a correct translation of the scriptural word for 'image' from the Latin and Greek. After scriptural exposition concerning this theme, Athanasius, Lactantius, Cyril, Epiphanius, Jerome, Ambrose and Augustine are brought in to support the argument against images. Then the *Ecclesiastical History* of Eusebius is used to trace the development of this trend from paintings to images. 'Wherefore let us beseech God, that we, being warned by his holy word forbidding all idolatry, and by the writings of the old godly doctors and *Ecclesiastical Histories,* written and preserved by God's ordinance for our admonition and warning, may flee from idolatry...'[22] Even though it may be argued that the present argument from the *consensus patrum* may not be accurate, the appeal to the Fathers is an unmistakeable reference to their authority. In the homily 'On Fasting' the argument turns on the issue of good works. St Augustine is invoked to make the point that good works do not bring forth grace but are brought forth by grace, while the practice of the early Church is cited from Eusebius's history.[23] In the homily on 'Common Prayer and the Sacraments' scriptural and patristic sanction is expounded. Concerning the receiving of Holy Communion reverently, Ambrose, John Chrysostom, Irenaeus, Ignatius, Dionysius, Origen, Cyprian and Athanasius are quoted:

> All which sayings, both of the Holy Scripture and godly men, truly attributed to this heavenly banquet and feast, if we would often call to mind, O how would they inflame our hearts to desire the participation of these mysteries, and oftentimes to covet after this bread, continually to thirst for this food.[24]

The Council of Nicaea's advice that 'we should lift up our minds by faith' is quoted. Then a passage is quoted from a sermon of Emissenus, a godly father, that when going 'to the reverend Communion ... thou look up with faith upon the Holy Body and Blood of thy God, thou marvel with reverence, thou touch it with thy mind, thou receive it with the hand of thy heart'.[25] The homily for Whitsunday speaks of the true Church, and states three notes or marks by which it is known:

> pure and sound doctrine, the Sacraments ministered according to Christ's holy institution, and the right use of the ecclesiastical discipline. This description of the Church is agreeable both to the Scriptures of God and also to the doctrine of the ancient fathers, so that none may justly find fault therewith.[26]

(v) Concluding Comments

More specific references could be listed. Suffice it to conclude with the fact that in the Index the names of thirty-four Fathers and others from the primitive church are listed. Here, the underlying principle of the English Reformation, the patristic mind, finds practical expression in homiletic teaching. Like the Fathers the

Reformers were preachers and pastors, concerned with the communication of the message of salvation to both theologians and ordinary people. In both, the all-embracing and integrating theme of salvation provides their principle of unity and makes their theology primarily pastoral, although at the same time it is soaked in Scripture and soundly academic. Before they could be used today there would have to be considerable pruning, and the repetitive use of similarly worded scriptural phrases and a battery of patristic quotations is not fashionable today. These homilies were written to meet their own contemporary needs, and therein lies their strength and weakness. Nevertheless, some could be easily adapted, and with an eloquence and vigour too often lacking today, speak to our contemporary society on such matters as 'good works', 'against strife and contention', 'on the right use of the Church', 'against swearing and perjury', 'whoredom and adultery', 'gluttony and drunkeness'. In a church that appears to have abandoned fasting, the relevant homily on this subject is informative for today.

The Book of Common Prayer

(i) Antecedents

All the early English service-books derive from materials provided from a Roman origin, but there were variations that originated from a common storehouse of materials that might be used in different ways. These incorporated certain non-Roman ingredients such as small features of a Celtic and Gallican origin. So while they were all of the Roman type there could be differences of detail in a time when strict liturgical uniformity was unknown. MS service-books differing from one another were provided for uses side by side in the same church. With the Norman conquest the arrival of French bishops and monks introduced a potential for further variation. The twelfth and thirteenth centuries saw a movement to remedy this liturgical diversity when Diocesan Uses in Salisbury, York and Hereford began to emerge with the Sarum Use becoming the most influential. It is this Sarum Use that directly influenced Cranmer's First Prayer Book when in the sixteenth century there was a desire for liturgical uniformity.

The 'Use of Sarum' in the later Middle Ages became increasingly influential throughout England, Wales, and Ireland.

Indeed in 1543 the use of the Sarum Breviary was imposed on
the whole of the southern Province, and it was from the books of
the Sarum Rite that the architects of First Prayer Book of Edward
VI took most of their material. On the eve of the Reformation,
the output of Sarum books was enormous; this fact, in itself,
indicating the position, influence and importance of this rite in
England.[27]

Hope goes on to point out, 'In essence the Sarum Rite was a "local
medieval modification of the Roman Rite in use at the cathedral
church of Salisbury"'. With a quotation from Archdale King he
contrasts 'the elaborate splendour of Sarum ceremonial' with the
'comparative simplicity of the practice of the Roman Church'. The
Breviary of Sarum, containing the daily services, together with the
Sarum Missal and *Sarum Manual,* are liturgical uses associated with
Richard Poore, dean and bishop, 1198–1228. These and some
other Service-Books constituted the 'Sarum Use' which became the
principal devotional Rule of the Church of England and had the
most direct bearing on the Prayer Book.

(ii) Principles of Liturgical Reform

It was in 1543 that Thomas Cranmer announced the King's intention to begin a reform of the service books, but with Henry's death
only some piecemeal revision had been achieved. Nevertheless
Cranmer continued, and the history of the Prayer Book down to
the end of Edward's reign is the biography of Cranmer. Mason
writes:

> It was a task to which he was well-fitted. So far as the study was
> possible in that age, Cranmer was a student of comparative litur-
> giology. 'A singularly clear answer to the supposition not
> infrequently entertained, that he was not well informed about
> liturgical order and ritual propriety, may be given' says Mr.
> Burbidge, [Liturgies and Offices of the Church p.xiv] 'by
> putting into the hands of his critics his copy of *Gemma Animae,*
> or *Directorium Sacerdotum secundum usum Sarum,* or Erasmus's
> version of the *Liturgy of St. John Chrysostom*; and by offering them
> a choice of his editions of Durandus's *Rationale Divinorum
> Officiorum'*. It was Cranmer who introduced into the West the
> now familiar 'prayer of St. Chrysostom'. Some features of the
> *Second Prayerbook* were very probably due to his acquaintance
> with the Mozarabic offices of Spain. He had paid attention to the
> various old English uses, some of which would have been lost to

memory if he had not happened to mention them in his Preface
to the Prayerbook.[28]

In two Acts of Uniformity Edward VI states that he had
appointed the Archbishop of Canterbury with other bishops and
learned divines to revise the Liturgy, 'having as well eye and
respect to the most sincere and pure Christian religion taught by
the Scripture, as to the usages in the Primitive Church'. In 1552,
the Act speaks of the Book of Common Prayer, 'a very godly order,
agreeable to the Word of God and the primitive Church ...'.[29] The
1552 Book arose from the agitation of Continental Reformers that
the Church of England had not gone far enough in its
Reformation. Nevertheless the theological principle of this English
Reformation, which is anti-papal but catholic, is maintained. The
Preface to the 1549 Book makes this plain, pointing out that in the
passage of time the Common Prayers of the Church have become
corrupted. The intention of the ancient Fathers, it points out, was
that such Divine Service was

> for a great advancement of godliness. For they so ordered the
> matter, that the whole Bible (or the greatest part thereof),
> should be read over once every year; intending thereby, that the
> Clergy, and especially such as were Ministers in the congrega-
> tion, should, (by often reading, and meditation in God's word)
> be stirred up to godliness themselves and more able to exhort
> others by wholesome doctrine, and to confute them that were
> adversaries to the Truth; and further, that the people (by daily
> hearing of holy Scripture read in the Church) might continually
> profit more and more in the knowledge of God, and be the
> more inflamed by the love of his true Religion.[30]

The Preface goes on to point out that '... this godly and decent
Order of the ancient Fathers hath been so altered...' and broken
up by additions of legends, Responds, Commemorations etc., that
while books of the Bible were read, they were never finished. The
ancient Fathers had also divided the psalms into seven Portions for
daily reading, but many of these were omitted. With a new
Kalendar providing for an orderly reading of Holy Scripture, and
certain Rules, 'here you have an Order for Prayer, and for the
reading of the Holy Scripture, much agreeable to the mind and
purpose of the old Fathers'.

(iii) Of Ceremonies

'Of Ceremonies', explains why some are retained and some abolished. Some have grown into abuse but others have been retained because they contribute to a decent order in the Church and to edification. St Augustine of Hippo is cited in support of this policy, since in his time he complained that ceremonies had grown to such a number that Christians were worse than the Jews in this respect. His counsel was that such a yoke and burden be taken away. This situation was much worse in the sixteenth century. The point is made that some ceremonies there must be for the keeping of any order or quiet discipline in the Church, and that the old ceremonies ought to be reverenced for their antiquity.

Evan Daniel writes,

> The principles which guided the Prayer Book revisers were very simple. In doctrinal matters they took for their standard of orthodoxy the Bible, and the belief of the Church of the first five centuries; in framing formularies for public worship, they retained whatsoever they could of the old service-books; in ritual matters they continued to follow the traditions of their own Church, deviating from them only where spiritual edification rendered such deviation necessary. Their object was not to revolutionise but reform; not to get as far away as possible from the Church of Rome, or from any other Church, but by retracing the steps whereby the primitive Church of England had 'fallen from herself' to return to Catholic faith and practice. Hence Queen Elizabeth was perfectly justified in saying in her letter to the Roman Catholic princes, 'that there was no new faith propagated in England, no new religion set up but that which was commanded by our Saviour, practised by the primitive Church and approved by the Fathers of the best antiquity'. The same principles are distinctly and authoritatively set forth in the 30th Canon Ecclesiastical which says: 'So far was it from the purpose of the Church of England to forsake and reject the Churches of Italy, France, Spain, Germany, or any such-like Churches, in all things which they held and practised, that, as the Apology of the Church of England confesseth, it doth with reverence retain those ceremonies which do neither endamage the Church of God nor offend the minds of sober men; only departed from them in those particular points wherein they were fallen both from themselves in their ancient integrity, and from the Apostolical Churches which were their first founders.[31]

Wordsworth[32] answered the question concerning the observation of rules in the prescribing of Rites and Ceremonies by pointing out that 'they must take care that the Rites which they ordain, be reasonable and decorous, and, as much as may be, in conformity with the ancient practice of the Universal Church ...'

(iv) Apology for the Book of Common Prayer

Wheatly prefaced his *A Rational Illustration of the Book of Common Prayer*,[33] with an Introduction in which he claimed that there was a need for an apologetic to those who disparage the Book of Common Prayer. His concern is to convince them of the Lawfulness and Necessity of National precomposed Liturgies in general. He appealed to the practice of the ancient Jews, Jesus, his Apostles, and the primitive Christians. Such precomposed forms of prayer are the Lord's Prayer, the Psalms and other set forms of prayer. He built his thesis from the internal evidence of the New Testament but also from the testimony of the primitive Church. 'It is plain then, that the three first centuries joined in the use of divers precomposed set forms of prayer, besides the Lord's Prayer and psalms: after which, (besides the Liturgies of St. Basil, St. Chrysostom, and St. Ambrose) we have also undeniable testimonies of the same', after which he cited Gregory Nazianzen, the Council of Laodicea and the Collection of the Canons of the Catholic Church; 'which Collection was established in the fourth general Council of Chalcedon, in the year 451; by which establishment the whole Christian Church was obliged to the use of Liturgies, so far as the authority of a general Council extends.'[34] Wheatly concluded that since a national precomposed Liturgy is warranted by

> ... the constant practice of all the ancient Jews, our Saviour himself, his Apostles, and the primitive Christians; and since it is a grievance to neither clergy nor laity, but appears quite, on the other hand, as well from their concurrent testimonies, as by our own experience, to be so highly expedient, as that there can be no decent or uniform performance of God's worship without it; our adversaries themselves must allow it to be necessary.[35]

(v) Reformation not Innovation

Wheatly also pointed out that in revising the Liturgy of the day,

> ... it was not the design of our Reformers (nor indeed ought it to have been) to introduce a new form of worship into the

church, but to correct and amend the old one; and to purge it
from those gross corruptions which had gradually crept into it,
and so to render the divine service more agreeable to the
Scriptures, and to the doctrine and practice of the primitive
church in the best and purest ages of Christianity.[36]

In which reformation they proceeded gradually, according as they
were able. Dr Comber is quoted as describing the character of the
Prayer Book, that 'its doctrine is pure and primitive; its ceremonies
so few and innocent, that most of the Christian world agree in
them; ... its language ... most of the words and phrases being
taken out of the Holy Scriptures, and the rest are the expression of
the first and purest ages...'.[37] In the opinion of Grotius the English
Liturgy comes so near to the primitive pattern, that none of the
Reformed Churches can compare with it.[38]

F. D. Maurice, one of Anglicanism's greatest theologians in the
nineteenth century whose theology had its roots in St John and the
Greek Fathers, could say, 'The Liturgy has been to me a great theological teacher; a perpetual testimony that the Father, the Son and
the Spirit, the one God blessed for ever, is the author of all life,
freedom, unity to men; that our prayers are nothing but responses
to His voice speaking to us and in us'.[39] One can see what Maurice
means by such a statement. The Prayer Book is not only a manual
of public devotion, it contains the fullest statement of the teaching
of the Church. In its lections from Holy Scripture, its creeds, its
prayers, its thanksgivings and exhortations, its confessions and
absolutions, the occasional offices, it brings before us the great
articles of the Christian faith in what we may call their natural
order and proportion, in their organic relation to other truths, and
with constant practical reference to their subjective aspects. In the
Thirty-Nine Articles these doctrines are set forth mainly as objective truths; the Prayer Book connects them directly with our
spiritual needs and our daily conduct.

The Source and Context of Theology

As the theology of Athanasius cannot be understood apart from
the liturgy of Bishop Serapion, so the theology of the Reformers
and their successors must find its origin and explanation in the
Book of Common Prayer. Here is a fundamental principle of
patristic theology, that the corporate worship of the Church is
the context of Christian thinking, the source of theology, where

theology and experience, intellect and intuition, thinking and praying are kept together. Rooted in the Fathers, Anglicanism has always sought to keep these things together, from Reformers and Carolines, to the Oxford Fathers, Butler, Maurice, Temple, Thornton and Ramsey, and one could cite many more. The concern has always been for an ideal of theology which was not divorced from prayer and liturgy, for a way of life and worship informed and structured by theological vision. We have a patristic theology when we rediscover the liturgical character of the Church's life in which we experience the Church, not as mere institution, doctrine or system but as the all-embracing *Life*, the passage into the reality of redemption and transfiguration. The *appeal to the Fathers* in the Reformers is much more than an historical reference to the past, but is an appeal to the *mind of the Fathers*, and to follow them means to acquire their mind.

The Ordinal

A question is posed in Wordsworth's *Theophilus Anglicanus*[40] asking whether the Church of England can stand the test applied by the ancient Fathers to test the catholicity of Christian communities. That is 'Whether her Ministers derive their commission from the Apostles', (Irenaeus iv. 43. p. 343 Grabe). In the words of Tertullian 'Let them produce the original records of their churches; let them unfold the roll of their bishops running down in due succession from the beginning ...', that is from the Apostles. (*De Praescript.Heret.* c. 32). The answer is that the Church of England can trace the Holy Orders of her bishops and priests in unbroken succession to the Apostles. Archbishop Bramhall[41] is cited: 'Apostolical succession is the nerve and sinew of Apostolic unity'; and Bishop Beveridge[42] 'They certainly hazard their salvation at a strange rate, who separate themselves from such a Church as ours, wherein Apostolical Succession, the root of all Christian communion, hath been so entirely preserved, and the Word and Sacraments are so effectually administered'.

The Preface to the Ordinal which has varied only in a few verbal alterations since 1549, testifies to this. Here it is stated that 'It is evident unto all men diligently reading the holy Scripture and Ancient Authors, that from the Apostles' time there have been these Orders of Ministers in Christ's Church; Bishops, Priests, and Deacons.' Article 36 approves this; 'The Book of Consecration of Archbishops and Bishops and ordering of Priests and Deacons, lately set forth in the time of Edward the Sixth and confirmed at the same time by authority of Parliament, doth contain all things necessary to such consecration and ordering.' The Canons of 1603 in Canon 36 affirm again what is expressed in the Preface to the Ordinal and in the quoted Article. This aspect of the English Church – its historic order, its sacramental life – is that in which she claims kinship with the pre-Reformation church, the church of antiquity, but also with acceptable Catholic elements still existing in the Church of Rome. The English Reformers may have been anti-papal, but they were not anti-catholic, and retained a sense of catholic faith and life to be preserved in a reformed idiom that was consistent with and in continuity with the church of antiquity.

Notes

1. Gee and Hardy, 'Selections from the Canons of 1571', *Documents Illustrative of the History of the English Church* (Macmillan & Co, London, 1896), pp. 476–7.
2. Georges Florovsky, 'The Catholicity of the Church,' in *Bible, Church and Tradition: An Eastern Orthodox View* (Nordland, USA, 1972), vol. i. The Collected Works of Georges Florovsky, pp. 40ff.
3. Florovsky, *ibid.*
4. C. Wordsworth, cited in *Theophilus Anglicanus* (Rivingtons, London, 1886), p. 185.
5. William Beveridge, *Works*, vol. i, Serm. vi (*LACT*, Oxford, 1844), p. 126.
6. Owen Chadwick, *The Mind of the Oxford Movement* (A. & C. Black Ltd, London, 1960), p. 25.
7. A. P. Forbes, 'Epistle Dedicatory', in *Explanation of the Thirty-Nine Articles* (Parker & Co, Oxford and London, 1871), p. xxx.
8. J. J. Blunt, *The Right Use of the Early Fathers* (John Murray, London, 1857), p. 6.
9. H. Chadwick, 'Traditions, Fathers and Councils', in *The Study of Anglicanism*, eds. Sykes and Booty (SPCK and Fortress Press, London, 1988), p. 99.
10. Forbes, *ibid.* xxxii.
11. A. M. Ramsey, *The Gospel and the Catholic Church* (Longmans, London, 1959), p. 206.
12. J. Ridley, *Thomas Cranmer* (Clarendon Press, Oxford, 1962), p. 266.
13. B. J. Kidd, *The Thirty-Nine Articles* (Rivingtons, London, 1911), p. 255.
14. P. Toon, 'The Articles and Homilies', in *The Study of Anglicanism*, eds. Sykes and Booty, p. 137.
15. C. Wheatly, *A Rational Illustration of the Book of Common Prayer of the*

Church of England, First published in 1710 and a standard work into the 19th century (J. Bohn, London, 1848), p. 272.

16. Wordsworth, *ibid.* pp.178–9.
17. J. Griffiths, ed. *The Two Books of the Homilies* (SPCK, London, 1908), pp. 2 and 3.
18. *Ibid.* pp. 24–5.
19. *Ibid.* pp. 48–9.
20. *Ibid.* p. 50.
21. *Ibid. Homilies*, 3, 4 and 5.
22. *Ibid.* p. 222.
23. *Ibid.* pp. 304–6.
24. *Ibid,* p. 476.
25. *Ibid.* p. 478.
26. *Ibid.* p. 494.
27. D. M. Hope, 'The Medieval Western Rites' in *The Study of Liturgy*, eds: Cheslyn Jones, Geoffrey Wainwright, Edward Yarnold, SJ (SPCK, London, 1978), p. 236. See also Ch. 1, in *A New History of the Book of Common Prayer* (Macmillan, London, 1958).
28. A. J. Mason, *Thomas Cranmer* (Methuen & Co, London 1898), pp. 139–40.
29. J. H. Blunt, *Annotated Book of Common Prayer* (Rivingtons, London, 1884), p. 46.
30. *Book of Common Prayer 1552*, ' Preface'.
31. Evan Daniel, *The Prayer Book, Its History, Language and Contents* (Gardner, Darton & Co, London, 1901), pp. 29–30.
32. Wordsworth, *ibid.* p. 313.
33. C. Wheatly, *ibid.* 'Preface'.
34. *Ibid.* p. 15.
35. *Ibid.* p. 21.
36. *Ibid.* p. 23.
37. *Ibid,* p. 34.
38. H. Grotius, *Ep. ad Boet.*
39. F. D. Maurice, *Life*, vol. ii, p. 359.
40. Wordsworth, *ibid.* p. 187.
41. J. Bramhall, *Works*, vol. i (*LACT*, Oxford, 1842), p. 126.
42. W. Beveridge, *Works*, vol. i, p. 23.

4

The Patristic Spirit of Reform

Darwell Stone points out that the English church from the beginning of the seventh century to the middle of the sixteenth possesses all the essential features of the Christianity of the patristic period. The earlier British church had episcopal representation at the Council of Arles in AD 314, possibly at Nicaea in AD 325 and Sardica in AD 343. Throughout the later church of the English nation there is the threefold ministry of bishops, priests, and deacons. 'With the ministry the sacraments were retained. Baptism and the Eucharist are habitually found as the means of bestowing and maintaining Christian life. Both ministry and sacraments were grouped round the preservation of the historic faith.'[1] Continuity with the primitive and undivided Church is a foundation fact of Anglicanism, rooted in the truth of history and nowhere weakened and destroyed by sixteenth century reform.

Archbishop Parker and the Argument from Antiquity

With Elizabeth I on the throne and Matthew Parker reluctantly at Canterbury (1559–75) this is the foundation on which Anglicanism was to be built. In Parker, deep study of the Bible and the Fathers strengthened a mind naturally mediating and judicial, in a scholar who was a great lover of antiquity. Anglican distinctiveness derives from theological method not content and emerged with Archbishop's Parker's theological interpretation of the Elizabethan Settlement in the 1571 Thirty-Nine Articles, the Second Book of the Homilies and the 'Canon of Preaching'. Michael Ramsey claimed that it was the nature of Elizabethan theology, rather than imitation of Cranmer or Hooker in the style of Lutherans to Luther and Calvinists to Calvin, that made it possible to appeal to Scripture and tradition, and it must remain so today. Even as a young man Parker had been concerned to immerse himself in the Scriptures and the Fathers, so that as a reformer this twofold appeal in theological matters comes as no surprise. While there was a diverse set of influences forming the mind of this reformer, from the Christian humanists Colet, Erasmus and More, to Martin Bucer the continental Protestant, the concern here is with Parker's appeal to Scripture and antiquity. He had studied patristics from the 1530s, had come to appreciate the value Cranmer placed on this appeal, and wrote a letter of commendation for Anne Lady Bacon's English version of Jewel's *Apologia,* which stressed the real antiquity of Anglican teaching and church order. Therefore it is not surprising that in Elizabethan England Parker was able to counter the accusation that the Church of England was an innovation that rested on no secure foundations.

A more special interest was the ancient history of the church in England and its records, which, explains Sir Edwyn Hoskyns, Parker needed for his specific purpose.[2] At Lambeth he kept scribes at his own expense who were skilled in copying ancient manuscripts. They were collected for a purpose and worked upon in Lambeth under the supervision of the archbishop. These records were in the form of Anglo-Saxon manuscripts, now in the possession of Corpus Christi College Library in Cambridge, and were completely English, written in England by Englishmen and illuminated in England by Englishmen. Originating from the Anglo-Saxon period to the reign of King Alfred, Thomas Fuller (1608–61), a seventeenth century commentator, described these manuscripts as 'the sun of English antiquity'. With the dissolution of the monasteries many of these manuscripts had been scattered far and wide, but Parker took the initiative in recovering them. His purpose was to find manuscripts that shed light on the ancient 'condition of England and upon the history of England'. Hoskyns quotes a letter of Parker's (20 January 1565) to Bishop Scory of Hereford, thanking him for searching the Hereford Library for Saxon books, and quoting a note from a Canon of Hereford (8 February 1865), saying he had sent three books to his bishop. In all, Corpus Christi College Cambridge holds thirty-seven Anglo-Saxon books from Parker, he gave another seven to the university library and one is in the Bodleian.

There is purpose in Parker's collection of these manuscripts. They were a necessary part of his research into the primitive church that existed in Britain in Anglo-Saxon times, and provided material for the publication of books at Lambeth in which the

results of this research were published. In addition there are the
Parker Books, private books of the Archbishop that are a key to the
way in which he used these manuscripts and to the mind behind
the research. The religious situation at the beginning of
Elizabeth's reign was delicate and difficult when in 1565, in
Antwerp, Thomas Stapleton published his translation of Bede's
History of the Church of England, with a dedication to the Queen. He
explained in the preface that his purpose was to demonstrate the
differences between the 'Primitive faith of England continued
almost through a thousand years and the pretended faith of protestants'. He reiterated the Roman charge that the Church of
England was a piece of *newfangledness,* supporting it by an appeal to
history. Parker's specific purpose was to respond to this charge of
newfangledness and to awaken confidence in the Church of
England. To this end he collected these manuscripts and
embarked upon his study.

> The wealth of Biblical manuscripts and of early commentaries
> upon the Bible, which are included among our manuscripts, is
> no doubt due to one great and important line of defence of
> the Church of England. The study of the Bible and of its
> meaning to the early Fathers of the Church, which was an
> appeal to sound biblical scholarship, enabled Parker to claim
> that many changes could be explained and justified by the
> authority of the Bible and of its earliest interpretation in the
> Primitive Church.[3]

More peculiar to his purpose was his concern to prove from his
Anglo-Saxon manuscripts that it was Rome that had erred and was
guilty of *newfangledness.* He found authority in the history of the
English church itself, as embodied in these manuscripts, for bible-
reading in the 'vulgar tongue', and that transubstantiation and the
celibacy of the clergy had no historic foundation in the Anglo-
Saxon Church. The Bampton Lectures (1830), *An Enquiry into the
Doctrines of the Anglo-Saxon Church* (Oxford, 1830), Sermon 2, cite
evidence of translations of the Bible in the vulgar tongue. Here
Henry Soames cites Bede's concern to translate the Scriptures into
the vernacular, and Bede's diocesan, the Bishop of Lindisfarne
(710), Eadfridus, 'who engaged in the task of rendering Holy
Scripture into his native idiom'. King Alfred promoted this diffusion of scriptural knowledge in the vernacular. Parker possessed
three manuscripts of the Gospels in Anglo-Saxon English, and
these manuscripts seemed to have been used in the liturgy of the
ancient English church. Parker had these Gospels set up in Anglo-

Saxon type and printed alongside the Elizabethan version of the Gospels. The title page reads:

> The Gospels of the Fower Evangelists translated in the Old Saxon tyme out of Latin into the vulgare tongue of the Saxons newly collected out of Ancient Monumentes of the said Saxons, and now published *for testimony of the same.* [London 1571, published under royal privilege].[4]

The preface by John Foxe explains the significance of the manuscripts:

> What a controversy, among other controversies, hath arisen of late in our days, whether it be convenient the Scriptures of God to be put in our English tongue. Wherein some more confidently than skilfully, contrary both to the evidence of Antiquity, as also against the open face of veritie, have thought it to be dangerous to have them in our popular language translated, considering partly the difficultie of the Scriptures in themselves, and partly the weakness of understanding in us. Some again have judged our native tongue unmeet to express God's secret mysteries, being so barbarous and imperfect a language, as they say it is.[5]

Foxe goes on to say that if anyone doubts the ancient usage of Scriptures in Anglo-Saxon the proof is to be seen in the said manuscripts where so much is translated into the 'old English tongue'. The reason for publishing the treatise is, so 'that the said book, imprinted thus in the Saxon letters may remain in the Church as a profitable example and precedent of old antiquitie *to the more confirmation of your* [Queen Elizabeth's] gratious proceedings now in the Church agreeable to the same'. Foxe then points out that this has been made possible by the researches of Parker. The primary purpose of all these researches and publications is then stated:

> We understand by the edition hereof, how religion presently taught and professed in the Church at thys present, is no reformation of things lately begun, but rather a reduction of the Church to the Pristine State ... as is manifestly proved not onely in this case of the vulgar translation of the Scriptures; but in other cases also in doctrine, as Transubstantiation, of priests restrained from marriage, of receiving under one kind, with many other points and articles newly thrust in.[6]

Two Anglo-Saxon homilies were printed with translations, one on the Sacrament of Holy Communion to be preached before the

people received the Sacrament, and the other on reservation for
the sick which was signed by the archbishop and twelve other
bishops. The purpose was to demonstrate that in Anglo-Saxon
times there was apparently no knowledge of the medieval doctrine
of transubstantiation. Therefore the Elizabethan church could not
be accused of innovation if such a doctrine was not taught. Parker
was also able to quote from early English chronicles to show that
the Anglo-Saxon clergy were married. In his book *A Defence of
Priest's Marriages* a statement of Henry of Huntingdon in his
Chronicle is quoted, that Archbishop Anselm had during a
Council in London forbade priests to marry, which had not been
the clergy discipline before Anselm.

> All this was no mere antiquarianism. It served to bring a sense of
> security and solid foundation in ancient tradition to a Church
> which had undoubtedly passed through revolutionary change. It
> was an appeal to sound learning and went along with the
> primary appeal of Anglicanism to the Scriptures, the 'ancient
> fathers' and the early Councils of the Church. At this stage of the
> struggle the controversy was mainly with Rome: it was against
> Rome that history was called to witness ... The importance of all
> this ... lies in the consistent refusal of the writers to allow any
> severance between the Scriptures and the early Church on the
> one hand and their Anglicanism on the other.[7]

The Reformers were dealing with a particular situation and
working out their theory in the light of it, and like every living
theology it springs out of and reflects the worship of the Church,
so that their theology finds its origin and explanation in the Book
of Common Prayer. A point made earlier is that there is a consistency between them and Athanasius, whose theology must be
understood in relation to the liturgy of Bishop Serapion, indeed
the whole patristic tradition in which prayer is the seed-bed of
belief. *Lex orandi legem statuat credendi:* let the law of prayer establish the law of belief. A theology that cannot be prayed is no
theology at all.

Their particular preoccupation with an anti-Roman
Reformation was soon to cease. Within their own church as well as
outside it there was soon to come a violent and able reaction from
those, who, comparing Anglicanism's Reformation with that of
Continental Protestantism, felt it had not gone far enough in
rejecting catholic institution and practice in doctrine, ministry and
observances. But the principle and course of Anglicanism was
already laid. Those principles

... can be summarily described as a strong attachment to the authority of Scripture, and of the early Church with its 'Fathers' and councils, to the tradition of an ordered liturgical worship and of the ancient threefold ministry of bishops, priests and deacons, and to the view that the Church of England, basing itself on sound reason in matters of relative indifference, 'may ordain, change, and abolish ... so that all things be done to edifying'.[8]

The Peculiar Character of Anglicanism

Henry Cary describes this *peculiar character* of Anglicanism.

> A principle which especially characterises the Church of England and distinguishes her from every other reformed communion, is her marked and avowed adherence to the catholic faith as received in the primitive and purest ages of Christianity. She has acted on this universally and acknowledged truth that whatsoever is new in the fundamentals of religion, must be false. On this ground, and believing that in the earliest ages the great truths of Christianity were known to, and plainly professed by the Church, she [and here he quotes from *The Peculiar Character of the Church of England* by Dr Jebb, the Bishop of Limerick] 'in the first instance, and as her grand foundation, derives all obligatory matter of faith', that is, to use her own expression, all 'that is to be believed for necessity of salvation,' from the Scripture alone: and herein she differs from the Church of Rome. But she systematically resorts to the concurrent sense of the Church catholic, both for assistance in the interpretation of the sacred text, and for guidance in those matters of religion, which the text has left at large: and herein she differs from every reformed communion.[9]

It is interesting to note what an Orthodox theologian makes of this *peculiar character* of our church. Nicholas Lossky points out that the mistake some Orthodox make is to seek in Anglicanism, past and present, statements which could be interpreted as symbolical texts. A symbolical text for an Orthodox is the expression of the Church's belief voiced by the episcopate as representative of the whole body. This means that a doctrinal statement made at a Council and confirmed by ecumenical assent on the part of the whole people is not merely an 'official statement of the Church's position on a given point, but the catholic expression of the one faith of the Church'. The Thirty-Nine Articles is not such a symbolical text, though Jewel's *Apologia* came nearest to being such. Lossky's advice to an Orthodox curious about Anglicanism is this.

> Instead of trying to organise quasi-symbolical texts such as the *Thirty Nine Articles* into a consistent doctrinal pattern [or] discussing the validity of Anglican orders on the basis of the Apostolic succession he should turn to other sources such as the actual works of Anglican divines, the *Book of Common Prayer*, and the *English Hymnal*, and study them ... The living tradition [of this *peculiar character* of Anglicanism] remains hidden in liturgical and devotional literature such as the Book of Common Prayer or the Hymnal and the works of those divines, without really finding catholic expression in a *statement* which might be described as a corporate act of the whole Church.[10]

Lossky makes a plea that an Orthodox read Anglicanism not from the outside but 'from the inside', meaning a sympathetic reading of the other's experience with total readiness to put one's own 'traditional' formulations in question and with absolute confidence in the indestructibility of truth. Returning to the Thirty-Nine Articles he says,

> ... it should perhaps be emphasised that instead of being the expression of the common spiritual experience of members of the Church of England, *in the light* of which the writings of such or such a divine, or this or that part of the English Liturgy, may or must be viewed to be rightly understood, it is the writings of the divine, the prayer, the hymn, which reflect an implicit, more or less grudging, more or less accepting, commentary on the formulations. They provide the further definition of certain terms lacking in the Articles themselves and will generally yield an impression of Anglican doctrine and spirituality very different from the conception too commonly prevalent among Orthodox Scholars.[11]

He illustrates this by comparing Article XIX and Hooker. The Article describes the Church as a 'visible congregation of faithful men where the pure Word of God is preached and the Sacraments ministered according to Christ's ordinance', which Lossky judges to be somewhat 'laconic'. In Hooker's *Laws of Ecclesiastical Polity*, we find (Bk. V, ch. lvi. 5–7) that the Church is not primarily a 'visible society of men' (Bk. III, ch. 1. v, 14), nor is the notion of a mystical body something apprehensible in 'our minds by intellectual conceit' (Bk. III, ch. 1. 2.); here the Church and Sacrament become really and truly one. McAdoo describes Book V as the first in-depth theological commentary on the Book of Common Prayer, '... a genre that would develop in a matter of decades with works such as those of Anthony Sparrow, Hamon L'Estrange and John Cosin'.

> It is a profound theological exposition of why Anglicans believe, think and worship as they do. Church, ministry, sacraments, liturgical principles and practice, are all discussed and not merely in the 'parochial' setting but in the context of participation in the Life of the Incarnate Lord through the grace of Word and Sacraments in the corporate fellowship of the Church.[12]

Throughout Hooker there is that wide vision of the continuity and wholeness of the church's Tradition, not in the sense of establishing a pedigree, but in the transmission of certain living qualities of faith and order. It is these living qualities that link the present church with the primitive church, being at once the assurance and norm of catholicity.

Lossky then gives two lengthy quotations from Lancelot Andrewes, from 'The Nativity Sermon'[13] and from a 'Pentecost Sermon'.[14] Here Andrewes expresses an essentially and much more explicitly Eucharistic conception of the Church, in which is a rich conception of symbolism and the full significance of the Eucharist in the Christian's life. The final vision on which the sermon ends, of man's partaking of the divine life in the Feast of the Kingdom, is, as Lossky claims, best expressed in the 'Pentecost Sermon' and the exposition of the mysterious presence, here and now, of the Eighth Day in the Church instituted at Pentecost. Here in his preaching, not only in the content that expresses an organic theology, but also in the style, Andrewes is most characteristically patristic. It was these successors of the Reformers who were to be called upon to defend and elucidate this *peculiar character* of Anglicanism into an expression of the primitive church on English soil, as within and without the Church of England they responded to attacks on its fundamental nature. Cary in 1835 lamented that this *peculiar character* of the English church was little regarded by the generality of its clergy, and H. B. Swete in 1904 wished that the clergy of every school would bring their convictions to that same test of the Fathers as previous generations of Anglican divines.

Reading from the 'Inside'

In Lossky's advice to the Orthodox in their reading of Anglicanism lies a clue for today's Anglican, to grasp in a living way from the 'inside' its *peculiar character*. This advice to the contemporary Orthodox, to put in question his own 'traditional' formulations and to have absolute confidence in the indestructibility of truth, has a lesson for Anglicans. The contemporary Anglican will need to suspend most of the responses and unlearn most of the habits of the modern mind that have created the great gulf between this and all preceding ages. As we do not translate Shakespeare into modern English in order to understand him, so in Greek, Latin and Caroline divine there is no easy process of changing the images. Such a tampering with their fashions of expression will only result in losing the substance of what they are saying. The images they use are what Bishop Ian Ramsey described as *disclosure models,* specific images with a depth of meaning that develop an understanding of what is presented in several directions at once. They 'are rooted in disclosures and born in insight' and hold together two things in such a way that thought about one produces some understanding in depth of the other. Hence the Anglican Fathers use the language and imagery of patristic theology because the poetic vision of these early Fathers could only be expressed as they, in fact, expressed it.

When all these divines are allowed to speak in their own voices, there is no substitute for reading what they say as they say it. One finds in them what Lossky found, a patristic theology in an English idiom, which was no mere repetition of what the Fathers said, nor the transforming of them into a formal and infallible authority, and theology into a patristic scholasticism. To do this would have been a betrayal of the very spirit of patristic theology. What is present in these Anglican divines is a recovery of the spirit of the Fathers and the secret inspiration that made them true witnesses of the Church. For the Reformers and Caroline divines the Fathers are not mere relics of the past but living witnesses and contemporaries with them. What constitutes the essential feature of the Fathers, their charismatic life in the Church, lives again in these Anglican Fathers in the apostolic tradition they have received. Thus it happens that the same faith of the Apostles which is relived and represented throughout all ages by the Fathers, and makes the age of the Fathers a perennial presence in the Church, is relived by the Anglican divines themselves. As they appropriate the *consensus patrum,* normatively and critically, in the development of that *peculiar character* of Anglicanism the age of the Fathers comes to life on English soil. It was this *peculiar character* of Anglicanism that Lossky was able to see, somewhat laconically, in its Formularies, but much more explicitly in the writings of her divines, the Book of Common

Prayer, and the *English Hymnal.* Looking at Anglicanism from the inside he was able to see a *return to the Fathers* in Hooker and Andrewes. We turn now to the writings of these divines and the reading of them from the 'inside'.

Notes

1. Darwell Stone, *The Christian Church,* 3rd edn. (Rivingtons, London, 1915), p. 183.
2. Sir Edwyn Hoskyns, 'The Importance of the Parker Manuscripts', in *Cambridge Sermons,* (SPCK, London, 1938), p. 204.
3. *Ibid.* p. 213.
4. Parker, cited by Hoskyns, *ibid.* p. 214.
5. John Foxe, 'Preface', *The Gospels of the Fower Evangelists* translated in the Olde Saxon tyme out of Latin into the vulgate tongue of the Saxons newly collected out of Ancient Monuments of the said Saxons, and now published *for testimonie of the same* (London, 1571), cited by Hoskyns, *ibid.* p. 215.
6. Foxe, 'Preface', cited by Hoskyns, *ibid,* p. 216.
7. A. T. P. Williams, *The Anglican Tradition* (SCM, London, 1947), pp. 18–19.
8. *Ibid.* p. 21.
9. Henry Cary, *Testimonies of the Fathers of the First Four Centuries to the Doctrine of the Church of England as set forth in The Thirty-Nine Articles* (D. A. Tolboys, Oxford, 1835), 'The Preface'.
10. Nicholas Lossky, 'An Orthodox Approach to Anglicanism', in *Sobornost,* series 6: no. 2. (Winter, 1971), p. 81.
11. *Ibid.* p. 82.
12. H. R. McAdoo, 'Richard Hooker', in *The English Religious Tradition and the Genius of Anglicanism* (Ikon, Wantage, 1992), ed. Geoffrey Rowell, p. 118.
13. Lancelot Andrewes, *Works,* vol. i, sermon 16 (*LACT,* Parker, Oxford, 1870), pp. 281–3.
14. Andrewes, *Works,* vol. iii, sermon i, pp. 107–9.

Part Two:

Fathers and Carolines

5

Successors and Builders

Newman and Routh

Thomas M. Parker speculates that when Newman spent two hours with Dr Routh of Magdalen to receive his opinion on his own work *The Arians of the Fourth Century,* Routh had no need in 1834, to introduce him to the Fathers. 'What he could do and may have done, was to point out that, besides Bull, many of the great Caroline divines were patristic students and based their theology upon the Fathers.'[1] Parker claims that with Newman writing *Tracts* and reviving doctrines submerged since the Nonjuring schism, it was natural for Routh to inform him that the interpretation of Scripture, the Anglican Formularies and the Fathers, to which Newman appealed, was not new but had previously appeared in a considerable corpus of Anglican theological writing. Parker's point is that Newman came to the Carolines by way of the Fathers and not vice versa. His dedication to Routh in *The Prophetical Office of the Church* in 1837, which speaks of Routh as having been preserved 'to report to a forgetful generation what was the theology of their Fathers', suggests that he has in mind the classic Anglican theologians. Routh revived patristic studies in Oxford, after a period of relative neglect, with the publication of his *Reliquae Sacrae.* Parker described him as 'the man who, even in his appearance, retaining as he did the old clerical dress, recalled the great figures of the classical Anglican age'. In the view of Oxford, Routh was the 'living representative of a tradition submerged by the metaphysical and apologetic trend of eighteenth century Anglican theology'.

These 'great figures' of Caroline divinity, the successors of the Reformers, were builders, their work being the natural outcome and growth of what the Reformers had laid not merely in the opinions of thinkers, but in the foundation documents of Anglicanism. If those foundations had not been there, Anglican theology in the

seventeenth century would have been quite different. These
Anglican divines of the seventeenth century continued to hold the
Fathers in special esteem, but as Michael Ramsey[2] points out:

> Whereas the Edwardian and Elizabethan divines had been inter-
> ested in the Fathers chiefly as a means of proving what had or
> had not been the primitive doctrine and practice, the Caroline
> divines went farther in using the thought and piety of the
> Fathers within the structure of their own theological exposition.
> Their use of the Fathers had these two noteworthy characteris-
> tics. (1) Not having, as did the Continental Reformers, a
> preoccupation with the doctrines of justification or predestina-
> tion they followed the Fathers of the Nicene age in treating the
> Incarnation as the central doctrine of the faith. Indeed a feeling
> of the centrality of the Incarnation became a recurring feature
> of Anglican divinity, albeit the Incarnation was seen as S.
> Athanasius saw it in its deeply redemptive aspect. (2) Finding
> amongst the Fathers the contrast of Greek and Latin divinity, the
> Anglican divines could be saved from western narrowness, and
> were conscious that just as the ancient undivided Church
> embraced both East and West so too the contemporary Catholic
> Church was incomplete without the little known Orthodox
> Church of the East as well as the Church in the West, Latin,
> Anglican and Reformed. The study of the Fathers created the
> desire to reach out to Eastern Christendom. Thus did Anglican
> theology find in the study of the Fathers first a gateway to the
> knowledge of what was scriptural and primitive, subsequently a
> living tradition which guided the interpretation of Scripture,
> and finally a clue to the Catholic Church of the past and the
> future: in the words of Lancelot Andrewes 'the whole Church
> Catholic, Eastern, Western, our own'.

Distinguished Writers

It is not surprising that no period in our Church's history is more
rich in writers of high distinction in the field of theology, a feature
which did not diminish until the end of the century in an age of
general intellectual ferment. These distinguished writers include
Hooker and Andrewes, Laud, Hammond, Overall, Field, Ussher,
Sanderson, Taylor, Pearson, Barrow and Bull, to name but a few.
Frere claims that with Hooker, Andrewes and Overall there came a
revulsion against the dominant Calvinism, which

introduced a more mature conception of the position of the
English Church, based upon the appeal to Scripture and the
principles of the undivided Church. The earlier theologians had
been able to recognise in principle the soundness of this appeal,
but they had hitherto been unable to work out in practice its
detailed results.[3]

If one were to define the ethos of these Caroline divines then it
would be found in the holding together of what Baron von Hügel
maintained as the necessary strands of the Christian life, the mystical, the intellectual and the institutional.

> It was marked by a time of massive scholarly activity. Following
> on the classical work of Richard Hooker (1554–1600) which only
> began to be assimilated in the years following his death, it saw
> the beginnings of a distinctively Anglican theological position,
> on the one side clearly distinguished from Rome, on the other
> from that of Calvinist Geneva. Above all it was marked by a
> renewal of the understanding and the practice of the Christian
> way of common and private prayer. And all these things were
> held together in a single focus.[4]

In the theology of these divines thinking and praying are indissolubly connected, in an orthodoxy which was not a static repetition
of the past but a living, growing pattern of truth.

The Love of Learning and the Desire for God

John Byrom points out that 'they were all soaked in the primitive
and medieval tradition of contemplation as the normal outcome of
a life of serious prayer.' He goes on to say that they all write as if
they held and would have given general assent to the Latin tag, *lex
orandi legem statuat credendi*, let the law of prayer establish the law of
belief. 'There is a sense of richness about these divines which gradually reveals itself as flowing from something deeper than
torrential intellect, or even high poetic gifts.' An unmistakable
mark of them is a love of learning and a desire for God, so deeply
intertwined that it is pointless to try and distinguish them, though
the manner of their lives makes clear that whenever the two came
into conflict it was invariably the love of learning which gave way,
making the point reinforced by Hegius, the fifteenth-century
German Christian humanist, that 'all learning is harmful which is
gained at the expense of piety'.[5] Canon Allchin tells us that it was

the fusion of thought and feeling in these theologians that drew T.
S. Eliot back to Christian faith and life. It prompted Eliot's small
book of essays *For Lancelot Andrewes,* who, for Eliot, embodied in
himself the learning, the theology and the devotion which marked
the best men of this age. Eliot believed that Hooker and Andrewes
made the English church more worthy of intellectual assent. In
them, as in the actual life and worship of the period, he found a
catholicism which was not ignorant either of the Renaissance or
the Reformation, a tradition which had already moved into the
modern world. 'It was a way of living and thinking the Christian
tradition which had taken humanism and criticism into itself,
without being destroyed by them.'[6]

Anglicanism's Distinctive Strength

Richard   Hooker   (1554–1600)   and   Lancelot   Andrewes
(1555–1626) are without doubt the two outstanding theologians of
this era, embodying in their own persons humility, piety and learning which made them men of moderation. By temperament
neither of them was suited to, nor attracted by, a spirit of controversy, but they both responded with their characteristic singleness
of mind and moderation. Their task was the establishment of the
catholic identity of Anglicanism, for Hooker in relation to
Puritanism, for Andrewes in relation to Roman Catholicism. Vital
to their theological method is the supremacy of Scripture, the
interpretation of which rested on an appeal to antiquity. The testimony of the undivided Church was fundamental to their
theological method, not only in their interpretation of Scripture
but also in matters of doctrine, liturgy and canonical matters, the
dogmatic decisions of the first four General Councils providing
their ground base.

This stance on the *constant* of Anglicanism, the *hapax* or *once-for-
allness* of the faith, does not imply a fossilized religion, the
precluding of any development. The faith that is set forth in the
Scriptures and the Catholic Creeds develops and grows under the
guidance of the Holy Spirit within the Church. Every age has to
apprehend, appropriate, re-present, and proclaim the *living revelation* in all the changes and varieties of human cultures throughout
history. But it must be a development *from* the *facts* of revelation
and not *away* from them. The criteria for such development must
be Scripture and Tradition conformable to Scripture, otherwise
one may end up with what Bishop Hanson described as 'a virtually

uncontrolled doctrinal space-flight'. In 1899 Francis Paget prefaced his *Introduction to the Fifth Book of Hooker's Laws of Ecclesiastical Polity* with the point that 'The distinctive strength of Anglicanism rests on equal loyalty to the unconflicting rights of reason, Scripture and Tradition'. McAdoo claims that a living church in a changing society needs to see why it is necessary that this classical way of doing theology and of being related to other Christians matters to Anglicans today. Such a method avoids the deadness of an atrophying traditionalism, for its concern is to allow *tradition* to live as a living process of transmission. 'Neither may we in this case lightly esteem what hath been allowed to *fit* in the judgement of antiquity, and by the long continued practice of the whole Church; from which *unnecessarily* to swerve, experience hath never as yet found it safe.'[7] Michael Ramsey said that the tests of true development are whether it bears witness to the Gospel, whether it expresses the general consciousness of Christians, and whether it serves the organic unity of the Body in all its parts. These tests are summed up in the Scriptures, wherein the historical gospel, the development of the redeemed and the nature of the one Body are described. So the Scriptures have a special authority to control and check the whole field of development in life and doctrine. These fundamental theological principles of the English Reformation we must now examine as they are developed in the theology of the Caroline divines.

Notes

1. Thomas M. Parker, 'The Rediscovery of the Fathers in the 17th Century Anglican Tradition', in *The Rediscovery of Newman* (Sheed & Ward, London, 1967), ed. J. Coulson, p. 46.
2. A. M. Ramsey, 'The Ancient Fathers and Modern Anglican Theology', in Sobornost, Series 4: no. 6 (Winter–Spring 1962), p. 290.
3. W. H. Frere, *A History of the English Church in the Reigns of Elizabeth and James I 1558–1625*, (Macmillan & Co, London, 1904), p. 284.
4. A. M. Allchin, *The Dynamic of Tradition* (DLT, London, 1981), p. 56.
5. J. Byrom, *The Glowing Mind* (SLG Press, Oxford, 1991), pp. 1–3.
6. Allchin, *ibid.* p. 57.
7. R. Hooker, 'The Laws of Ecclesiastical Polity' in *The Works of that Learned and Judicious Divine Mr Richard Hooker: with an Account of his Life and Death,* by Isaac Walton in two volumes (Oxford University Press, Oxford, 1880), vol. i, Bk v, vii, 1. p. 442.

6

Richard Hooker and the Puritans

Controversy and *The Laws of Ecclesiastical Polity*

In 1585, on his appointment as Master of the Temple, Hooker came into conflict with English Puritanism in the Presbyterian Walter Travers, who was one of its recognized leaders, second only to Cartwright himself. Travers as Lecturer and Hooker as Master were not compatible in their principles, but the notion of 'the pulpit speaking pure Canterbury in the morning and Geneva in the afternoon' is questioned by Richard Bauckham[1] as having small foundation in fact. Travers not only opposed episcopacy; he also denounced the Prayer Book, along with Hooker's charitable teaching that God would be merciful to those who had lived 'in popish superstition'. According to Bauckham there were two levels of conflict: the one over matters of church polity and liturgical conduct which was Anglican versus Puritan; the other was over matters of Calvinist doctrine. The latter was Travers's position as a Calvinist over against Hooker who was not, as yet, the official champion of Anglican orthodoxy. Bauckham is concerned not, as some students of Hooker do, to treat Calvinism and Puritanism as synonymous. Bauckham maintains that their disputes on ecclesiastical and liturgical issues, matters of controversy between Anglican and Puritan, were conducted in private, not in the pulpit of the Temple. Furthermore, Hooker 'did not deliberately oppose Travers's doctrine. In his occasional divergences from Calvinist orthodoxy Hooker was establishing his independence as a theologian, not promoting an Anglican party line against Geneva.'[2]

The controversy came to a head in March 1586, when on three successive Sundays Travers used his sermon to refute the doctrine preached by Hooker in the morning. It centred round Faith and Justification, and whether the Romanists who denied or obscured justification by faith could hope for salvation. Hooker affirmed this possibility, if in other respects they were sincere Christians, and maintained that God would be merciful and save the thousands of our forefathers that had died 'though they lived in popish super-stitions, inasmuch as they sinned ignorantly'. To the Puritan and Calvinist mind this was a betrayal of the Reformation. Whitgift, the Archbishop of Canterbury, removed Travers from his lectureship and gave judgement in favour of Hooker. It was the shock of this first direct experience of the workings of the Puritan mind that motivated Hooker's return to first principles, and the working out of his own position more adequately. It signalled the need for a constructive theology of a new type.

Away from the Temple, but not in the quiet country living of Boscombe, which according to Professor Sisson[3] Hooker never inhabited, he worked out his *Laws of Ecclesiastical Polity*, in which he reviews the whole of the Puritan controversy from its inception at the beginning of Elizabeth's reign. He remained in London until moving to another country living near Canterbury in 1595. Sisson has also shown, in his *Judicious Marriage of Mr. Hooker*, that the *Laws* was written in London, where the author could draw on the help of his friends Edwin Sandys, a trained lawyer and MP, and George Cranmer, so that it was no lone secret venture and was backed by Whitgift. At Whitgift's request he also found himself resuming the Archbishop's unfinished controversy with Thomas Cartwright, the Presbyterian Lady Margaret Professor of Divinity at Cambridge. This controversy between Anglican and Puritan made a notable contribution to theological method, for the 'Admonition to Parliament' in 1572 was a comprehensive plan of change whose primary interest was theological, identifying a type of authoritative viewpoint that was subsequently always identified with Puritanism. Hooker's task was to confute this by outlining a method, providing a distinctively Anglican ethos in which, as McAdoo points out, the distinctiveness lies in the method rather than the content.[4] Anglicanism is not committed to believing anything because it is Anglican, but only because it is true. So Hooker stands in the larger room of the Christian centuries, with the Fathers who were always conscious of the problem of fusing faith and reason, and with Anselm who brought new vigour to theological method before the Reformation period with his 'faith seeking understanding'. He also stood with Aquinas, who is the forerunner of an approach to reason and to a synthesis of faith and reason which left its mark on this seventeenth century Anglican theologian. In his ecclesiastical and theological position in the Church of England,

Hooker was a close follower of his early friend and patron, Bishop Jewel. Jewel, in his celebrated *Apology of the Church of England,* had clearly defined the Catholic foundation principles of the Reformed English Church and especially in its appeal to Apostolic and Catholic antiquity. Hooker practically applied this position to the discipline of the Anglican Church, against the clamour of the Puritan party for the enforcement of the discipline of Geneva. Jewel had defended the English Church against the denunciatory attacks of Rome, Hooker defended it against the scurrilous attacks of the Puritans. It is specially interesting to notice how closely Hooker follows and often amplifies the theological teaching of the great Anglican Apologist, whom he described as 'the worthiest divine that Christendom hath bred for the space of some hundreds of years'.[5]

More specific to the purpose of this book is Hooker's use of the Fathers, which, while not a creation of the seventeenth century, became during this century an integral part of the Anglican approach to theological questions. This appeal to antiquity was not simply a search for guarantors of some specific teaching and practice. In addition to establishing an identity of doctrine with the early period, the concern was to discover what kind of church existed in the first three centuries and to show a resemblance between it and the contemporary church. This appeal to antiquity was not peculiar to Hooker; others were concerned to use their understanding of the teaching and ecclesiastical polity of the primitive church. The Puritans wanted a system on *Sola Scriptura*; others among reformed churches were more historically-minded and sought to establish their position from the first three centuries. So Hooker found himself having to deal with people who believed not only that they had rediscovered the Gospel in its original purity, but also that they held in their hands a master key to its re-establishment, a divinely-willed and pre-ordained church polity. For them the Genevan platform of church order embodied the express will of God.

The Appeal to Antiquity

It is natural that Hooker's *Ecclesiastical Polity* should be a development of his ministry of preaching at the Temple. Documents relating to Hooker's controversy with Travers and three Sermons on the Book of Habakkuk have a direct connection with the arguments of Books I–IV. His third sermon on 'The Nature of Pride', discusses Justice and includes an outline of the distinctions of law that he elaborates in more detail in Book I, and the Preface to his *Polity* prepares for the argument in Books I–III. His second sermon tackles the subject of 'Justification, Works, and How the Foundation of Faith is Overthrown', and within it he raises what he sees should be the right attitude to Roman Catholics, that they are not beyond God's salvation. Book IV discusses this issue in a positive light, for which the Puritans condemned Hooker, and leads by way of preparation into the argument of Book V. Again in his Preface in ch. vii, 5, Hooker claims a continuity and coherence in the argument of his eight books of the *Ecclesiastical Polity*. Hooker's first four books establish the foundations upon which the later ones are built, making a thread of continuity to run through Books I–V, with Books I–IV laying the foundations upon which the whole argument of the remaining four books is built. The enquiry is impressive in its scope and in the range of authorities on which it is founded. Hooker's vision encompasses the whole universe of angels and men subordinated under God to the reign of law, which in all its various forms is essentially an expression of the Divine reason. Aristotle and the philosophy of Greece, the Greek and Latin Fathers, St Thomas and the schoolmen, are co-ordinated with the teaching of the Bible in support of an analysis which establishes the position that 'to measure by any one kind of law all the actions of men were to confound the admirable order, wherein God hath disposed all laws, each as in nature, so in degree, distinct from other'. Novelty or innovation is the last thing Hooker would have claimed. His starting point was a set of common assumptions central to the debate, commanding assent on both sides. He integrated them into a new synthesis, at the centre of which was a novel and distinctive vision that he was concerned to impress upon the Puritans as the logical consequence of the premises of these assumptions. In the Preface, he establishes an independence of mind from Calvin, which is what the Church of England at this time needed, but could not expect, from Whitgift whose doctrinal convictions were Calvinist. This placed him and the Church of England at a disadvantage when he had to defend catholic institutions. With Hooker there emerges that independence of Calvin's influence that was vital if the Church of England was to think out her own position.

So Hooker's *Laws of Ecclesiastical Polity* represents a new stage in the argument between Anglican and Puritan. To quote the words of Arthur B. Ferguson as cited by John Luoma:

Both Whitgift and his opponents had, after all, continued to treat the past mainly as a reservoir of authorities and had gone about as far in pitting authority against authority, as it was reasonable to go – and at times further. Experience of this sort of thing undoubtedly convinced Hooker of its futility.[6]

Luoma goes on to say that the unhistorical nature of this argument for the restoration of the primitive church by the Puritans, forced Hooker into making an historical refutation. Hooker's use of the Fathers is an advance in historical understanding, in his setting of patristic scholarship on a new level, which 'one might even argue, forces an abandonment of the Fathers as a source of authority for the Puritans while establishing it as a bulwark in the Anglican defence.'[7]

Jewel had maintained that the English church was reforming itself along the lines of the primitive church. As they argued among themselves the English Reformers turned Jewel's argument, directed at the Roman church, against the defenders of the Elizabethan settlement, maintaining that the English church was not yet in correspondence with the primitive pattern. Whitgift had to defend the English Church against this charge in his debate with Thomas Cartwright.[8] Both these men shared a high regard for the primitive church and a reverence for the Fathers as one of the chief testimonies to its structure. 'However, neither succeeded in clearly defining the role of the Fathers in determining the nature of the primitive Church. The Fathers appear more as an appendage than an integral part of the argument.'[9] They merely used the Fathers as a kind of fortress theology, using them in a piecemeal manner to bolster the didactic requirements of the moment. Furthermore, the weakness of Whitgift's defence lay in his agreement with Cartwright's basic premise that there is in Scripture a perfect pattern for the Church.[10] Wasinger's conclusion is that only by examining the way the Holy Spirit works through Scripture could a successful critique of this Puritan claim be provided and this is what Hooker provided.[11]

> The manner in which Hooker employs the Fathers serves as a chief example of the way in which he overcomes Cartwright and the Puritan concept of inspiration, advancing beyond Whitgift and transforming the role of the Fathers in the argument over the nature of the Church from tangential to integral.[12]

In contrasting Cartwright and Hooker in the use of the Fathers, Luoma makes a number of points. In relation to Cartwright's use of the Fathers his first point is that their testimony is subordinate to Scripture properly interpreted, which means through the inspiration of the Holy Spirit, and which in principle is patristic. In no way can they operate as an independent source of authority and he rejects the Augustinian canon which permits following the practice of the Church when there is no clear command of Scripture. Patristic testimony without clear scriptural testimony has no authority. His second rule is that the consensus of the Fathers, especially the Councils, is preferred to the testimony of the few. The most important consensus for Cartwright is the primitive church or the Reformed church of his own day, which he regards as the embodiment of the primitive discipline. His final rule is that owing to the increasing corruption of the church since the sixth century, the use of patristic consensus must be restricted to the first five centuries. In Cartwright's use of the Fathers there is a dearth of quotations from the early church, and fewer than ten per cent of his references are drawn from the Fathers of the first two centuries. Tertullian provides more than half the references, and the majority of the citations date from the late fourth and fifth centuries, principally Latins and especially the Africans. Luoma finds it odd that a theologian trying to establish the character of the early church should have so few references from the early period yet use the later sources he has so warned against. Furthermore, his use of Flacius Illyricus suggests that he does not have an in-depth knowledge of the Fathers. His method is typical of the time, a mere listing of authorities as from a reservoir of patristic sources rather than attempting to expound what they say and employ their argument within his own, making his use of the Fathers highly subjective. In the end Cartwright's use of the Fathers ends up by serving an 'anti-historical purpose', paradoxically the revolutionaries becoming reactionary, while the conservative *apologia* for an institution which prided itself on being *semper eadem*, was more sensitive to the historical process involved in the unfolding of tradition.[13]

In relation to Hooker Luoma makes the following points. First, the key word in his use of the Fathers is 'consensus', which is misused by the Puritans because they misunderstand the true nature of reason and revelation, denying that revelation presupposes reason.[14] Hooker's concern is for credible belief. Scripture contains all doctrine necessary for salvation[15] and so there is no need for any other source of revealed law.[16] Secondly, the establishment of discipline is a matter of reason and therefore decided by a consensus of the wise[17] who have learned it from Nature whose

voice is the instrument of God.[18] Unable to distinguish between
revelation and reason, the Puritans, in putting all God's truth on
one level, are trapped into making everything in Scripture an
unchanging law which is necessary to salvation. So in a scriptural
condemnation of the Church of England,[19] they confuse doctrine
and discipline, using a text from Galatians which is concerned with
unchanging doctrine[20] rather than the laws of discipline which can
be altered according to time and place. Reason determines discipline with the help of Scripture, which gives no prescription for
one form of church polity.[21] Resorting to reason is to follow
Augustine whose principle was to accept in church discipline that
which was grounded in scripture or in a reason not contrary to
scripture.[22]

Thirdly, such a rule allows for dependence on tradition, and
Hooker cites Augustine as his authority:[23] 'That the custom of the
people of God and the decrees of our forefathers are to be kept,
touching those things whereof the Scripture hath neither one way
nor other given us any charge'. He goes on to comment, 'St.
Augustine's speech therefore doth import, that where we have no
divine precept, if yet we have the custom of the people of God or a
decree of our forefathers, this is a law and must be kept.' Again he
cites Augustine in relation to apostolic succession 'that whatsoever
positive order the whole Church everywhere doth observe, the
same it must needs have received from the very apostles themselves, unless perhaps some general council were the authors of
it'.[24] Tradition is not a rival authority to Scripture as the source of
revelation and, as he points out,[25] it is not given the same obedience and reverence that is given to the written law nor regarded
with equal honour. 'For Hooker tradition is not an immutable
body of truths which is a rival to revealed doctrine. It is a body of
ordinances established by the authority that Christ has given the
Church in things indifferent. These ordinances are binding until
the Church has cause to change them'.[26] This places the Puritans
in a cul-de-sac situation, because with the fallenness of the church
spanning a thousand years as their premise, the only credible forefathers who can be followed are the apostles. This binds them in
the assertion that there is one polity in Scripture which they are
unable to prove out of Scripture alone. They ruled out Augustine's
suggestion to take the tradition of the Church as apostolic and so
destroyed any authority the Fathers may have for them. Hooker
therefore demonstrates that though Cartwright quotes the Fathers,
they have no authority in his argument because he has negated it
by his doctrine of the fall of the church. He asks [27] where they are

to draw the boundary line to delineate the prime of the church and concludes that their use of the Fathers is very subjective. Therefore they are unfit to judge 'What things have necessary use in the Church ... who bend themselves purposely against whatsoever the Church useth...' and only give 'grace and countenance' to what pleases them 'which they willingly do not yield unto any part of church polity'.

Fourthly, Hooker's argument illustrates how the Puritans have torpedoed any claim to consensus by virtue of their own method, which will only validate primitive discipline if it is found in a scriptural context, and this becomes impossible. Their appeal to the practice of the first five hundred years is also negated by a subjectivism that makes their selection of evidence arbitrary. Hooker's concept of consensus allows him to use the Fathers not only where the consensus is grounded in Scripture, but also where it is not against Scripture in matters of doctrine and discipline. Furthermore, consensus for Hooker is much wider, because he will not draw limiting boundaries at a particular century. He disagrees with the Puritan understanding of the fallenness of the church, in which from the beginning there has always been a 'continual consensus of truth'. Thus he can write, 'We hope therefore that to reform ourselves, if at any time we have done amiss, is not to sever ourselves from the Church we were of before.'[28] This frees him, not only in his use of the Fathers but in widening his consensus to the wisest men in every age. This is the major difference between Hooker and Cartwright.

Fifthly, Hooker unlike Cartwright did not cite the Fathers merely as authorities but always proved their relevance to his argument. Luoma exemplifies Hooker's skill in this by citing his defence of fasting[29] in Bk. V. lxxii, where he trawls for the natural basis of this discipline, its grounding in Scripture and the Fathers, and concludes by highlighting differences and agreements to put consensus into perspective. The result is a multi-faceted consensus, in which Scripture, reason and the Fathers contribute to the argument. This illustrates how Hooker's sense of history is central rather than peripheral to his theology, but also in an implicit way his dependence on St Thomas Aquinas in his use of Scripture and reason, whom Munz claims he had so thoroughly assimilated and had no need to explicate.[30] With Hooker there is developing a new sense of history that A. B. Ferguson sees as a necessary precondition for a revolution in historical scholarship.[31] Munz can see in Hooker the development of a sense of perspective and process heralding a new attitude, and that he is the exception among the

Reformers who, as Greenslade pointed out, exhibited little sense of the development of patristic theology.

> Hooker's use of the Fathers represents a real advance in patristic scholarship. In exposing Cartwright he uses the Fathers consistently and critically. The primitive church is revered, but it is revered as part of a continuing consensus. In his realization that the purpose of the Church will remain the same, but must be adapted to the circumstances, one might argue that Hooker is truer to the primitive church than Cartwright ...[32]

For the Puritans the Fathers were extraneous to their arguments, being reservoirs of authorities.

> Hooker on the contrary could critically use the Fathers and delineate a theology that made room for them as part of the continuing activity of the Spirit in the Church. In his attempt to develop a theological method that achieved a proper balance between revelation and reason Hooker exposed Cartwright's subjectivism. This left Hooker in the enviable position of being able to appropriate the long-held and revered authority of the primitive Church while removing the Fathers as a weapon from the Puritan arsenal. [33]

The Incarnation

Hooker's concern, in differing from the Reformers, as the quotation from Michael Ramsey points out, and as the foregoing elucidates in relation to the Puritans, is not to use the Fathers as a quarry for proof authorities. He wants to use the thought and piety of the Fathers, to incorporate within his own theological exposition what we may call the patristic mind,

> ... the central idea which generally governed the policy of the Fathers ... But this mind is clarified neither by one Father alone, nor again by all the Fathers as a whole, but by some who were able to combine wisdom with right action. Such Fathers are to be found in all periods of Church history from the times of the Apostles to the present century.[34]

The technical term *Phronēma* is used for what is called *the patristic mind,* whose real foundation Hooker found to be in Scripture, Tradition and Reason. This placed him in a much larger room than his contemporary opponents, and made him more quickly and more acutely aware of dangers in the wider theological scene, which in their preoccupation with changes of belief in the secondary doctrines of the Reformation they had been slow to spot. The dangers that threatened were in the form of old heresies in a new dress, which were directed at fundamental doctrines such as the Trinity and the Incarnation, and came from Anabaptists and Socinians. His awareness finds its focus in Hooker's exposition of the Incarnation and in his doctrine of the sacraments, which are implied by a religion of the Incarnation and organically connected with it.

> The section of Book V which deals with the Incarnation (cc.1ff), occupies a unique position in Hooker's work. It stands on a level with the central chapters of Book I. These are the two peaks of the *Ecclesiastical Polity* by which the whole must be judged. To change the metaphor, if Book I lays down distinctions of thought which are the foundations of the whole edifice, the section on the theology of the Incarnation is like a central tower round which the whole is grouped.[35]

In making the Incarnation central, Hooker differed from his opponents who were preoccupied with doctrines of justification, grace and predestination and the grounding of their reality in a subjectivism, where personal experience and private judgement counted most. Here individualism is set up over against the corporate and affects attitudes towards religious institutions, among them creeds and sacraments. Hooker's concern is with objectivity in religion and the right balance of priorities in the mutual relations between the objective and the subjective. Fundamental to Hooker's theology is the presence of creeds, without which corporate religion has no ground and when faith is reduced to a purely personal and individual possession, finds itself inadequate to its task.

> A common religious life with its worship and organisation must be based upon communal experience, upon convictions corporately expressed and emphasised with a continuity of tradition from age to age. The creeds serve this purpose and so give objectivity to our faith, for they lay stress upon the object of faith rather than upon the experience of the faith itself.[36]

The objectivity of faith he sets forth in his exposition of Chalcedonian Christology,[37] but not before rooting the validity and reality of our 'life in Christ', in the objectivity of sacraments which are a natural outcome of the Incarnation.

Sacraments are the powerful instruments of God to eternal life. For as our natural life consisteth in the union of the body with the soul; so our life supernatural in the union of the soul with God. And forasmuch as there is no union of God with man without that mean between both which is both, it seemeth requisite that we first consider how God is in Christ, then how Christ is in us, and how the Sacraments do serve to make us partakers of Christ. In other things we may be more brief, but the weight of these requireth largeness.[38]

No form of personal experience could be the ground of religion, only God who bestows faith and whose self-revelation of himself is to that gift of faith he has given, making the Incarnation the true foundation for Christianity. In Christ, the perfect union of God and Man, 'we may expect to find the norm of all true thought about both God and Man ... all our practical activity as Christians must proceed from the Incarnation as its source and must be enshrined in and supported by institutions which exhibit its principles and perpetuate its life.'[39] In this most theological section of the *Laws*, Hooker, in building this 'central tower', is sensitive to its importance in determining not only the stability but also the overall final shape of the whole 'building'. Incarnation and sacraments cannot therefore be separated, because the sacraments are the means by which the purpose of the Incarnation is effected in us, namely 'the union of the soul with God'.

Hooker sets this discussion significantly within the context of his defence of the liturgical institutions of the Book of Common Prayer, which provided the liturgical experience that gave an ecclesial context to Anglican divinity. This understands the Church as bearing witness to the truth, not by reminiscence, or from the words of others, but from its own living, unceasing experience, from its catholic fullness which has its roots in continuity with the primitive church. Is not this what we mean by Tradition in theological method? It is a life mystical and sacramental, the constant abiding Spirit, not merely the memory of words, and is therefore a charismatic not a historical principle. Together with Scripture it contains the truth of divine revelation, a truth that lives in the Church. On this Catholic and patristic foundation, Incarnation in relation to the sacraments, Hooker built his theology. It was an implicit criticism not only of those Reformed theologies where the Incarnation had ceased to be taken as the centre of gravity, but also of those old heresies such as Gnosticism and Arianism that he saw emerging in a new key.

He begins his exposition of the Incarnation with an assertion of the oneness of God in the indivisible Trinity. 'So that in every Person there is implied both the substance of God which is one, and also that property which causeth the same Person really and truly to differ from the other two.'[40] God becomes man in the Person of the Son so that 'the Father and the Holy Ghost (saith Damascene) have no communion with the Incarnation of the Word otherwise than only by approbation and assent',[41] but is not denied to that nature which is common to all three. He is expressing the mind of Scripture as found in 2 Cor. 5: 19; Heb. 2: 10, Col: 1: 15–18, Heb. 4, where he explains why God should save man by man himself, and the necessity for Christ to take manhood. Attempts to explain the union of the two natures in the one Person have led to a succession of heresies that the Church has had to counter. Individual Fathers have had to correct misrepresentations of relations between the Persons of the Trinity, the nature of the Persons, and depreciation and exaltation of one or other of the divine or human, or confusion of both in the Person of Christ. In consequence synods and councils of bishops have been called to define the Church's understanding of such matters. Hooker begins by going through these various heresies[42] with judicious quotations from Scripture and the Fathers, including Theodoret, Cyril of Alexandria, Gregory of Nyssa, Hilary of Poitiers, Irenaeus, Leo the Great, John Damascene, Augustine and Origen. He weaves into the substance of his argument that *phronēma* of the Fathers as found in them and sums up his discussion of the nature of Christ in relation to these heresies.

> To gather therefore into one sum all that hath hitherto been spoken touching this point, there are but four things which concur to make complete the whole state of our Lord Jesus Christ: his Deity, his manhood, the conjunction of both, and the distinction of the one from the other being joined in one. Four principal heresies there are which have in those things withstood the truth: Arians by bending themselves against the Deity of Christ; Apollinarians by maiming and misinterpreting that which belongeth to his human nature; Nestorians by rending Christ asunder, and dividing him into two persons; the followers of Eutyches by confounding in his person those natures which they should distinguish. Against these there have been four most ancient general councils: the Council of Nice to define against Arians, against Apollinarians the Council of Constantinople, the Council of Ephesus against Nestorians, against Eutyches the

Chalcedon Council. In four words ἀληθῶς, τελέως, ἀδιαιρέτως ἀσυγχύτως truly, perfectly, indivisibly, distinctly; the first applied to his being God, and the second to his being Man, the third to his being of both One, and the fourth to his still continuing in that one Both: we may fully by way of abridgement comprise whatsoever antiquity hath at large handled either in declaration of Christian belief or in refutation of the foresaid heresies. Within the compass of which four heads I may truly affirm, that all heresies which touch but the Person of Jesus Christ, whether they have risen in these latter days, or in any age heretofore, may be with great facility brought to confine themselves. We conclude therefore that to save the world it was of necessity the Son of God should be thus incarnate, and that God should so be in Christ as hath been declared.[43] [NB. It is interesting to note that only two of the original four words from the Chalcedonian Creed are right! ἄτρεπτως and ἀχώριστως are missing. For 'distinctly', *unconfusedly* is a more exact translation].

Reformed theology differed from Hooker not in its divergence from orthodoxy in Christology, but in its failure to make the Incarnation the normative principle of their religion. In Johannine and Pauline Christianity it is the kernel, with the consequences of sacramental participation in that life through eating the flesh and drinking the blood of Christ. This is thoroughly patristic and central to the thought of Hooker and leads naturally to a doctrine of the mystical body of Christ where Christ's saving presence in the world manifests itself. Our coinherence with Jesus Christ is not through a mere kinship of human nature.

The Church is in Christ as Eve was in Adam. Yea by grace we are everyone of us in Christ and in his Church as by nature we are in those our first parents. God made Eve out of the rib of Adam. And his Church he frameth out of the very flesh, the very wounded and bleeding side of the Son of Man. His body crucified and his blood shed for the life of the world are the true elements of that heavenly being which maketh us such as himself is of whom we come. For which cause the words of Adam may fitly be the words of Christ concerning his Church 'flesh of my flesh and bone of my bones', a true native extract out of my own body.[44]

This was the contextual framework from within which Hooker understood and expounded the sacraments as major instruments through which we are incorporated into the mystical body of Christ.

Through them 'the medicine that doth cure the world' – God in Christ – was distributed to the members of Christ's body the Church. Hooker thus went out of his way to emphasize that the sacraments had real objective effects; not mere signs, they really did confer grace. 'We take not baptism nor the eucharist for bare resemblances or memorials of things absent neither for naked signs and testimonies assuring us of grace received before but ... for means effectual whereby God when we take the sacraments delivereth into our hands that grace available unto eternal life, which grace the sacraments represent or signify'.[45]

For Hooker, therefore, the sacrament was not a subject for debate so much as an object for devotional contemplation. As such it provided the centre-piece for his vision of the Church; here the visible and invisible churches met, as Christ's presence in his mystical body the Church was made manifest in the sacrament. Since man was created in God's image it was axiomatic that 'life' had been 'proposed unto all men as their end'. Sin had damaged, if not destroyed the naturalness of that end, but grace could restore the damage. It was Hooker's vision of 'God in Christ' as 'the medicine that doth cure the world' and of 'Christ in us' as the means by which that medicine was applied to a wounded human nature, which underlay his account of the sacrament. For through Christ's presence in the sacrament, God's causative presence in the world was transformed into his saving presence in the Church.[46]

Here we find a clear break from an approach to the sacrament through an attempt to find an alternative to transubstantiation, such as preoccupied the focus of reformers like Cranmer, Jewel, and Grindal. Hooker's focus is elsewhere and is much larger because it is in that which is more fundamental, the Incarnation and its organic connection with the Church as Christ's mystical body. In this Hooker diverged fundamentally from the Puritans whose religion was certainly Christocentric in making the value of Christ to the soul a central and dominating idea, but their emphasis was on our experience of Christ as Saviour, rather than on the Incarnation as an objective fact. This made the efficacy of the sacraments dependent on the preaching of the word, reducing the sacraments to a position of inherent inferiority to the proclamation of the word. They were seen not as the 'medicine of souls' but as

mere signs, and 'some . . . assign unto them no end but only to teach
the mind, by other senses, that which the Word doth teach by
hearing.'[47] The sermon becomes more important than the sacrament. Hooker has much to say on the way in which preaching is
valued by the Puritans, almost to the exclusion of worship, prayer
and sacraments; they tilt the vision of ministry away from Hooker's
and the Fathers' sacrament-centred direction, and so tie the efficacy of the sacraments closely to an instructive imparting of
knowledge. In this they are not far from the Valentinian heresy,
which claimed that 'the full redemption of the inward man . . . must
needs belong unto knowledge'.[48] This lowered the whole significance of sacramental or external religion, creating a theology aloof
from the intimate traits of a Gospel. This made separation rather
than union dominant, the separation of the spiritual from the material, which for man is its natural field of expression and had been
claimed by God in Christ in the Incarnation.

> . . . in Hooker's day all the old tendencies of earlier heresies were
> at work. The Reformed combined orthodox Christology with a
> Manichaean dislike to any thorough and consistent application
> of the principles of the Incarnation to religion as a whole; the
> Anabaptists ceased to attach any importance to the historic
> Christ, substituting an interior Word for both written and
> Incarnate Word. The Socinians denied the possibility of any
> union of Godhead and Manhood in one Person. Lutherans
> mistook confusion for union and opened the doors for others to
> deny the difference between the human and the Divine.
> Hooker's solution is to return to the Christological principles of
> the Council of Chalcedon and to make the Incarnation, so
> understood, the norm and centre of the Christian religion. In
> much that he says he seems to be simply travelling over old
> ground and saying nothing that could not be learnt from the
> Fathers. Yet novelty is not always synonymous with truth and
> Hooker accepts the old ground deliberately; for no other would
> have been compatible with his general theological principles.
> His formula for the Incarnation is 'Union in distinction.'. . . All
> these principles are seen to meet in the doctrine of the
> Incarnation as understood by the Fathers and Councils and as
> restated by Hooker in these pages of Book V. In chapters li–liii
> the main lessons learnt by the Primitive Church are thus
> restated; and then in the chapters which immediately follow
> (liv–lvii) we are given Hooker's own handling of this great
> scheme on the highest dogmatic level.[49]

Participation

For Hooker, as Thornton points out,[50] the grace of the sacraments is the last link in a series whose terminus is the participation of the Saints in the life of God. 'If we are looking for the key concepts in Hooker's theological thought, we shall find them in terms such as mutual participation and conjunction, coinherence and perichoresis. God is in Christ; Christ is in us; we are in him.'[51] The archetype of participation is the mutual indwelling of the Father, Son and Holy Spirit in the oneness of the Blessed Trinity in which there is a law of self-impartation alongside that mutual indwelling of divine life and love that exists between the Father and the Son.

> Life as all other gifts and benefits groweth originally from the Father, and cometh not to us but by the Son,[(i)] nor by the Son to any of us in particular but through the Spirit.[(ii)] For this cause the Apostle wisheth to the Church of Corinth 'The grace of our Lord Jesus Christ, and the love of God, and the fellowship of the Holy Ghost.'[(iii)] Which three St. Peter comprehendeth in one, 'The participation of the divine Nature.'[(iv)] We are therefore in God through Christ eternally according to that intent and purpose whereby we were chosen to be made his in this present world ... we are in God through the knowledge which is had of us, and the love which is borne towards us from everlasting ... Our being in Christ by eternal foreknowledge saveth us not without our actual and real adoption into the fellowship of his saints in this present world. For in him we actually are by our actual incorporation into that society which hath him for their head,[(v)] and doth make together with him one Body, (he and they in that respect having one name,[(vi)] for which cause by virtue of this mystical conjunction, we are of him and in him even as though our very flesh and bones should be made continuate with his.[(vii)] We are in Christ[(viii)] because he knoweth and loveth us even as parts of himself. No man actually is in him but they in whom he actually is. 'For he which hath not the Son of God hath not life'[(ix)].

Hooker is careful to point out that there is more to our coinherence[(x)] than that Christ and we share the self-same human nature.

> The Church is in Christ as Eve was in Adam. Yea by grace are every one of us in Christ and in his Church, as by nature we are in those first parents. God made Eve of the rib of Adam. And his

Church he frameth out of the very flesh, the very wounded and
bleeding side of the Son of Man. His body crucified and his
blood shed for the life of the world, are the true elements of that
heavenly being, which maketh us such as himself is of whom we
come(xi) .52

Canon Allchin writes, 'It is true that Hooker here avoids the
explicit language of *theosis* (or deification), but it does not escape
our attention that when he speaks of Christ 'making us such as
himself is' he affirms the underlying mystery which the word
expresses'53 On both the divine and human levels of the
Incarnation there is a mutual indwelling between the Father and
the Son. As a consequence of this unique participation of the Son
in the Father by mutual indwelling, all created things are enabled
to participate in the life of God and in some degree enjoy mutual
indwelling with him. This means that because of the Incarnation
the self-impartation that exists within the Godhead finds expression in a self-impartation of God to his creation, allowing creation
and redemption to become the two modes in which created beings
participate in the life of God.

John Booty54 is reluctant to admit that Hooker understood
participation in terms of deification. He speculates from a basis of
probability, that Hooker probably had four other New Testament
Greek words in mind in his use of the word participation. The first
two of these words, μετουσία (μετέχω) meaning to share or
partake in (1 Cor. 9: 10,12; 20: 17,21 etc.), and μεταλαμβάνω,
meaning to partake or share in (Acts 2: 4 etc.). The two words of
greater importance to Hooker are κοινωνία and μένω (μενεῖν).
The former means fellowship, a two-sided relationship with
emphasis on giving and receiving. He explains that κοινωνία
draws on the concern of primitive religion for the inward recep-
tion of divine power (*mana*) in eating and drinking, and therefore
the logical consequence is to find this word used in connection
with the Eucharist. The word μένω, means to abide in or be in
union with, as in John 6: 54, and so describes a community of life
between the Father and the Son, and the disciples' sharing in
Christ's life as they do his works. He argues further from Hooker's
awareness of misrepresentations of participation in terms of deification or mystical union as being irrational. There seems little
capacity and no effort made to understand what deification in its
patristic context actually is, and the tendency is to confuse it with
pantheism, which is certainly what Hooker argued against.
However, his strictures against the misrepresentations of deifica-

tion cannot be used as a basis for giving the impression that this is what deification actually is, nor for discounting it from Hooker's way of understanding participation. The impression is that Booty has not grasped what the Fathers actually mean by the mystery of *theosis*, confusing it with pantheism of which he is rightly fearful. Furthermore, because Hooker is sensitive to the mood of controversy in which he has to express his polemic, his language is moderate and restrained rather than explicit. So Booty is either unable to see in the essence and context of what Hooker is expressing, an affirmation of the underlying mystery of *theosis*, or has dismissed such an interpretation of Hooker's understanding of participation as pantheistic. Then he attributes his own view of participation to Hooker by positing the probability that Hooker may or may not have had in his mind these other four New Testament Greek words for participation which cannot be interpreted in terms of deification.

Canon Allchin affirms again in another context Hooker's understanding of participation in terms of deification.[55] C. S. Lewis, whose theology was greatly influenced by Hooker, is quoted by Allchin, from his work on Hooker in the *Oxford Dictionary of English Literature*.[56] Here Lewis speaks of Hooker's model universe as being 'drenched with Deity', and Hooker's words 'All things that are of God, have God in them and they in himself likewise, and yet their substance and his are very different'. Lewis spells out what this presence of the transcendent God in his world implies, keeping together things that can easily be set in opposition,

> reason as well as revelation, nature as well as grace, the commonwealth as well as the Church, are equally though diversely, 'of God' ... All kinds of knowledge, all good arts, sciences and disciplines ... we meet in all levels the divine wisdom shining out through 'the beautiful variety of things' in 'their manifold and yet harmonious dissimilitude'.

This is nothing less than the patristic vision of God's creation filled with his energy and wisdom, the presence of God participating in his world which can be the only context within which to speak of man's participation in God in terms of deification. 'The Word of God, who is God wills in all things and at all times to work the mystery of his embodiment'.[57] Within this context Hooker expounds a vision of man which finds its fulfilment in God, a theocentric humanism. 'If then in him we are blessed, it is by force of participation and conjunction with him ... so that although we be men, yet being into God united we live as it were the life of God.'[58]

The theme of deification emerges in Hooker's description of man's relationship to God in terms of conjunction and participation, terms with a technical significance which occur frequently in this context. Because man is made for God and can only find fulfilment in him there is a restlessness and longing for self-transcendence, 'that which exceeds the reach of sense; yea somewhat above the capacity of reason, somewhat divine and heavenly, which with hidden exultation, he rather surmiseth than conceiveth'.[59] God's initiative in Christ leads man into the kingdom of heaven where life becomes a constant growth into everlasting life.

Canon Allchin cites Olivier Loyer speaking of Hooker's vision of man as of 'a being whose end is God himself ', a being inhabited by 'a natural desire for a supernatural end'. Loyer shows how for Hooker the concept of participation becomes a key to be used to unlock many different areas of theological thought, 'not only the economy of creation, but also the Trinitarian economy and the economy of salvation. In the heart of the Trinity, participation becomes procession of the persons, the circumincession, underlining at once their distinction and their mutual coinherence. At the level of redemption it expresses the mystery of our adoption.' God is in us, we are in him by way of a mutual participation, in which creature and Creator remain distinct while being no longer separate.

> Following this line of thought and working within the terminology of the western scholastic tradition, Hooker opens up the way for a reaffirmation of the patristic conviction that man can indeed become a partaker of the divine nature, but only and always by gift and grace, never by right and nature.[60]

The theological implications of this have already been spelt out in the exposition of Hooker's doctrine of the Church and sacraments that he organically connects with his reaffirmation of the Chalcedonian Christology.

A Theology of Synthesis

Hooker presents a constructive synthesis in which the mystical, the intellectual and the institutional are mutually related and balanced. The mystical dimension is rooted in the *sui generis* experience of the Church which constitutes the source and context of his theology, expounded not only in terms of 'intellectual clarity, but of a union of human lives with God in the way of holiness'. As a synthesis this theology is rooted in the Greek and Latin Fathers, and embraces the legitimate concerns of Christian thought in the medieval schoolmen as well as the contemporary concerns of the seventeenth century. It is a dynamic presentation of the orthodox doctrine of the Trinity as the basis of ecclesiology and anthropology, while assuming into his theological vision the totality of creation, the world and human culture by referring it to its ultimate fulfilment in its restoration and transfiguration. Here in Hooker's vision of the *divine order* Redemption extends to the whole universe, expressing that comprehensiveness of the Fathers that was a characteristic of their account of the central doctrine of the Christian faith. Set within this wider context of creation and redemption is the mystery of the complementarity of all things, each with its distinctive contribution within the overall context of God's law that holds within it the *laws of an ecclesiastical polity*. In this vision *continuity* and *wholeness* are of the *esse*, because of their sacramental character within the *divine order*. The patristic wholeness of vision enabled Hooker to avoid the damaging dualism of natural and supernatural. His vision is of a Christian mysticism that is rooted in the incarnate life of God. As such, it is grounded in history, and within it is the world as sacrament in contrast to the purely spiritual mysticism acquired by special transcendental techniques in Eastern religions.

The influence exerted by Hooker on the Church of England cannot be confined to the contents of this great work of literature and theology. It extends beyond his literary activity to the creation of a school of writers who looked to him as their master. They not only carried on the great tradition of his teaching, but like him they worked in a spirit of independent enquiry, and thus enabled and made permanent the adhesion of the Anglican Reformation to the principles of Apostolic order as well as primitive truth. After three hundred years Hooker's way of interpreting the continuing life of what became Anglicanism still speaks to issues facing contemporary Anglicans in an age of ecumenism. In a century dominated by empiricism in debates about our knowledge of God, Hooker's *Polity* can still contribute, while his ecclesiology can address the dominant individualism of our times in its conflict with the corporate nature of Christianity. Finally, in the face of a rising biblical fundamentalism, Hooker's hermeneutical principles are a positive antidote.

Notes

1. R. Bauckham, ' Hooker, Travers and the Church of Rome in 1580', in *Journal of Ecclesiastical History,* vol. 29 (January 1978), p. 41.
2. *Ibid.* p. 42.
3. V. J. K. Brook, citing Sisson, *Whitgift and the English Church* (English Universities Press, London, 1957), p. 147.
4. H. R. McAdoo, *The Spirit of Anglicanism* (A. & C. Black, London, 1965), p. 1.
5. Sidney C. Carter, 'Richard Hooker', in *Church Quarterly Review* vol. cxl (Jan–Mar. 1945), pp. 222–3.
6. John Luoma, citing Arthur B. Ferguson, 'The Historical Perspective of Richard Hooker: A Renaissance Paradox', in *The Journal of Medieval and Renaissance Studies,* vol. iii (1973), p. 22; 'Who Owns the Fathers? Hooker and Cartwright on the Authority of the Primitive Church', in *Sixteenth Century Journal,* vol. viii, 3 (1977), p. 45.
7. *Ibid.*
8. John Whitgift, *Defence of the Answer to the Admonition against the Reply of T.C.*(1574).
9. Luoma, *ibid.* p. 46.
10. *Ibid.* p. 46, citing Stephen S. Wasinger, 'Politics and the Full Persuasion: An Inquiry into the Source of the Puritan Project' (unpublished Ph.D. Dissertation, University of Notre Dame, 1972), pp. 119–20.
11. *Ibid.*
12. *Ibid.*
13. *Ibid.* citing Arthur B. Ferguson, 'Circumstances and the Sense of History in Tudor England: The Coming of the Historical Revolution' in *Medieval and Renaisance Studies,* ed. John M. Headley (Chapel Hill: University of North Carolina Press, 1968). p. 173.
14. Richard Hooker, 'The Laws of Ecclesiastical Polity', in *The Works of that Learned and Judicious Divine, Mr Richard Hooker: with an account of His Life and death* by Isaac Walton in two volumes (Oxford University Press, Oxford, 1880), vol. i, bk I, xiv, 4–5.
15. *Ibid.* 'Preface', 3: 2.
16. *Ibid.* bk. I, xiii, 2.
17. *Ibid.* bk. I, x, 7.
18. *Ibid.* bk. I, viii, 3.
19. Galatians 1: 8.
20. Hooker, 'Preface', 6, 3; bk. V, viii, 2.
21. *Ibid.* bk. IV, ii, 2.
22. *Ibid.* bk. II, iv, 7.
23. *Ibid.* bk. IV, v, 1.
24. *Ibid.* bk. VII, v, 3.
25. *Ibid.* bk. I, xiii, 2.
26. Luoma, p. 55.
27. Hooker, bk. VII, xiii.

28. *Ibid.* bk. III, i, 10.
29. *Ibid.* bk. V. lxxii.
30. Luoma, pp. 57–8, citing P. Munz, *The Place of Hooker in the History of Thought* (Routledge, Kegan Paul Ltd, London, 1952).
31. *Ibid.* p. 58, citing Ferguson.
32. *Ibid.* p. 59, citing Munz.
33. *Ibid.*
34. Methodius, Archbishop of Thyateira and Great Britain, 'The Mind (Phronema) of the Fathers of the Church', in *Patristic Byzantine Review*, vol. iv, pt. i (1985), p. 14.
35. L. Thornton, *Richard Hooker* (SPCK, London, 1924), p. 54.
36. *Ibid.* pp. 55–6.
37. Hooker, *Laws*, bk. V, li.
38. *Ibid.* bk. V, i, 3.
39. Thornton, *ibid.* p. 56.
40. Hooker, bk. V, li, 1.
41. *Ibid.* citing John Damascene, *De Orthod Fid.*, bk. V, li, 2.
42. *Ibid.* bk .V. lii.
43. *Ibid.* bk. V, liv, 10.
44. *Ibid.*, bk.V. lvi, 7.
45. *Ibid.*
46. Peter Lake, *Anglicans and Puritans* (Allen & Unwin, London, 1988), p. 175.
47. Hooker, bk. V. lvii, 1.
48. *Ibid.* bk. V. lvii, 1; lx, 4.
49. Thornton, pp. 64–5.
50. *Ibid.* p. 71.
51. A. M. Allchin, *The Kingdom of Love and Knowledge* (DLT, London, 1979), p. 96.
52. Hooker, Bk. V, lvi, 7, citing i) 1 John 5: 11 ; ii) Rom. 8: 10; iii) 2 Cor. 13: 13; iv) 2 Pet. 1: 4; v) Col. 2: 10; vi) 1 Cor. 12: 12 ; vii) Eph. 5: 20. viii) John 15: 9; ix) 1 John 5: 12; x) John 14: 2; 15: 4; xi) John 1: 4–9.
53. Allchin, p. 97.
54. John Booty, 'Richard Hooker,' in *The Spirit of Anglicanism,* ed. W. J. Wolf (T. & T. Clark, Edinburgh, 1979), p. 17.
55. A. M. Allchin, *Participation in God* (DLT, London, 1988), p. 8.
56. C. S. Lewis, 'English Literature in the Sixteenth Century, excluding drama', in *The Oxford Dictionary of English Literature* (Oxford, 1954), p. 460.
57. A. M. Allchin, *Participation in God,* p. 9, citing a text from 'The Ambigua', Maximus the Confessor.
58. Hooker, bk. I. xi, 2.
59. *Ibid.* bk. I. xi, 4.
60. Allchin, *ibid.* pp. 12–13, citing Olivier Loyer, *L'Anglicanisme de Richard Hooker* (Paris, 1979), vol. i, pp. 353ff.

7

Lancelot Andrewes and the Roman Catholics

In the Preface to his biography, Douglas Macleane[1] states that the career of this Caroline divine stood in an important relation to the critical sub-Reformation era, and did much to determine the subsequent life and thought of the Church of England. He describes his writings as representative of the best apologetic of Anglican divinity but that it is the 'holy and patristic character of the man' that has impressed itself on succeeding generations as a truly apostolic bishop of the Catholic Church. He is the kind of person one would have expected to find among the fathers of Nicaea or Ephesus. Andrewes has about him 'so primitive and reverend an exterior also that,' says Thomas Fuller, 'the Fathers are not more faithfully cited in his books than lively copied out in his countenance and carriage'. Macleane quotes from Dean Church's essay[2] that Andrewes

> recalled an age which else would have stifled in the looms of Protestant scholasticism into a diviner, purer, freer air, back to the many-sided thought, to the sanctified divinity of the undivided Church, by the influence of which his contemporaries might be led from a theology which ended in cross-grained and perverse conscientiousness to a theology which ended in adoration, self-surrender and blessing, and in the awe and joy of welcoming the Eternal Beauty, the Eternal Sanctity and the Eternal Love, the Sacrifice and Reconciliation of the world.

In their theological opinions Hooker and Andrewes shared much in common, and had been formed under the same circumstances, both strongly recoiling from the popular systems and traditions which, under Elizabeth, had claimed to interpret and represent exclusively the English Reformation. They also stood together on the same positive ground and identified it as the true and positive basis of the teaching of the English church. As Church points out,

they also shared 'that devotional temper, those keen and deep
emotions of awe, reverence and delight, which arise when the
objects of theological thought and interest are adequately realised
according to their greatness by the imagination and the heart.'[3]
Their differences lay in the fact that Hooker was an obscure
country parson, while Andrewes held high office as a bishop and
counselled in the nation's corridors of power. Nevertheless, he it
was who followed for twenty-five years after Hooker's death the
theological method Hooker had opened up.

His Theological Base

It is not insignificant that in 1957 the English translation of
Vladimir Lossky's *The Mystical Theology of the Eastern Church* was
published. 'Mystical theology' he defines as meaning specifically a
spirituality that expresses a doctrinal attitude, reaffirming the vital
link between dogma and spirituality. The roots of such a theology
lie in the praying and worshipping Church, beyond mere intellectual apprehension. From that same family and Eastern Orthodox
perspective in 1991 comes Nicholas Lossky's *Lancelot Andrewes the
Preacher (1555–1626), The Origins of the Mystical Theology of the Church
of England*. His theology is mystical in that same sense, that it is a
spirituality that expresses a doctrinal attitude.

> For Andrewes, not only are spirituality and theology not
> opposed, but the one could not be conceived without the other.
> Spirituality (a modern term that Andrewes does not use, be it
> understood) is, as has been suggested, the ecclesial experience,
> in the Church, of the union of man with God, and not an indi-
> vidualistic pietism. Theology, far from being for Andrewes a
> speculative intellectual system to do with God, is a translation in
> terms that can be transmitted of this same ecclesial experience.
> It is consequently a vision of God and not a system of thought.[4]

So the aim of his preaching becomes

> to convert his hearers to the experience of God in the rectitude
> of the *lex credendi,* which cannot but be in profound harmony
> with the *lex orandi.* Therefore, he cannot be content merely to
> quote the fathers; he has integrated their essential attitude to
> theology itself, which is not thinking about God but the attempt
> to translate into intelligible terms the experience of life in God.[5]

His theological base is best summarized in his own words, 'One canon reduced to writing by God himself, two testaments, three creeds, four general councils, five centuries, and the series of Fathers in that period ... determine the boundary of our faith.'[6] His point is that the authority of the Church of England is based on the Scriptures, and on the fact that her faith is that of the Church of the first five centuries, and she holds as *de fide* neither more nor less than did the Fathers. On the Roman front he argues from this base that novelties introduced by Rome are rejected by Anglicanism, and on the Puritan front he uses the same argument with opposite effect claiming that nothing should be rejected that finds support in the primitive church. Welsby[7] points out that the writings of Andrewes demonstrate that his knowledge of the Fathers was far wider than any of his contemporaries, but it never reduced him to being purely antiquarian. He did not condemn all subsequent developments as long as they were not held to be *de fide*, nor was his concern to return to the precise conditions of the primitive church. He quotes Ness, 'What he desired was to provide a standard within the history of the Church itself, by which the development of doctrines and institutions might be tested.'[8] For Andrewes that standard or norm of faith for the Church was iden- tified in its purest form in the New Testament and in the first five centuries of church history. The continuity of Anglicanism with antiquity meant that the Anglican Church was part of the Catholic and Universal Church. Although this was unacceptable to Rome and Geneva, Andrewes claimed that the authority which Rome confined to the Pope and which Puritans restricted to the invisible church, belonged to the universal, historical Church, and there- fore to Anglicanism. Andrewes's vindication, says Welsby, became the norm of Anglican apologetic. This *primitivism* of Andrewes's is not a retreat into a simplistic return to the past, to a *traditionalism*, nor can it ever be, claims Lossky, a search for some 'golden age', as a period of reference *par excellence*.

> The 'tradition' of the Church is not the simple conservation of what has been said and done in the past. It is a dynamic process that transcends linear time, without in any way abolishing it. It is, in fact, a way of living in time in the light of eternity, which recapitulates past, present, and future because everything is lived in contemporaneity with the reality of the Gospel. 'What the Churches of God have done at all times' is of importance to Andrewes, not in a spirit of imitation or conservatism, but to the extent that they have done it in a consciousness of living by 'memorial', 'anamnesis' (ἀνάμνησις), the past events of the

Gospel and their consequences to come, in the Church of the present.[9]

His work is as significant as Hooker's, whom he supplemented in various ways. 'But his real significance', McAdoo points out, 'is due to his contribution to theological method which was of a formative nature. It was something he inherited from Jewel whose work he valued (*Opuscula* p. 91) ... What he inherited and shared he also enriched and it passed into the theology of the century, its origin often unnoticed.'[10] He goes on to say that in Anglicanism there is an absence of theologians who created a system or body of teaching distinctive because of its theological method. Anglicanism produced theologians, rather than theologians producing Anglicanism. Andrewes is a prime example, in that the whole theme of his work states that Anglicanism had no specific teaching other than that of Scripture interpreted by the primitive church with which it had a continuity, historical and doctrinal. It was not his creation, but an inheritance which in Andrewes finds a positive orientation as he brings it into association with the distinction between what was and what was not fundamental, and with freedom in matters not defined. Isaac Casaubon became one of his friends (1610); he was attracted to Anglicanism after studying the patristic writings amidst doubts and difficulties which two communions in his own country were unable to satisfy. Andrewes found in him 'a welcome and unsought confirmation of the position by one who had studied the Fathers unprejudiced by inherited allegiance or chosen affiliation'.[11]

Some have accused the theology of Andrewes as lacking in originality, which, as Lossky points out, is true if by theology one means the elaboration of a coherent system of thought about God.

But if ... to make a theology means to make more and more truly one's own, by experience, the mystery of the relation of God to man that has been traditionally lived by the Church, then originality will consist not so much in innovation, as in enabling the whole era to grasp the genuine essence of the Christian message. In fact, the more a theologian penetrates into the heart of the mystery, the more his teaching will be personal, and consequently original. Seen like this, Andrewes seems to deserve to be counted amongst the great hierarchs of the history of Christianity, who, speaking to their contemporaries, have been able to do so in such a way that their message continues to live beyond their own time.[12]

The Apologist

The day of Andrewes's consecration as bishop, 3 November 1605, was also the day the King learned of the Gunpowder Plot, which, in adding intensity to the Roman controversy forced this bishop into the forefront of polemic. He found himself in the shoes occupied by Jewel in an earlier generation, which, in the words of Frere, 'forced from him what was deeply rooted in him and might not have been expressed'. Frere describes Andrewes's great contribution, 'viz. a statement of the position of the English church from one man who by his position, his learning and his piety was pre-eminently qualified to do it.'[13] The time of his entry into the controversial field was the moment when the needs of the English Church were becoming sufficiently clear. The great need of the time had arrived when she had to put on a real and positive basis the reason for boldly breaking with the papacy. This would involve determining the true nature of the authority she exercised over her members, which was needed to vindicate her from the accusation of schism. It was crucial that the Church of England now elucidate her first principles to demonstrate the issues at stake in the English Reformation and the greatness of the objects in view.[14]

His controversial works were sparked by a dispute between the papacy and King James I, who after the Gunpowder Conspiracy had issued an Oath of Allegiance, which repudiated the papal decree that princes excommunicated by the Pope might be deposed or murdered by their subjects. Bellarmine, under the name of his chaplain, Matthew Tortus, declared this oath unlawful. Tortus refused to see the Oath of Allegiance as the King saw it, involving only the matter of civil disobedience. For Tortus it raised the whole question of papal authority, and thereby for Roman Catholics touched the centre of religion. Directed by King James, Andrewes replied with *Tortura Torti*, in which he moves the central argument from the special to the general ground, maintaining that the primacy of the Pope is not *de fide catholica*. Even supposing the oath to be incompatible with holding the primacy of the Pope, it was not incompatible with the catholic faith. While the main attack is on what Andrewes regarded as the excessive powers of the papacy, some passages present a positive defence of Anglicanism, and when Bellarmine replied in his own name, Andrewes followed up with *Responsio ad Bellarmine*. Here his concern is to present positive principles in defence of his cause, the catholicity of Anglicanism as patristic rather than papal, in a tone that is 'apologetic, constructive, and catholic'.[15] Of equal significance is the

polemic with Cardinal Perron, in his *Two Answers to Cardinal Perron,*
who had taken exception to King James's claim to the title of
catholic. This latter answer, together with the *Responsio,* is perhaps
the nearest positive statement of belief on the essential points of
difference between Anglicanism and Rome. The method of
Bellarmine and Perron is refutation rather than systematic and
consistent argument, the refutation of the English church's claim
to be catholic because this depended on certain doctrines she
rejected, transubstantiation, the temporal claims of the papacy,
and the invocation of saints. Bellarmine's thesis was supported by
Cardinal Perron, who in correspondence with Casaubon had
refused to acknowledge James's right to the name 'catholic'.
Andrewes met the challenge historically and theologically.

He maintained that the acceptance of such doctrines could not
constitute the test of catholicity since they were unknown in the
first thousand years of Christian history.[16] The relevance of this
debate lies in the way in which Andrewes based the vindication of
his position on the historical and theological testimony of antiquity. 'If opinions are new' he writes, 'they are not ours. We appeal
to antiquity, and to the most extreme antiquity ... We do not inno-
vate; it may be we renovate what was customary among the ancients
but with you has disappeared in novelties.'[17] For Andrewes, the

> Catholicity of the Church was not dependent on propositions
> (as per Bellarmine), nor (as per the Puritans) was it an attribute
> of the invisible Church. It emerged from continuity with the
> Primitive Church, and the establishing of that continuity by
> reference to the standard evolving within the first five centuries
> was for Andrewes and his successors the reason for the emphasis
> on antiquity, and the explanation of the continual preoccupa-
> tion with historicity in Anglican theological method.[18]

In the *Responsio*[19] he appeals to Vincent of Lérins: 'Let that be reckoned Catholic which always obtained everywhere among all, and
which always and everywhere and by all was believed.' What the
English church needed was not a coercive jurisdiction but a moral
authority and Andrewes found that in the primitive church, which
in continuity with Anglicanism still preserved in England, as elsewhere, the tokens of apostolic descent, that doctrine, discipline
and polity once delivered to the saints. His understanding of ecclesiastical authority was qualified by his distinguishing between
different degrees of authority, in drawing a distinction between
what is *de fide* as being a matter of revelation and what is probable
and a matter of opinion. Rome had put everything on the same

level since Trent, therefore belief in transubstantiation and in the pope's deposing power are as important and binding as belief in the existence of the Church. From this standpoint of truths which have primary authority, tested by the Vincentian Canon, Andrewes dismisses Bellarmine's theses, in that transubstantiation is a 'new doctrine' unheard-of for centuries, and therefore not *de fide*. It is over the mode of the presence that differences occur; and Andrewes asserts a real sacramental presence of Christ in the Eucharist and declared that the Church of England admitted the catholic conception of the Eucharist as a commemorative sacrifice. So, too, is the primacy of the Roman see interpreted by modern popes and exemplified in the claim to depose princes. Andrewes examines Bellarmine's authorities for the invocation of the saints, convicting him of misquotation and of using passages of disputable authenticity, dismissing his contention as 'not proven'. As to the adoration of relics, a tendency to it had been condemned by the Fathers, therefore the practice is not catholic.

Chapters I and VIII discuss a wide range of patristic references. In the same work he writes, 'there is no principal dogma in which we do not agree with the Fathers and they with us'.[20] It is sufficient 'if one should believe the canonical Scriptures, freely affirm the three Creeds, respect the first four Councils, and allow the unanimous consent of the Fathers in anything necessary to salvation'.[21] He elaborates this in great detail,[22] and as McAdoo points out, his method of handling the subject is with reference to history and the teaching of the primitive church as seen in the writings of the Fathers. While Andrewes cites medieval writers as valuable in other matters his exclusion of them here is because of their distance from the Apostles. This limitation to the first five centuries is no arbitrary matter, but is controlled by reference back to Scripture and the period after the Apostles, by which the appeal to antiquity interpreting Scripture is justified on the premise that this period interprets it best, being the period of the Creeds, four Councils, and outstanding patristic writers at the time when the Canon of Scripture was being established. This reflection of the mind of the Church in the first centuries is what gives meaning to the idea of continuity. For Andrewes this was no mechanical concept 'but the transmission of certain living qualities of faith and order, the possession of which linked the present church with the primitive church, being at once the assurance and norm of catholicity.'[23]

Under twenty-six heads, Perron had drawn a comparison between the church of St Augustine's day and what he regarded as the tenets of the Church of England. Andrewes's response is to use the same method of appeal to the Fathers by answering him point by point, convicting him of mistatement and misrepresentation. In dealing first with Eucharistic doctrine, he demonstrates that for Anglicanism this is consistent with the Fathers in that it is an effectual means of grace, and that the Presence is real but not corporal. Concerning Eucharistic adoration Perron cites Cyril, Austin, Chrysostom and Theodoret, Andrewes writes, 'I trust no Christian man will ever refuse to do – that is, to adore the Flesh of Christ.'[24] However, he goes on to point out that St Austin speaks of the eating as being after a heavenly and mysterious manner and so Perron's quotations, he points out, are not supportive of transubstantiation. There is no conflict with Reservation of the Blessed Sacrament for the sick, since 'It cannot be denied but reserving the Sacrament was suffered a long time in the primitive Church ...'[25] He goes on to point out that since the sick can always have private communion and viaticum, the need is not there, though the intent still exists. On sacrifice he is explicit:

> The Eucharist ever was, and by us is, considered both as a Sacrament and as a Sacrifice. The Sacrifice of Christ's death is available for present, absent, living, dead, yea, for them that are unborn (because we are all members of the one Body) ... If we agree about Sacrifice, there will be no difference about the Altar.[26]

Frere[27] comments that it took time for the English church to recover the pure truth and express it in this mature statement of Andrewes, but it was there in Jewel and Bilson, who both maintained sacrifice as consistent with Scripture and antiquity. 'Sacrifice of Christ's death' implies Eucharistic sacrifice as well as the sacrifice of Calvary being available for present and absent, meaning in the Liturgy. Furthermore, the allowing of prayer for the dead is consistent with Andrewes's practice in his *Preces Privatae,* and being consistent with the Bible and antiquity he is expressing the maturer view of the English church. While refusing worship of relics, 'the uncounterfeit are to be given the regard that becometh us', and while giving no countenance to prayers addressed to martyrs in his own devotions, there are Greek prayers with explicit commemoration of the Blessed Virgin Mary and of All Saints. He asserts there is no interruption in the succession of our church.

In effect, Andrewes is saying to Perron that the English church has some of what he defines as characteristics of catholicity, but others so defined are immaterial and not essential to catholicity.

'We partly agree with you and we partly differ; so far as Rome is
Catholic, England agrees; but where Rome parts company with
antiquity, England parts company with her.'[28] Frere continues,

> We owe it largely to Andrewes that we were set upon a sounder
> foundation, with a firm line laid down for us upon fundamen-
> tals, as being fundamental, and a wide margin of liberty and
> toleration allowed for us in things of secondary importance ...
> we owe largely to Andrewes the constructive view and positive
> statement of our position. The work of earlier reformers was to
> protest, to formulate our differences from Papist or Puritan. The
> Thirty-nine Articles express this attitude; it is at once both the
> weakness and the strength of that document. But the later
> divines, with Andrewes at their head, reversed the situation,
> went down to the positive foundations of the reconstructed
> building, and emphasized not our Protestantism but our
> catholicity.[29]

The Preacher

For the contemplative mind of Andrewes, preaching was more
congenial than controversy and it is where he was more at home.
The practical import of Andrewes' prayers for the illumination of
his mind can be discerned in his sermons, in the close connection
and continuity between the *Private Devotions* and the sermons that
is always maintained, and which F. E. Brightman's edition of the
Devotions elucidates. While there is in the sermons a strong ascetical strain, they are also theological works that demonstrate the
Bishop's theological creativity. 'The essence of this creativity lies in
[his] assimilation of classical Christian doctrine and his artful
application of it to the doctrinal, liturgical, and ascetical needs of
his day ... despite the tremendous theological and scholarly
acumen the sermons display, their genius issues from a rootedness
in prayer and the truly graceful creativity of the mind that illu-
mines them.'[30]

In a style peculiar to himself he impresses the reader 'not by a
sustained chain of reasoning, but by the wealth of biblical illustration and patristic comment with which they enforce and give
substance to a leading thought.'[31] Ottley compares his style with St
Leo the Great's for its 'inelegance' and 'antithetic treatment of
Christian facts'. Church describes him as theologian first and foremost, whose deepest belief is the importance of his theology and

who profoundly reverences the truth. What he is aiming at is the giving of accuracy and breadth to dogma and 'to put life into its expression, in the manner of St Augustine, St Chrysostom and the great Greek Fathers'. As a preacher he is not interested in plumbing the depths of the unknown, of that which it is impossible to know, but of focusing his hearers' thoughts 'on the certainties and realities, passing all wonder, that we believe *are* known'.[32] His concern in the pulpit is the presentation of a pattern of faith akin to all that was ancient and universal in Christianity and rose above the contemporary controversies, and in this he enlarged the teaching of the Reformation without departing from its fundamental principles. So we find him fearlessly supplying, from those authorities to whom appeal had always been made, that which was necessary to complete the fullness and harmony of doctrine.

> Full of discrimination for what really had the authority of the ancient Church, he was the most fearless of English divines when he had that authority. English theology would be in danger of being much less Catholic, much more disconnected with that of the earlier ages, much more arbitrarily limited in all directions, except towards Geneva or else towards simple latitude, but that a man of Andrewes' character and weight had dared to break through the prescription which the Puritans were trying to establish against the doctrinal language, at once more accurate and more free, of the ancient Church.[33]

Without Andrewes, the Church of England would not have had Jeremy Taylor, Bull and hardly Waterland. Commenting on the presentation of the Incarnation in the seventeen Christmas sermons, Lossky stresses that Andrewes's concern is to lead his hearers into a practical way of incarnating this mystery into their own lives by a personal engagement. The implication is always the old patristic adage, which Andrewes reformulates for his own time: 'God has become man, that man might become God.'

> What I am trying to show here is that at the heart of an era dominated by polemic, which necessarily hardens positions, Andrewes does his utmost to preach the mystery without rationalizing it or evading it or drowning it in lyrical pietism. He preaches it in patristic language, that is to say, using the vocabulary of that thought as well as its symbolism, always striving towards the limit the human mind can attain, but also recognizing that limit. He never seeks to rationalize beyond that point, nor to deny human intelligence its proper place in the

pursuit of the mystery. From this way of proceeding there results a great economy, in the sense that everything that is said is directed towards a precise goal which is never a gratuitous effect ... The play on words, the bold comparisons, the para- doxes, force the mind to look again at one or another aspect of the Christian mystery, just as the same kind of procedures were used with similar intention and an analogous result in the patristic and liturgical tradition that Andrewes knew so well, as all his biographers have remarked, and as it quite evident from the sermons themselves and a glance, however brief, at the *Preces Privatae* .[34]

There is a difference in the way Andrewes used the Fathers in his sermons and how he employed them for controversial purposes. In the latter his method is a straightforward citing of his authoritative reference in Scripture, Creeds and Council in the historical context of patristic writings. What makes his sermons impressive in their appeal to the Fathers is the incidental nature of this appeal. 'But let me also tell you a saying. It is St. Basil's, and well worth remembering, ... "I had rather you heard St Augustine, than myself."' On the theme of Fasting (Matt. 6: 16) 'Which of the Fathers have not homilies yet extant in praise of it ? ... either we must cancel all antiquity or we must acknowledge the constant use and observation of it.'[35] There is an ease in the way in which he slips into his sermons, allusions to and quotations from the Fathers; 'There was saith St Gregory, no error of the Disciples'.[36] 'To conclude, it is St Augustine, and so say all the rest'.[37] In a sermon on 'Dives and Lazarus' he uses Chrysostom (*de Laz. con.* 20) without quoting[38] and St Chrysostom's[39] two points are just slipped in to introduce a point, that Dives behaved as if there was no life but this and forgot Lazarus and so he received his just reward. He incorporates in his sermon Chrysostom's meditation on this theme and his concern about a right use of wealth. 'But the Fathers press a farther matter yet out of *Verbum Caro factum;* that we also after our manner *verbum carnem facere,* "to incarnate the word"'[40] 'When the world shall bid us goodnight, then, as St. Augustine expresseth it, *videre in nocte saeculi diem Christi.*'[41] Preaching on what good can come out of Bethlehem, he exclaims 'What good,' and then 'Nazianzen tells us; ... it gives us our intro- duction to Paradise Bethlehem'.[42] An Easter sermon[43] explores the custom of keeping Easter, where he sets out to demonstrate the nature and purpose of ecclesiastical custom. Existence of customs is not sufficient authority for them; their apostolic and catholic institution must be proven. His text, 'the Church hath her customs' (1 Cor. 11: 16) and the custom of keeping Easter is linked with 1 Cor. 5: 7–8 to prove its existence from the beginning. Here the practice of the Church is clear enough from 'custom' and no further authority is necessary. He then distinguishes between customs and traditions, the former concerned with *agenda*, the latter with *credenda*. However, custom must be in agreement with Scripture, and he cites the respect of the first Nicene Council for customs in existence from the beginning, the test being that it must be general and ancient. The keeping of Easter is then discussed in the light of this, always and everywhere observed, though the timing of it had raised questions. He discusses it in the light of the first five centuries, citing calendars for estimating the timing of it, the Easter letters of Alexandria and the writings of the Greek and Latin Fathers in their Easter discourses, Easter hymns, commentaries, and particular instances of recorded practice 'all these ways, by singing, by saying, by writing, by doing'.

Then he turns from the Fathers to the first councils, citing evidence from all four. It is not merely the citing of quotation to buttress what he preaches, but the expression of *the patristic mind* in his own thought and words as it is embedded in the theme of his sermon. So we find him committed not only to the *kerygma* of the Apostles but also to the *dogmata* of the Fathers. For Andrewes the Church is indeed Apostolic, but she is also Patristic, and only by being Patristic can she be continuously Apostolic, and the teaching of the Fathers is a permanent category of Christian faith, a constant and ultimate measure or criterion of right belief. His appeal, as our own contemporary appeal to the Fathers, cannot be reduced to a mere historical reference to the past.

Like Hooker he has grasped the *phronēma* of the Fathers, which he does not separate from the interpretation of Holy Scripture because together they are an intrinsic reference point in his theology. In his exegesis of Holy Scripture he systematically follows the Fathers, because,

> The ancient Fathers thought it meet that they that would take upon them to interpret 'the apostles' doctrine' should put in sureties that their senses they gave were no other than the Church in former time hath acknowledged. It is true the apostles, indeed, spake from the Spirit; but that, I take it, was their peculiar privilege. But all that are after them speak not by revelation, but by labouring in the word and learning; are not to utter their own fancies, and to desire to be believed upon their

bare word; ... but only on condition that the sense they now give
is not a feigned sense, as St. Peter termeth it, but such an one as
hath been before given by our fathers and forerunners in the
Christian faith ...[44]

With this interpreter there grows the capacity to link exact statements of doctrine to the scriptural imagery, not merely because of
his profound knowledge of the Bible, but because he has caught
the 'spirit of revelation'. There has been formed in him a deep and
strong sense of the range and comprehensiveness of Christian
truth in its organic wholeness, each part connected with and
related to every other part. Through the Fathers there is formed in
him *the scriptural mind,* which is the result of bending one's own
thought to the mental habits of the biblical language to relearn the
idiom of the Bible. Repentance must precede the receiving of the
Gospel, and this is more than mere acknowledgement of sin. It is a
profound change of one's own mental and emotional attitude, an
integral renewal of oneself that begins in self-renunciation and is
accomplished and sealed by the Spirit. This is what makes the
difference between a mere thinker and a witness. The reference to
the Fathers is not to abstract tradition in formula and proposition,
to thinkers, but is primarily an appeal to persons, to witnesses,
which in his turn Andrewes himself became. The witness of such
people belongs integrally and intrinsically to the very structure of
Christian faith and life.

In his understanding of continuity, Andrewes, in keeping
Scripture and the Fathers together, visualizes the Catholic Church
of all ages, and the Church of England in part with it, as a living
expression of the church of the Fathers.

> If one considers the whole preaching of Lancelot Andrewes, one
> will notice that the fathers of the Church are not only present in
> the form of quotations illustrating this or that point of interpre-
> tation or doctrine. There is a true incorporation of the patristic
> body of thought which results in the preacher very often speak-
> ing like the Fathers, because he comes to know his own time as
> he has come to know theirs, that is to say in the light of
> Christianity lived in deep unity with the experience and renewed
> reception of the dogma of Chalcedon.[45]

An example of this is found in his understanding and exposition
of *Symbol,* where he is completely in tune with the patristic mind.
In his discussion of this, Lossky first defines the patristic understanding of *symbol,* that it signifies the coexistence of two realities,

that of what signifies and that of what is signified, the image participating in the reality signified.

> A symbolic name of Christ is an image, but an image not at all in
> the abstract sense of a reminder, by certain conventionally
> recognizable traits, of the existence of an absent reality. It is an
> image in the concrete sense of participation in the reality of
> what it represents by the likeness of the representation to that
> which is represented.[46]

He goes on to point out that the application to Christ of the name
'Lamb', is no mere poetic allegory, but that name and image
acquire a sacred character by virtue of the presence in them of the
grace of the One they evoke. Such symbols are bearers of two realities, 'the human reality and the divine reality, after the image of
the Godmanhood of the Person of the Incarnate Christ'. This
experience of such human and divine realities is not the subjective
product of human psychology; rather does it come as 'an "objective" revealed reality, grasped by the movement of faith'. It is in this
sense that Andrewes understands symbol and Lossky goes on to
illustrate this from a sermon,[47] in which he speaks of the Eucharist.
Andrewes is speaking of the elements of bread and wine, the recapitulation of the seasons of the year, and of Christ, the heavenly
recapitulation of the Bread of Life and of the true Vine. He goes
on to say, 'And the gathering or vintage of these two in the blessed
Eucharist, is as I may say a kind of hypostatical union of the sign
and the thing signified, so united together as are the two natures
of Christ.' His use of the term 'hypostatical' is to make precise the
difference between 'person' and 'individual' which in the patristic
mind 'is conceived precisely as the recapitulation of the whole'.
Lossky goes on to show how this conception of symbolism throws
light on the use Andrewes makes of symbolic language in other
contexts in his sermons.

This is what places not only his thought but his preaching in a
larger room which raises it above the controversies and theological
fashions of his age. It is therefore inevitable that in thinking and
style he is thoroughly patristic. As Ottley points out,

> His aim is ever to bring out the full content of dogma; to exhibit
> its bearings on life; to give reality and vividness to men's appre-
> hension of it. In this respect there is affinity, both in the
> structure and tone of his sermons, between him and the Father
> he so often quotes – St. Chrysostom ... the same tendency to a
> 'running commentary,' each verse of a passage being

expounded in its order; (*On the Resurrection*, xiv, vol. 3. p. 3.) the same lucidity; the same insistence on practical aspects of known truth, and the avoidance of speculation on the 'secret things' of the Most High.[48]

To quote Canon Allchin,

> ... in Andrewes's sermons we have a kerygmatic and liturgical theology, a theology of praise and proclamation, whose models are patristic rather than medieval. It is a theology which reaffirms and represents in London in the first twenty-five years of the seventeenth century that particular synthesis of dogma and experience, of thought and intuition, of learning and devotion which we find in the fathers of the first ten centuries, alike in East and West. This patristic quality has often been noticed in Andrewes' preaching, though some have thought that it was more a matter of external application, of laborious scholarship, than a living part of his thought. Such a supposition has been convincingly refuted ... Nicholas Lossky shows in the preaching of the seventeenth-century bishop a living and dynamic presence of the understanding of the mystery of Christ which is characteristic of the teaching of the Fathers, and especially of the fathers of the East.[49]

This in-depth observation of Andrewes by Lossky is pertinent because it comes from within an Eastern Orthodoxy that recognizes something of its own image mirrored in this Anglican divine.

Deification

An essential and important strand in the fabric of Andrewes's theology is the doctrine of *theosis* as the consequence and completion of the doctrine of the Incarnation. Canon A. M. Allchin discusses this in two of his works, an essay, 'Trinity and Incarnation in the Anglican Tradition',[50] and his book, *Participation in God.*[51] In the former he quotes from a sermon for Pentecost,[52] comparing the work of Christ with the Holy Spirit. Here Andrewes speaks of the mystery of his Incarnation and the mystery of our inspiration as 'great mysteries of godliness', in both, God being 'manifested in the flesh',

> In the former by the union of his Son; in the latter by the communion of his blessed Spirit ... without either of them we are not complete, we have not our accomplishment; but by both

of them we have, and that fully, even by this day's royal exchange. Whereby, as before he of ours, so now we of his are made partakers, he clothed with our flesh, and we invested with his Spirit. The great promise of the Old Testament accomplished, that he should partake our human nature; and the great and precious promise of the New, that we should be *consortes divinae naturae,* 'partakers of his divine nature', both are this day accomplished.

Here, as Allchin remarks, there is no reticence about the doctrine of *theosis* that is characteristic of other Western theologians. 'Rather we find a renewal of the teaching of the Fathers in its fullness, a fullness which includes such themes as the constant progress into God described by Gregory of Nyssa.' Christian life is continuous growth, Gregory's idea of *epektasis,* of never having arrived, but of the pressing on in pursuit of still purer, more vital experience of God's light and truth, where each fulfilment contains in itself the impulse to further growth.

> ... to be made partakers of the Spirit, is to be made partakers 'of the divine nature' ... Partakers of the Spirit we are, by receiving grace; ... The state of grace is the perfection of this life, to grow still from grace to grace, to profit in it. As to go on still forward is the perfection of a traveller, to draw still nearer and nearer to his journey's end.[53]

In his second work, after establishing Andrewes's capacity to preach a coherent and organic theology, Allchin cites T. S. Eliot's essay *For Lancelot Andrewes,* to emphasize with this 'a quality or depth in his writing'. Eliot speaks of Andrewes as being completely absorbed in his subject, his emotion growing the more deeply he penetrates the mystery he seeks to grasp. This emotion Eliot describes as contemplative, something evoked by the object of contemplation, wholly contained in and explained by its object. In Andrewes, Allchin points out, thinking and feeling have been fused together,

> ... a man in whom what is within, what is subjective, is wholly evoked by what is beyond, the object of his contemplation, in whom subjective and objective are thus reconciled and at one. A man ... totally absorbed in his subject ... which is more than metaphorical ... such a one should be able to speak to us about participation in the divine nature, for he speaks from experience.[54]

Andrewes expounds the meaning of *Emmanuel,* what 'God with us' means, in a Christmas sermon where he demonstrates a living integration of the doctrines of incarnation, adoption, deification, virgin birth, baptismal birth, and the life-giving action of the Holy Spirit in womb and font. God is with us:

> to make us that to God that he was this day to man. And this indeed was the chief end of his being 'With us'; to give us a *posse fieri,* a capacity, 'a power to be made sons of God', by being born again of water and the Spirit; *Originem quam sumpsit ex utero Virginis posuit in fonte Baptismatis,* the same original that himself took in the womb of the virgin to us ward the same hath he placed for us in the fountain of baptism to Godward', well therefore called the womb of the Church *sustoichon* to the Virgin's womb, with a power given it of *concipiet et pariet filios* to God. So his being conceived and born of the Son of man doth conceive and bring forth *(filiatio, filiationem)* our being born, our being sons of God, his participation of our human, our participation of his divine nature.[55]

In no way can Easter be separated from Christmas, nor Resurrection from Incarnation, nor the consequences of this Christian mystery imply any disjunction between the union of human and divine. Christmas needs Easter, '... the still greater mystery of death and resurrection, where we see the divine–human interchange in a new and still more striking perspective',[56] in a new birth from the dead. Here a quotation compares and contrasts these two births in which Easter is described as a second Christmas. Christmas unites Christ with humankind, not in its sin, but in its natural infirmities, mortality and death and in a brotherhood which death dissolves. Easter heralds his second birth from the womb of the grave,

> ... he begins a new brotherhood, founds a new fraternity straight; adopts us, we see, anew again by his *fratres meos;* and thereby he that was *primogenitus a mortuis* becomes *primogenitus inter multos fratres;* when 'the first begotten from the dead', then 'the first begotten of many brethren'. Before he was ours, now we are his. That was by the mother's side; so he ours. This is *Patrem vestrum,* the Father's side; so we his. But half-brothers before, never the whole blood till now. Now by the Father and mother both, *fratres germani, fratres fraterrimi,* we can not be more ... This day's is the better birth by far.[57]

Returning to Nicholas Lossky's perceptions of the patristic

quality of Andrewes's theology, a comment on the coherence of this vision of Christian doctrine is cited [*ibid.* p.18. *Lancelot Andrewes: Le Predicateur* (Paris, 1986)].

> In the theological movement characteristic of Andrewes's preaching, it can be said that the Christmas sermons, treating of the dogma of the Incarnation, underline time and again the paradox of the most high God, of the heavens, who limits himself to become fully man, consubstantial with us, becoming participant in human nature, in its entirety, sin only excepted. In the Easter sermons, the accent will constantly be placed on what could be called the corollary of this paradox; this suffering servant, who has reached the last degree of the human condition, is the almighty God, consubstantial with the Father, who with the Father has created the world. In his resurrection, which is due to his consubstantiality with the Father, he remains fully consubstantial with men, and there ensues a new life and a new destiny for creation. Easter is then the feast, *par excellence,* of springtime joy for creation re-created and become the heir of a great destiny.
>
> Lancelot Andrewes's Easter preaching, resounding with the hope and joy that emanate from the Passion–Resurrection of Christ is certainly not in that respect novel in the general history of preaching. However, it cannot be denied that at the end of the sixteenth and the beginning of the seventeenth century in England, it had been a long time since such accents had been heard.[58]

Any understanding of Andrewes's teaching on deification cannot be fully understood without seeing its organic connection with his pneumatology, which Lossky says is given significance by the stress he puts on the deification of man as the supreme goal of the way of salvation.

> It is a matter of man with God in Christ through the Holy Spirit. If his theology is at once christocentric and pneumatological, it is because in his vision of salvation he has made profoundly his own the image of St Irenaeus according to which the Son and the Spirit are 'the two hands of the Father'. This image expresses the complementarity, reciprocity, the unity and the distinction of the two Persons in the divine economy. At the same time, and above all, it shows clearly that the divine economy is the action of all Three Persons of the Holy Trinity. As we have seen, Andrewes never forgets this.[59]

Andrewes's vision is Trinitarian; he is a pastoral theologian with a theology to be preached, and therefore with a practical purpose, nothing less than to participate in the divine life Christ lives with the Father in the Holy Spirit. It is a life within the Church, a sacramental life in worship and prayer, a life of continual movement and growth in the very life of God himself. This is saving life, salvation. In this work, Christ and the Spirit cannot be separated.

> The Holy Spirit reveals the divinity of the Son who is the image of the Father (2 Cor. 4: 4). The man who becomes a 'partaker of the divine nature' (2 Pet. 1: 4) enters into communion with the common nature of the Three Persons as it is manifested from the Father, through the Son, in the Holy Spirit. By the uncreated grace of the Holy Spirit, God, that is to say the Trinity, comes to dwell in him, and man comes, one could say, 'in the Holy Spirit, through the Son, to the Father', to take over the inversion of the ancient doxology, as used by Fr Boris Bobrinskoy.[60]

The Incarnation of God is for the breathing into man of the very life of God, and this keeping together of Incarnation and Inspiration, *Incarnatio* and *Inspiratio*, God clothed in flesh and man invested with divinity, dominates Andrewes's sermons for Pentecost. Thereby are we caught up in the very life and being of the Trinity.

Prayer

A man is what he prays. The person who prays is a theologian and a theologian is a person who prays, or to put it in the words of St John Klimakos, *the climax of purity is the threshold of theology.* In this patristic and Evagrian sense Andrewes is a theologian. The character of Andrewes's theology can only be grasped when it is realized that for him the mind and intellect must also be offered to God. Human reason must be subjected to prayer. The sense of the need for such subjection is found in some prayers 'at the Eucharist'.

> Prior to reception he prays for illumination of the mind. The word *dianoia* refers specifically to the faculty of thinking, to the intellect. In the same context he prays for 'the fullness of wisdom' and, finally, for 'a proper exercise of human reason'. In these few but significant precations we can discern Andrewes' realization of the need to subject even the processes of rational reflection to the searching gaze of God's Holy Spirit. To be a

theologian was indeed to pray truly, and, more than that, to submit one's mind to the illumination of grace which alone makes genuine theology possible.[61]

In the *Preces Privatae* is the hidden life of worship, self-discipline, and self-consecration of this Anglican divine. Speaking of their sources, F. E. Brightman,[62] describes them as 'a mosaic of quotations. The first and principal source is Holy Scripture,' but he also used existing 'precatory collections of eastern and western Christendom,' as well as drawing copiously from the Fathers and saints. Andrewes arranges and articulates them in an orderly scheme of penitence, intercession, praise and thanksgiving. H. B. Swete describes these prayers as a devotional handling of the Creeds, and their theology as being for the most part an interpretation of the Apostles' and Nicene Creeds read in the light of the experience of life, embodying recollections from Irenaeus, Tertullian, Cyprian, the Gregories, Chrysostom, Jerome, Augustine. 'Of the ancient liturgical books free use is made: we recognise portions of the great Horology and Euchology, of the Liturgy of St. James and St. Basil; the Western Hours and Missal and manual ...'[63]

Swete highlights the way in which 'certain elements of devotion, such as commemoration, petition, intercession', are combined with minuteness of detail, and the unobtrusive way in which use is made of extracts from the liturgies. There is no evidence here of our modern pseudo-problem, a conflict between personal and public prayer; not only is the liturgy Andrewes's theological teacher, it is also his tutor in prayer. Dean Church has commented on the liturgical quality of these devotions,

> ... incorporating bursts of adoration and Eucharistic triumph from the Liturgies of St. James or St. Chrysostom, recalling the most ancient Greek hymns of the Church, the *Gloria in Excelsis*, and the Evening Hymn preserved at the end of the Alexandrian manuscript of the New Testament, (translated in the *Lyra Apostolica*, No. 62. See Bingham's *Antiquities*, Vol. IV, p. 411.) – all this is in the strongest contrast to anything that I know of in the devotions of the time. It was the reflection, in private prayer, of the tone and language of the Book of Common Prayer, its Psalms, and its Offices; it supplemented the public book, and carried on its spirit from the Church to the closet. And this was the counterpart of what Andrewes taught in the pulpit. To us it shows how real and deeply held his theology was.[64]

The predominant disposition of Andrewes's prayer is that of the publican, not the Pharisee. His *Devotions* have as their context two essential elements of Christian prayer, adoration and penitence. The same moment that expresses adoration to God keeps within it remembrance and expression of sorrow for human weakness. This is what 'changes the mind', one's mental and emotional attitude, that integral renewal of oneself, which begins in self-renunciation and is accomplished and sealed by the Spirit. This is what was noted earlier as the precondition to the formation of the 'scriptural mind', the result of the bending of one's own thought to the mental habits of the biblical language to relearn the idiom of the Bible. Here in the *Devotions* lies the clue to the formation of that 'scriptural mind' in Andrewes. Andrewes belonged to that seventeenth-century school of thought in which, with Hooker, Thorndike, Cosin, Taylor and others, the concern was to penetrate beneath the outward trappings of liturgy and comprehend its inner meaning and principles. For them liturgy has something to do with dogma and life, and their understanding of the Church as an organism means that dogma, prayer and life are one whole. This organic relationship between dogma, prayer and life transforms theology into life, living reality, and it is noteworthy that the *Devotions* focus on the created order with its manifest variety of human life and experience.

> Such a focus points to a personality shaped by the new Renaissance learning, as well as to an interest in natural science which was confirmed and encouraged, no doubt, by Andrewes' close friend, Francis Bacon. This fascination, however, was not a function of Andrewes' intellect and personality alone; it was primarily ascetical and theological. Every aspect of the world and human experience is offered to God – and in that offering becomes a means to know God.[65]

Furthermore, there is continuity in outline in its main features between the primitive liturgies and the Book of Common Prayer. References in his sermons bear out this interest and the comment of Swete that the 'whole tone of the *Preces Privatae* is akin to that of Greek liturgies'. Swete goes on to draw attention to an interesting point, in that this bishop, in the spirit of some early Greek liturgies, seems to have attributed the consecration of the elements to the Son rather than the Spirit. 'Thou' he says addressing our Lord, 'art with us invisibly to hallow the gifts that are set forth, and those for whom they are brought.' McAdoo,[66] reinforcing Swete's point about the kinship between the *Preces Privatae* and the early liturgies, cites a point in Andrewes's sermons 'to very good purpose it was that the ancient Fathers in the Greek Church in their liturgy...' as an example illustrating such interest. Another is on the use of Psalm 85, illustrating his wish to underline liturgical continuity, 'one of the psalms selected of old by the Primitive Church, and so still retained by ours, as part of our office, or service of this day'. His interest in liturgy was also practical, and in the spirit of the Fathers he produced a liturgy where the Book of Common Prayer provided none. His knowledge of the early liturgies was of great value in such ventures as the 'Form for the Consecration of a Church or Churchyard', a 'Form for Consecrating Church Plate', a 'Form of Induction', and a 'Manual for the Sick'.

A Mystical Theologian

The contemporary Russian Orthodox theologian Nicholas Lossky describes Andrewes as a 'mystical theologian'.

> The final goal of the spiritual life being union with God, one can say that the theology of Lancelot Andrewes is a mystical theology, as long as one elucidates the meaning of the word 'mystical'. It is not a question of an exceptional experience, reserved for a few, in some way outside the traditional ways of theology. On the contrary, it is a question of the interiorisation of the revealed Christian mystery, to which Andrewes calls all the baptised. This theology is mystical in the sense that it is not an abstract reflection, but a concrete way of living the mystery in the deepening of the faith through prayer and the renunciation of one's own will. It is a way of the submission of the human to the divine will, which allows the grace of the Holy Spirit to impregnate human nature. For Andrewes it is altogether clear that this is only possible in fidelity to the given realities of revelation, that is to say in the scriptural and patristic tradition, or in other words in the catholicity of the Church. [67]

Fr Walter Frere of the Community of the Resurrection finds Andrewes not only as a character that has been formed by what is best in the Christian tradition, but also as 'the firstfruits of the working out of the principles of the English Reform of Religion.'[68]

Andrewes represents in the Anglican context, the manifestation of the patristic character which is common to the catholic Fathers of Eastern and Western Christendom. This is plainly revealed by the way in which *the patristic mind* informs every aspect of his thought and life. As an apologist for Anglicanism, the Fathers and Councils are for him the authoritative basis for its catholic integrity, which he defines as primitive rather than papal, thereby recognizing the *consensus patrum* not as a period piece, nor a stereotype in which to freeze the theology of future generations. For Andrewes it is a continuity of life, mystical and sacramental, in which theology ends in adoration, because for him and for the Fathers, theology is not merely thinking about God but attempting to translate into intelligible terms the experience of life in God. Hence, for Andrewes as for Hooker, the grace of the sacraments is the last link in a series whose terminus is the participation of the Saints in the life of God. Therefore, as a preacher and pastor, the style and content of his preaching is akin to the Fathers in its primary concern with salvation in terms of that *partaking of the divine nature,* and the presentation of an organic theology in which the emphasis is on grace rather than knowledge, and preaching is subordinated to participation in the sacraments. Theology is then truly mystical, the description of an experience rather than definition, and therein lies not only the patristic quality of Andrewes's theology but also his originality as a theologian.

Notes

1. Douglas Macleane, *Lancelot Andrewes and the Reaction* (George Allen & Sons, London, 1910), 'Preface'.
2. Richard W. Church, 'Lancelot Andrewes', in A. Barry, ed. *Masters of English Theology* (London, 1877), p. 90.
3. Church, 'Sermon III, Bishop Andrewes', in *Pascal and Other Sermons* (Macmillan & Co, London, 1895), p. 64.
4. Nicholas Lossky, *Lancelot Andrewes the Preacher (1655–1626) The Origins of the Mystical Theology of the Church of England,* translated by A. Louth (Clarendon Press, Oxford, 1991), p. 31.
5. *Ibid.* p. 350.
6. Andrewes, *Works,* Opuscula (*LACT.,* 1841–54, Parker, Oxford), p. 91.
7. Paul Welsby, *Lancelot Andrewes, 1555–1626* (SPCK, London, 1958), p. 156.
8. Welsby, p. 156, citing W. H. Ness, 'Lancelot Andrewes and the English Church', *Theology* (Sept. 1926).
9. Lossky, *ibid.* p. 340.
10. H. R. McAdoo, *The Spirit of Anglicanism* (A. & C. Black, London, 1965), p. 321.
11. *Ibid.* p. 323.
12. Lossky, *ibid.* p. 6.

13. W. H. Frere, *Bishop Lancelot Andrewes, as a Representative of Anglican Principles* (SPCK Pamphlet for the Church Historical Society, 1897), pp. 11–12.
14. R. L. Ottley, *Lancelot Andrewes* (Methuen & Co, London, 1905), 2nd edn revised, p. 152.
15. *Ibid.* p. 156.
16. Andrewes, *Responsio ad Apologiam Card. Bellarmini* (*LACT*, Parker, Oxford, 1846), p. 7.
17. Ottley, citing Andrewes, *Tortura Torti* (*LACT*, Parker, Oxford, 1846), pp. 96, 158.
18. McAdoo, *ibid.* p. 334.
19. Andrewes, *Responsio* p. 25.
20. *Ibid.* p. 70.
21. *Ibid.* p. 208.
22. *Ibid.* pp. 208–33.
23. McAdoo, *ibid.* p. 335.
24. Andrewes, *Answer to Cardinal Perron* (*LACT*, Parker, Oxford, 1846) ii, 3.
25. *Ibid.* iii.
26. *Ibid.* v and vi.
27. Frere, *ibid.* p. 16.
28. *Ibid.* p. 21.
29. *Ibid.* p. 22.
30. E. C. Miller Jr, *Towards a Fuller Vision* (Morehouse Barlow, Wilton, CT, 1984), pp. 10–11.
31. Ottley, *ibid.* p. 127.
32. Church, *ibid,* p. 83.
33. *Ibid.* pp. 85–6.
34. Lossky, *ibid.* p. 33.
35. Andrewes, *The Sermons of Lancelot Andrewes,* ed. Marianne Dorman (Pentland Press, Bishop Auckland, 1992), vol. i, p. 135.
36. Andrewes, 'Sermon III', *Works,* vol. ii (*LACT*, Parker, Oxford, 1870), p. 48.
37. *Ibid.* p. 52.
38. 'Sermon V', *Works,* vol. ii, p. 92.
39. *Ibid.* p. 94.
40. Andrewes, 'Sermon VI', *Works (LACT)*, vol. i, p. 99.
41. Andrewes, 'Sermon VIII', *Works (LACT)*, vol. i, p. 124.
42. Andrewes, 'Sermon X', *Works (LACT)*, vol.i, p. 162.
43. Andrewes, *Works (LACT)*, vol. iii, p. 517.
44. Andrewes, 'Of the Worshipping of the Imagination', *Works (LACT)*, vol. v, p. 57.
45. Lossky, 'La Patristique dans la Prédication Anglaise du debut du XVIIe Siècle; Un Exemple, Lancelot Andrewes', *Messager de L'Exarchat du Patriarche Russe en Europe Occidentale*, p. 121.
46. Lossky, *ibid.* pp. 62ff.
47. Andrewes, *Works (LACT)*, vol. i, Nativity 16, p. 281.

48. Ottley, *ibid.* p. 133.
49. Allchin, *Participation in God* (DLT, London, 1988), p. 15.
50. Allchin, 'Trinity and Incarnation in the Anglican Tradition', in *The Kingdom of Love and Knowledge* (DLT, London, 1979), p. 98.
51. Allchin, *Participation in God,* pp. 15–23.
52. Andrewes, *Works* (*LACT*), vol. iii, pp. 108–9.
53. Andrewes, *ibid.* p. 367.
54. Allchin, '*Participation in God*', p. 16.
55. Andrewes, *Works,* vol. i, p. 150.
56. Allchin, '*Participation in God*', p. 17.
57. *Ibid.* pp. 17–18, citing Andrewes, *Works,* vol. i, p. 122.
58. Lossky, pp. 153–4.
59. *Ibid.* pp. 334–5.
60. *Ibid.* p. 335.
61. Miller Jr, p. 10.
62. F. E. Brightman, 'Introduction', *The Preces Privatae of Lancelot Andrewes* (Methuen, London, 1903).
63. H. B. Swete, 'Introduction', *The Devotions of Bishop Andrewes,* vol. i, translated from the Greek by J. H. Newman (London, 1840, SPCK, and London, 1920).
64. Church, p. 89.
65. Miller Jr, *ibid.* p. 10.
66. McAdoo, *ibid.* p. 327.
67. Lossky, *ibid.* p. 335.
68. Frere, *ibid.* p. 27.

8

William Laud (1573–1645) and Calvinism

The Man and his Assessors

William Laud described the death of Andrewes as a great light going out in the Christian world, and though their lives did overlap and Andrewes died in Charles I's reign, his life belongs to the earlier period. Laud, who became prominent in James's reign, did his life's work in the later period. Though there were obvious differences in character and circumstances between the two men, nevertheless Laud was the 'heir' to Andrewes, who was for him and for his tutor Buckeridge, a kind of intellectual father figure, and in Oxford Laud emulated his predecessor's 'quiet rebellion to the Calvinism in Cambridge'. Both had passed from the highest academic honours to a deanery and bishopric and though different in temperament they complemented each other, as the bustling energetic Laud carried on and brought to good effect the quiet work of Andrewes. Laud would have been more overbearing if he had not imbibed some of Andrewes's gentleness that found expression in his heroic stand during his time of trial and execution.[1]

His sermons were modelled on those of Andrewes, and Laud's own book of *Private Devotions* was obviously influenced by the late Reverend Bishop of Winchester, as he called him, because Andrewes entrusted to Laud his own book of *Private Devotions* before he died. Despite the influence of Andrewes, the mere mention of Laud can often provoke a dismissive and biased comment, because too often he has been judged from the narrow perspective of his involvement in the political arena, so that his fame as a theologian is entirely obscured. Nicholas Tyacke[2] rates him as one of the greatest Archbishops of Canterbury since the Reformation, which is not giving Laud complete approval, but recognizing that his contribution to the future of the English church was of major importance. Our concern here is with Laud as

a theologian and in particular with the way in which he completely
accepted the theology of Andrewes, and rooted that theology in
the Fathers. The Greek Fathers especially provided a powerful
court of appeal from certain aspects of modern Protestantism.
His tutor, John Buckeridge, preaching against Scottish
Presbyterianism in 1606, said that 'in a reformation [of a Church]
we should conform ourselves ... to the rule of the ancient
Scriptures, apostles and fathers: Chrysostom, Nazianzen, Basil,
Ambrose, Jerome. Augustine, Gregory and the like, rather than
after the new cut of those who have not above the life of a man on
their backs, sixty or seventy years'.[3] At a time when predestination
was a crucial issue among Elizabethan bishops with Calvinist
sympathies and with reservations about the orthodoxy of the Greek
Fathers, especially Chrysostom, on the subject of predestination,
this is a significant statement. In Laud's time the principle of the
English Reformation looked to the faith and discipline of the primitive church for a non-papal Catholicism, and was confronted by
the Puritan spirit of Calvinism that threatened the integrity of the
English church. The Puritans resented the fact that predestination
and its corollary reprobation had no place in the doctrine of the
Church of England because of a deeper understanding of
Scripture and primitive theology. Puritanism objected to the
doctrine of the Prayer Book. In such circumstances there is no exaggeration in claiming that the stance for which Laud eventually was
martyred, safeguarded the future of Anglicanism in Creeds,
Episcopacy and Sacraments. Nevertheless, Macaulay's spiteful cari-
cature of him as 'a ridiculous bigot' or as 'intolerant and
meddlesome' has stuck as serious history 'in quarters which might
be expected to know better'.[4] Ballard goes on to quote from S. R.
Gardiner,[5] whose judgement on Laud is 'sufficiently free from the
twin evils of antithesis and debunking'. Gardiner's point is that
'there was a fruitful seed in his teaching which was not to be smoth-
ered in blood' but also that 'his nobler aims were too much in
accordance with the needs of the age to be altogether baffled '.
Three centuries later the parish churches and their worship
expressed a realization of his hopes concerning uniformity which,
with some variations, the Book of Common Prayer was to achieve.
'It is far more that his refusal to submit his mind to the dogmatism
of Puritanism, and his appeal to the cultivated intelligence for the
solution of religious problems has received an ever-increasing
response.' What this priest-martyr became was the champion of
theological liberty.

Dean Hutton declares that he was 'the man who preserved for the Church of England both her catholicity and her freedom.' Laud completed what Elizabeth had begun, and did much more. He not only saved the English Church from the Puritans; he established her right to regard herself, not as the creation of either Parliament or King, but as part of the One Holy Catholic and Apostolic Church, national in her liturgy, but faithful to primitive doctrine.[6]

This accords with J. B. Mozley's judgement, that Laud, the lad from humble origins in Reading who became England's Archbishop, 'saved the English Church'.[7] Mozley is critical of biography that shrinks from doing justice to the combination of bishop and politician, and claimed that 'The political department, e.g. in Laud, throws depth on the ecclesiastical, and each benefits the other'.[8] For Mozley, Laud's contemporary biographer Heylyn fails to do justice to the *homo interior,* where there existed 'a whole inward sphere of thought and feeling in which Laud's mind was moving all the time'. His political involvement in Church and State covers an interior depth and feeling and 'it is only when this courtier, statesman, and man of the world kneels before the cross that we gain a different idea of him altogether'.[9]

Fundamentally he was a priest who loved his church and whose ministry was exercised in the nation's corridors of power, and though with more active involvement than Andrewes, it was exercised in that same spirit of prayer and with the theological outlook that Laud and Andrewes shared with Hooker.

> Laud's object was a doctrinal clearance; the subjugation of the Calvinistic spirit in the Reformed Church of England. The restoration of Church ceremonial and external worship was not so much his object as this doctrinal one. The Church was overrun with heresy, for we cannot call the Puritanical movement of the seventeenth century by any other name; and he was bent on expelling it, on the view that nothing could be made of the Church till it was got rid of. He was a doctrinal reformer.[10]

Too often the inner life of this great priest, who always remained first and foremost an ecclesiastic, has been overlooked, and his achievement in laying the principles and practices for the future of Anglicanism underestimated.

The Theologian

From the start Laud was swimming against the tide of the prevalent
Calvinist theology of his day. It confronted him in the university
authorities, among the bishops and clergy, and in Parliament. He
was greatly influenced by John Buckeridge, his tutor, who in the
closing years of Elizabeth's reign was a leading light in the universities in the reaction against the dominant Calvinism of the day.
Buckeridge stressed the primary importance of sacramental grace
and the episcopal organisation of the Church of England. He
guided Laud's studies in the spirit of the Canon of 1571, which
prescribed the study of the Fathers and ancient doctors as the best
commentary on Holy Scripture. It was from Dr Buckeridge, who
became Bishop of Rochester, that Laud derived his conviction that
the Church of England is part of the Catholic Church of Christ.
This conviction, developed by the uncompromising logic of Laud's
mind, was deepened by his wide and intelligent study of the
Fathers which led him to affirm the Church of Rome, although
corrupt, as the true church in Italy, while the non-episcopal continental bodies had forfeited that claim. When in 1602 he had to
read the Divinity Lecture on Mrs May's foundation in his college,
he opposed the contrary opinion of the post-Reformation theologians that from the Apostles until Luther and Calvin, the Church
had apostatized and become papal, implying that Romanism was as
old as AD 100. On page 49 of his biography, Heylyn tells us that in
this lecture Laud maintained 'the constant and perpetual visibility
of the Church of Christ, derived from the Apostles to the Church
of Rome, and continued in that Church, as in others of the East
and South, until the Reformation.' He also claimed a regular legitimate existence for the medieval English church. For him the
authority of the present church rested upon that basis because its
orders and genealogy were traceable through the Roman Catholic
hierarchy, up to the Apostles and primitive church. It brought
upon Laud the wrath of Dr Abbot, the Vice-Chancellor and future
Puritan Archbishop, and others. From then onwards he was persistently misrepresented by Abbot and his partisans as a confederate
of Rome and an enemy of the Gospel of Christ. Undaunted, Laud
later delivered publicly a thesis, required before passing to a divinity degree, in which he boldly proclaimed the necessity of
baptismal regeneration using the arguments of the Roman
Catholic Bellarmine, and the episcopal form of church government, in the face of more fury from the academic community.

'He appears before us, in short, in the first instance, as an innovator upon the dominant and authorised theology of the day',[11] the school of Geneva being prominent among the greater part of the clergy and laity, and Calvin being regarded as a greater authority than St Augustine or St Jerome. The authority of the Church, its existence as a visible body and Apostolic succession were all called in question. In fact it was heresy to speak to him, and suspicion of heresy to acknowledge him in the street, because his divinity was constructed on the foundations of the Fathers, the Councils and the ecclesiastical historians. His friends were 'perplexed and suspicious of the formal ecclesiastical bearing of his theology'. Mozley goes on to point out that Laud's orthodoxy raised itself and 'was the growth of his own mind in opposition to the prevailing system, and had to be maintained by the force of his own judgement and taste against a whole uncongenial and hostile state of contemporary theology'.[12] He was ordained in 1601 by Bishop Young of Rochester. Bishop Young 'found his study raised above the system and opinions of the age, upon the noble foundation of the Fathers, Councils, and the ecclesiastical historians, and presaged that, if he lived, he would be an instrument of restoring the Church from the narrow and private principles of modern times',[13] which Young regarded as being the more free, large and public sentiments of the purest and best ages. The post-Reformation theologians of Laud's day had severed the Church of England from her medieval past, therefore it was anathema that she should derive authority from what was the fountainhead of the Roman church, so that antiquity for them had no dignity but only pollution. For Laud then, the greater problem was from within, from among those ordained ministers who worked to overthrow a system they had solemnly sworn to protect, and set up an order completely contrary to that established by the Anglican reformers.

This does not reduce Laud to a traditionalist whose views reflect nothing more than a blind acceptance of the thought of the past. He was a man of the Tradition because his own thought and experience convinced him of its essential rightness. As a scholar his knowledge of patristics was monumental and his works, including his sermons, are littered with quotations from the early Fathers. As for his predecessors Hooker and Andrewes, they were not so much rigid authorities to whom he appealed in support of a thesis, but examples of the mind and wisdom of the past from which it was presumptuous and unwise to depart without careful consideration. It became fundamental to his own thought and life, embedded into his own pattern of thinking. Like his predecessors Cranmer, Jewel, Parker and Hooker, he believed profoundly in the Catholic

Church, visible in its continuity, the Church of England essentially part of it.

> Laud had caught a glimpse of the Church moving through the upheavals of history and like Andrewes he saw the significance of the first five centuries for later times, and he concluded that 'the Church of England is nearest of any Church now in being to the Primitive Church'.[14]

His attitude to the whole problem is expounded in the account he published of the famous controversy with 'Mr Fisher the Jesuit'.

His Apologia

Charles I made an analysis of Laud's *Conference with Fisher,* and gave it to his daughter Elizabeth, putting it alongside Andrewes's *Sermons* and Hooker's *Ecclesiastical Polity.* This *Conference* became the authoritative statement of the position of Anglicanism in opposition to the Roman claims. It is at King James's command that Laud, then Bishop of St David's, engages in dispute with the Jesuit Fisher, the latter maintaining that the main question requiring an answer was, 'Is there an Infallible Church?' It is here that he illustrates in conviction and scholarship his own firm belief in the catholicity of Anglicanism's faith and order in an unbroken continuity with its patristic roots. *A Relation of the Conference*[15] is prefaced by *An Epistle Dedicatory* to King Charles, in which Laud is concerned to justify his attempts to ensure uniformity. Without uniform and decent order there is chaos and it is such chaos, that draws people away from the sincerity of religion professed in the Church of England. While worship has an inner reality without which there is no true worship, nevertheless this cannot be separated from its outward expression, for such 'external worship of God in his Church is the great witness to the world.'[16] Such separation destroys true worship and is Laud's reason for trying to secure

> decency and an orderly settlement of the external worship of God in the Church. For of that which is inward there can be no witness among men. Now no external action in the world can be uniform without some ceremonies. And these in religion, the ancienter they be, the better, so they may fit time and place.

The Church of England he understands to be positioned between Roman Catholics and Puritans, a *via media* which is not deliberately chosen, 'but is incidental to the fact that "she professes the ancient Catholic Faith".' Laud maintains that there is in fact no innovation but a return to the teaching of Scripture and the Fathers, and that 'she practises church government as it hath been in use in all ages and all places.'[17] McAdoo comments that Andrewes and Laud see the criterion of antiquity in relation to continuity and catholicity which is not a 'narrow conclave'. Laud's purpose in the Conference is 'to lay open those wider gates of the Catholic Church, confined to no age, time or place; nor knowing any bounds but that faith which was once (and but once for all) delivered to the saints.'[18] The Church is founded on the Faith not the Faith, on the Church.

In the discussion with Fisher he contends that infallibility cannot be asserted of any particular church, citing Bellarmine, who studied the past to provide a basis for present faith, and claimed that the pope and the Roman church are unable to err. The latter is the important question, whether inerrancy for all time in matters of faith belongs to the Church of Rome. Bellarmine's proof was based on three passages from Cyprian, Jerome and Gregory Nazianzen, while referring to but not referencing Cyril and Rufinus. Examining and quoting from these authors, Laud establishes that no infallibility attributable to the Roman church can be proved from them. He points out that the six of the popes Bellarmine appeals to 'have less cause with me than any other six of the more ancient Fathers.'[19] He then instances that the Church of Rome has erred in allowing the worship of images and in taking the cup from the laity. On the general question of the Church's infallibility he cites the Greek church, a large part of the church in Eastern Europe which had never acknowledged the growing claims of the papacy. Fisher dismisses the Greeks on the *filioque,* a clause in the Creed which they themselves had asserted. Quoting from the tradition, Laud dismisses this with a statement from the esteemed medieval, Peter Lombard, that 'The Greeks differ from us in expression, none the less they do not differ in meaning.' After pointing out that it should be no easy thing to 'condemn a man of heresy in foundation of faith, much less a Church, least of all so ample and large a Church as the Greek, especially so as to make them no Church', he quotes Alphonsus a Castro, one of their own, against them: 'Let them consider that pronounce easily of heresy how easy it is for themselves to err.'[20] On this basis he will not allow Rome to arrogate to themselves alone the word 'Catholic', because in a real sense they were less 'Catholic' than the Church of England by virtue of the doctrines Rome had asserted on her own authority. From these Anglicanism had demurred because as later additions they were contrary to the doctrine *quod ubique, quod semper, quod ab omnibus,* which is the only fundamental basis of the Catholic Faith. Laud found confirmation for these convictions in the Greek church, and was convinced of the importance of being able to show that the English position had the approval of the early Christian Fathers. His interpretation of Christ's promise, 'upon this rock I will build my Church', he explains as being addressed not to Peter personally, but with regard to the faith which he had just professed, and in which he was the spokesman of the others. He claimed support from Ignatius, Hilary, Gregory of Nyssa, Isidore, Cyril, Theodore, Gregory the Great, Theophylact, Augustine, Justin Martyr, Chrysostom and Ambrose.[21]

The main argument concerns which articles of faith are fundamental, where Laud expounds the Anglican principle established by Hooker and Andrewes of primary and secondary articles, and demonstrates that the English church is firm in its adherence to catholic doctrine. He opposes the Roman position, that all points defined by the Church are fundamental, with the thesis that only the credal articles come into this category, to which the Church has no power to add or subtract from that foundation. Even what the Church defines in council is not fundamental because the Church has defined it. Here in his stance that the Church is to witness and explain he is in harmony with a theological tradition that is traceable through Ockham to Augustine. 'The Church is founded on the Faith, not the Faith on the Church. It is her duty to guard the principles of faith, the *dogmata deposita,* and keep them unblemished and uncorrupted.'[22] Such an appeal to antiquity depends for Laud, as it did for Andrewes, on Scripture being central, and therefore the section dealing with the authority of Scripture is one of the most important parts of his work. Only by holding the two in balance can a true and stable belief be maintained.

> While the one faction cries up the Church above the Scripture, and the other the Scripture to the neglect and contempt of the Church, which the Scripture itself teaches men both to honour and obey; they have so far endangered the belief of the one, and the authority of the other, as that neither has its due from a great part of men; whereas, according to Christ's institution, the Scripture where it is plain, should guide the Church; and the Church, where there is doubt or difficulty, should expound the Scripture; yet so, as neither the Scripture should be forced, nor

the Church so bound up, as that upon just and further evidence she may not revise that which in any case hath slipped by her.[23]

Therefore, Laud contends, because Scripture contains all fundamentals not only held by the Church of England but also by the Fathers and does not exclude universal traditions, and because all the present articles of the present Church of England are grounded upon Scripture, Anglicanism is content to be judged by the joint and constant belief of the Fathers. For Laud this means the first five hundred years after Christ, which was when the Church was at its best, and also by the Councils held within that time.

> The Fathers are plain, the Schoolmen not strangers in it. And have we not reason then to account it, as it is, the foundation of our faith ? ... and if the Scripture be the foundation to which we are to go for witness, if there be any doubt about the faith, and in which we are to find the thing that is to be believed, as necessary in the faith; we never did, nor never will refuse any tradition that is universal and apostolic for the better exposition of the Scripture; nor any definition of the Church in which she goes to the Scripture for what she teaches; and thrusts nothing as fundamental in the faith upon the world, but what the scripture makes fundamentally '*materiam credendorum*', 'the substance of that which is so to be believed', whether immediately and expressly in words, or more remotely, where a clear and full declaration draws it out.[24]

The most important part of the whole work is to be found in the arguments on the authority of Scripture. His overall concern is to limit the extent of 'soul-saving' faith and establish that the foundations of faith were 'Scriptures and the Creeds'. Here the teaching of Hooker and Andrewes is unmistakeable, as Laud adopts and defends Hooker's own statement that 'Scripture is the ground of our belief '[25] and therefore contains in itself all things necessary to salvation. Grounds for the confirmation of this can be found in many quarters, but the strength of his argument is its convergence along two lines. There is the argument from tradition establishing the Church as the continuous living organization in which Scriptural truth is enshrined: 'the authority of man (that is the name he [Hooker] gives to tradition) is the key which openeth the door of entrance into the knowledge of the Scripture'. The Apostolic teaching, the writings of the Fathers, the decisions of Councils, all witness to this fundamental ground of Holy Scripture as containing all things necessary to salvation.

> Tradition and Scripture do mutually, yet do they not equally,
> confirm the authority either of other. For Scripture doth infalli-
> bly confirm the authority of Church tradition truly so called. But
> Tradition doth but morally and probably confirm the authority
> of Scripture.[26]

Scripture and Tradition or the Church are not two authorities but
one mutually inclusive authority, authenticating each other.

> The key that lets men into the Scriptures, even to this knowledge
> of them, that they are the word of God, is the tradition of the
> Church ... For a beginner in the faith, or a weakling or a
> doubter about it, begins at tradition and proves Scripture by the
> Church; but a man strong and grown up in the faith, and under-
> standably conversant in the word of God proves the Church by
> the Scripture. And then upon the matter we have a double
> divine testimony. Altogether infallible, to confirm unto us, that
> Scripture is the word of God. The first is the tradition of the
> Church of the apostles themselves, who delivered immediately
> to the world the word of Christ; the other, the Scripture itself;
> but after it hath received this testimony. And into these we do,
> and may safely, resolve our faith.[27]

To this must be added reason which both suggests and justifies
that which tradition formulates. Here Laud[28] argues that, as in
other sciences there are authoritative texts from which novices may
come to knowledge of what they may authoritatively and reason-
ably accept as the basis of their scientific knowledge, so too it is
reasonable for novices in theology to have an authoritative text.
Scripture, as a rule, is something that novices may be taught to
believe in order to come to knowledge of those things from which
rich principle and treasure are deducible. It is reasonable to
assume such grounds, making it possible for the natural man to be
convinced that the text of God is a credible text. The uninstructed
mind then discovers that it is reasonable to suppose the likelihood
that there should be an inspired and divine guide. As Tradition
points to Scripture as that guide, reason and Tradition alone are
powerless to make anyone embrace such teaching and submit their
will to it. Faith alone does this and the power of Scripture to induce
such faith credits it with divine power; and while it is the tradition
of the Church that persuades us of this, the light of nature
convinces us of the need of revelation. Finally there is the text of
Scripture itself, wherein we encounter the presence of the living
God in his Word, inwardly inclining our hearts to seal an assurance

of the sufficiency of all three into us, giving certainty by faith and not by knowledge.[29]

In the settling of doubts concerning doctrines about the faith Laud claims that the 'best judge on earth' is a lawful and free General Council, determining according to Scripture. His concern is to narrow the scope of dogmatism, allowing views not necessary to salvation to be freely and publicly discussed by authorized exponents rather than being decided at the bar of an infallible authority. What Laud is answering is a fallacy he found present in both Jesuit and Puritan, the assumption of God's special guidance overriding man's free will and liability to err.

> I have often heard some wise men say, that the Jesuit in the Church of Rome, and the precise party in the reformed Churches, agree in many things, though they would seem most to differ. And surely this is one; for both of them differ extremely about tradition; the one magnifying it, and exalting it into a divine authority; the other vilifying and depressing it almost below human. And yet, even in these different ways, both agree in this consequent, – That the sermons and preachings by word of mouth of the lawfully sent pastors and doctors of the Church, are able to breed in us divine and infallible faith; nay are the very word of God.[30]

For the Jesuit there is the necessity of an infallible Church, and for the Puritan the need of an infallible Bible. Laud will not allow infallibility in either. For him Church and Bible are mutually dependent and one without the other does not make sense. He provides four possible ways of 'proving' that the Bible is the Word of God. First, by the tradition of the Church; secondly, 'by the light and testimony which the Scripture gives to itself'; thirdly, by the testimony of the Holy Spirit; fourthly, by the testimony of natural reason. They will not stand by themselves; they are mutually inclusive.[31] This is in line with Andrewes, except for the addition of the special revelation given by the Holy Spirit, and exhibits Laud's attitude to the Bible as being a reasonable one. In this he follows Hooker and Andrewes and the finest medieval tradition. His concern is to present a reasonable faith, and in so doing he finds himself confronted by two adversaries in the Jesuit and Puritan. The Laudian position is that 'Scripture must not be tested by any man's opinions, neither those of the Pope nor those of Calvin. It is itself the test, and the true interpretation is that placed on it from the earliest times. Its main points are determined in the Apostles' Creed'.[32]

R. P. C. Hanson's *Tradition in the Early Church* supports the seventeenth century writers concerning the appeal to antiquity in their
claim that the Fathers proved the rule of faith from Scripture, and
so disposes of the suggestion that tradition was treated as an independent authority in early times. 'The idea of the rule of faith as
supplementing or complementing, or indeed adding anything
whatever, to the Bible, is wholly absent from their thought.'[33]
Hanson points out that all the Fathers believed that the rule of
faith was in its content identical with the content of the Bible and
regarded the rule as open to being proved from the Bible. For
McAdoo the thought-out quality of what Laud produced is notable
in that it 'is the outline of a balanced theology, a middle way, and
this position he regards as due, not to a conscious effort to assess
the arguments on either side, but to the undifferentiated nature of
its sources in Scripture and antiquity.'[34] It was to the primitive
Church that he always looked as his interpreter of the Faith.

> I have always lived, and shall, God willing, die, in the faith of
> Christ as it was professed in the ancient Primitive Church, and as
> it is professed in the present Church of England. As for the rule
> that governs me herein, if I cannot be confident in my soul upon
> the Scripture, and upon the Primitive Church expounding it, I
> will be confident upon no other.[35]

Laud's contribution here is of real value, and is clear proof of
the injustice of the charge brought against him that he was a
Romanizer, one favourable to the Church of Rome. Hooker,
Andrewes, Laud and others of their school will always be open to
this charge from those that will admit of no other authority than
the letter of Scripture. Laud, in line with his Caroline predecessors
and successors, found, in the principles he recognized as primitive
and catholic, a defence, not only against a papal Catholicism but
also against the dogmatism of Puritanism.

His views on the Eucharist in no way depart from Catholic
doctrine in his assertion that the Church of England believes and
teaches a true and real presence of Christ in the Eucharist, the
difference between Rome and Canterbury lying 'in the way and
manner of being'. For Laud the Eucharist was a source of grace to
all believers and he even described the altar as 'the greatest place
of God's residence on earth'. Like Andrewes he understood the
Eucharist as '. . . the conduit-pipe of grace' and after receiving the
sacrament of Holy Communion he prays 'enrich me with all those
graces which come from the precious body and blood, even till I be
possessed of eternal life in Christ'.[36] He asserts the doctrine of

Eucharistic sacrifice, maintaining that we offer three sacrifices: the first being the commemorative sacrifice of Christ's death made by the priest only, the second by priest and people together, which is the sacrifice of praise and thanksgiving; and the third by every worshipper for himself, which is the sacrifice of each person's soul and body to serve him in both all the days of his life.

Episcopacy

One of the chief targets of the Puritans was the episcopal order of ministry, for they claimed that the organization of the Church should be the same as that which existed in New Testament times. This ruled out episcopacy as traditionally practised. Bishop and presbyter are synonymous in their New Testament context, and the difference between ministers of the Gospel is not one of order but ability. Authority for ministry depends on the inward call of God, not on episcopal ordination or the grace of orders, a view quite contrary to the Anglican Ordinal. Against this argument Anglicanism urged that episcopacy had the unanimous agreement of the Fathers concerning not only its Apostolic origin, but also the special position of the bishops among the other presbyters. Ignatius, Irenaeus, Tertullian, the Cappadocians, Jerome, Augustine and the general consent of the Fathers, testify to this universal order of episcopal government in the Church. There is a threefold distinction between bishop and priest from the earliest days. The bishop not only has authority to ordain and confirm, but he also has the right of jurisdiction and excommunication. The three distinctions derive from the Apostolic origin of the episcopate and ultimately from Christ himself. Bishops hold them *jure divino*, and therefore they are not a purely convenient human institution.

Laud developed an extremely exalted view of episcopacy very early, both as divinely instituted and as an essential mark of the Church. He argued that only a bishop can confer orders. In 1608 he wrote a doctoral thesis on this, the effect of which was to unchurch most European and Scottish Protestants. The correspondence that Laud had with Bishop Hall[37] concurs with this view of episcopacy. Hall had asked the Archbishop for his critical advice on his book *Episcopacy of Divine Right*. Here Laud's concern is not only with the answer to the Puritans, but to express the truly Anglican understanding of episcopacy that lies midway between that of Rome and Geneva. Therefore his point to Hall is that episcopal superiority is not merely one of jurisdiction in ecclesiastical matters, otherwise not only archdeacons but the Moderator of the Presbyterian Assembly would qualify. It stems from that which is intrinsical and original in the power of excommunication. Furthermore the first feature of the body of a church is episcopacy, and where it has been denied there it is by abdication. He will not allow presbyterian government as a substitute where episcopacy cannot be had,

> for there is no place where it may not be had if there be a Church more than in title only ... since they challenge their Presbyterian fiction to be Christ's kingdom and ordinance (as yourself expresseth), and cast out episcopacy as opposite to it, we must not use any mincing terms but unmask them plainly ...

At the same time he wishes to make plain that an episcopacy that subordinates the bishops completely to the pope is also contrary to the historic tradition. He also makes the point that the bishop's is not a mere title of honour, in that the distinction between a bishop and a priest is one of Order, not just one of degree.[38] The Anglican understanding of episcopacy as defined by our English Reformers is a necessary part of a 'right' Church, of the *esse* of the Church, not only of the *bene esse,* and to reject it is to depart from the implicit directions of Christ himself. It is part of that threefold Order of ministry essential to the Church 'everywhere, at all times, and by all men accepted.' Its abolition would be a betrayal of the Faith.

John Keble's judgement is that what came to be the Laudian view of episcopacy rather than Hooker's view, represents the high water mark of Anglicanism.

> There is, he says, 'a marked distinction between that which now perhaps we may venture to call the school of Hooker and that of Laud, Hammond and Leslie.' And Mr. Keble goes on: 'He, as well as they, regarded the order of bishops as being immediately and properly of Divine right; he as well as they laid down principles which, strictly followed up, would make this claim exclusive. But he, in common with most of his contemporaries, shrunk from the legitimate result of his own premises, the rather, as the fulness of apostolic authority on this point had never come within his cognizance; whereas the next generation of divines entered on the subject, as was before observed, fresh from the study of St Ignatius.'[39]

His Achievements

Queen Elizabeth I is reported to have said that she knew what amount of concession would satisfy the adherents of Rome, but she never could discover what would satisfy the Puritans. Archbishop Abbot's policy of conciliation failed, even when he had yielded almost everything, but without satisfying the Puritans, because *everything* was not yielded. Laud was more discerning and refused to yield more, because he knew they hated the whole church system in creeds, episcopacy, sacraments, order, ceremonial, vestments, holy seasons and reverence. The issue was not about ceremonial, but was far more fundamental, because it was about the very nature of the Church, catholicism or Calvinism, communion with the primitive ages or with Geneva. Their aim was the destruction of the primitive Catholic character of the Church of England. This was proved after Laud was executed, when their pretence for amendment was exposed in their ruthless sweeping away of everything. Laud knew that the battle was not about rites and ceremonies but for Anglicanism against Calvinism, for the Church of England in its adherence to primitive doctrine against Geneva.

Nevertheless, the failure of the Laudian reformation was apparent rather than real, its effect on the Church of England being for its ultimate good. In doctrine and discipline the principle of the English Reformation was safeguarded in the appeal to Holy Scripture as interpreted by the undivided Church in the pure and primitive ages, an appeal which is embodied in its canons and laid down by its apologists. The same appeal is spoken of in the Prayer Book as being agreeable 'to the mind and purpose of the old Fathers'. Mozley[40] tells us that a new theological race of clergy sprang up under Laud's administration.

> The tone of the clerical body was altered; and a theological school, which was a mere handful when he commenced life at Oxford, had spread over the country in all directions. Oxford itself, from being a focus of Calvinism, had come round, and hardly knew its new reflections in the theology of Jeremy Taylor and Hammond. A Puritan remnant remained ... but they felt their occupation of the place gone, and another standard on the ascendant, a new genius loci penetrating the air. The crowds of clergy whom the Rebellion and directory threw out of their places show the strong growth that had been going on in the Church at large, and the change of the Church of England theology that a few years had brought about.

It was in that sense, of effecting a doctrinal reformation of the Calvinism that had supplanted Anglican practice but not Anglican formularies, that Laud was a theological innovator. He was behind the royal injunctions that ordered the study of the Fathers rather than the moderns in the Universities, and the patronage given to Wren, Montague, Taylor, Cosin, Mede, and Bramhall. In their turn, these men trained another generation, and in a great degree influence our own. Here in this Caroline era are some of the most powerful and consistent exponents of Anglicanism, because Laud obeyed the instructions of his church in following the primitive interpretation of Holy Scripture, and in so doing, effected a revolution in English theology. In less than twenty years after Laud's martyrdom they were able to procure a revision of the Book of Common Prayer on its own principles, and to turn the whole current of English theology.

It was through these pupils of Laud and their disciples that the fruit of those theological principles for which he was martyred were to blossom in the Church and to prove that he had not laboured in vain. With Juxon at Canterbury, and with fellow-bishops, Wren at Ely and Cosin at Durham, Laud's principles lived on in men whom he had taught what the Church of England is. To them was entrusted the work denied to their leader of bringing the church's liturgy nearer to the models of primitive antiquity. They were responsible for the 1662 Book of Common Prayer with its more catholic spirit in the restoration of the oblation and the commemoration of the faithful departed in the Liturgy; manual signs in the prayer of consecration, the improvement of the Ordinal and the prohibiting of all but the episcopally ordained from ministering at our altars. The baptismal water is to be blessed and baptismal regeneration affirmed, along with the sign of the Cross, absolution restricted to priests, a table of Vigils, prayers for Ember seasons, for All Sorts and Conditions of Men, and especially for the good estate of the Catholic Church. Requests from the Presbyterians, that the Communion Office be performed at the desk and the season of Lent be abolished, were ignored.

In fact, the greatest triumph for Laud is the adoption by the whole English church of a prominent position for the altar at the east end, fenced by communion rails where communicants kneel to receive the Sacrament. This illustrates the central focus of Laud's theology in the Incarnation as an objective fact and its organic connection with the Church as Christ's mystical body. This is patristic and quite alien to the Puritans, whose theology was certainly Christocentric in making the value of Christ to the soul a central and dominating idea, but their emphasis was on our experience of Christ as Saviour, rather than on the Incarnation as objective fact. Hence for them the efficacy of the sacraments was dependent upon the preaching of the Word, reducing the sacraments to a position of inherent inferiority, so that the sermon becomes more important than the Sacrament. The logical consequence is, as was discussed in relation to Hooker, that preaching becomes valued by the Puritans almost to the exclusion of worship, prayer, and sacrament. Therefore to Laud the position of the altar and the ordering of the Liturgy is crucial in demonstrating that the Christian life and ministry must be centred in the sacraments, whose efficacy does not depend upon an instructive imparting of knowledge, but on divine grace. Laud taught that this must be central to all sound restoration.

Such a theology and piety centred in the sacraments was able to encourage those yearnings after holier and stricter lives which, it is often forgotten, Laud personally fostered, not only by example but by his own pastoral ministry. It issues in outward expressions of sanctity. His own life witnessed to the necessity of spiritual discipline in celibacy, his prayers seven times a day, his fastings and vigils and the penitential spirit of his own personal devotions. Such a disposition enabled him to give his patronage to Little Gidding, which the Puritans would have destroyed, and his influence on the saintliness of George Herbert cannot be underestimated. Other systems might make people good, religious, even holy, but not in the highest sense saints, because sanctity is the fruit of humanity's participation in divinity which sacraments effect.

Laud's patristic foundation

Laud takes his stand on the principle of the English Reformation in his appeal against Rome and Geneva, to Holy Scripture as interpreted by the primitive church. In line with the Reformers, Hooker and Andrewes, he uses the patristic argument at a time when Rome wanted to deny the English church any catholicity and the Puritans wanted to destroy her identity with primitive ancient catholic Christianity. Like his study, his mind and spirit was raised above the opinions and systems of his age, because his foundation was the apostolic doctrine that found expression in Fathers, Councils and ecclesiastical historians. On this rock this apologist ably safeguards Anglicanism's catholicity in the face of Rome, but also prevents the destruction of the patristic nature of Anglicanism by the Puritans.

The presence of this patristic mind maintains the episcopal government of the Church of England and provides Anglicanism with that Laudian school of theology that established itself through a revised Book of Common Prayer, in the ethos of an English religious tradition that found expression not only in the ordering of worship, but also in the ordering and care of buildings and the yearnings for sanctity.

> As far as doctrine was concerned Laud carried on the teaching of Cranmer and Hooker. He held that the basis of belief was the Bible, but that the Bible was to be interpreted by the tradition of the early Church, and that all doubtful points were to be subjected, not to heated arguments in the pulpits, but to sober discussion by learned men. His mind, in short, like those of the earlier English reformers, combined the Protestant reliance on the Scriptures with reverence for ancient tradition and with the critical spirit of the Renascence ... What was peculiar to Laud was his perception that intellectual religion could not maintain itself by intellect alone. Hooker's appeal to Church history and to the supremacy of reason had rolled over the heads of men who knew nothing about Church history and who did not reason ... [41]

The Laudian era widened the intellectual vision of mankind and produced a landmark in the progress of thought. This was done by enabling the progress of theological thought to move away from the barren region of mere rival assertions of the infallibility of either Scripture or tradition by attempting to harmonize both by the action of reason inspired by faith.

Notes

1. W. H. Frere, *A History of the English Church in the Reigns of Elizabeth and James, 1558–1625* (Macmillan & Co, London, 1911), 2nd edn, pp. 387–388.
2. N. Tyacke, 'Archbishop Laud', in *The Early Stuart Church 1603–1642* (Macmillan, London 1993), p. 51.
3. John Buckeridge, *A Sermon preached at Hampton Court* (1606); cited by Tyacke, *ibid.* p. 56.
4. A. W. Ballard, 'Laud: A Vindication', in *Church Quarterly Review*, vol. cxl (Oct.–Dec. 1945), p. 98.
5. *Ibid.* p. 108, citing S. R. Gardiner, *The History of the Civil War, 1642–1649*, vol. ii, in ch, xxiv (1898 edn).
6. Sidney Dark, *Seven Archbishops* (Eyre & Spottiswoode, London, 1944), p. 147.

7. J. B. Mozley, 'Archbishop Laud', in *Essays Historical and Theological,* vol. i (Rivingtons, London, 1878), p. 107.
8. *Ibid.*
9. *Ibid.* p. 109.
10. *Ibid.* p. 163.
11. *Ibid.* p. 115.
12. *Ibid,* p. 116.
13. *Ibid.*
14. H. R. McAdoo, p. 338, citing W. Laud, 'A Relation of the Conference (between Laud and Fisher)', 3rd edn, Dedicatory Preface, *The Spirit of Anglicanism* (A. & C. Black, London, 1965), p. 338.
15. W. Laud, *Works,* (*LACT,* Oxford, 1849), 6th edn, vol. ii.
16. *Ibid.* p. xvi.
17. *Ibid.* p. xiii.
18. *Ibid. Epistle Dedicatory,* p. xvii.
19. Laud, *Works,* vol. ii, p. 21.
20. *Ibid.* p. 29.
21. *Ibid.* p. 257.
22. A. S. Duncan-Jones, *Archbishop Laud* (Macmillan, London, 1923), p. 60.
23. Laud, *Works,* vol. ii, p. xv.
24. *Ibid.* pp. 61–2.
25. W. Laud, *The Conference with Fisher the Jesuit* (Macmillan, 1901) 4th edn, p. 103.
26. *Ibid.* p. 112.
27. *Ibid.* p. 116.
28. *Ibid.* p. 120.
29. *Ibid.* pp. 131ff.
30. *Ibid.* p. 113.
31. *Ibid.* p. 131.
32. Dark, p. 124.
33. R. P. C. Hanson, *Tradition in the Early Church* (SCM, London, 1962), pp. 74 and 65.
34. H. R. McAdoo, p. 342.
35. Laud, cited by E. C. E. Bourne, in *The Anglicanism of William Laud* (SPCK, London, 1947), p. 87.
36. W. Laud, *A Summarie of Devotions* (William Hall, Oxford, 1667), p. 219.
37. Laud, 'Letter 178', *Works,* vol. vi, pp. 573–5.
38. 'Letter 179', *ibid.* p. 577
39. William Clark, *The Anglican Reformation* (T. & T. Clark, Edinburgh, 1897), p. 357.
40. Mozley, p. 151.
41. Ballard, *ibid.* p. 103, citing Gardiner in *The History of the Great Civil War, 1642–1649* (London, 1898) vol. ii, ch. 24.

9

The Laudians and Henry Hammond

The Laudians

'Laudian' describes those who shared the theological viewpoint of Laud, the High Churchmen who were in whole-hearted agreement in their method of defending the church's interests before and after the Restoration. This is not to say that they were unswerving followers of the Archbishop, nor can any overtones which the word Laudian may have acquired be applied to them. The word 'Canterburian' was another term used to describe them in Henry Hickman's *Laudensian Apostasia* (1660) – sub-titled 'The Canterburians Apostasie from the Doctrine Received in the Church of England'.[1] They did not consider themselves a party, believing they represented the true Church of England, and it would be wrong to describe them as such. At this stage of the seventeenth century, groups and individuals were connected by an interchange of ideas and an emphasis on an existing measure of agreement that cut across differences of outlook. Such differences were contained and admitted by a theological method with a firm but adaptable centre, that was capable of contact with a variety of subjects and situations and able to readjust emphases in order to cope with new ideas. McAdoo points out that 'this more than anything else is the basis for that general agreement that existed between individuals and groups which a later age, with some justification, would assign to different and more or less opposing schools of thought' and includes in such general agreement Hooker, Andrewes, Jeremy Taylor, William Chillingworth, Henry Hammond and Gilbert Sheldon.

> It might be described as the spirit of Anglicanism, including as it does the centrality of Scripture and the visibility and continuity of the Church, both confirmed by antiquity, and

illuminated by the freedom of reason and liberality of view-point. It constitutes the shared attitude of the seventeenth century, and although one group may lay the main emphasis on one aspect and another may criticise it, the awareness of a common ground of agreement was a fact until the appearance of parties as a result of events in the closing years of the century.[2]

It was difficult to base both faith and practice upon the same foundations as the Church of Rome and raise something quite separate. Yet seventeenth-century Anglicanism claimed to be rooted in Catholic tradition and historically descended therefrom, while maintaining a vigorous growth through the translated services and the Book of Common Prayer. Hence the Romanists and the Puritans continually attacked her official formulae, but this dual offensive produced from the Laudian loyalists a spate of explanatory and defensive literature. The added pressure of laws against her required the stressing of the continuity and visibility of the church, and in a large number of works the Laudians set out to illustrate this. The result was a considerable emphasis on the appeal to antiquity in relation to the form of church government. It was a time of *defensive* and *offensive* theology in the face of a concerted attack on the content of Anglican teaching as embodied in the Liturgy. A century before, the Book of Common Prayer had been the rallying point of reformed Anglicanism against Popery. Now it was regarded as a popish superstition, and a sign of episcopal order, and the two must stand or fall together.

Henry Hammond (1605–60) was the leading light, and with others preserved the traditional balance of a theological method in which the beginnings of a specific orientation can be seen. Bull, Pearson, Dodwell and Beveridge took it a stage further, McAdoo points out that, combined with the events of the 1689 Revolution these people produced an alignment so that High Church and Latitudinarian became descriptions of parties in a way that would not have been the case earlier.

Henry Hammond

When the Church of England was suffering persecution in the time of Cromwell, it was to Dr. Hammond, more than to any other single man, that she owed the continuance of her existence ... It was by his holiness, charity and devoted labours, that a tone was given to the clergy of that period which bore good fruit afterwards.[3]

He is the embodiment of Anglicanism in the seventeenth century in the tradition of Hooker and Andrewes, expressing himself in the same kind of way and through his writings illustrating the impact of the *Ecclesiastical Polity* in the thought of the day. It is not surprising to find that a balanced relationship between Scripture, Antiquity and Reason form the core of his theological method. There is a resemblance to Andrewes not in the style of his general approach but in interests, both finding a common concern for antiquity and history, biblical texts and language, liturgical and devotional matters. Their common strain of Arminianism is not surprising in Hammond, who was influenced by Grotius, the Dutch Arminian scholar whom he defended more than once from the charges of Socinianism and Papistry. He shared the basic conviction of Hammond's ecclesiology, that the Church of England was 'the most careful observer, and transcriber of primitive antiquity'.[4]

His reasonable theology

At a time when the outward organization of the Church was collapsing, Hammond was the first to realize that a defence of Anglicanism must be intellectually sound. His aim and that of his circle was to build an edifice of reasoned theology in support of Laudian church principles, which not only moderated them but made them intelligible to their opponents. In their respect for the autonomy of reason there is a kinship not only with Hooker and Andrewes but also with the Latitudinarians. Reason and the argument from natural law need to be supplemented, but that does not dispense with the need for reasonableness in the supplementary data. What is 'superadded to the law of nature, right reason will of its own accord commend as best'.[5]

Of the Reasonableness of the Christian Religion

McAdoo points out that while Hammond has been regarded a Laudian *pur sang*, it is necessary to highlight where he relates to the underlying agreement of the period. This lies in the 'curious similarity in his writings with certain points of view usually looked on as being distinctively Latitudinarian'.[6] On this front he sees a resemblance to Tillotson and Wilkins in the style of his approach in *Of the Reasonableness of the Christian Religion*. Hammond's aim is to demonstrate a valid basis for Christianity and then its advantages; 'the first will render the belief rational ... the second will render the belief gainful'.[7] The first point rests on the authority of the biblical records, and McAdoo claims, that like Stillingfleet, he refers to miracles and to 'the success which attended them'.[8] Apart from the evidence of witnesses, 'there is no rational evidence imaginable for those who lived not in that age', nor can there be any more authentic proof of 'matter of fact'.[9] Hammond considers the New Testament historically and the case against it, and concludes that the nature of the biblical testimony and its basis makes it 'a rational ground of belief'.[10] Hammond expresses in detail his awareness of the limitations placed on reason by the authority of this testimony. McAdoo goes on to explain that there is a suggestion of the later attitude which is heightened in his words, 'that which is really advantageous is always most rational, most prudent for man to choose'.[11]

McAdoo identifies this as the true note of latitudinarianism, which he sees Hammond developing in the same way as Wilkins, with a division of the advantages into outward and inward, the former affecting the public life and the latter the well-being of the individual person and relationships in general. Behind them are the advantages of grace, faith, and hope. He regards present and future advantages as 'evidence of the rationalness of religion'.[12]

> Hence the conclusion is, that right reason is able to judge of all merely moral subjects, whether anything be good or bad morally; of natural objects in matter of fact, whether such a thing be done or no, by the help of the means specified, and by discourse, and analogy from things that we see are done, to judge that such another thing is possible. But of supernatural truths, such things as it never discerned in nature, either in the kind or the like, it cannot judge any further than thus: either first, that though we cannot do it, yet, for aught we know, it is possible (nay it hath being) with God; or secondly, that God hath affirmed it so, therefore I am sure it is; or thirdly, what comes to me from authority, that I have no reason to suspect, but, on the contrary, concurrence of all reasons to be persuaded by it; nay, there are some inward characters in the thing itself, that make me cast off all jealousy or doubt of such affirmations, and therefore I believe it so. But generally, and *in thesi*, it is no way judge of these last kind of controversies.[13]

McAdoo comments:

> This is one of those agreements which are unexpected only if
> the fact of basic and underlying agreement in the seventeenth
> century is ignored. Whether the work had any direct influence
> on Stillingfleet and Wilkins is not known, although the date of
> its publication makes this a possibility, but in itself it is an indi-
> cation of the way in which this line of thought was not confined
> to any group but was making itself generally felt in the middle of
> the century.[14]

His *Practical Catechism*

In his concern for practical divinity there is the same importance
attached to its reasonableness. The foreword, 'To the Reader', in
his *Practical Catechism,* identifies the fundamental error of
Christianity in his time. 'Christianity hath been taken, if not with
the Atheist for an art or trick, yet with the scholastic for a science,
a matter of speculation; and so, that he that knows most, that
believes most, is the only sanctified person.'[15] This expresses the
seventeenth-century Gnosticism which Hammond sought to
counter with a method in the tradition of religious teaching, the
catechetical method, which had its roots in the Fathers, and is liturgical in character. While the aim is to establish a firm intellectual
foundation for the faith, it is to be done not by mere speculative
methods but by bringing the individual into the life of the visible
church. Its concern is with edification, the building up of a
member of the Body of Christ. The design of all Christian teaching
as Hammond understood it, is 'in effect the reformation of lives,
and the heightening of Christian Practice to the most elevated
pitch'. Catechizing had been neglected in parish churches, and
had been replaced by discourses and sermons on speculative and
national things. As a *Practical Catechism* it presupposed the Church
Catechism, and by such arguments Hammond was building up an
edifice of doctrine that would contribute much to the re-establishment of the Church of England in 1660. It was also necessary in a
time of subjective individualism, when introspective illuminism in
Hammond's view undermined not only the basis of historicity and
reason, but also the implications of the visible church. The visibility of the church was to form the essence of later controversy, and
so it became the concern of Hammond and his circle to set themselves to establish a reasoned defence of the Church of England

against the Roman claims and Puritan teachings. This was done by appeal to Reason, Scripture and the Fathers.

His approach to the Bible

Hammond brought the same reasonableness that characterized the arguments of his catechetical and apologetic defences to the field of biblical scholarship. 'It is not too much to say that Dr. Hammond is the father of English biblical criticism.'[16] He was the first English scholar to compare the MSS of the New Testament, and examine the language in which it was written, to discover its true meaning. Laudian apologetic could not be sustained by 'the Bible only' dictum of Chillingworth, but Scripture must be fundamental in the defence of the Church of England, not only as the ground of historical and doctrinal arguments but also in the defence of the Book of Common Prayer and the teachings, rites and ceremonies derived from it. In Hammond they had a biblical scholar whose primary concern was a critical exegesis of the text, a solid foundation of biblical scholarship against the attacks on episcopacy and the Book of Common Prayer from Presbyterians and Independents.

In 1653 Hammond published *A Paraphrase and Annotations upon all the Books of the New Testament*. His forerunner was Hugo Grotius (1583–1645) who had published in 1642 *Annotationes in Vetus et Novum Testamentum,* a critical study of the text discarding literal inspiration, though acknowledging the importance of ecclesiastical tradition for a right understanding of the Scriptures, but subsidiary to detailed interpretation of the original text. Hammond supported his methods, though he did not go as far in rejecting the traditional authorship of 1 and 2 John, Jude and 2 Peter. On 4 January 1652 he wrote to Thomas Smith of Christ's College Cambridge, 'Be confident the true Protestant (i.e. Church of England's) cause will never suffer at that Tribunal of the Primitive Church, or Apostolicall Tradition, sufficiently testified to be such; ... that Grotius saith ...'[17] He acknowledges his debt to Chrysostom and Grotius,[18] but also to James Ussher who was doing a similar job between 1650–4 in his *Annales Veteris et Novi Testamenti.*[19] His biblical scholarship admits of the 'use of ordinary means', in the study and the interpretation of Holy Scripture, which includes 'the use of learning, study, meditation, rational inference, collation of places, consulting of the original languages, and ancient copies, and expositions of the Fathers of the Church'.[20] A Postcript in the Preface points out that pretensions to a divine illumination or an introspective illuminism which is given precedence over such 'ordinary means', is a pretension and leads to the superseding of the 'written canon' undermining not only historicity and reason but also the implications of the visible church. 'The understanding of the word of God contain'd in the Scripture, is no work of extraordinary illumination, but must be attained by the same means, or the like, by which other writings of men are expounded, and no otherwise.'[21] This predates the emergence of biblical criticism but illustrates the path by which it progressed.

His understanding of the authoritative foundation

The battle which Hammond and his circle had to fight centred around two main issues, Episcopacy and the Book of Common Prayer. Defending episcopacy involved not only a close scrutiny of the biblical evidence but also a detailed examination of the practice and teaching of the early church. Similarly, an apologia for the Book of Common Prayer and the doctrines in it would also involve that third strand in the theological method of Hammond, the use of antiquity. It is for him a criterion of history and part of the wider dependence on 'antiquity, or Scripture, or rational deductions from either'[22] which constitutes the whole Anglican theological approach.[23] John Fell describes Hammond as '... learned in school divinity, and a master in church antiquity, perfect and ready in the sense of the fathers, councils, ecclesiastical historians and liturgies ...'[24] He points out that Hammond took a course of reading quite different from that which was most usual, 'conceiving it most reasonable to search for primitive truth in the primitive writers, and not to suffer his understanding to be prepossessed by the contrived and interested schemes of modern, and with all obnoxious authors'.[25] The use of antiquity is integral to Hammond's whole theological approach. However, it is not devoid of liberality, and his understanding of fundamentals that the *foundation* or *depositum fidei* is to be found in Scripture or the Creeds of the universal Church,[26] finds agreement not only with Laud, but also with William Chillingworth of the Tew circle.

> ... it is the affirmation of the first writers of the Church, as frequently appears in Tertullian, Irenaeus, &c., and there is no reason of doubt of the truth of it, that all those articles which were thought fit to be laid as the foundation of Christian life, were by them distinctly delivered; and this being a matter of fact,

of which – as of the canon of Scripture, or of this or that book in it, – only the records and stories of the first times are competent judges, that Creed which is delivered down to us by the ancient Churches thus planted, I mean those of the first three hundred years, and by them entitled to the name 'the Apostles', and expounded in the homilies of the fathers, some extant, others mentioned by Rufinus, *illustrious tractors* which had gone before him in that work, is in all reason to be deemed the sum of that foundation.[27]

In affirming the catholicity of a reformed catholicism that protested against papal supremacy as the criterion of being catholic, it was necessary to affirm what is fundamental and basic. This Hammond identifies in *Of Fundamentals*, as that which is contained in Scripture, or in that which is derived and deduced from Scripture, 'the creeds or confessions of the universal Church'.[28] There is a 'deposit' or 'foundation', that which was handed on, the *paradosis* or 'the faith once for all delivered'. There is a consensus of agreement among the Fathers that this 'foundation' is that which has been handed on to them. Hammond quotes St Theophylact: 'the faith is ... the foundation', and St Augustine: 'this is the faith which being comprised in few words is in the creed delivered'.[29] That this is consistent with the New Testament Hammond has no doubt, quoting St Paul that 'other foundation can no man lay than that is laid, which is Jesus Christ,'[30] which 'foundation' Hammond identifies as the contents of the Apostles' Creed. This credal foundation is what is expounded in the homilies of the Fathers.

> Having viewed the Apostles' Creed, and of it premised this one thing, that it was a complete catalogue of all that they, being directed by the Holy Ghost in their ministry, thought fit, to lay the foundation of Christian obedience in every Church, and consequently that there was no more in their opinion necessary in order to this end of working reformation in the world.[31]

What Hammond is really identifying is the 'rule of faith', which is identified with the Creeds, but is not a separate and independent authority from Scripture, and is identical in its contents with the contents of the Bible and open to proof from the Bible. This is consistent with Laud's understanding when he asserts that 'the Fathers make the Creed the rule of faith'.[32] The approach is not peculiar to Hammond, because with Laud, as McAdoo points out, the approach is similar with a correspondence of ideas in questions on the surface. Their agreement results from a common method. Basic to it is a deep-seated conviction about the nature of fundamentals. So Laud quotes Chillingworth stressing that 'the creed contains all necessary points of belief', noting that it was so regarded 'upon the authority of the ancient Church, and written tradition, which ... gave this constant testimony unto it'.[33] The transmission of such an authoritative foundation Hammond envisages by way of apostolical writings and apostolical traditions, and the test of their authenticity must be the Fathers and Councils who form part of that same tradition. The criteria for testing such testimonies must be those in the Vincentian Canon, the marks of universality, (in terms of time this is to be understood as the first and purest ages of the Church), antiquity, and consent. Furthermore, such patristic testimony must be consistent with Scripture,

> the universal consent of the doctors of the first ages, bearing testimony that such a doctrine was from the apostles' preachings delivered to all churches by them planted, or their general conform testimony herein, without any considerable dissenters producible, is, I acknowledge ... authentic or worthy of belief, and so hath been made use of by the orthodox of all time as sufficient for the rejecting of any new doctrine. [34]

This for Hammond, and indeed for Anglicanism, is the authoritative foundation, which excludes for him any solifidian or fiduciary ideas, because they preclude the freedom of the human will. Response and obedience to that authoritative foundation finds expression in the visible church through its sacramental life, preaching of the Word, catechizing and Confirmation, in short through liturgical involvement which has always been the universal practice of the Church.

Episcopacy

For Hammond, the test of true doctrine in any debate was by way of appeal to that which was the source of apostolical, original doctrine and tradition, and to the trustworthy and competent testifiers in such doctrine, councils and Fathers universally received or other testimony truly universal. The defence of episcopacy fell to the Laudian party and particularly to Hammond, and the establishment of the authenticity of the Ignatian Epistles was the most significant contribution. Ignatius regarded episcopacy as the best safeguard of the unity of the Church, and without the bishop's authority the Eucharist could not be celebrated. If it could be proved that the authority of Ignatius's support for episcopacy was genuine, a severe blow would be dealt to those opposed to bishops. The works of outstanding critical scholarship which authenticated these epistles were produced by James Ussher, Archbishop of Armagh, who in 1644 published *Polycarpi et Ignatii Epistolae*. In 1646 Isaak Voss, a classicist and ecclesiastical historian, a friend of Grotius and professor at Leyden, edited the corresponding Greek text which Ussher had traced to a manuscript in the Medicean Library at Florence. This not only completed the critical analysis of the Ignatian letters, but also produced the strongest evidence for episcopacy in the early church.

In 1647 Hammond published *Of The Power of the Keyes; or Of Binding and Loosing,* in which he examines the evidence of Scripture and the Fathers for evidence concerning the nature of church government. There is a detailed examination of the support given by the Fathers to the Order of bishops, and a special appeal to the Ignatian letters. With Ussher and Voss he argues for the authenticity of the Ignatian Epistles and their support of episcopacy as a distinct Order in the Church. His *Dissertationes Quatuor* was published in 1651 in response to the attacks of Salmasius and Blondel, being four dissertations prefaced by a fifth. Here he asserts the episcopal ordination of presbyters and deacons and in the second dissertation defends the Ignatian epistles. The third and fourth examine the scriptural evidence for the government of the Church from the Gospels, Acts, and Epistles. A fifth examines the evidence of Clement of Rome and others in the sub-Apostolic age.

> *The Dissertationes Quatuor, quibus Episcopatus Jura ex S. Scripturis et primaeva Antiquitate adstruuntur, contra sententiam D. Blondelli et Aliorem &c.,* ... are a fine example of exact scholarship with detailed biblical and patristic references in an age when Latin was still the medium for international discussion ... The whole discussion is a fine piece of apologetic for the government of the Church by bishops, as established from the seven epistles of Ignatius whose genuineness has been proved by Ussher and Voss. The central argument is then supported from Scripture and from the Fathers.[35]

Dr Anne Whiteman comments that,

> Hammond's comprehensive restatement of a view of episcopacy now commonly held by Anglicans at a time when the need was

so keenly felt to assert the identity of the episcopal Church of England was of incalculable importance both during the Interregnum and at the Restoration.[36]

The Book of Common Prayer

Hammond stood firmly opposed to Parliament's attempt to replace the Book of Common Prayer with a *Directory of Worship*, and his stance was grounded on fundamental theological principles. The aim of the *Directory* was to replace the rites and ceremonies of the Church of England with a way of worship on Presbyterian lines. It contained no set forms of service and no general instructions for the conduct of worship and the King described it as 'a means to open the way, and give liberty to all ignorant, factious or evil men to broach their own fancies and conceits'. Hammond's concern for liturgy is integral to his theological vision because it has a theological function in being a general statement of belief. Hence the Book of Common Prayer is a general statement of the Anglican position and to abolish it would effectively obliterate Anglicanism.[37] The theological function of liturgy, indeed its very authority, has always been to act as a boundary to keep out errors, *lex orandi, lex credendi*, so that it must always presuppose creed or catechism. Hammond published his *View of the New Directory* and a *Vindication of the Ancient Liturgy of the Church of England*. He identifies six Extrinsic Forms of Worship that relate to the action, and fourteen Intrinsical or Parts of the Service, which deal with the actual forms of liturgy.[38] He defends each section with Jewish, biblical and patristic evidence, finding support for set forms of liturgy in the liturgies of St Basil, St James and St Chrysostom, the compiler of the *Apostolic Constitutions* and liturgical writers. Chapter Two defends the changes made by the Reformers in the Anglican Liturgy, in that they 'retained nothing but what the Papists received from purer Antiquity', so that there was no justification for the charge of popery. It was Anglicanism's concern for maintaining continuity with antiquity that inspired Casaubon's approval of the Church of England. An interesting point worthy of notice is the comment in a postscript, that his opponents had betrayed their own cause by issuing a book for use on ships which contained a set form of prayer. In the third and concluding chapter he summarizes his argument, making the point that having critically examined the difference between the *Directory* and the Liturgy he has 'demonstrated no-necessity but the plain unreasonableness of the change'.

McAdoo aptly sums up the significance of this Laudian theologian.

> Hammond's work reveals a balanced theological method by which, building on a clear-cut understanding as to what may legitimately be regarded as constituting fundamentals, Scripture and antiquity are held in such a relationship with reason that the claims of authority and freedom hardly trench upon each other.[39]

Lex Orandi, Lex Credendi

It was Hammond's biographer Dr Fell who remarked of him that 'his closet was his library, and that he studied most upon his knees', which could also have been said of Andrewes. As with all these Carolines, the law of prayer has an integral part in establishing the law of belief through a life of devotion soaked in the primitive and medieval tradition of contemplation which gives a richness to their doctrine because it issues from something far deeper than mere reason. This did not depreciate Hammond's concern for reasonableness in his catechetical and apologetic writings, because it was an appeal balanced by the reasonableness of his biblical scholarship which was tested by the tribunal of the primitive church. Such patristic testimony, the authoritative foundation identified as the Apostles' Creed, must be consistent with Scripture, and finds expression in the sacramental and liturgical life of the Church, making continuity and visibility essential marks of authentic church life.

Hammond was the most prominent member of the Laudian party whose continued insistence on the continuity and visibility of the Church of England resulted in many of his contemporaries, as well as the Tractarians in a later age, regarding him as the very embodiment of Anglicanism in the seventeenth century. His massive learning, deep personal devotion, and, in consequence discernment, placed him in a prominent position as architect of the reconstruction of the Anglican Church. Restoration Laudianism, because of Hammond and those around him, was rooted in sound scholarship with a patristic foundation, where the primary appeal was to Scripture tested and interpreted by the undivided primitive church in Creeds and Councils. This led to a renewal of patristic study which identified a kinship between the church in East and West and fostered a desire for closer links with the Orthodox churches of the East. In its struggle with presbyterianism in which episcopacy and the liturgy of the Book of Common Prayer were threatened with extinction, the Church of England emerged with its liturgy intact and the episcopal character of its ministry strengthened.

Notes

1. Anne Whiteman, 'The Church of England Restored', in *From Uniformity to Unity 1662–1962*, edited by Geoffrey Nuttall and Owen Chadwick (SPCK, London, 1962), p. 38.
2. H. R. McAdoo, *The Spirit of Anglicanism* (A & C Black, London, 1965), p. 357.
3. J. W. Packer, *The Transformation of Anglicanism* 1643–1660 (Manchester University Press, 1969), p. 15, citing G. G. Perry, *Life of Henry Hammond* (no date, suggests 1864 in catalogue), p. 3.
4. Henry Hammond, *Works,* vol. ii (*LACT,* Parker, Oxford, 1849), 'A Continuation of the Defence of Hugo Grotius (1656)', p. 93.
5. Hammond, *Works,* vol. ii, 'Of the Reasonableness of the Christian Religion', p. 30.
6. McAdoo, *ibid.* p. 360.
7. Hammond, *Works,* vol. ii, p. 7.
8. *Ibid.* p. 25.
9. *Ibid.* p. 20.
10. *Ibid.* p. 28.
11. *Ibid.* p. 39.
12. *Ibid.* ch. 4, pp. 39–50.
13. *Ibid.* p. 32.
14. McAdoo, *ibid.* p. 361.
15. Hammond, *Works,* 'A Practical Catechism', 16th Edition, (*LACT,* Parker, Oxford, 1847), p. cxxx.
16. G. G. Perry, *Life of Henry Hammond* (SPCK, no date), p. 67.
17. Packer, *ibid,* p. 90, citing Perry, *Life,* Lambeth MS, vii, p. 14, 595, Cod. Wharton.
18. Packer, *ibid,* p. 94 citing Perry, *Life,* Fulman: *Works,* vol. iii, 'A Necessary Advertisement'.
19. *Ibid.*
20. Hammond, *Works,* vol. iv, (*LACT,* Parker, Oxford, 1849), 'Paraphrase and Annotations'.
21. *Ibid.* 'Preface', Postscript paragraph 26.
22. Hammond, *Miscellaneous Works,* vol. ii, (*LACT,* Parker, Oxford, 1849), p. 126.
23. John Fell, 'The Life of Dr H. Hammond', prefixed to *A Practical Catechism,* p. xvii.

24. *Ibid.* p. xx.
25. McAdoo, *ibid.* p. 363.
26. Hammond, 'Of Fundamentals', *Hammond's Miscellaneous Theological Works,* (*LACT,* Parker, Oxford, 1849), p. 98.
27. *Ibid.*
28. *Ibid.* p. 75.
29. *Ibid.* p. 82.
30. *Ibid.* p. 110.
31. *Ibid.*
32. W. Laud, *Conference with Fisher,* edition of C. H. Simkinson (Macmillan, London, 1901), p. 49.
33. McAdoo, pp. 363–4, citing W. Chillingworth, *Religion of Protestants* (1674 edition), ch. 4, p. 152.
34. Hammond, 'Paraenesis', *Miscellaneous Theological Works,* (Parker, Oxford, 1849), Vol. ii, p. 335.
35. Packer, *ibid.* p. 114, citing G. G. Perry's *Life.*
36. Whiteman, *ibid.* p. 46.
37. Hammond, 'A View of the Directory', Preface.
38. Hammond, *Works,* vol. i, pp. 135–6.
39. McAdoo, p. 367.

10

Literature and Laudians

Space precludes detailed analysis of other significant members of
the Laudian circle, but a summary overview of some representatives, their thought and some of the literature they produced is
attempted.

Richard Field (1561–1616)

Richard Field, who took his master's degree at Oxford in 1584, was
appointed to the 'Catechism Lecture', a private lecture which he
made so interesting that he drew hearers from the whole university. He was famous for his knowledge of school divinity and had
the reputation of being one of the best disputants in the university.
Though Field pre-dated the Laudians, the influence of his
published work *Of the Church* cannot be underestimated. The first
four books of this work were published in 1606, the fifth in 1610,
then in 1628 a considerably enlarged second edition was
published. It was directed mainly at the Romanists, those who
would unchurch the Church of England and disclaim her catholicity. His attitude towards the Romanists was more extreme than
Hooker, who was attacked by his opponents for describing the
Church of Rome as 'a part of the house of God, a limb of the visible
Church of Christ'.[1] Field declared that the Church of Rome is 'the
synagogue of Satan, the faction of antichrist, and that Babylon out
of which we must fly, unless we will be partakers of her plagues.'[2]
This affirmed a position from which the Church of England, in its
official statements, had been careful to abstain, so that we would
agree with Hooker rather than Field. Nevertheless, there was a
great friendship between Hooker and Field and, as Field's son
pointed out, there was much agreement in the tenor of their
thought and judgements. Despite Field's extremist attitude

towards Rome his work is a piece of constructive theology and is a permanent contribution to Anglican theology. At a time when the visibility and continuity of Anglicanism was threatened and there was much confusion about the visible and the invisible church, it was destined to have an influence on the Laudian theology of the Church. His definition of the Church is,

> ... the multitude and number of those whom Almighty God severeth from the rest of the world by the work of His grace, and calleth to the participation of eternal happiness, by the knowledge of such supernatural verities as concerning their everlasting good He hath revealed in Christ His Son, and such other and precious and happy means as He hath appointed to further and set forward the work of their salvation.[3]

Field asserts that the visible and the invisible are but two aspects of one and the same Church. The visibility of the Church finds expression in creeds and formularies, ministry and sacraments, and those participating can be properly identified, since those are 'discernible that do communicate therein'. What cannot be discerned are the elect who are known only to God, in the sense that Nathanael was identified by the disciples as an Israelite, but only by Christ as a true Israelite,[4] 'in respect of those most precious effects and happy benefits of saving grace wherein only the elect do communicate'. The Church is distinguished by three permanent marks or notes.

> First, the entire profession of those supernatural verities which God hath revealed in Christ His Son; Secondly, the use of such holy ceremonies and Sacraments as He hath instituted and appointed to serve as provocations to godliness, preservations from sin, memorials of the benefits of Christ, warrants for the greater security of our belief, and marks of distinction to separate His Own from strangers; Thirdly, an union or connexion of men in this profession and use of these Sacraments under lawful pastors and guides, appointed, authorized, and sanctified, to direct and lead them in the happy ways of eternal salvation ... these are Notes of the Church ... and they are essential, and such things as give being to the Church, and therefore are in nature more clear and evident, and such as that from them the perfect knowledge of the Church may and must be derived.[5]

On the question of apostolical succession, Field claims the need for more than a mere succession of persons; such a succession of bishops must also hold 'the faith their predecessors did'. This is entirely patristic in principle, that '... truth of doctrine is a necessary note whereby the Church must be known and discerned, and not ministry or succession, or anything else without it'. For the faith the Fathers defended was not something peculiar to themselves, but something they had all received and shared with each other. Field's sole work breathes the spirit of antiquity in the writings of which he is well versed. The 'power of ordination'[6] is invested in 'bishops alone': in the ordination of presbyters, other presbyters join with the bishop in the laying on of hands, but without the bishop this cannot be done. According to the 'old canons, all ordinations made otherwise are pronounced void'; while bishops and presbyters share the same power of order, he claims that in extreme cases, such as episcopal apostasy in a church or country, the presbyters remaining catholic may elect their own chief and with him continue to ordain. On the question of ecumenical Councils,[7] Field considers first, their use and necessity; secondly, 'of whom they may consist'; thirdly, 'what assurance they have of divine assistance and direction'; and fourthly, 'who must call them'. In so far as such general Councils were called to address the life and soul of the Christian faith, and 'in respect of the manner and form of their proceeding, and the evidence of proof brought in them', they are to be believed. The first six councils are in this category but he has reservations about the seventh, because it may 'have opened the way unto that gross idolatry which afterwards entered into the church'. He admits that the complete certainty of a General Council cannot be undoubtedly affirmed, nevertheless, 'unless we most certainly know the contrary,' the presumption is so strong that they are to be accepted.[8] He allows 'a primacy of honour and order found in blessed Peter', but not in terms of the papacy.[9] Peter's commission from Christ was not different or greater than that of the other apostles, but was more in terms of 'honourable precedence, pre-eminence and priority' such as one might find in a duke chosen to represent the state amongst the great lords of that state, but unable to do anything without the consent of the others. Peter received the keys, not for himself, but as chief of the company of the apostles, 'receiving for himself in the first place that which in him was intended to them all'. 'This primacy and honour found in blessed Peter ... is the original of all that superiority that metropolitans have over bishops of their provinces, and primates and patriarchs over metropolitans, and, in a word, of all that order that is in the Church, and amongst her guides, whereby unity is preserved'.

He discusses degees of infallibility in the church. 'If we speak of the Church, as it comprehendeth the whole number of believers that are and have been since Christ appeared in the flesh, it is absolutely free from all error and ignorance of divine things that are to be known by revelation, *Quid enim latuit Petrum, &c.*' Not only is the whole church in this sense 'freed from error in matters of faith', in such matters 'we think it impossible also that any error whatsoever should be found in all the pastors and guides of the Church thus generally taken'.[10] However, all might be deceived 'in things that cannot be clearly deduced from the rule of faith and word of divine and heavenly truth'. Baptism[11] is 'the ordinary and set means of salvation ... so that no man carelessly neglecting, or wilfully comtemning it, can be saved ...' He goes on to say that the Fathers teach that if people have been excluded from Baptism by 'inevitable impossibility', they may be saved without it, 'faith and the inward conversion of the heart flying unto God in Christ, through the gracious instinct and sweet motion of the sanctifying Spirit, may be reckoned a kind of baptism: because thereby they obtain all that which should have been sought in the baptism of water.' He also affirms with the Fathers that martyrdom is 'fitly named baptism'. Baptism, the means of salvation, is the beginning of the justified and sanctified life, the root of the life of faith, hope and love, while in the Eucharist[12] the elements of bread and wine after consecration are no mere 'naked figure or similitude only' but 'consisteth of two things, the one earthly, and the other heavenly; and that the body of Christ is truly present in the sacrament and communicated to us ...' in a sacrificial commemoration of Christ's passion and death.

John Bramhall (1594–1663)

It is not surprising that when the continuity and visibility of the Church was threatened, Field's handling of the appeal to antiquity should commend itself to John Bramhall. Not only was Field's influence strong, but so too was that of Andrewes and Hammond, and the tradition of Hooker in which Bramhall stood, behind which was Aquinas. It was Samuel Ward, the Master of Sidney Sussex College, Cambridge, who first turned Bramhall's attention in the direction of antiquity. He told him that it was impossible

that the present controversies of the Church should be rightly determined or reconciled without a deep insight into the doctrine of the primitive fathers, and a competent skill in school

theology. The first affordeth us a right pattern, and the second
smootheth it over, and planeth away the knots.[13]

The nature of the task confronting him takes the form of responses
or vindications. He wrote his *Just Vindication of the Church of England*,
in response to the charge of being in criminal schism; *An Answer to
de la Milletière* was written in answer to a letter to the King by de la
Milletière inviting him to become a Roman Catholic. Other literary
responses coming from Bramhall included *A Replication to the Bishop
of Chalcedon's Survey, Schism Guarded, The Consecration of Protestant
Bishops Vindicated, A Fair Warning to take heed of the Scottish Discipline*,
and *A Vindication from the Presbyterian charge of Popery*. McAdoo
comments that 'In his writings he is not simply meeting issues as
they are raised but rather confronting them from a stable and
coherent standpoint. His approach is a positive and constructive
application of Scripture, antiquity and reason.'[14]

Bramhall's position is consistent throughout his writings and its
criterion is antiquity linked with continuity. In his *Just Vindication*,
he makes the point that the Britannic church is more ancient than
the Roman, using in his argument the medieval legend that it was
planted by Joseph of Arimathea in Tiberius Caesar's reign (AD
14–41) whereas St Peter did not establish the Roman Church until
the second year of Claudius (AD 41–54). Aside from the truth or
falsity of the legend, the point he is making is that from the beginning the Britannic church was free from papal jurisdiction, and
therefore the Catholic Church has gone on continuously from the
time of the apostles and continues as the Church of England while
the Roman church is in schism. For the sake of the unity of the
Church Bramhall defines what he would accept,

> ... if the Bishop of Rome were reduced from his universality of
> sovereign jurisdiction *jure Divino*, to his *"principium unitatis"*, and
> his Court regulated by the Canons of the Fathers, which was the
> sense of the Councils of Constance and Basle, and is desired by
> many Roman Catholics as well as we: secondly, if the creed or
> necessary points of faith were reduced to what they were in the
> time of the four first Oecumenical Councils, according to the
> decree of the third general Council (who dare say that the faith
> of the primitive Fathers was insufficient?), admitting no addi-
> tional articles, but only necessary explications; and those to be
> made by the authority of a general Council ... and lastly,[15]

he wishes things which cause offence to be removed. The same is
summarized in *Schism Guarded*, 'to reduce the present Papacy to

the primitive form, the essentials of faith to the primitive creed, and public and private devotions to the primitive liturgies.'

In his funeral oration Jeremy Taylor describes Bramhall's apologia for the Church of England as demonstrating 'that the Church of England only returned to her primitive purity, that she joined with Christ and his Apostles, and that she agreed in all the sentiments of the primitive Church'.[16] He goes on to say that 'in him were visible the great lines of Hooker's judiciousness, of Jewel's learning, of the acuteness of bishop Andrewes.' As in Hammond, so in Bramhall there is that which is fundamental, the authoritative foundation; the 'ground for unity of faith is the creed; and unity of government, the same form of discipline which was used in the Primitive Church, and is derived from them to us'.[17] That foundation is 'the authority of the primitive Fathers and the General Councils, which are the representative body of the universal Church.'[18] or again, 'the old faith of the whole Christian world, that is the creed of the apostles, explicated by the Nicene, Constantinopolitan, Ephesine, and Chalcedonian Fathers.'[19] 'We retain whatsoever the primitive Fathers judged to be necessary, or the Catholic Church of this present age doth unanimously retain ... We know no other necessary articles of faith but those which are comprehended in the Apostles' Creed.'[20]

For Bramhall therefore catholicity means the keeping together of this authoritative foundation and continuity, which implies the acceptance of the authority of the universal Church and its representative a General Council, the maintenance of communion, and avoiding change without lawful authority on sufficient grounds. Continuity in an uninterrupted line of apostolic succession is integral to it, as are the acceptance of Scripture and the unanimous and universal practice of the Church. Like other Laudians he was pro-catholic but anti-papal, and his identification of Anglicanism with the catholic doctrine of the Primitive Church brought the charge of popery from Puritans and Presbyterians who were unable to distinguish between the primitive and the papal. By 'catholic' he meant the doctrine enshrined in the Creeds as the fundamentals of primitive doctrine, and continuity with the primitive church not only in sucession but also doctrine with the appeal to scripture and antiquity. One of the principal motives for rejection of the papacy was the Church of Rome's departure from 'the constant Tradition of the primitive church'. Yet his concern for the unity of the Church enabled him to propose such a primitive doctrinal basis for such union, a point of contemporary relevance for today's ecumenical movement. Bramhall also embodies that liberality of outlook on secondary questions that one finds in the Carolines.

> Bramhall's writings furnish an instance of the combination of the appeal to Scripture and the appeal to antiquity with the liberal approach to other matters, an approach which stems as much from an attitude to reason and the reality of freedom as it does from the conviction that only fundamentals are authoritative.[21]

Herbert Thorndike (1598–1672)

The Church of England in the seventeenth century in the opinion of Herbert Thorndike, was fighting for the preservation of two things it believed necessary to the life of the Church: the episcopate and the liturgy.[22] To this end his first publication in 1641, *Of the Government of Churches,* enlarged into a new edition in 1649 as *The Primitive Government of Churches* , was concerned to expound the patristic understanding of episcopacy. A liturgical work, *Of Religious Assemblies and the Publick Service of God,* first published in 1642, was also reissued in a new edition, and enlarged with a Review in 1649 as *The Service of God.* The latter appeared because of the prescribed use of the *Directory.*

His principal work, *Epilogue to the Tragedy of the Church of England,* was published in 1659. His fundamental point is that the Reformation, as a durable settlement, would only work on the basis of a return to the discipline and teaching of the primitive catholic church. It is a clear and unhesitating exposition of the doctrine espoused by the Laudians, not something peculiar to them, but that which had been received, inherited from the Reformation and their historical ancestry. His principle was the appeal to Scripture as interpreted by the primitive church.

> Whatsoever then is said of the Rule of Faith in the writings of the Fathers is to be understood of the Creed; ... I would not have any hereupon to think that the matter of this rule is not, in my conceit, contained in the Scriptures. For I find St. Cyril (*Catech.* v.) protesting, that it contains nothing but that which concerned our salvation, selected out of the Scriptures ... And to the same effect, Eucherius, Paschasius, and after them Thomas Aquinas, all agree that the form of the Creed was made up out of the Scriptures, giving such reasons as no reasonable Christian can

refuse; ... I will think I give sufficient reason why God should provide Tradition as well as Scripture to bound the sense of it ... For I beseech you what had they, whosoever they were that first framed the Creed, but Tradition, whereby to distinguish that which is substantial from that which is not?[23]

He claims Origen's support for his exposition of Tradition from the preface to *De Principiis* and the Vincentian Canon. Outside of this there was no compromise possible for churchmen. His work was written in Latin in order to secure a wider circulation, though he did not include either the Roman Church or the continental Protestants in his plan of reunion. His chief aim was to define the patristic integrity of Anglicanism as the basis of a non-papal catholicism, that *peculiar character* which distinguishes her from every other reformed communion. To this visible catholic church so defined he professed an allegiance to which his duty to the Church of England itself was subordinate. In *Just Weights and Measures* (1662), Thorndike maintains that the standard of the primitive church is that by which all change must be measured in its concern for visible unity. The arguments of the *Epilogue*, and treatises on the same subject, were refined and recast in more methodical and finished form in 1670 in the first part of *De Ratione ac Jure finiendi Controversias Ecclesiae Disputatio*.

In 1661 he was appointed to assist at the Savoy Conference, and as a member of Convocation he took a leading part in the revision of the Prayer Book. He saw the Eucharist as central to the Church's life, in which is to be found the whole content of the Christian religion. Not only is it the centre, the crown of the liturgy, but on it the liturgy depends for its true functioning. Newman regarded Thorndike as the only writer of any authority in the English church who held the true catholic theory of the Eucharist. In arguing for the Real Presence in the Eucharistic elements but rejecting the theories of Transubstantiation, Zwinglianism, Calvinism, and Lutheranism, he maintains in a long and elaborate argument that the consecration of the elements is effected, not by the recital of the words, *This is My body, This is My blood*, but by the use of prayer. This is scriptural, because when our Lord had said these words he had already by actions of blessing and thanksgiving made the elements to be his body and blood. He supports this with the evidence of the ancient liturgies and Fathers who agree that prayer is the means of consecration.[24]

In his unpublished D.Phil. thesis (Oxford 1990),[25] Dr Charles Miller Jr discusses the principles of Thorndike's theological method as he expounds them in the first six chapters of his *Principles of Christian Truth*. The 'truth' for which Thorndike is searching is an understanding of the credal profession of the one catholic and apostolic Church. He is committed to a rational theological exercise in the tradition of Aquinas and Hooker, in which reason is applied to the content of the divine revelation in Scripture, and tradition becomes a reasonable aid in the search for scriptural truth. In Thorndike's own words, 'there will be no cause why the tradition of the Church should not be joined with the Scripture, in deciding the controversies of faith ... to clear and determine the sense of Scripture.' Miller goes on to say, 'This is the theological basis upon which his appeal to history and the fathers, such distinctive features of his writings, is based'.[26] Such an appeal to an interpretative church tradition must not be allowed to inhibit his foundational appeal to reason.

John Pearson (1613–86)

The remarkable achievement of the schoolboy Pearson is that he had read many of the Greek and Latin Fathers before leaving school. It is not surprising that among his generation he could be described as 'the ablest scholar and systematic theologian'. 'Burnet describes him "in all respects the greatest divine of the age", Menage "le plus savant des Anglais", and Bentley writes of "the most excellent Bishop Pearson, the very dust of whose writings is gold".'[27] Archdeacon Cheetham claimed that,

> Probably no other Englishman, few of any nation, had the same accurate knowledge of antiquity which Pearson possessed, and the same power of using it with skill and judgement ... No English theologian has less claim to originality or imagination; he proceeds always upon authorities, and his distinctive skill is in the discrimination and use of authorities.[28]

His two greatest works, on which his reputation rests, is his *Exposition of the Creed* (1659), and *Vindiciae Epistolarum S. Ignatii*, the latter of which is discussed in Chapter 11 on the Ignatian Controversy. A quotation from the dedication to his *Exposition* will illustrate his theological approach; 'in Christianity there can be no concerning truth which is not ancient; and whatsoever is truly new, is certainly false'. There is a resistance to novelty and innovation in doctrine. Pearson's concern is to expound 'the first faith' and nowhere can there be 'a more probable guide than the Creed, received in all ages of the Church' for it brings us to that in which the Rule of Faith was conceived, 'the Scriptures from whence it was at first deduced'.

His work has remained a standard book in English divinity. Henry Hallam, the eminent historian and critic, said of it that 'It expands beyond the literal purport of the Creed itself to most articles of orthodox belief, and is a valuable summary of arguments and authorities on that side. The closeness of Pearson and his judicious selection of proofs distinguish him from many, especially the earlier, theologians'.[29] The work emerged from a series of addresses he preached at St Clement's Eastcheap, and the resulting exposition has been described, within its limits, as the most perfect and complete production of English dogmatic theology. The notes within the *Exposition* are a rich quarry of patristic and general learning, providing a rich *catena* of the best authorities on doctrinal points. Numerous editions of the work were published until the nineteenth century. Like Peter Gunning (1614–84), he was well read in the Fathers and Councils, and his purpose is to illustrate the consonance between Creed and Scripture from such sources, 'so my design aimeth at nothing else but that the Primitive Faith may be revived'.

Darwell Stone points out that a complete impression of his thought and methods can be formed only by comparing the *Exposition*, written for ordinary readers, with the *Minor Works* written for scholars. While he sees the most valuable part of the *Exposition* in the noted quotations from the Fathers, it expresses a clear grasp on the truths concerning the being of God, the Holy Trinity, and the Incarnation. Stone's qualified criticisms are that he omits a sufficient treatment of any other than the intellectual elements of faith, his emphasis on a supposed time-scale for creation, his ignoring of the intermediate state and his apparent view that the material particles of our present bodies will be restored and reunited in the resurrection, and finally that the extent to which he associates local movements 'through all the regions of the air, through all the celestial orbs' with the Ascension of our Lord. Nevertheless, despite the qualifications, '. . . it remains a splendid example of strong and solid treatment of fundamental theology and a permanently valuable exposition of orthodox belief'.[30]

John Cosin (1594–1672)

John Cosin became a member of the Laudians through Bishop
Neile of Durham, in whose London residence, Durham House,
they met. On his son's defection to Rome a correspondence with
the French Roman Catholics revealed the shaping of his thought.
He views the Church of England as catholic and protestant, and
draws a distinction between the catholicism of antiquity and that of
Trent. In exile he produced three large-scale works of polemical
scholarship: a series of letters on the *Validity of Anglican Orders,*
Historia Transubstantiationis Papalis (1656), *and A Scholastical History*
of the Canon of Holy Scripture (1657). Geoffrey Cuming points out
that today Cosin's reputation rests chiefly on his liturgical work,
'but these writings reveal him as a very learned patristic scholar ...
the approach is historical rather than doctrinal, the appeal to
antiquity rather than to unaided reason'.[31] At the Savoy
Conference in 1661, Richard Baxter 'commends him for his excellent memory for canons, Councils and the fathers ...'[32]

> He was almost without a rival in any age for acquaintance with
> Liturgical lore, the decrees of Councils, and Patristic teaching.
> In his early days he had sat at the feet of Andrewes and Overall
> (he owed so much to Overall that he used to designate him his
> 'lord and master'). He became his librarian in 1616 and after-
> wards, when Chaplain to the Bishop of the See to which he
> succeeded, he drank in the opinions of Laud and other like-
> minded divines, for Durham House in London was the centre of
> high Ecclesiastical society.[33]

Luckock comments that the Presbyterians must have felt somewhat
dismayed when he joined their opponents at the Savoy
Conference, for while of generous temper 'he stood firm and
unbending to the principles for which he had suffered'. These
principles Cosin set out in a letter to the Countess of Peterborough
which he sets out in two sections: first, the differences between
Roman Catholics and the Church of England, and then second,
points of agreement which Anglicans profess and are ready to
embrace, 'if Roman Catholics would be as ready to accord with us
in the same'. He summarizes each section in fourteen points that
give a general overview of the main tenets of Caroline theology,
allowing that some individuals might differ in certain particulars.[34]

Cosin's *Works* were published in five volumes in the Library of
Anglo-Catholic Theology 1843–55. When Dean of Peterborough in
1652, Cosin published *The Catholic Religion of the Realm of England,*

Primitive, Pure, Purged. This treatise is in volume iv. The first chapter, reprinted here, is entitled 'The Perpetual Standard of Religion' and is reminiscent of the theological base of Lancelot Andrewes.

> To us in the Church of England the perpetual standard of our Religion and our Faith is this:
> One Canon of Scripture delivered by God in two Testaments.
> For in those truths which manifestly rest on Holy Scripture
> are contained all things that regard faith and morals.
> After them our authentic Instruments are these:
> The Three Creeds.
> The Four Councils.
> The First Five Centuries, and throughout them the succession and consent of the Catholic Fathers.
> For in them is discovered and set forth that early Faith once for all delivered to the Saints,—primitive, pure, and purged from defilement, apart from human corruptions and later accretions.
> Further, such Theology in succeeding centuries as is not at variance with this earliest Theology.

Jeremy Taylor (1613–1667)

As a theologian, moral theologian and writer of devotional works, Jeremy Taylor was erudite and expert in the patristic tradition, but had a sharp independence of mind that contained a quality of liberality. Taylor's Anglicanism was rooted in the Scriptures as well as the faith and practice of the primitive church, and this determined his theological method which was rooted in Scripture, antiquity and reason. Like his fellow Laudians he had a sense of the visibility and continuity of the Church as well as a profound knowledge and love of the Fathers. His use of the Fathers was not credulous but critical, an understanding and grasp of that patristic sense of tradition that sees it as nothing less than an expression of the Scriptural mind.

> That the Scripture is a full and sufficient rule to Christians in faith and manners, a full and perfect declaration of the Will of God, is therefore certain, because we have no other. For if we consider the grounds upon which all Christians believe the Scriptures to be the Word of God, the same grounds prove that nothing else is. These indeed have a testimony that is credible as

any that makes faith to men, the universal testimony of all
Christians; in respect of which St. Austin said *Evangelio non cred-
erem, etc.* 'I should not believe the Gospel if the authority of the
Church' (that is of the Universal Church) 'did not move me.'[35]

In the first chapter of Part I of the *Dissuasive,* he shows that the
faith of the Church of England is Catholic, Apostolic and Primitive,
whereas, because the Roman church has added new articles and
introduced innovations, she cannot make this claim in these
instances. The Scriptures, the Creeds, the Four General Councils
and 'that which is agreeable to the Old and New Testament and
collected out of the same by the ancient fathers and catholic
bishops of the church' are the foundation upon which the Church
of England rests. This was and is the faith of the primitive church.
He then elaborates on this in relation to what the Church of
England rejected in the Roman innovations and where she stands
vis-à-vis antiquity in relation to them. The Second Part was written
in response to the criticisms of the Roman apologist John Serjeant
and an anonymous critic A.L., both of whom attacked Part I.

In *Episcopacy Asserted* (1642) he contributed to the debate
concerning the government of the Church by bishops, arguing
from Scripture and the Fathers for its divine institution. As with all
the Carolines the aim of the appeal to antiquity was to establish
identity of doctrine with the primitive church, and not the establishing of tradition and the writings of the Fathers as a separate and
independent source of received doctrine. In the *Liberty of
Prophesying* he emphasizes that no new truth can be added to the
Creed because Christ and the Apostles proclaimed all things necessary to salvation, and these truths are enshrined in the Apostles'
Creed. Deductions can be made from the Creed but cannot be
made articles of faith.[36] The foundation of the Church is Christ
and is therefore unchangeable, and since the faith was not evolved
by but committed to, the Church, the Church cannot enlarge it.
The function of the Church is to bear witness to, and make 'more
evident', the faith once and for all time delivered to the saints. This
is not inconsistent with the guidance of the Holy Spirit in the
Church, for the Spirit's task is that of guiding the Church to interpret unchanging truths in terms of the thought and life which
prevail at any given time. Only in this way can the faith become
intelligible and convincing. Again we return to the important
premise of Caroline theology, that which is fundamental,
Hammond's authoritative foundation which must remain
constant, and that which is secondary. For Taylor that rule of faith

is the Apostles' Creed, and while he accepts the Council of Nicaea, he regrets its extension to the Creed. He sums up his position with a quotation from Tertullian:

> This symbol is the one sufficient, immoveable, unalterable, and unchangeable rule of faith, that admits no increment or decrement; but if the integrity and unity of this be preserved, in all other things men may take a liberty of enlarging their knowledges and prophesyings, according as they are assisted by the grace of God.[37]

Nevertheless, in his discussion of the general features of Taylor's theology in *The Eucharistic Theology of Jeremy Taylor Today*, McAdoo can write,

> ... he is no modernist, subordinating tradition to harmonise it with current concepts and fashions. Yet there is in his thought, and frequently expressed, *a certain quality which is congenial with the way we think nowadays* [McAdoo's italics] and which makes us feel, for a passing moment, that somehow Jeremy Taylor is our contemporary too.[38]

William Beveridge (1638–1708)

This account would be incomplete without the mention of a number of eminent patristic scholars whose work made a major contribution to the continuing presence of the patristic mind within Anglicanism. William Beveridge, though not included in Bosher's list of Laudians, stands in the High Church tradition despite his Calvinistic views on predestination.[39] However, in the Preface to his *Works* the Editor claims '... his mind was too essentially practical to entertain Calvinistic opinions'.[40] He also tells us that

> ... the circumstances of Beveridge's early years would either involve him in the confusion and disputes of those troubled times, or they would throw him, as in fact they did, for direction, and guidance, and comfort, amidst these confusions and disputes, on the earlier and better ages of the Church, and on the study of Ecclesiastical Antiquity, yet ever with a view to the elucidation of fundamental truth, and the promotion of practical piety.[41]

His first published work at the age of twenty was a treatise on the

Importance and the use of the Oriental Languages, especially Hebrew, Chaldee, Syriac, Arabic, and Samaritan, together with a Syriac Grammar (1658). On the next page the same Preface speaks of a '... coincidence in the lives and pursuits and writings of Bishop Beveridge ... with that of William Cave', another giant in the patristic field at this time, in birth, locality, education, and then later as parish priests, but also in their scholarship and writings.

   Two great works by which he is best known are the Συνοδικόν, *sive Pandectae Canonum SS. Apostolorum at Conciliorum, necnon Canonicarum SS. Patrum Epistolarum cum Scoliis* (Oxford, 1672) and *the Codex Canonum Eccl. Primitivae Vindicatus, ac Illustratus.* (1679), which are connected with the canon law of the early church which is still followed by the Eastern Orthodox churches. It is a collection of the apostolic canons and decrees of the councils received by the Greek church together with the canonical epistles of the Fathers. It is not only the production of accurate text, but the claiming of apostolic origin and sanction for what were long post-apostolic. These works include an exposition of primitive doctrine and practice as defined in these source documents and seen to be consistent with the claims of the Church of England in its appeal to antiquity. They are quoted by the nineteenth-century author William Andrew Hammond in his *The Definitions of Faith and Canons of Discipline of the Six Oecumenical Councils, with the Remaining Canons of the Code of the Universal Church,* added to which are *The Apostolical Canons* (Oxford, 1843) and Hammond points out that the translation of these canons is made from the copy in Beveridge's *Synodicon.* Almost all the notes he has added on the canons are from Beveridge's *Annotations,* but there are a good number from Bingham's *Antiquities of the Christian Church,* and they come at the end of each series of translations.

   Beveridge earned for himself the title of 'The Great Reviver and Restorer of Primitive Piety', for the spirit of this divine is pastoral, not purely academic. This is evidenced in his works of practical divinity, his preaching and catechizing, the aim of which is the recalling of the Church of England to conformity with the primitive doctrine and models she claims as her authoritative foundation. His sermon on 'The Exemplary Holiness of the Primitive Christians' is the best example in his preaching. Pointing out that it is not sufficient to be baptized, but, in the words of his text, it is necessary to continue 'steadfastly in the Apostles' Doctrine and Fellowship, and in the Breaking of Bread, and in the Prayers',[42] the first and great thing that Christians in all ages ought to be steadfast in, is the doctrine which Christ and his Apostles taught. He points out that the Church of England requires nothing to be believed but what the Apostles taught as expressed now in the New Testament,

> ... and what the Church of Christ in all ages hath believed to be consonant to the doctrine delivered in their writings ... the surest way is to keep close to the doctrine of our Church, contained in our Articles and Common Prayer Book, which is plainly the same with that of the Apostles in all points.[43]

The second section points out the need for continuing in fellowship and communion, 'not only receiving and believing the doctrine ... but likewise observing the rules and orders which they appointed, and using all the means of grace and Salvation as administered by them, and such as were deputed by them in the Name of Christ to do it'.[44] The third section points out that the purpose of this communion and fellowship is for the celebration of the Eucharist, and is critical of those who laid more emphasis on the sermon. A fourth section stresses the need of coming together for 'the public prayers of the Church.'

> In short, I know nothing that can contribute more effectually to keep up a due sense of God, and the true Christian religion in any place, than frequent Communions and daily prayers. This was the way wherein the Saints of God walked in the Apostles' days.[45]

In commending such principles of Christian devotion and life as necessary for our salvation, there is certainly no trace of Calvinistic predestination.

He returns to these themes in *The Great Necessity of Public Prayer and Frequent Communion*, and the same spirit breathes in his *Catechism*, seeing Anglicanism declaring its primitive and catholic character in the ordering of daily services and frequent communions, and a vigorous discipline in awakening her members to a higher and livelier estimation of the ministration and ordinances of the Church. It is not surprising that he opposed the proposal of the *Directory of Worship*.

A work of great weight is his *Ecclesia Anglicana Ecclesia Catholica*,[46] and is a discourse on the Thirty-Nine Articles, expounding the doctrine of the Church of England as consonant with Scripture, Reason, and the Fathers. In the 'Preface to the Reader',[47] Beveridge tells us that his method

> ... was first to shew that each article for the sum and substance

of it is grounded upon the Scriptures, so that of it be not expressly contained in them, howsoever it may by good and undeniable consequence be deduced from them. Having shewn it to be grounded upon the scriptures, I usually prove it to be consonant to right reason too, even such a truth, that though scripture did not, reason itself would command us to believe it. And lastly, for the further confirmation of it, I still shew each article to be believed and acknowledged by the Fathers of the primitive church, that so we may see how though in many things we differ from others and from the present church of Rome, yet we recede not in anything from the primitive and more unspotted church of Christ. These are the three heads I ordinarily insist upon ...

He then goes on to cite Augustine's authority for the basis of his method, keeping in his mind that Father's words, 'No sober man will think or hold an opinion against reason, no Christian against the scripture, and no lover of peace against the church'.[48] Already it has been acknowledged that Cary's *Testimonies of the Fathers* (1835) cites this work as a source.

In a discussion of authority under '"Confessional" formularies',[49] Dr Gillian Evans cites Beveridge's *Ecclesia Anglicana* in relation to autonomy in a church's authority.

William Beveridge (1637–1708) picks out 'two things' as belonging in some autonomously deteminable way to a Church's authority: 'the decreeing of ceremonies' and 'the determining of controversies'. The matter is further compounded by the legitimate existence both of traditions which are 'customs of the Church produced by the frequent and long-continued usage of the great part of the community' and which are rightly precious to that group of Christians; and also traditions of the Church universal, that is, of the whole community over time. So long as it is without prejudice to theological consensus, there must be room for variety in practice. The difficulty is to define the limits of that variation which must operate if there is not to be a consequent division in matters of faith.

In the 1851 edition of *Against Heresy* by Vincent of Lérins, (Latin and English) there is an extract from Bishop Beveridge included as a preface to the English translation because it forms a suitable introduction to the argument of Vincentius. It is a translation from the Preface to *Codex Canonum Ecclesiae Primitivae vindicatus ac illustratus, Autore Gulielemo Beveregio, Ecclesiae Anglicanae presbytero,*

Lond. (1678). In it William Beveridge elaborates his understanding of catholicity, these fixed and common principles of the *Catholic or Universal Church* in a number of points. First, Holy Scripture is fundamental because from it the rest arises, and all Christians everywhere have agreed that these are inspired writings containing doctrine necessary for every man's salvation. To safeguard the interpretation of Holy Scripture from becoming merely a matter of private opinion and conjecture the need is to have recourse to how the ancient church interpreted them and accepted the consent of Christians in all ages, because the consent of all Christians 'may be deservedly accounted the voice of the Gospel'. Secondly, there are many things not expressly stated in Scripture, but drawn out from it, which have always had the common consent of all Christians. 'For example: "that there are in the ever-blessed Trinity three distinct Persons to be worshipped, the Father, the Son, and the Holy Ghost, and that these are, each of them, truly God, and yet that there is but one God; that Christ is God and man, θεάνθρωπος, truly God, and truly man, in one and the same person."' The doctrine of the Trinity, infant baptism, the commemoration of Sunday as the first day of the week, celebrating Passiontide, Eastertide, Ascensiontide and Pentecost, the government of the Church by bishops distinguished from presbyters, are not explicitly enjoined by Holy Scripture.

> So that there have been, as it were, certain *common notions* from the beginning implanted in the minds of all Christians, not so much from any particular passages of holy Scripture, as from all; from the general scope and tenor of the whole Gospel; from the very nature and purpose of the religion therein established; and finally, from the constant tradition of the Apostles, so to speak, ... For on any other supposition it would be incredible, or even impossible, that they should have been received with so unanimous a consent every where, always, and by all.[50]

On the basis of this Beveridge makes his third point, that more confidence is to be placed in the whole body than in individual Christians, and more in the universal Church than in any particular churches whatsoever because there are many points in which the universal Church, during many ages after that of the Apostles, agreed. Therefore, it is this consent of the universal Church that is the surest interpretation of Holy Scripture on those points on which it has agreed, making those ancient Fathers and other writers of all ages of the Church of great value, because in the prosecution of ecclesiastical controversies the heart of the matter for them is either their own salvation or the peace of the Church.

His fourth point defines that this *consensio* of the universal Church on matters of faith and order is not to be confined to a minority of writers, or one or two passages in a particular writer apart from the rest. It must comprise the greater part of those 'who in all ages of the Church, (and especially the earlier), were the authors of any written works in which they treated on these subjects'. While this *consensio* does not include the opinions of every individual Christian through all the ages, handed down to us, it does contain what amounts to the same effect. For while the laity have never been admitted to deliver their judgement on the doctrine and discipline of the Church, nevertheless by electing their bishops and testifying to those whom they elected, they openly demonstrated consent to their doctrine and discipline. Therefore, whatever the bishop's doctrine and discipline it could be assumed that the people over whom he presided would be in agreement. In consequence, following Vincent of Lérins, the *consensio* of the Church is to be sought not from the people but from their bishops, from the teachers. This very point the universal Church agreed about, in that the laity were never present nor voted when these ecclesiastical matters were discussed, for there is no evidence of this in any of the Councils. These matters were transacted by bishops, or occasionally by presbyters representing their bishops; if held in a province represented that *provincial* Church alone, and if attended by them conjointly, or by the majority of them, they then represented the *universal Church.* From the acts and decrees of these Councils, and the testimony of individual bishops, it is possible to know the mind of the Church in these matters.

His fifth point is concerned with *the right use of the Fathers,* in response to those whose objection to the testimony of the Fathers is that they have erred in points of religion, not only separately as individuals but conjointly, and at times have disagreed among themselves on matters of great moment. Beveridge's point is that this is no objection, since we are thinking of the Fathers not as individuals taken separately, but taken together conjointly. So, though there may be errors, and even on great matters they may appear to disagree, there are many things on which agreement prevails among the Fathers universally, and very many to which a majority of them have given their united assent. This takes nothing from their authority on those points on which they agree, but rather confirms it.

The sixth point is that the English Reformers in their resolve to

avoid rushing from one extreme to another were concerned that
the English church should embrace 'whatsoever things had been at
all times, believed and observed, by all Churches, in all places ...
For they well knew, that all particular Churches are to be formed
on the model of the Universal Church'. As a result, though the
Church of England at this time is out of communion with the
Roman church and other particular churches, 'yet have we abiding
communion with the universal and catholic Church, of which
evidently ours as by the aid of God first constituted, and by His pity
still preserved, is the perfect image and representation'.

Beveridge's final point is that in considering the universal
Church and its agreement, a special regard has to be paid to the
primitive church because it is universally agreed to be the more
pure and genuine part. His concern is that as ancient customs have
been allowed to fall into disuse they have been replaced by 'new
institutions ... devised by the wanton imaginations of men's minds,
which very fault is above all other to be eschewed in religion'. The
general consensus of all Christians is that 'the Apostolic Church as
constituted by the Apostles of our Lord in person, under the guidance of Divine inspiration, and by them whilst yet living
administered, was of all churches the purest and most perfect'.
Furthermore, their successors in those primitive ages kept the
Church inviolate and uncorrupted, and though the Church was
harassed by new heresies she was in no way corrupted because they
were immediately rejected by the Catholic Church as she appealed
to the primitive church as the rule of other churches.

> For if any one endeavoured to bring any thing new into the
> doctrine and discipline of the Church, those Fathers who
> opposed themselves to him, whether individually or assembled
> together in a body, sought their arguments, as out of the Holy
> Scriptures, so also out of the doctrines and traditions of the
> Church of the first ages. For this is observable in nearly all acts
> of councils, and commentaries of individual Fathers, wherever,
> that is, ecclesisastical controversies are discussed. And indeed
> nothing still is more rational, nothing certainly more desirable,
> than that all particular Churches at this day, wherever consti-
> tuted, were reformed after the model of the Primitive Church.
> For this measure would immediately cast forth whatever corrup-
> tions have crept in during later ages, and would restore to their
> original vigour, on the other hand, all things which are required
> for the true constitution of a Christian Church.[51]

William Cave (1637–1713)

William Cave, whose reputation as a patristic scholar rests upon his writings on church history, was described by J. H. Overton as '. . . a classical divine, whose *Primitive Christianity* and *Historia Literaria* ought to live as long as the English language lives.'[52] His writings are voluminous and valuable, and include numerous historical works on themes of Primitive Christianity; Lives, Acts, Deaths and Martydoms of Apostles and Fathers; Writings of Eminent Fathers; Arianism, Paganism, and other sects; the Government of the Ancient Church; and Sermons. In his letter to Nathanael, Bishop of Durham, he writes, 'Our inbred thirst after knowledge naturally obliges us to pursue the notices of former times, which are recommended to us with this peculiar advantage, that the stream must needs be purer and clearer, the nearer it comes to the fountain'. Describing the character of the times,

> . . . wherein religion is almost wholly disputed into talk and clamour; men wrangle eternally about useless and insignificant notions, and which have no tendency to make a man either wiser or better: and in these quarrels the laws of charity are violated, and men persecute one another . . . And . . . the peace and order of an excellent church . . . is broken down . . . To avoid the press and troublesome importunity of such uncomfortable reflections, I find no better way, than to retire into those primitive and better times, those first purest ages of the gospel, when men really were what they pretended to be, when a solid piety and devotion, a strict temperance and sobriety, a catholic and unbounded charity, an exemplary honesty and integrity, a great reverence for everything that was divine and sacred, rendered Christianity venerable to the world, and led not only the rude and the barbarous, but the learned and politer part of mankind in triumph after it.[53]

As the Preface to Beveridge's *Works* puts it, while the *Historia* shews the working of a mind weary of controversy and gradually feeling back as best it could to primitive doctrine and practice, the Dedications and Prefaces to Cave's English works 'evidence a mind throwing itself back upon the contemplation of the Primitive Church, as seen in its government and worship, and exemplified in the lives of the early Christians'.[54]

He began his great work early in life, the *Scriptorum Ecclesiasticorum Historia Literaria*, in two volumes, folio 1688–98, is the most valuable piece of work. The best edition is Oxford

(1740–3) (superintended by Waterland). It is the most elaborate of all his works and what is called today 'reader-friendly'. His style and method is to divide his subject into fifteen sections defined in terms of the age in relation to *Apostolicum, Gnosticicum, &c.* each introduced with a short summary, and then an exhaustive account of the writers in it.

His *Primitive Christianity* reached a fourth edition in 1682 and was reprinted in 1839 and 1849. The first part deals systematically with the charges against the early Christians in the novelty of their doctrines, their mean condition and the manner of their life before concentrating on 'the positive parts of their religion, their piety, places of worship, fasts and festivals, ministry and sacraments'. Part Two surveys the character of these early Christians in relation to their religion, humility, heavenly-mindedness, sobriety of dress, temperance, chastity, religious constancy and patience in suffering. Part Three concentrates on their religion in relation to other men such as their justice and honesty, love and charity, unity and peaceableness, obedience to civil government, and discipline and penance.

The Lives of the Apostles was republished in a new and carefully revised edition by Henry Cary in 1840. Cave's Introductory, 'To the Reader', explains his concern to present the state of things in the preceding periods of the Church, to let him see 'what methods God in all ages made use of to conduct mankind in the paths of piety and virtue'. After the failure of patriarchs and prophets, God sent his Son, 'and being born of a virgin, conversed in the world, and bore our sorrows and infirmities, that by rescuing human nature from under the weight and burden of sin, he might exalt it to eternal life. A brief account of these things is the main intent of the following discourse'. *The Lives of the most Eminent Fathers of the Church* was also popular, and covered the first four centuries, with an historical account of the state of paganism under the first Christian emperors. Again it was republished in a carefully-revised edition in two volumes in 1840 by Henry Cary, who found that Cave's references needed some correction because of his use of inferior editions of the Fathers. As Cave states in the *Preface,*

> For herein, as in a glass, we have the true face of the Church in its several ages represented to us ... those divine records, which are the great instruments of our eternal happiness, have through the several periods of time been conveyed down to us ... With how incomparable a zeal good men have 'contended earnestly for that faith which was once delivered to the saints.'[55]

In the *Preface* to Volume Two Cave writes,

> The work contains the noblest work of church history, this
> being, in many respects, the most considerable age of the
> church. For besides what concerns particular persons, whose
> lives and actions are here related, he will here find an account
> of the fall and supression of paganism ... of the conversion of
> princes to the faith; the adopting of Christianity to be the reli-
> gion of the empire; the acts and proceedings of the first two
> general councils; the advancement of the church to its greatest
> height of splendour; and those lamentable ruptures that soon
> after were made in it by schism and faction, by covetousness and
> ambition, and 'the cunning craftiness of those that lie in wait to
> deceive'.[56]

J. H. Overton states that Cave's merits as a writer consists in 'the
thoroughness of his research, the clearness of his style, and, above
all, the admirably lucid method of his arrangement'. The charge
against him of Socinianism was groundless but, as Overton points
out, there is a little more reason in the charge by Le Clerc that he
wrote panegyrics rather than lives, and also that he forced the
Arian Eusebius to the side of the orthodox and made a Trinitarian
of him.[57]

Joseph Bingham (1668–1723)

Joseph Bingham, a man of blameless life, ranks as one of the greatest in a long line of scholar parish priests in which excellence
dominates his work as scholar and priest. He 'was one who during
the reign of Anne maintained and advanced the reputation of the
Church of England for learning'.[58] His claim to such esteem lies in
his monumental contribution to English theological literature and
learning, as he concentrated his attention on the writings of
Christian antiquity, which made him one of Anglicanism's greatest
patristic scholars. His major work, *Origines Ecclesiasticae* or
Antiquities of the Christian Church, was first published in an imperfect
edition in two volumes (folio) in 1726. A nine-volume edition was
published by his great-grandson Richard (1821–9), that includes
the three sermons on the Trinity and a memoir prefixed to vol. i.
There were other editions, the latest being a two-volume publication in 1875 by Chatto & Windus of London.

Bingham had a sad life and had to cope with a delicate constitu-
tion, a shortage of money and deprivation of the necessary literary

resources that his scholarship required. He was deprived of his Fellowship through involvement in the Trinitarian controversy in Oxford, after a sermon he preached before the university in St Peter-in-the East in October 1695. Here he expressed a sense of responsibility to proclaim what the Fathers rather than the Schoolmen had to say on the Trinity. His text was 1 John 5: 7: 'There are three that bear record in heaven, the Father, the Word, and the Holy Ghost: and these three are one.' He aimed at expounding the patristic understanding of *persona*, and despite his masterful handling of his subject he was misunderstood and accused of heresy. The public press accused him of being Arian, guilty of Tritheism and even of the heresy of Valentinian. In later life he wrote a preface to the sermon, to illustrate that his primary concern was an appeal to Christian antiquity. In this preface,[59] which was never published, Bingham pointed out that his only concern 'was to follow the doctrine of the primitive Fathers and the judgement of antiquity'. In no way did he 'deny the three Persons to be *unius substantiae,* of one substance or consubstantial, in any sense that the primitive Fathers believed them to be so'. He was concerned to defend one substance and three Persons in the sense in which the first four General Councils understood these words, which is how the Church of England has always understood them. 'And then it could be no innovation, much less heresy or Tritheism to endeavour to reduce old words to their first and prim-itive signification'.

He went to the living of Headbourne Worthy near Winchester, and in May 1696 and September 1697 he was invited to preach two Visitation sermons. Again he defended his University sermon, using extensive reference to Scripture and the Fathers. His first sermon concluded with these words:

> Therefore I cannot but think, that all calm and sober men, who consider things impartially without heat and prejudices will bear a just regard to that hypothesis, which besides its Catholicism and antiquity, contributes so much towards a clear understand-ing of all the necessary articles of the Christian faith. And if that be the true advantage of this hypothesis then it can be no disser-vice to the Christian religion to have endeavoured to give a fair and just account of it: if such an attempt deserves no more, yet I hope it may pretend to deserve a favourable construction; which I am willing to persuade myself Gentlemen, it has already had from you.[60]

He began writing his *Antiquities of the Christian Church* in 1702, despite his lack of patristic sources, though he did have the use of Bishop Morley's patristic library bequeathed to the Dean and Chapter of Winchester. Twenty years later his work was completed. He had gone through the whole state of the primitive church, giving an account of the several parts of her public worship and offices of divine service. In the preface he stated,

> The design which I have formed to myself is to give such a methodical account of the antiquities of the Christian church as others have done of the Greek and Roman and Jewish antiquities, by reducing the ancient customs, usages, and practices of the church under certain proper heads, whereby the reader may take a view at once of any particular usage or custom of Christians for four or five centuries.[61]

A German writer claimed that Bingham was the first to publish a complete archaeology of the Christian church worthy of the name. His concern was not merely that of academic scholarship: as a pastor, he loved God's Church and was concerned for her peace and unity. In the preface to a projected second edition of the *Antiquities* he argues for reunion on the basis of a real and primitive episcopacy. His first preface also ends with the hope that his scholarship will be of benefit to the 'present' church.

> That this essay may prove useful both to the learned and unlearned, to instruct the one, who cannot read these things in their originals, and refresh the memories of the other, who may know many things that they cannot always readily have recourse to. Or, if it be of no use to greater proficients, it may at least be some help to young students and new beginners, and both provoke them to the study of ancient learning, and a little prepare them for their entrance upon it. Besides, I considered there were some who might have a good inclination toward the study of these things, who yet have neither ability to purchase, nor time and opportunity to read over many ancient fathers and councils; and to such, a work of this nature, composed ready to their hands, might be of considerable use, to acquaint them with the state and practice of the primitive church, when they have no better opportunities to be informed about it. If, in any of these respects, these collections (which were designed for the honour of the ancient church, and the benefit of the present) may prove serviceable toward those ends, I shall not think my time and pains ill-bestowed.[62]

He claimed that another book, more of miscellaneous rites might be added, but having worked for twenty years, with frequent illness inhibiting hard study, and the things themselves being of no great moment, he chose to give the reader a complete and finished work with an index, rather attempt too much and be forced to leave it incomplete.[63]

Bingham's *Antiquities* was the first work of its kind. There had been no other comparable work on the hierarchy, ecclesiology, territorial organization, rites, discipline, and calendar of the primitive church. Its basis was the original documents, but Bingham also had an immense knowledge of the later literature on this subject. He worked from 1702–22, staggering the publication in ten volumes as they were completed. Books I and II covers such subjects as the 'Titles and Appellations of Christians'; the 'Names of Reproach cast upon the Church'; the 'power and independence of bishops'; the 'privilege of Bishops to intercede for criminals'; of 'Primates, Metropolitans, Patriarchs, Presbyters, Deacons, Archdeacons, and Deaconesses'. Book III considers the inferior Orders, and Book IV 'the qualifications and method of electing clergy'. Book V contains information relating to 'the privileges, immunities and revenues of the clergy in the primitive church' while Book VI considers 'the laws and rules relating to the employment, life, and conversation of the clergy'.

Book VII discusses *ascetics and monks, virgins and widows*, Book VIII *church buildings, baptisteries, consecration of churches* and *the origin of asylums* and *places of refuge in Christian places of worship*. Book IX describes *the geography of the primitive Church*. Books X–XII describe *the origin of the Catechumenate, the classes of catechumens, the origin of the Creeds, the rites and customs associated with Baptism, Confirmation* and *other post-baptismal ceremonies*. Book XIII discusses *Worship*, Book XIV the *Missa Catechumenorum*, Book XV the *Missa Fidelium*, Book XVI, *Unity and Discipline in the Early Church*, Book XVII *Clergy Discipline*, Book XVIII, *Orders of Penance*, Book XX *Festivals*, Book XXI *Marriage Rites*, Book XXII *Funeral Rites*, and Book XXIII, *The Method of Burying the Dead*.

His work is not a mere catalogue of information but a compendium of critically-evaluated evidence for the living tradition of patristic church life. He discusses second-century metropolitans,[64] pointing out on Eusebius's evidence that Irenaeus had the superintendency as such in the Gallican dioceses, and listing other examples, which are acceptable proofs of the existence of metropolitans, but notes that these do not prove this matter. 'For presiding in Council does not necessarily infer metropolitical power, as those presiding may only be doing so as senior bishops'. He cites Eusebius's example; Palmas was presiding not as bishop of Amastris, because Heraclea and not Amstris was the civil metropolis of Pontus, but as the most ancient bishop among them. Similarly, he disagrees with Blondel, who concluded from this evidence that in the second century the senior bishops were the metropolitans. Only in Africa was this the case. His wider knowledge of the Roman empire assisted him in the evaluation of evidence and the establishing of conclusions, particularly in the immunity of the clergy from civil taxation.

While others have superseded Bingham in various areas of the field he covered, his work is a remarkable achievement for one man: such immense erudition, critical judgement and reasonable application. He must be considered the foremost patristic scholar of his generation. His concern, which he sets out in his prefaces, is solely to recover what the early church believed and to release it for the enlivening of God's church in succeeding generations. A concluding quotation will suffice to indicate a way forward:

> if ... we have that zeal which we profess, we shall be careful to demonstrate it in all our actions; observing those necessary rules and measures, which raised the primitive Church to its glory ... confining ourselves to the proper business of our calling and not intermeddling or distracting ourselves with other cares; employing our thoughts and time in useful studies, and directing them to their proper end, the edification of the Church.[65]

A controversy that engaged Bingham's use of the Fathers was the argument concerning lay baptism where his concern was to correct mistakes made by learned writers, chief among whom was Roger Laurence, a learned Nonjuror. Laurence published his *Lay-baptism Invalid* in 1712–13. Bingham responded with *A Scholastical History* pt. ii (1714), and to Laurence's *Supplement* (1714) with *A Dissertation on the Eighth Canon of Nice* (1714). It is interesting to note that it was the Calvinists and Puritans, such as Whitgift and Cartwright, who on scriptural grounds opposed lay baptism, whereas Hooker, giving due place to antiquity with Scripture and reason, accepted it. Barnard[66] points out that central to this dispute between Laurence and Bingham was the interpretation of the authority of heretics and schismatics in the ancient church. In censuring the heretical clergy by removal of their commission the Church had reduced them in status to laymen, but in receiving their baptisms had accepted lay baptism. This was where Bingham stood consistently. He was also able to quote authorities in support of lay baptism *in extremis*. These authorities included Tertullian, *De*

Bapt. 17; the Spanish Council of Eliberis; Jerome, *Adv. Lucifer, 4;*
Augustine, *Ep. ad Fortunatus* (in Gratian, *De Cons. Distinct.* 4) and
Adv. Parmenian. 36; Gelasius, *Ep. ad Episc. Lucan.* 9; Isidore, *de Offic.
Eccles.* 24 and others.[67] (Works 9, 27–37). The clue to Bingham's
assessment of this issue in patristic terms is the distinction he draws
between unauthorized and invalid baptisms. Heretical baptism
might be unauthorized but it did not automatically follow that it
was invalid – in the spirit of Augustine, who claimed that the
Church did not repeat heretical baptism because the baptism of
Christ could never be lost. So Bingham can demonstrate that there
is sufficient patristic evidence to prove that heretical baptism was
allowed so long as it was baptism in the threefold name of the
Trinity. Any deficiencies such as not conveying the remission of
sins, were rectified by the imposition of hands upon repentance
and reconciliation to the Church. The evidence is there in the first
six General Councils.[68] (*Works,* 9, 62, 66–7, 77–8). Laurence had
made the mistake of equating unauthorized with invalid baptisms.
Even with Cyprian the Church agreed that the commissions of
heretics and schismatics should be voided, but would not agree
with Cyprian in concluding that the baptisms of heretics are
absolutely invalid and make a case for rebaptism.

There was no doubt about the quality of Bingham's patristic
scholarship, which had a distinctive pastoral orientation because
he was an effective parish priest, even if he ended up almost by
default in the parochial situation. There was an integration
between this scholar priest and pastor in the high spiritual and
moral standards of a holy life which had its roots in the discipline
of the ancient Fathers, where he found a wisdom with which he
could discern and find solutions to the problems of his age.

Caroline Scholarship

What is illustrated here in relation to the Laudians characterizes
these Caroline divines as a whole; they read the Bible and the
Fathers for themselves, and found that their theology was consistent with what was ancient rather than with the modern or 'new
theology' of their day. Hence, in starting from the Bible and the
statement of Anglican formularies, they discovered that the interpretation of Holy Scripture was to be in accordance with that of the
ancient doctors of the Church. For them the government of the
Church is episcopal, and while some saw it as the *bene esse,* the
majority believed it was of the *esse.* Andrewes may be regarded as

the father of this school, but Laud is its most prominent member, and while among them there were differences on points of detail and expression, they were of one mind concerning the main principles of church government and doctrine. This Caroline era was a time when historical learning was at a high premium, and English scholarship highly regarded throughout Europe. These scholars

> fostered qualties in the English character which have in no small measure been responsible for the greatness of this land. They reflected in the nation a reverence for the past, and during an age of change they taught her to rely on traditional wisdom rather than novel doctrine ... These scholars who made the motives of public policy depend so strictly upon an examination of past history, who made even change subserve an inherent continuity, fortified the mind of England.[69]

A. T. P. Williams[70] describes them as having a due place in an age of giants, and while as thinkers they were not in the same league as Francis Bacon or Joseph Butler, 'They were scholars, historians, interpreters of history, theologians in a theological age, reasoning upon material drawn from Scripture and antiquity for the exposition and defence of their cause'. He goes on to say that rather than producing new ideas and speculations in divinity 'their special distinction is to have collected, ordered, and applied to the defence of Anglicanism, a great body of ancient learning'. While they may have been lacking in originality in that sense, this is not to say that originality is absent from these scholars, if originality is taken in the sense in which Lossky describes it in relation to Lancelot Andrewes.[71] To be a genuine theologian is to make ever more truly one's own, by experience, the mystery of the relation of God to man that has been traditionally lived by the Church. For such a theologian, claims Lossky, originality then consists, 'not so much in innovation, as in enabling the whole era to grasp the genuine essence of the Christian message'. Like the poet, the theologian is to live at a required depth at the creative centre face to face with the divine reality, and the more he penetrates into the heart of that mystery the more his theology will be personal, intuitive and in consequence original. What he studies is a present reality, the self-disclosure of God in Christ made present in the life of the Church whose true *Sitz-im-Leben* is the life of grace where of necessity there is the intertwining of past and present. Any creative theology arises out of the actual life of the Church, the life of grace, so that originality in this sense springs from something far deeper than the intellect – from lives where there is a deep desire for God, which is the well-spring from which their desire for learning is generated in its richness and peculiar originality. Thereby did these Caroline theologians make a permanent mark on subsequent English thought about the nature and authority of the Church. It made the English church in their age widely respected in the world of scholarship and brought the respect of men like Casaubon and Grotius, 'the universal minds of the time', because they found an openmindedness, a genuine historical outlook and a liberality that was a generosity of spirit distinct from the rigidity of Rome and the dogmatism of Calvinism. In our own day T. S. Eliot[72] described them as bringing into the Church a breadth of culture and an ease with humanism and Renaissance learning, both hitherto conspicuously lacking. Their intellectual achievements and prose style did for the Church of England what thirteenth-century philosophy did for medieval Christianity; they completed its structure and gave it form and shape. At the same time it enabled Anglicans to reach out to Orthodox churches of the East, when those who travelled found themselves in Orthodox surroundings, face to face with a non-Roman catholicism and an ancient form of church government with its rule of faith in the ancient creeds, enabling even in those early days a reaching-out to Eastern Orthodoxy.

What characterizes them is a singleness of purpose, that of restoration. They had no agenda for the producing of something new, nor the emasculation of Christian truth by adapting it to the spirit of the age. Their single-minded aim was to restore the grandeur of Christian truth, and teach it once again to their contemporaries who had forgotten it in the turbulence of the Reformation. In their *return to the Fathers,* their theology is given a wholeness with its centre in the Incarnation and in this they found what Dean Church described as something '... to enrich, to enlarge, to invigorate, to give beauty, proportion and force to their theology.'[73] With the *consensus patrum* as the ground of 'their theology it becomes something *sui generis',* and 'by no means provincial', giving to it what distinguished it from some of the new and prevalent conceptions of Christianity planned in the minds of theologians and having no connection with the past nor the life of the Church. Hence it was 'something quite different from Tridentinism and Continental Protestantism.'[74] Small wonder that they were given the title *Stupor Mundi* and found themselves with a reputation in Europe, as they restored the dignity of theology that made it once more the Queen of the Sciences. What further differentiated them was the pastoral orientation of their theology, emanating as it did from the parishes in which they ministered among ordinary people, rather than the cloister or university. What resulted was a theology in the language and form that the laity of their day could understand, in sermons to ordinary people as well as in learned treatises.

In consequence, Patristic church creeds and doctrine, Patristic canon law, Patristic liturgies and church practice were all investigated with rigour and presented as the perennial basis on which the Reformed Church of England sought or ought to be structured. This was done, not in a blindfolded way, but positively, critically, and constructively, and especially preserving continuity and consensus with the primitive Church of the Apostles and Fathers.

Notes

1. Hooker, *Laws* Bk.V, lxviii, 9.
2. Richard Field, *Of the Church*, (English Historical Society, Cambridge, 1847), Appendix Part iii, *ad fin.*
3. *Ibid.* Bk. 1, vi.
4. *Ibid.* Bk. 1, x.
5. *Ibid.* Bk. 2, ii; see also vi, on succession of doctrine.
6. *Ibid.* Bk. 5, lvi.
7. *Ibid.* Bk. 5, xlviii–lii.
8. *Ibid.* Bk. 5, li.
9. *Ibid* Bk. 5, xxiii, xxiv.
10. *Ibid.* Bk. 4, ii.
11. *Ibid.* Bk. 3, xxi, xliv.
12. *Ibid.* Bk. 3, xxxviii, and Appendix.
13. H. R. McAdoo, *The Spirit of Anglicanism* (A. & C. Black, London, 1965), p. 369, citing John Bramhall, *Works* (1672 edition), p. 636.
14. H. R. McAdoo, *ibid.* p. 373.
15. Bramhall, *Works,* vol. i (*LACT,* John Henry Parker, Oxford, 1842), p. 279.
16. Jeremy Taylor, 'Funeral Sermon', in Bramhall, *Works,* Vol. i, p. lxix.
17. H. R. McAdoo, citing Bramhall, *Works* (1676), p. 375
18. *Ibid.* citing Bramhall, p. 375.
19. *Ibid.* citing Bramhall, p. 376.
20. Bramhall, *Works,* vol. ii (*LACT,* Parker, Oxford, 1842) , pp. 313 and 314.
21. McAdoo, *ibid,* p. 379.
22. Herbert Thorndike, *Works* (*LACT,* Parker, Oxford, 1845), vol. ii, pp. 4–7.
23. Thorndike, 'An Epilogue to the Tragedy of the C of E', Bk. 1, ch. vii, 15–21, *Works,* vol. ii, Part i, pp. 120–4.
24. Thorndike, *Works,* vol. iv, pp. 50–68.
25. E. C. Miller Jr., 'The Doctrine of the Church in the Thought of

Herbert Thorndike (1598–1672),' Unpublished D.Phil. thesis (Oxford, 1990), pp. 30ff.

26. *Ibid.* p. 37.
27. F. Sanders, 'John Pearson', *DNB*, vol. xv, p. 613, citing Bentley, *Dissertations on Phalaris*, pp. 424–5 (edn 1699).
28. *Ibid.* citing Cheetham .
29. *Ibid.* citing Hallam, *Lit. Hist. Eur.* Pt. iv, ii.
30. Darwell Stone, ' John Pearson', *Dictionary of English Church History*, eds. Ollard and Crosse, (Mowbrays, London, 1912), pp. 451–2.
31. G. Cuming, *The Anglicanism of John Cosin* (Durham Cathedral Lecture, City Printing Works Ltd, Chester-le-Street, 1975), p. 9.
32. *Ibid.* p. 14.
33. H. M. Luckock, *Studies in the History of the Prayer Book* (Rivingtons, London, 1882), p. 164.
34. J. Cosin, *Works,* vol. iv (*LACT*, Parker, Oxford, 1843–55), pp. 332–6.
35. J. Taylor, 'A Dissuasive from Popery', Pt. ii, Bk. i, 2, *Works*, ed. R. Heber, vol. x, pp. 384–6 (ed. C. P. Eden, vol. vi, pp. 380–2). *Anglicanism,* (SPCK, 1951), More and Cross, p. 91.
36. Jeremy Taylor, 'The Liberty of Prophesying', in *Works* (Revised and improved edition by C. P. Eden, 1847–52, 10 vols), p. 375.
37. Tertullian, cited by Taylor in 'The Liberty of Prophesying', *Works,* p. 378. Taylor is discussing the nature of fundamentals in belief and agreeing with Tertullian that the Apostles' Creed is the authoritative foundation. Taylor supports this, not with a direct quotation from Tertullian but with a conflation of what he remembers from Tertullian, as he probably did not have the necessary texts available. The sense of Tertullian's mind is right on this matter though the exact words are not. The nearest is *De Virg. Vel.* ch. 1: 'The rule of faith, indeed, is one, alone, immoveable and irreformable', then he goes on to state the articles of the Apostles' Creed. *ANF*, vol. iv. p. 27. The second is in *De Praescriptione*, 13, where he spells out the rule of faith as being the articles of the same Apostles' Creed. *ANF*, vol. iii, p. 249. A third is in *Adversus Praxeam*, ch. 2, where again he rehearses the articles of the Apostles' Creed as the rule of faith. *ANF*, vol. iii, p. 598.
38. McAdoo, *The Eucharistic Theology of Jeremy Taylor Today* (Canterbury Press, 1988), p. 16.
39. F. L. Cross ed., *Oxford Dictionary of the Christian Church* (1st edn), p. 164.
40. W. Beveridge, *Works* (*LACT*, Parker, Oxford, 1845), vol. i, p. ix.
41. *Ibid.* p. iii.
42. Beveridge, *Works,* vol. iv, p. 441; Acts 2: 42.
43. *Ibid.* p. 444.
44. *Ibid.* p. 445.
45. *Ibid.* p. 450.
46. Beveridge, *'Ecclesia Anglicana Ecclesia Catholica, The Thirty-Nine Articles',* 3rd edn, (OUP, Oxford, 1847).

47. *Ibid.* p. x.
48. Beveridge, citing Augustine, *De Trinitate,* I. iv. c. 6.
49. G. R. Evans, *Authority in the Church* (Canterbury Press , 1990), p. 98.
50. Beveridge, 'Preface' in *Vincentius Against Heresy,* Vincent of Lérins
     (J. H. Parker, Oxford, 1851), p. xv.
51. *Ibid.* p. xxx.
52. J. H. Overton, *Life in the English Church 1660–1714* (Longmans,
     Green & Co, London, 1885), p. 104.
53. William Cave, *Lives of the Apostles and the Two Evangelists St. Mark and
     St. Luke,* with Introductory Discourse Concerning Patriarchal,
     Mosaical and Evangelical Dispensations. A New Edition carefully
     revised by Henry Cary (J. Vincent, Oxford, 1840), pp. vii–viii.
54. Beveridge, *Works,* vol. i, p. vi.
55. Cave, Preface in *Lives of the most Eminent Fathers of the Church, that
     flourished in the First Four Centuries:With A Historical Account of the State
     of Paganism uner the First Christian Emperors,* vol. i, revised by Henry
     Cary (J. Vincent, Oxford, 1840), p. ix.
56. Cave, *ibid.* vol. ii, p. iii.
57. J. H. Overton, 'William Cave', *DNB,* vol. iii, p. 1250.
58. G. W. Hutton, *The English Church from the Accession of Charles I to the
     Death of Anne* (Macmillan & Co, London, 1903), p. 302.
59. Joseph Bingham, *Antiquities of the Christian Church,* vol. viii, pp. 290–8,
     Eight-Volume Edition published in 1821, by Richard Bingham.
60. Bingham, *ibid.*
61. Bingham, Preface, *Antiquities of the Christian Church,* (Chatto &
     Windus, London, 1875), vol. i. p. viii.
62. Bingham, *ibid,* p. xi.
63. Bingham, *Antiquities,* vol. ii (London, 1875), p. 1261.
64. *Ibid.,* vol. i, ch. xvi, sect. 4. p. 61.
65. Bingham, *Works* (1821 edn), vol. i, p. 605.
66. L. W. Barnard, 'The Use of the Patristic Tradition in the Late
     Seventeenth and Early Eighteenth Centuries', in *Scripture, Tradition
     and Reason, A Study in the Criteria of Christian Doctrine,* ed. Benjamin
     Drewery and Richard Bauckham (T & T Clark, Edinburgh, 1988)
     pp. 195-201, for a full discussion of the Lay-baptism controversy.
67. Bingham, *Works,* 9, 27–37 (1821 edn).
68. *Ibid,* 62, 66–7, 77–8.
69. D. C. Douglas, *English Scholars 1660–1730* (London, 1951), p. 283
70. A. T. P. Williams, *The Anglican Tradition in the Life of England* (SCM
     Press, London, 1947) p. 37.
71. see ch.7, p. 000.
72. T. S. Eliot, 'For Lancelot Andrewes', *Selected Essays* (London, 1928),
     p. 319.
73. R. W. Church, 'Bishop Andrewes', in *Pascal and Other Sermons,*
     (Macmillan & Co, London, 1895), p. 92.
74. G. W. O. Addleshaw, *The High Church Tradition* (Faber & Faber Ltd,
     London, 1941), p. 25.

Part Three:

Objections and Responses

11

Direct Objections and Responses

Fathers and controversy

The Fathers are no strangers to controversy. It was in controversy with those intent on distorting or destroying the faith once delivered to the saints that their works were conceived and born. In their own day it was the heretics who assailed them on every side but within the Church.

> During the fourth and fifth centuries, which are the Augustan age of ecclesiastical literature, the numerous authors who then flourished prove, by continual quotations, the integrity of the antecedent writings that have come down to us. They speak of their predecessors, not indeed in terms of blind zeal and indiscriminate attachment, but with respect and confidence: and this testimony is weighty, because it is immediate, moderate and reasonable.[1]

That same moderate and reasonable testimony to the integrity of the Fathers is demonstrated here in the English Reformers and the Caroline Divines, in their claim that the catholic integrity of Anglicanism is patristic not papal.

Continental Protestantism had always claimed that the Reformation within Anglicanism did not go far enough, and in the struggles for Anglican identity the pressure from that ethos and polity has always tried to pull it in that direction, even to the present day. The attacks on the Fathers were to some extent part of that design, for to undermine the very patristic foundation which Anglicanism claimed authenticated its polity and catholicity, would be an effective way of adjusting it to the claims of continental Protestantism. At the same time there was the argument against the Roman church's misuse of the Fathers, in that they were read and quoted not for the illustrating of the great truths of Christian doctrine, but in support of established institutions. The doctrines of the Church were not to be regulated by the sentiments of the Fathers, but the Fathers were to speak the language of the Church. The method was to bring forward quotations that were often partial and perverted in their meaning and sense, and sometimes quite mistaken. It was a time when genuine copies of the texts were rare, and *catenae* of quotations were used as working texts which were appended to texts of scripture, but without order and exposition. 'The authority of the Fathers was not only exaggerated ... their sentiments were also partially extracted, and misrepresented: and the credit of their influence ... directed to extend a temporal jurisdiction'.[2] Hence the Fathers came to be seen as being more favourable to the papal cause, though this was more a generally-supposed impression of the primitive writings than one based upon strict examination of these texts. Fr Tavard SJ, quoted in chapter 1 (n. 4) above, maintained that in making Scripture and Tradition the mutually inclusive and self-evident basis of Anglicanism, she maintains a consistency with the patristic spirit. This makes her a better representative of the catholic eras, patristic and medieval, than many of the catholic writers of the Counter-Reformation period. It was not surprising that Protestantism should be suspicious, even perhaps confused, when Anglicanism found in these same Fathers the source of their catholic integrity, and that Anglican protest to Rome in Reformers and Carolines should be concerned with maintaining catholic doctrine and institution in their primitive similitude. Hence the fundamental point of Anglican protest is that 'catholic' need not be synonymous with 'papal', and this protest rested on the appeal to Scripture and antiquity.

In his Bampton Lectures,[3] John Collinson, a former Rector of Boldon (1840–57) who is buried in its churchyard, points out that it was Erasmus who led the way in attacking the method of the School-Divines, 'and reduced within legitimate bounds the credit of the Fathers'. Luther, in a tract in 1520 responding to the Pope's bull of excommunication, makes a plea for the setting aside of 'an implicit dependence on all human writings', and urges 'let us strenuously adhere to the Scriptures alone'.[4] This mood within Protestantism was assisted by the invention of the printing press, which made available editions of the works of the Fathers before 1530 in Germany, Venice, and particularly at Basle by Froben overseen by Erasmus, and by Henry Stephens in Paris. The Centuriators of Magdeburg published their History of the Church from its beginnings to 1400, dividing it into centuries. It was published in Latin at Basle, 1559–74, as the *Historia Ecclesiae Christi*. Its principal author was M. Flacius, and his rigid Lutheranism and anti-Romanism prevails in the work, as he views the pure Christianity of the New Testament progressively dominated by the power of the papal Antichrist until liberated by Martin Luther. 'In its breadth and conception the work was a landmark in ecclesiastical history; but its inaccuracies, and esp. the liberties it took with the texts of original documents, made it an easy target for C. Baronius in his *Annales Ecclesiastici*.'[5] A counter-polemic of the Roman church came towards the end of the sixteenth century, in these *Annals of Baronius,* twenty years in the making, issued under the express patronage of the papacy, and whose primary aim was to vindicate papal catholicism in its appeal to antiquity.

Polemic was the aim and context of the approach to the Fathers in the sixteenth century: on the one hand, the affirmation of them to vindicate catholic doctrine and institutions, papal as well as Anglican; on the other, a negating of them to make credible Protestant doctrine and institutions. A new turn emerged in the controversy with the publication in 1631 of Jean Daillé's treatise *Concerning the Right Use of the Fathers in the Decision of the Controversies that are at this day in Religion.* The first edition was published in French followed by a Latin translation, but then in 1651 came an English translation by Thomas Smith, Fellow of Christ's College Cambridge. Daillé (1594–1670) was a French Reformed minister, a theologian and controversialist. This was the beginning of a number of direct attacks on the Fathers. A second, not from an ecclesiastic but from a lawyer, came in the form of Barbeyrac's 'On the Morality of the Fathers', an incidental attack by a Professor of Law at Gröningen in a Preface he wrote to Pufendorf's *Of the Law of Nature and Nations.* A reply came from the great French Benedictine patristic scholar Remi Ceillier (1688–1763), to which Barbeyrac responded with an essay too large for inclusion in a new edition of Pufendorf, so it was published as an independent essay. J. J. Blunt comments that in their approach to the Fathers their only object 'is to single out whatever imperfections they present, and place them before their readers in continuous succession, and without one lucid interval of merit.'[6] Nearer home other direct attacks came from the historian Edward Gibbon (1737–94) in the fifteenth and sixteenth chapters of his *Decline and Fall of the Roman Empire.* The Puritan John Milton (1608–74), poet and controversialist, attacked the Fathers in his *Treatise of Prelatical Episcopacy,* and again in his dissertation *Of Reformation in England,* in vol. I. of his *Prose Works.* In 1748 Dr Conyers Middleton severely attacked the

Fathers in his *Free Enquiry into the Miraculous Powers ascribed to the early Christian Church,* which in 1790 Henry Kett refuted in his Bampton Lectures. Related to these direct attempts to discredit the Fathers is the Ignatian Controversy, which centred around the doctrine of episcopacy: if this was to be validated as apostolic, then the genuineness of the Ignatian epistles must be vindicated.

The indirect assaults on the Fathers took the form of a doctrinal attack in the resurgence of *Arianism,* the rise of *Socinianism* and its English form *Unitarianism,* along with *Deism* and *Rationalism.* Not only was there open contradiction of patristic doctrine, but misrepresentation of the Fathers by the attempts to demonstrate that the writings of the first three centuries are not inconsistent with the modern tenets of Unitarianism.

> The authenticity of primitive tradition and its records, of scripture and its doctrines, and of Christianity as a revelation, stand or fall together. It is not the defence of any particular doctrine which is involved in the question of the credibility of tradition: the whole fabric of Christianity is vitally connected with it. In former ages infidelity openly assailed the truth of Christianity: in later times it has assumed the name of Christianity itself, in order to pursue with more success its plans for the subversion of the faith.[7]

In Tract 89, 'On the Mysticism Attributed to the Early Fathers of the Church', which Church[8] described as an inopportune piece of work, John Keble asserts that it is curious how the assailants of primitive antiquity have shifted their ground, since the beginning of the seventeenth century. The feeling at the Reformation was that the Fathers were against them, whether in theological enquiry or ecclesiastical practice.

> It was not until divines of his class had thoroughly wearied themselves in vain endeavours to reconcile the three first centuries with Calvin and Zwingli, that Daillé published his celebrated treatise 'Of the Right Use of the Fathers', in which, under pretence of impugning their sufficiency as judges between Papist and Protestant, he has dexterously insinuated every topic most likely to impair their general credit.

As Keble points out, Daillé became the standard author for all who took that side of the question, but differs from those who came after him in the ground and substance of his argument. First, his concern is to confine himself to those points at dispute between Protestant and Romanist, and secondly he puts the chief emphasis of his objections on the scantiness of the remains, their corruption and interpolation and the difficulty of discerning their real sense. When he challenges their authority he is careful to cite their own disclaimers to such authority before instancing their supposed errors and inconsistencies. At the beginning of the eighteenth century, the same quotations are appealed to, the same particulars insisted upon, but with more open defiance and a more direct and avowed purpose of impugning their credit in all questions of Christian religion. Daniel Whitby (1638–1726), who in later years was a Unitarian, declares his debt to collections of patristic expositions of Scripture in his Preface to a *Paraphrase and Commentary on the New Testament* (2 vols, 1703). He wished to exclude appeals to Antiquity, as to the transmission of the Rule of Faith (i.e. the great fundamental doctrines), no less than in facts of general history, or in controversies between England and Rome. In 1749, Conyers Middleton published *Introductory Discourse, etc., to the Free Inquiry into the Miraculous Powers which are supposed to have subsisted in the Christian Church from the Earliest Ages through Several Successive Centuries*. It is in this work that he claims to be able to prove that the Fathers were characterized by a weak and crafty understanding that only confirmed those prejudices with which they happened to be possessed, especially where religion was the subject.

In *The Use and Value of Ecclesiastical Antiquity*, Daniel Waterland (1683–1740) claimed that, like Athanasius and Basil, the concern of the Church of England was not for something modern, but for the pure and ancient faith. In making antiquity the handmaid of Scripture, she appealed to Scripture first, speaking for itself and so proving its own reasonableness according to the rules of grammar and criticism. After that she referred to the faith of the ancient and undivided Church for confirmation of the same rational and natural construction. On this foundation a distinctively Anglican tradition was built, which was that neither of Rome nor Geneva. At a time when episcopacy and liturgy were under attack, the Protestant concern was to undermine the integrity of the Fathers as guides for the Post-Reformation Church. Daillé's concern was to demonstrate that there is no *consensus patrum* that is relevant or authoritative in settling the controversies between Papist and Protestant. For the Romanist, the primary aim of the appeal to the Fathers was the vindication of Papal Catholicism. Therefore, for the Roman and Anglican there is a positive and negative approach in their appeal to the Fathers; on the one hand, the affirmation of catholic doctrine and institution, on the other, for the Anglican, the negating of medieval accretions to the primitive faith, for the

Romanist the negating of Anglicanism and Protestantism. The same negative and positive approach is found in the Protestant, but the aim was to undermine the Fathers as arbiters and authorities in the settling of differences in doctrine and practice between Rome and Geneva, and thereby affirm Protestantism.

John Daillé and *The Right Use of the Fathers*

The work was printed in London 'for John Martin, and [are] to be sold at the sign of the Bell in St. Paul's Churchyard MDCLI.' The late Baron of St Hermine had told Daillé that people who wanted to win support for the Roman Church and who despised the Reformed, used as their chief argument, *Antiquity,* and the *general consent* of all the Fathers of the first ages of Christianity. Though the baron claimed to know the 'vanity of this argument of theirs', nevertheless, he invited Daillé to discover for him 'the very Bottom, and Depth of this business'. Collinson pointed out that, despite the efforts of patristic scholars and editors in different parts of Christendom, 'it should seem that since M. Daillé's publication, the writings of the Fathers have not recovered in public estimation that veneration which before attached to them'.[9] Daillé's introductory chapter sets out 'The Design of the Whole Work,' which is in two books, making the point that the Fathers cannot be judges of the sixteenth-century controversies between papist and Protestant and giving two main reasons. First, because it is difficult to find out what their sense is 'touching the same'. Secondly, their 'sense of judgement' of these things (supposing it to be clearly understood), cannot claim infallibility or freedom from error and therefore is an insufficient authority for the satisfying of the understanding. Such understanding cannot, nor ought it to believe, anything in religion but what it knows to be true. The First Book argues from eleven proofs to validate the first reason, and the Second Book deals with six such proofs in support of the second reason.

In the Preface, Daillé presupposes two things. First, that if passages from the Fathers are to be used to substantiate certain things, then the meaning and sense of them must be clear and their authorship not in doubt. Secondly, in deciding these controversies from the writings of the Fathers, it means attributing to them very great authority. If such authority is lacking, the two things which need examination are, whether we can know clearly now, for certain, the opinions of the Fathers about these differences and whether their authority is such that anyone clearly knowing their opinion on any Article of Religion, can receive it as true. If the Church of Rome can and is able to prove both these points, then there is no dispute, but if either or both these things be found doubtful then the way of proof they have used hitherto is insufficient. Therefore, of necessity, they ought to seek a more sound way of proving the truth of the said opinions that Protestants will not receive.

Daillé's arguments are considered here in relation to the direct responses made to them by Anglican divines. These responses came in various works which included Matthew Scrivener's *Apologia pro Ecclesiae Patribus adversus J. Dalleum De Usu Patrum (1672)*; *Vindiciae Epistolarum S. Ignatii*, John Pearson (1672); *The Use and Value of Ecclesiastical Antiquity with respect to Controversies of Faith*, in Daniel Waterland's Works; *An Essay on the Right Use of the Fathers*, William Reeves (1709) in (*Apostolic Fathers of the Second Century*, ed. Wake and Burton, vol. ii, p. 195); preliminary Discourse in *The Apostolic Fathers* by Archbishop Wake [Sir John Lubbock's Hundred Books edition]; *On the Right Use of the Early Fathers*, J. J. Blunt, Two Series of Lectures delivered in Cambridge in 1845–46.

Daillé's first general objection

He accuses the Fathers of being vague, uncertain, and obscure. Daillé then lists his reasons and this obscurity of the Fathers takes up half his treatise. Waterland claimed that Daillé's declamation of the Fathers is frequently laboured, and since he wrote, many things have been cleared up, some by himself and more by others after him. He notes that several answers have been given to him, listing Scrivener's *Adversus Dalleum*, Reeves's *Essay* and Beveridge's *Cod. Can. Vindicat, Proem Sect. viii* (*Vindication of his Collection of Canons*) but also new editions of the Fathers and Bibliothèques or critical dissertations.

Daillé brings eleven points to support his first objection. First, that it is difficult to know what the true sense of the Fathers was, because most of the writings for the first three centuries have been lost. They might contain something quite different to what is found in the extant writings. Reeves argues that this objection is not grounded in the true sense of the Fathers which we have, but in a presumptive question grounded in the lost writings which we do not have,[10] so that without evidence the objection is imaginary. 'Historical certainty is at an end if the loss of some writings invalidates those in being.' Eusebius's[11] point that no writings specific to ecclesiastical history were written to serve him as a precedent, he miscontrues into a staement about writings in general. He then gives the impression that only fragments remained. The lost writings were once extant, read, and approved, and many fragments are preserved by Eusebius and others. Eusebius, Blunt[12] claims, meant that no writings specific to ecclesiastical history or regular church annals were written that would serve him as a precedent. Blunt[13] cites Dr Routh, who gathered such fragments, editing them with notes, and regarding them as valuable documents throwing great light on points in the primitive church that were otherwise obscure, 'and as worthy of acceptation for their piety, learning and authority'. Such titles are now in circulation in the Ante-Nicene Fathers, where in Clement's letter light is shed on the churches of Rome and Corinth, and in Hippolytus there are scriptural commentary, histories and treatises of doctrinal significance.

Secondly, Daillé claims these writings of the first centuries are concerned with matters far different from Reformation controversies. Nobody expects to find a patristic handbook detailing Reformation controversies about Papal Supremacy, Infallibility, Image Worship, or whatever. Nevertheless, this does not diminish the significance of the patristic heritage. The perennial value of the patristic writings lies in the principles they supply by which one may distinguish rightness or wrongness. The same point may be made about the Scriptures inasmuch as they do not supply direct evidence for polemical discourse or treatise on controversial issues between Papist and Protestant. They do indicate the first principles of theological discourse. Patristic literature enlarges on the Scriptures, elucidating hints and obscure passages, explaining apostolic traditions, rites and customs, and 'unless there is patience and precision in reading them, much will be lost.'[14]

Justin describes primitive Sunday worship and valuable information about primitive ecclesiastical usage. Clement's *Paedogogus* provides valuable evidence for the practice of infant baptism among precepts relating to the application of Christian principles. Irenaeus prescribes the necessary circumstances for guaranteeing the truth of tradition in his argument with the Gnostics. In his discussion of Aeons he mentions the Eucharist, illustrating indirectly that there was a set liturgy. Such seemingly casual passages, a characteristic feature of patristic literature, have a perennial relevance, even for Daillé's time. Comments of Irenaeus, Cyprian, Tertullian and Justin, about the Eucharist and Real Presence may contribute decisively to the debate on Transubstantiation. What

Clement of Rome says about his own authority, and the exchanges between Irenaeus and Victor of Rome, or Cyprian and Stephanas, on church authority, may be used as indirect evidence on the controversy over papal supremacy, between the Roman Catholics and Protestants of Daillé's time. Blunt's concern is that the Fathers should not be misrepresented as irrelevant by Daillé, whom he believes to be deliberately misleading the kind of people who would not check such authorities.

Daillé's third point, the charge of forgery, will not stand. He alleges as examples of the first accusation Rufinus, whose treatise on the Apostles' Creed is attributed to Cyprian, and the same Rufinus, of Aquileia, who, he says, to vindicate Origen's honour wrote an *Apology* under the name of Pamphylus, a renowned martyr. Part of it was from the Fifth and Sixth Books of Eusebius, who had written on the same subject, and part was his own invention; or certain Latin scribes, monks and clergy from the eighth century altered and invented, interpreted or changed texts whenever it was to the advantage of their own religion. Justin and Theophilus are criticised for using arguments from the *Sybil*, claiming for them an authority that they did not possess. To these points adequate responses were supplied by Blunt instancing evidence in Justin for incidents in Christ's life in the *Acts of Cyrenius* and the *Acts of Pilate*,[15] and for the mystical power of the Cross to Plato.[16] These are instances of the Fathers reinforcing their arguments by appealing to the heathen through evidence with which they would be familiar and which they respected in non-Christian writings.

Daillé failed to acknowledge that doubts about the patristic works he mentions had long been admitted and dismissed as required reading. His argument cannot invalidate genuine works. Also the Fathers used sentiments known to the pagans to establish the facts and doctrines of revelation. The *Sybil*[17] had been a point of contact with pagans and was used to attract the pagans to the Gospel. Blunt lists similar examples from the Epistles of Barnabas and from Hermas which had been used by Clement as genuine. Modern patristic research has distinguished the genuine from what was spurious and proved that lack of historical accuracy does not necessarily imply doctrinal error. To devalue patristic authority on one level and then use it on another, as in the case of establishing the Canon of Scripture, betrays an unacceptable inconsistency.

A fourth point is that legitimate writings of the Fathers have been in many places corrupted by Time, Ignorance, and Fraud. He uses complaints from the Fathers concerning the interpolations of heretics. Rufinus is accused of 'licentiously confounding' the writings of Origen, Eusebius and others, and Jerome is accused of suppressing everything 'that was not consonant to the common judgement and opinions of his Time'. Hilary[18] and Eusebius are accused of similar behaviour. There are accusations of altered Liturgies, and of Latins[19] subtracting and adding to the Canons of Councils.

Marcion, Tertullian told us, took a knife instead of a stylus to Scripture, not to corrupt it but to cut it to his liking and Augustine was well aware of this practice. He also knew how a critical approach to the texts prevented the Fathers from being misled by spurious texts.

> But does not St. Austin tell Faustus, that if any dispute arises about various readings i.e. Scripture, which are but few in number, and sufficiently known to the learned, we have recourse to the books of those countries, from whence we received our copies and religion together, and are willing they should determine the controversy, or if there still appear any difference, the greater number of copies ought to be preferred before the less; those which are most ancient, to those of a later date, are the original languages to all others. Thus do they proceed, who, when they meet with any difficulties in the Holy Scriptures, search and examine things with a desire to be instructed, and not merely for dispute and cavil.[20]

This same rule should hold for the Fathers as well as the apostles and Daillé's argument can be used for any ancient book when the subject-matter is not to our taste. Joseph Priestley[21] (1733–1804) illustrated this when he disposed of the evidence of the Socinian question and the divinity of the Son, which was an extraordinary way of conducting an historical enquiry.[22] For Daillé this argument helps him dispose of the Roman question.

With the tools of the critical art, errata and frauds can be detected and remedied by the comparison of manuscripts and the checking of early translations in Greek and Latin, pre-900, before the corruptions began, and many passages appear as fragments in other authors authenticating old translations. This has been proved in the texts of Barnabas, Hermas, and the Ignatian Letters. The charges that the Romanists have tampered with texts previous to Cyprian can be discounted by looking at the context to prove otherwise, and particularly in Justin where passages contrary to transubstantiation[23] and purgatory[24] are to be found. Similarly with Irenaeus, there is no way in which it can be construed that the text has been tampered with and given a bias towards Rome, as for example in the text III. c. iii. 2, cited as favouring Roman supremacy. The argument in its total context is against it, as are other passages in Irenaeus. What he writes about the Blessed Virgin, comparing and contrasting her with Eve, (c. xix. 1.) is to demonstrate to the Gnostics that Old and New Testaments worship the same God; and in Bk. III. c. xxii. 4, Mary is seen as the remote cause of our salvation. Justin, who obviously influenced what Irenaeus wrote about the Blessed Virgin, cannot be seen as the ground of Roman mariology. Anyone tampering with his text because of its appalling translation would not have been able to disguise the fact. Furthermore, as Blunt goes on to point out, Irenaeus's understanding of Tradition is consonant with Anglicanism rather than the papal understanding, and this surely would have been altered by a textual tamperer.

Finally, Daillé is wrong; doctrines have not been built on suspicious or doubtful passages. This is alien to the spirit of the Fathers, who never built any doctrine upon the thinking of a single Father, but upon the unanimous consent which clearly can be deduced from many of their works. The Fathers, as they stand corrected in the best editions, agree with the Scriptures in faith, manners, and church polity. The concern of such critics is 'to undermine their credit and bring them into general suspicion, to check any curiosity about them, and divert people from a course of study which would not be favourable on many accounts to the class of opinions they are disposed to support and propagate'.[25] He points out that there is no evidence in the patristic writings of any evidence of alteration by Roman authorities, the damage being from neglect rather than from interference, and that the Romanists were saved from the temptation to debase these texts by ignorance of their contents. Dodwell[26] points out that the old Ante-Nicene Fathers were neglected, so that the Romanists were not accustomed to test their decrees (as they ought to have done) by such Fathers. On the contrary, they indulged themselves in heavy censure of the most ancient Fathers, on the strength of modern decrees and established dogmas, in ignorance of these Fathers rather than in informed judgements. Daillé cites Leo the Great's legate Paschasinus as fraudulently interpolating a canon of the Council of Chalcedon, but as Blunt points out, he was guilty of misreading the sixth Canon, not of fraud.

Daillé's fifth charge is that the literary style of the Fathers is obscure and complicated, so 'that there is hardly any knowing what they would be at'.[27] He exaggerates their obscurity, claiming that a knowledge of Latin and Greek is essential if their sense is to be understood. To support his point he selects original Greek passages from Latin translations and highlights the mistakes, accusing the Latin translators of lacking the necessary knowledge of Greek,[28] and concluding that the translators are not to be trusted because they make their authors speak more than they meant. In the theological concerns of the patristic writers there may well be certain fundamental matters of principle that have an indirect reference to Reformation controversies. The Fathers who predated the Arian controversy can have only an incidental value, and the same holds in the religious disputations of our own time, yet it is in the incidental nature of their evidence, claims Blunt, that the value of these patristic writings lies. Daillé's citing of incautious expressions concerning the nature of the Son in Justin and Tertullian does not detract from the main thrust of the evidence for their belief in the Son's divinity and consubstantiality with the Father. Exact technical theological language was not available, so look at any Ante-Nicene Father and the result will be the same. As Bull[29] and Waterland[30] have maintained, the testimony of the Fathers even before the Arians is against Arius, and they express it in a language of their own.

Similarly with writings on the Eucharist, where Daillé is blinkered by a continental Protestant bias that deprecates patristic authority on the Eucharist and magnifies the difficulty of getting at the Fathers' sense. This *wilful* obscurity is blamed on a patristic reserve concerning disclosure about the nature of the Sacraments. Persecution necessitated a certain natural reserve but there is certainly an openness to be communicative for the sake of the Gospel, as in Justin's[31] description of Baptism and Eucharist to the Emperor, and Irenaeus and Tertullian would bear this out. Daillé cites Clement of Alexandria's[32] deliberate reserve, which Clement claims is a safeguard against misleading his readers, to vindicate his point. His concern is to communicate the truth in a manner that would recommend it to the heathen people to whom he writes. Hence his reserve is prudence for fear of giving offence. Daillé is not reading these writings within the context of the times which laid upon these Fathers certain constraints, that inevitably affected the way in which they thought it best to communicate the Gospel. Such charges of obscurity of style are therefore misplaced.

Blunt claims that Daillé has an ulterior aim, and that is to weaken the testimony of the Fathers to the dignity of the Eucharist, to the claims of episcopacy, and in general to what are called 'high church views'. He senses in Daillé a strong Post-Nicene influence, where some inflated expressions might justifiably be modified, but such modification is not justified in the Ante-Nicene Fathers where even figurative language cannot be misunderstood. Irenaeus's[33] language on the Eucharist in terms of sacrifice, epiclesis,[34] on the elements, mixed chalice, episcopacy,[35] representing the office of government from the apostles, is what Daillé would not support.

Another objection to style is the change in the meaning of words. He sees the ancient discipline, the Canons, Baptism and the Eucharist, and Ordination as defunct. A new age calls for new customs. Words such as pope, patriarch, mass, oblation, have changed their meaning. They should be discontinued as antiquated. Surely, however, if such offices and institutions as discipline, orders and sacraments observed in the modern church, have been distorted from what they were in the primitive church, it is the distortion that should be charged with obscurity and corrected. The original form of these should not be charged with obscurity, and we should conclude that they are no longer what they were in the least corrupt period of the church. Therefore, instead of dismissing the Fathers with complaints of their obscurity, we should cherish them because they witness to continuity with antiquity when they are found within Anglicanism. Figurative language is not an invention of the Fathers, Scripture itself is full of such language, as converted Jews speak to unconverted Jews and Gentiles, in an idiom that will make contact with the hearers. This does not weaken the historical part, and so in the Fathers, the way they write does not weaken their testimony in matters of fact. Our concern is not with figures of speech, but whether the Fathers have expressed themselves intelligibly in matters of fact.

The sixth point accuses the Fathers of concealing their own private opinions and speaking of things they did not believe when they report the opinions of others, or when disputing with an opponent. He has three kinds of literature[36] in mind: Commentary, Homily and Polemic or Disputation. Jerome is cited in his *Epistola ad Pammah et Marc* and *Apologia adversus Rufinus* as defining a commentary to be the placing of various interpretations and expositions before the reader without comment or clarification. Daillé finds Jerome's view strange because it leaves the reader uncertain about the true interpretation in a commentary when no comment is given. With the Fathers using the same mind and method it is difficult to discern the author's opinion, and the sense and opinion of the Father under whose name such a commentary goes cannot be clarified because the words and opinions of others are expressed as if they were his own. Daillé[37] is being dishonest here, because he leaves out a passage that would completely undermine what he is saying, where Jerome does say that in such commentaries it was openly declared which opinions were catholic and which heretical. Reeves continues, that such a way of commentary is not confined to the ancient Fathers but features in modern commentators, so why should it be less reliable in the Fathers? Yet why should Daillé, who is so doubtful of Jerome's reliability, depend on him to such an extent? This raises a question about other Fathers who are not commentators and who have written testimonies of fact concerning the faith and manners of Christians in their time; are they merely giving the opinions of others?

A further accusation is that in their preaching they are arrant jugglers: in expounding Scripture they would extract their text from its context and use it for the purpose of amusement, especially if the catechumens were present; if preaching on the sacraments they would use their text to disguise these mysteries. This is contrary to the spirit of catechetical instruction among the Fathers, which Justin Martyr's *First Apology* explains. Strict discipline was exercised in the instruction of catechumens in the way of reverence, knowledge, and probation for initiation into these Christian mysteries. The spirit of Cyril of Jerusalem's *Catechetical Lectures* completely destroys any such accusation, as does the seriousness of the Lenten preparation for the celebration of the Paschal Mystery and the admission of the catechumens into church membership.

Another objection[38] is that in their polemics the Fathers stopped at nothing in order to secure the victory, urging arguments which were in their favour, though they knew them faulty, and suppressing arguments which they knew to be sound. Daillé adds that this further difficulty prevents us from knowing the real sentiments of the Fathers, and cites Jerome as his solitary authority. It proves nothing except that like fencing, in the art of disputing 'we threaten one part to hit another; and moreover, that they often argued from the concessions of an adversary, which are a good argument, *ad hominem*, whether the concessions be true or false'.[39] This is a common argument with the Fathers, and it creates no difficulty for those who approach it in the regular study of these authors, because the general drift of their reasoning establishes their point. However, they must be read carefully in order to discern the complexion of their argument and the basis on which it is built, so that the necessary allowance for the circumstances can be made. It is an easy matter to choose from the whole some detached passage, and a meaning will be assigned to it quite at variance with the real sentiments of the authors. A prime example of such an approach to the Fathers is present in the Socinians who frequently use the Fathers in this way, taking extracts out of context and giving the impression that the Fathers were Socinians, which would succeed if these extracts had been the only surviving fragments from their works.

If concealment of their true opinions was their aim there would not have been such a willingness among so many of them to die for truth when a lie could have saved them.

In his seventh charge Daillé claims that the Fathers have not always held one and the same belief, and that they have sometimes changed some of their opinions, as their judgements have matured through study or age. His argument is that non-biblical writers do not have an inspired knowledge of divine things, but an acquired knowledge by means of Instruction, Reading and Meditation, so that their writings are not all of the same weight and value, since these depend on their maturity of vision which progressively increases. Daillé maintains that those who, after maturer delibera- tion and further study, have changed their opinions cannot be credited; this invalidates most people and books, for the expecta- tion is infallibility. His unproven point is that learned and honest men when they make a mistake are not to be trusted again in anything they write: because St Augustine retracted many things, therefore he is to be credited in nothing. Daillé quotes Augustine in his *Retractiones*, and a confession of Origen's recorded by Jerome in *Epistle 65*, that they repented in their old age of many things they had written and taught in their youth. Such alterations in their sentiments do occur and will be found if the Fathers are compared with themselves, as would be the case with any writer.

Blunt[40] explains apparent inconsistencies in Clement of Alexandria and Tertullian, making the point that in the peculiar circumstances an explanation is found. For example Clement of Alexandria and most of the primitive Fathers are at variance with themselves on the subject of the corruption of human nature, sometimes arguing extremely, at other times arguing as if it were trifling. So Clement writes 'the heart of natural man is an habi- tation of devils'[41] but also 'man being by nature a high and lofty animal that seeks after what is good'.[42] Blunt points out, that the Fathers were embarrassed not only by what Scripture expressed on this subject and by the testimony of their own hearts, but also by the Gnostic heresy that viewed the world as evil and corrupt, created by an evil demiurge. This view is quite contrary to the Christian doctrine of the Creator God who had made all things good. Clement is also inconsistent with himself on the question of asceticism, but in Tertullian the inconsistencies are more numerous and decisive. Daillé exaggerates this feature and its effects, in his efforts to undermine the general testimony of the Fathers.

Daillé also accuses them of not holding *one and the same belief.* There were indeed differences among the Fathers, but the issue is the significance of the difference, not the fact. Such accepted differences are found in the observance of Easter,[43] and on the Rule of Faith in Tertullian.[44] These examples only illustrate a patristic acceptance of differences in the relative importance of questions. The difficulty of ascertaining the emphasis with which they spoke on any given subject does not detract from their value. The same objections could be brought against the Scriptures, Creeds, Churches and Liturgies. There must be a considerable margin of opinion within which the individual is left to range, so that we cannot expect the Fathers to be categorical on subjects that do not admit of it. Hooker and Andrewes distinguished between belief that was primary and fundamental and necessary for salvation, and that which was secondary and allowed a measure of liberality of opinion. There is no evidence suggesting fundamental difference of belief on the Creed, the divinity of Christ, or the necessity of being in communion with the Church. If the Fathers are unanimous in these matters, they must also be credited with the discernment that would enable them to know whether writings were Scripture and what practices were valid in the church of their time, and thereby be of value in settling what in the seventeenth century was not in accord with antiquity.

Daillé's eighth point is that it is difficult to discover how the Fathers have held all their several opinions. He claims that it is necessary to know not only what the Fathers believed or did not believe, but how they believed or did not believe, whether they held them as propositions necessarily or probably, either true or false, and in what degree of necessity of probability they placed them. He illustrates his point from two propositions; that Christ is God, and that Christ suffered death when he was thirty-four or thirty-five years old. The former proposition is necessary, because Christ could not but be God and we cannot deny it without denying Christianity. The second is contingent, since he could have delayed his suffering until he was older and though taken from Scripture it may be denied as false without great danger. However, both are expressed in Scripture, not as necessary but as true, and it is not a matter of being necessary or contingent but whether it is a matter of divine revelation that cannot be dismissed without great danger.

The Fathers did recognize a great difference in the relative importance of questions they handled from time to time, a point which scarcely required proof. The Fathers were reasonable men, but they might not be prepared to draw up a scale or the exact estimate they took of such differences. It seems odd that their writings should be devalued because of the difficulty of ascertaining the *emphasis* with which they spoke on any given subject. The testimony of the Fathers to the Scriptures, the apostolic doctrine and the customs and polity of the Church, is not dependent on how they held some opinions, whether as necessary or probable. How they held them does not matter, since an error in opinion can never prejudice a testimony concerning fact. One only has to note how they proclaimed the faith among pagans and heretics, instructed the catechumens, expounded the creed, defined the Faith in Council and ruled the Church in Canon;

> to object against the Fathers for not letting us know how they held their opinions, is very disingenuous, not to say dishonest; and this objection I am afraid, falls heavier upon the apostles than their successors, who surely are more large and explicit in their expositions of the Christian religion, and in their condemnation of heresies, than the apostles were, as strange doctrines increased in every age.[45]

The last three points supporting Daillé's first argument, nine, ten and eleven, are so similar that they can be discussed together. He claims we need to know the opinion of the whole ancient Church, and it is very difficult to discover this or whether the opinions of the Fathers concerning the controversies of Daillé's time were received by the universal Church or only by part of it. Furthermore, it is difficult to know exactly what the belief of the church has been, universal or particular, concerning the controversies in Daillé's time.

It is not a difficult task to find out the opinion of the ancient Church in what is to be believed as necessary to salvation. Is it likely that when so few Christian writings have been preserved by the Church, that those should have happened to be preserved which were not on the whole in accordance with her? The Church must have seen some merit in them as expressive of the mind of the Church. The heretical writings were lost except for fragments preserved in those who wrote against the heretics. Furthermore, Eusebius in his *History*, adopts the Fathers as his authorities, using not only many other Fathers whose works are now lost, but great use of those volumes we now possess. In them he finds witnesses to the life and doctrine of the ancient church.[46] The status and character of these Fathers identifies them with their respective churches. Clement of Rome, Ignatius of Antioch, Irenaeus of Lyons, Cyprian of Carthage, were all bishops, and among them also were distinguished presbyters. As for the further objection of Daillé, that recognition of a doctrine by the universal Church is the only guarantee of its soundness, then one only has to note that these very Fathers are drawn from all parts of the Christian world. In almost all of the substantial questions of the Christian Creed they will be found to concur, including many points which touch Daillé and come within the category of controversies. There will also be found differences and contradictions which Daillé disparages, questions about the baptism of heretics and the date of Easter, and the millennarianism which confronted Justin. Allowances have to be made that this is before the age of General Councils; and these Fathers are the raw material out of which these Councils might emerge, and they are not equivalent to General Councils. What is certain is that the interpretations and testimonies of the earliest Fathers (many of which are now lost) were the great helps and authorities, and became the basis on which later councils condemned heresy, established Creeds and settled the Canon of Scripture. Yet Daillé wants to find in the Fathers tracts against the papal supremacy and transubstantiation etc., controversies which came centuries later. The fact is that the Fathers are silent on such matters, though, as Blunt maintains, there is incidental evidence as to where their sympathies would have been in these controversies. The fact of silence on direct evidence becomes an argument to dismiss their relevance and usefulness in relation to such controversies. The same silence becomes a negative argument in their polemic against the Romanists, where it is claimed that no article ought to be imposed as necessary, which was unheard of in the purest times of Christianity. Such a reason can affect only notions and opinions, and not testimonies about fact, which are the main things for which subsequent generations of Christians are dependent upon the Fathers. Is it reasonable to reject such testimony concerning the Sunday Eucharist or the writings of apostles, because some may have held the contrary but did not write about it, or their writings are lost? While some would answer this question negatively, our view is that such a conclusion would be an unsubstantiated supposition, in which imagination has run riot and been, allowed to supplant argument.

Daillé's second general objection

Even if their testimony were clearer, the Fathers are not of sufficient authority to decide modern controversies; this is the
argument of Daillé's Second Book and he makes six points in its
support. First, the testimonies given by the Fathers, concerning the
belief of the Church, are not always true and certain. Errors of fact
may found among the Fathers, but to invalidate their witness to the
belief of the Church for that reason is to expect them to be infallible. Even the most honest people can be mistaken in what they
thought they had seen and, like the Fathers, be innocently
deceived. Goodness does not render people infallible. However, as
Reeves points out, he had always thought

> a matter of sense, of sight especially, no such perplexed matter;
> and to see a king *de facto* full as easy, as to know a king *de jure*. If
> goodness then will not render them infallible, I hope it may
> render them credible witnesses of fact, or else why do we receive
> the canon of Scripture upon testimony? Or where shall we find
> credible witness upon earth, if it be so, he must needs be infalli-
> ble?[47]

The supposition is that none of them could see and hear well
enough to be believed, and the instances used to invalidate their
testimony are some philosophical disputes about the traduction of
human souls[48] and the corporeity of angels.[49] Such opinions were
never claimed as beliefs of the Church. Daillé[50] also instances
Petavius's correction of Epiphanius concerning the Eucharist
being celebrated three times a week by apostolical institution, and
also his correction of an error in the Venerable Bede.

Secondly, Daillé declares, the Fathers themselves testify against
themselves, that they are not to be believed absolutely, and upon
their own bare word. This, however, is not an argument against
their integrity, but rather proof of their honesty and fallibility,
which must give their testimony credibility. They do not declare
that they are not to be believed on their own bare word in matters
of fact. Daillé's anxiety that their writings are regarded with equal
authority to Scripture is unfounded, and his citing of Augustine on
the authority of the Greek writers[51] is to make the point that the
writings of the Fathers are grounded, not upon their bare authority but upon their reasons. We are to examine the Fathers by the
Scriptures, not the Scriptures by the Fathers, and are not to accept
the truth of any Father until it has been proved by Scripture and
Reason. This has been the way of Anglican divines, who have

regarded the Scriptures only as divinely inspired, and therefore as binding in themselves, and the Fathers as interpreters of the Scriptures with better qualifications than the moderns. Daillé heaps up quotations from numerous Fathers, including Augustine, Jerome, and Ambrose, to prove that the opinions of the Fathers are binding only in so far as they are consonant either with Scripture or Reason, 'therefore all this outcry against appealing from God to man, from Scripture to the ancients, is mere paralogism; for the appeal is only to the best human judges, about the meaning of the Word of God'.[52]

Thirdly, the Fathers have written in a way that makes clear that when they wrote, they had no intention of being our judges in matters of religion. This claim is based on a hasty statement by Jerome[53] in which he claims[54] that he had allowed himself three days for the translating of Proverbs, Ecclesiastes, and the Song of Songs, and that he did almost everything at full speed and in haste. Some writings were extempore utterances as in Origen, and in occasional homilies of Augustine and Chrysostom. Writing with such incaution, carelessness, and negligence, says Daillé, only indicates that these Fathers did not regard themselves as oracles to whom we were to listen.[55] His illustrations of errors come mainly from the Post-Nicene Fathers, though he does include Origen's off-the-cuff homilies. Such utterances would be a poor authoritative basis for the doctrines of the Church, but then only a small part of Ante-Nicene theology is contained in homilies. He also lists errors from Justin,[56] who in his handling of the LXX version misdates David 1500 years before Christ and claims the Greek Ptolemy, King of Egypt, sent messengers to Herod, king of Judea, for copies of the writings of the prophets. It was two hundred years before Herod's time that Ptolemy sent his messengers to Eleazer the High Priest.[57] Despite his numerous errors Justin is described by one of his editors, as *aetate antiquissimum, auctoritate gravissimum*,[58] and Blunt says such would be the impression on anyone who read him carefully, fairly, and candidly, for these are accidental lapses and comprise a small proportion of his work. Blunt says that this is what gives effect to Daillé's criticism in the whole of his second book, 'that ranging over the writings of the Fathers, he selects nothing whatever from them but their mistakes and defects; and having done this with an air of seeming triumph, he exclaims, these are the authors you are disposed to regard with reverence'.[59] The same criticism could be made about the Bible, but would not be allowed to invalidate the biblical witness. So Justin's slips of memory do not materially affect his credit as a witness of the church. It may be due to the difficult circumstances under which he wrote. He was a man who lived in persecution, not in a quiet scholar's study, and he died a martyr.

Another class of errors listed stems from the Fathers' ignorance of Hebrew and occurs in their attempts at etymology, as in Justin's[60] derivation of Satanas from Satan, an apostate, and Irenaeus's[61] saying that Jesus in Hebrew means 'that Lord who contains heaven and earth'. Clement of Alexandria is also cited among others.[62] The Fathers' ignorance of Hebrew, with one or two exceptions, cannot impair their authority as witnesses of the practices and doctrine of the primitive church, though it may make them less able expositors of the Old Testament. Their value and authority lies in their nearness in time to the apostles on whom the Holy Spirit had been outpoured and who was leading them into all truth; and being themselves entrusted with high office, they can scarcely fail to have reflected and communicated the doctrine and ordinances to be observed, which were not dependent on their knowledge of Hebrew. Similar was their use of allegory, which Daillé draws mainly from the Post-Nicene Fathers, though the Ante-Nicene Fathers are governed by a figurative interpretation of Holy Scripture. Its primary aim was to illustrate that the Scriptures speak of a Saviour, or in other words, that the primitive church sanctioned an evangelical construction of Scripture. Individual extravagances in an allegory might damage an individual while he was using an allegory to point to Christ; but 'their authority as witnesses, that the interpretation of Scripture went very much upon that principle, would not suffer by it; nay, would be rather promoted. And this, we must always remember, is the matter at issue, what authority is due to the Fathers as witnesses of the character of the Primitive Church'.[63] Waterland's[64] comment is that they were probably in most instances not intended to be interpretations of Scripture, as uses or improvements of it, but rather pious meditations upon Scripture to attract attention and win hearers.

In taking points four and five together, it is noted that Daillé claims that many of the Fathers have erred in different points of religion: and moreover, strongly contradicted one another, and maintained different opinions, in matters of very great importance. Daillé[65] deals with these two accusations, making a list in chapter 4 of his second book. As Reeves points out, their several errors fall into the categories of grammar, history, philosophy, chronology, geography and astronomy, some of which may be errors, some in dispute in Reeves' own time, but most of them cleared up and vindicated by critics of another sort. The inference is that because the Fathers have erred in these matters then their authority in matters of faith is destroyed. The same accusation could be brought to the biblical writers and personages on the basis of similar kinds of error in the Scriptures, and similarly in relation to Justin and his views about the millennium, and to Irenaeus[66] contending that our Lord was between forty and fifty years old when he died. Clement of Alexandria[67] would also be included for teaching that the Gentiles were justified by philosophy. These are only a few instances that could be cited. Such errors are private conjectures on speculative points of subordinate importance, which do not affect the great doctrines of Christianity on which all these Fathers are agreed. Furthermore, no one has claimed infallibility for them, which would then have put this argument in a different light.

Their disagreement with one another is an old accusation of Father against Father. Among the Ante-Nicene Fathers are the various opinions about the millennium, the observance of Easter, the baptism of heretics, differences between Cyprian and Stephanus, the age of Jesus at his crucifixion, the difference between Irenaeus and Tertullian, and Justin and Tertullian's difference concerning the soul of Samuel. Then come the differences between Ante-Nicene and Post-Nicene, as Tertullian's differing view from Augustine on the nature of the soul's generation, and the Post-Nicene Fathers differing from one another. The discrepancies between the Ante-Nicene Fathers are few and unimportant, and those who would devalue them always raise the baptismal and paschal controversies. Their determination to stick out for what both parties considered primitive usage is an indication of how certain we might be that the same persons would not have submitted to any unsound compromise on matters more serious. Our conclusion can be that if on such matters they are so unanimous, their unanimity is the result of their confidence that the faith they hold in these particulars was that once delivered to the saints.

Daillé's final point in support of his second argument claims that neither the Church of Rome, nor the Protestants, acknowledge the Fathers for their judges in their disputes, but accept and reject them at pleasure, and in a degree that suits their own convenience. Reeves points out that it is a shrewd sign that the Church of Rome is conscious of the weakness of its cause, that it will not stand the test of antiquity. However, our own Reformers appealed to the judgement of the Fathers, not only for the refutation of Rome's novelties, but also for the establishment of the primitive doctrine that Anglicanism claimed as its foundation. They are not infallible, but are seen as the best-appointed judges since the apostles and it is not the role of a judge to make laws, as Daillé seems to suppose, but to interpret those already made.

Protestants admit nothing but the canonical Scriptures as their rule of faith, which Daillé claims is the very cornerstone of the Reformation, citing Calvin, Bucer, Melanchthon, Luther and Beza, though admitting that the chief among them did refer to the works of the Fathers. John Jewel is introduced in this respect, but Daillé says that the English Reformers used the Fathers not to establish their own opinions but to refute the Romanists. The discussion of John Jewel in the first part of this book would contradict this, so too would Jewel himself who in the beginning of his *Apology* proposes to make the works of the Fathers an element of his demonstration that the Reformers had right on their side. So also would the Sixth Article contradict Daillé concerning his maxim of the Reformation in which he involves the Church of England. To quote Daniel Waterland,

> We allow no doctrine as necessary, which stands only on Fathers or on tradition, oral or written; we admit none for such, but what is contained in Scripture, and proved by Scripture, rightly inter-preted. And we know of no way more safe in necessaries, to preserve the right interpretation, than to take the ancients along with us. We think it is a good method to secure our rule of faith against impostures of all kinds, whether of enthusiasm or false criticism, or conceited reason, or oral tradition, or the assuming dictates of an infallible chair. If we thus preserve the true sense of Scripture, and upon that sense build our faith, we then build upon Scripture only; for the sense of Scripture is Scripture. Suppose a man were to prove his legal title to an estate, he appeals to the laws; the true sense and meaning of the laws must be proved by the best rules of interpretation; but after all it is the law that gives the title, and that only. In like manner, after using all proper means to come at the sense of Scripture (which is Scripture), it is that, and that only which we ground our faith upon, and prove our faith by. We allege not Fathers as grounds, or principles, or foundations of our faith, but as witnesses, and as interpreters and faithful conveyors.[68]

The Ignatian controversy

This controversy concerning the genuineness of the Ignatian epistles has already been discussed in relation to its bearing upon the
debate about episcopacy and the work of Henry Hammond, in
which it was the most important contribution.[69] As Lightfoot
points out, in England it was never considered on its own merits
because of the burning question of episcopacy, which was crucial
in predetermining not only the sides of the combatants but also
their attitude towards this question.[70] The Ignatian epistles, which
had begun to be published from stray Greek and Latin copies in
1495, settled into what came to be known as the 'Long Recension'
of twelve Greek and three Latin epistles. They became the storm-
centre of untold controversy because of the way in which they
vigorously asserted the necessity of episcopacy. Calvin, the first to
grapple with them, condemned them as 'impudent forgeries'.
Chemnitz, a Lutheran theologian, and after him Whitaker, noted
that the twelve published letters do not correspond with references
to Ignatius in Eusebius and Jerome, who only mention seven and
not twelve; while a quotation from Ignatius in Theodoret does not
appear in the published edition. Baronius and Bellarmine
discount the three Latin letters, accepting the twelve Greek as
undoubtedly genuine, but Socinus dismisses them all. Casaubon
defends the antiquity of some but Petavius regards them all as
interpolated.

An attempt to separate the spurious from the genuine Ignatian
literature was made in 1623 by Vedelius, a Genevan professor, but
the question remained insoluble until 1644 when James Ussher,
Archbishop of Armagh, published his *Polycarpi et Ignatii Epistolae,*
an outstanding work of critical scholarship in the seventeenth
century. He found quotations in three medieval English theologians referring to St Ignatius for that very passage which was found
quoted from Ignatius in Theodoret, and yet was missing from the
twelve letters. Ussher concluded that Faber's text, the 'Long
Recension', must be spurious and that some genuine MSS probably existed in England which represented the Ignatius known to
Theodoret. His search uncovered two Latin copies of Ignatius's
letters; one in Caius College, Cambridge, the other in Bishop
Richard Montagu's library in Norwich. These copies of the text
corresponded with that quoted by the Fathers, and not with the
Long Recension. Lightfoot,[71] while describing Ussher's work as
one of marvellous erudition and critical genius, claimed that it was
marred by one blot. Ussher will only receive six of the letters

mentioned by Eusebius, disclaiming the *Epistle to Polycarp* on the authority of Jerome, who misunderstood the language of Eusebius and confused the *Epistle to the Smyrnaeans* with the *Epistle to Polycarp*. Jerome's error was based on ignorance, that Ussher failed to spot, for the letter to Polycarp, substantially the same in all three recensions, is the best standard and the safest test of the style of Ignatius. While this part of Ussher's theory was universally rejected, his main argument was beyond dispute. His work was further assisted by Isaak Voss, a Genevan professor, who in 1646 edited a Greek text of the 'Middle Recension' from a MS Ussher had traced to the Medicean Library in Florence. Voss published six out of the seven epistles of the 'Middle Recension', the missing Epistle to the Romans being due to the MS being imperfect at the end. This epistle, says Lightfoot,[72] must have been incorporated in the *Acts of Martyrdom* of the saint, with which the volume would close, as was the case in the corresponding Latin version, and both together must have disappeared with the missing sheets. Fifty years later the missing Greek *Acts of Ignatius* with the incorporated *Epistle to the Romans* were discovered in a MS belonging to the Colbert collection, and published by Ruinart (Paris, AD 1689) in his *Acta Martyrum Sincera*. Thus the Greek text of the seven epistles of the 'Middle Recension' was completed.

The work of Ussher and Voss, 'not only completed the critical analysis of the Ignatian Letters but also produced the strongest evidence for episcopacy in the early church.'[73] It could not be denied that the seven epistles contained passages as difficult to be overcome by the advocates of Presbyterianism as any in the 'Long Recension', so it is not surprising that the first opposition came from those who were anti-bishop, the French Protestants. They claimed the testimony of the epistles to the early spread of episcopacy to be untrue. In 1645 Claudius Salmasius (1588–1653) a French classical scholar, declared himself against the Ignatian letters in *Adparatus ad Libros de Primatu Papae*, declaring them to be the false lies of an impostor, in the days perhaps of Antoninus or Marcus Aurelius, and he is quoted by Pearson.[74] The following year David Blondel (1590–1655) goes still further in his *Apologia pro Sententia Hieronymi de Episcopis et Presbyteris*,[75] maintaining that the epistles are spurious and of a later date. As Lightfoot pointed out, 'It did not occur to them to ask whether Ussher's discovery did not require them to reconsider their fundamental position as regards episcopacy.'[76] The part played by Henry Hammond in this controversy has already been discussed, a response also occasioned by the English Puritans who used the weapons of the French armoury.

Daillé had already dismissed the Ignatian epistles as spurious in his *Right Use of the Fathers*. Here he argues that if the epistles Eusebius[77] mentions had been extant in the time of Irenaeus, he would have known them and used them against the heretics as he used Clement of Rome and Polycarp, and they would not have escaped the attention of Clement of Alexandria or Tertullian. This argument cannot be sustained, because the epistles are concerned with such simpler matters as denials of the divinity and humanity of Christ, while Irenaeus is concerned with more elaborate and more complicated heresies. A paragraph in Irenaeus, preserved in Eusebius, concerning 'one of our brethren', who when condemned to the wild beasts saw himself as 'corn being ground into pure bread', might well be a reference to Ignatius and identical to the same passage in his *Letter to the Romans*. Daillé admits this but claims it is a forgery to give the epistle a colouring of truth. Blunt[78] produces from Bishop Bull[79] evidence of another reference from Ignatius in Irenaeus.[80] Polycarp's *Epistle to the Philippians*,[81] speaks of the epistles of Ignatius being sent to him by Ignatius himself, and is decisive against Daillé in having 'said' instead of 'wrote', proving that there were written epistles for Irenaeus to read. Polycarp83 describes them and uses them with their many phrases and peculiar forms of speech. Clement of Alexandria is said never to quote from these epistles, but there are many distinguished writers before him whom he never mentions. Tertullian is also cited as never mentioning Ignatius, but *De carne Christi* c.v. has a passage that resembles one in Ignatius *Ad Ephes.* ch. vii. Here Tertullian uses the same antithetical style as Ignatius in describing the divine and the human in the one Person. Daillé completely by-passes Origen, the next Father to Tertullian and prior to Eusebius, because he directly and repeatedly testifies, not to the sayings, but to the Epistles. As Blunt goes on to say, Daillé's suppressing of a witness because he is against him can only suggest a less than honest search for truth.

In 1666 Daillé published his famous work *De Scripturis circumferuntur*. His assertion of the spuriousness of the Areopagite writings has been endorsed and maintained; Lightfoot's view is that his treatment of the Ignatian writings does not deserve the same praise.

> It is marked indeed by very considerable learning and great vivacity of style; but something more than knowledge and vigour is required to constitute genuine criticism. The critical spirit is essentially judicial. Its main function is, as the word itself

implies, to discriminate. The spirit of Daillé's work is the reverse of this. It is characterized throughout by deliberate confusion.[83]

In 1672 Pearson's great work, *Vindiciae Epistolarum S. Ignatii*, appeared. The vindication rests on two main arguments: (1) Ignatius certainly wrote the letters; (2) The seven letters of Voss are certainly the letters attributed to Ignatius by Eusebius. With these propositions as his starting point, he analyses the attack of Daillé, and sifts the various editions, concluding that the seven can hardly be other than the genuine work of Ignatius, recognized as they are by Irenaeus, Origen, Eusebius, Athanasius, Chrysostom, Jerome, and Theodoret. Lightfoot described it as

> ... incomparably the most valuable contribution to the subject which had hitherto appeared, with the single exception of Ussher's work. Pearson's learning, critical ability, clearness of statement, and moderation of tone, nowhere appear to greater advantage than in this work. If here and there, an argument is overstrained, this was the almost inevitable consequence of the writer's position, as the champion of a cause which had been recklessly and violently assailed on all sides ... The true solution was reserved to our own age, when the correct text has been restored by the aid of newly-discovered authorities. But on the whole, compared with Daillé's attack, Pearson's reply was light to darkness. In England at all events his work seemed to be accepted as closing the controversy.[84]

Lightfoot makes the following points. First, while stating the facts concerning the different recensions in the light of Ussher, Daillé treats the whole of the Ignatian literature as if it was the work of one author, making the Vossian letters bear all the odium of the charges brought against the letters of the 'Long Recension'. Secondly, half of his sixty-six objections against the Ignatian Epistles only apply to the 'Long Recension' and several others are chiefly, though not entirely, occupied with it; and two or three deal only with the medieval Latin correspondence. Ussher had already discounted the spurious and interpolated letters. Thirdly, sane critics would discount Daillé's arguments and positions today. These were: that the Ignatian writings were unknown until they were forged in AD 300; that Origen's quotations from Ignatius were by a Latin interpolator; that a reference to evangelical narratives or incidents not contained in the Canonical Gospels is an argument against the early date of the writings which contain them; and that an author who persistently distinguishes between bishops and presbyters could not have written in the second century.

> The literary ability of this work is undeniable; but it has contributed nothing, or next to nothing, of permanent value to the solution of the Ignatian question. Its true claim to our gratitude is of a wholly different kind. If Daillé had not attacked the Ignatian letters, Pearson would not have stepped forward as their champion.[85]

Opponent of the Fathers

Daillé's objections that the testimony of the Fathers is vague, uncertain, and obscure, and that even if their testimony was clearer, they are not sufficiently authoritative to decide modern controversies, strikes at the foundation upon which Reformers and Carolines established their English catholicism. By implication it destroys the integration of the threefold appeal to Scripture, antiquity and reason, while his dismissal of the Ignatian epistles attempts to destroy patristic authority for the necessity of episcopal government. His aim had been, not to examine the Fathers for themselves alone, but to find reasons in support of an argument he wished to prove, that the Fathers cannot be authoritative judges in the Post-Reformation controversies between Papist and Protestant. As J. J. Blunt pointed out in his Preliminary Lecture, Daillé's only concern in fulfilling this aim was to single out whatever imperfections they present, and place them before his readers without one lucid interval of merit. 'For were the writings of the Fathers such as they are here represented, the reader, but especially the translator, ought both to be sent to the workhouse for better employment.'[86] He goes on to point out that that anyone wishing to malign someone can find something to pin on the wisest and best, and might well imitate Daillé in describing David by his adultery or Peter by his denial. 'It is a much easier matter to cut than cure, to be witty than wise, and a very ordinary hand will serve to deface, what a Pearson or Grabe only can restore and beautify.'[87]

John Barbeyrac and *The Morality of the Fathers*

Another attack on the Fathers came from a different direction in *c.*1716–7, not from an ecclesiastic but from a lawyer. He had been appointed Professor of Law at the University of Gröningen in 1716. He translated several works of Samuel Pufendorf (1632–94) and Grotius (1583–1645) from Latin into French, adding to them notes and additions that attracted attention. Pufendorf's *Of the Law of Nature and Nations* was published in 1672 and an English translation was published in 1710. The work had a subtitle *A General System of the most important principles of Morality, Jurisprudence, and Politics*, and was translated from the Latin by Basil Kennett, DD. The fifth edition was published in 1769 and is in the Bodleian Library). The Preface by Barbeyrac originated as an incidental attack and is entitled '*An Historical and Critical Account of the Science of Morality and the Progress it has made in the world, from the earliest times to the publication of this work*'. It contains thirty-three sections, and in sections IX and X, beginning on page sixteen, is the attack on the Fathers. Here Barbeyrac writes,

> In fact it appears, both by those books we have transmitted down to us, and by the catalogue of such as are lost; that the greatest part of those we call the Fathers of the Church, scarce ever took pen in hand to write on any other subject, besides matters purely speculative; or relating to ecclesiastical discipline. It was but rarely, if at all that they handled points of morality, and that too only occasionally; and always in a very inaccurate and careless manner. The sermons which they sometimes made on this subject, were so stuffed with vain ornaments of false rhetoric; that the Truth, as it were, lay smothered under a heap of metaphors and pompous declamations. And the greatest part of those moral reflections, which they scattered here and there in their Works, were extracted by force and far-fetched allegories, from a thousand different places of Scripture, where the pure literal sense itself made nothing to their purpose. To be convinced of this we need only read those Collections, which some of the most extravagant admirers of Ecclesiastical Antiquity have given us of the most shining passages which they found in the Works of the Fathers. Besides, these ancient Doctors, even in their very best treatises of morality, perpetually confound the Duties of Mankind in general with the particular duties of the Christian, precisely considered as such; as well as the principles of morality purely natural, with those of Christian morality. On the other hand you will often find them putting too great a difference between the Man and the Christian; and by pushing this distinction too far, run themselves into the absurdity of laying down Rules that are impracticable.[88]

This attack was responded to in 1718 by the French Benedictine patristic scholar Rémi Ceillier, in his first great work, *An Apology of the Morality of the Fathers against the unjust accusations of John Barbeyrac*. The work, a dissertation of forty pages, is devoted to establishing the authority of the Fathers, in which Ceillier follows step by step the arguments of Barbeyrac to defend individually those Fathers whom he attacked – Athenagoras, Clement of Alexandria, Augustine, and others. He accuses Barbeyrac of plagiarizing Daillé's treatise and from the *Bibliothèque Universelle,* to which Barbeyrac's rejoinder was that he may as well have made the same accusation in his use of those writers he quoted, such as Dupin, Ussher, Fleury, Grabe and others. Barbeyrac defends his choice of examples in the *Preface*. He had purposely chosen his examples because of their appearance before and their citation in 'very common books'. The success of this work of Ceillier led him to undertake another, similar in character, but wider in scope, and dealing with all the sacred and ecclesiastical writings. Barbeyrac's response to Ceillier's *Apology* was a longer essay, too large for inclusion in subsequent editions of the *Preface*, and in consequence it was published separately with the title, *On the Morality of the Fathers*.

Another response, *The Spirit of Infidelity Detected,* was published in London in 1723 by A Believer, and was printed for T. Payne, near Stationers Hall. The title page points out that it is 'In Answer to a Scandalous Pamphlet, entitled The Spirit of Ecclesiasticks of all Sects, and Ages, as to the Doctrines of Morality; and more particularly the Spirit of the Ancient Fathers of the Church, Examined by Mons. Barbeyrac'. It points out that 'the Fathers are vindicated, the gross Falsehoods of that writer exposed, and his innumerable inconsistencies, as well as those of his Infidel Prefacer, are fully lay'd open'. The author deplores the spirit of Barbeyrac's essay in response to Ceillier, comparing it to Milton's in his *Of Prelatical Episcopacy,* in which he describes the Fathers as 'an undigested heap and fry of authors which they call antiquity'; and to the deists Toland, the author of *Christianity Not Mysterious,* and Tindal, who wrote *The Rights of the Church Vindicated against Romish and all other Priests,* where he describes the religion of the clergy of the fourth and fifth centuries as consisting mostly of cursing. It is the manner in which these authors run down the primitive Fathers and martyrs that the Believer deplores. His suspicion is that the Prefacer of Barbeyrac's essay is a clergyman, and 'the universal belief is that he assumed the guise of a Quaker, in order to vilify and traduce some of the most worthy and valuable men of his own order'. *The Spirit of Infidelity* is a page-by-page approach to Barbeyrac's essay, and replies to his criticisms from the Fathers themselves in a way which illustrates the Believer's considerable patristic knowledge. He accuses Barbeyrac of having very little knowledge of the Fathers, a knowledge limited to their names,[89] regarding him as a Deist and a Sceptic.

The Revd. J. J. Blunt's two series of lectures on *The Right Use of The Early Fathers* delivered in the Michaemas terms of 1845 and 1846 in the University of Cambridge, addressed his remarks not only to Daillé's *The Right Use of the Fathers,* but also dealt with Barbeyrac's criticisms. He wrote of criticisms 'so far as they affect the credit of the *Ante-Nicene* Fathers, especially as I shall thus have a convenient opportunity of clearing away *in limine* certain objections to the study of the Fathers, which one constantly hears alleged, for they comprise nearly all.' Blunt's concern was to prepare his students for the positive advantages of the study of the Fathers. He claimed[90] that the two books by Daillé and Barbeyrac have contributed more to disparagement of the Fathers than any other work, probably affecting even people like Chillingworth and giving his theology the bias it has. As for Barbeyrac himself, Blunt claimed that

> ... it seems very doubtful whether its author had carefully read the Fathers, on whose morality he comments; or had his mind imbued with the spirit, which the actual perusal of them would have left on it. Indeed the review of them which he takes, extending over the first six centuries, renders it impossible that he should have mastered all the Fathers on his list; or should have known more or many of them than he could get at second hand from indexes, abridgements, and extracts, which others might have furnished him with.[91]

Blunt's approach is different from the approach in *The Spirit of Infidelity,* in not following through in order the instances Barbeyrac considers to be defective morality in the Fathers, but rather using them as convenient illustrations of his proposition, that one defect pervades Barbeyrac's reasoning throughout almost all of them: that of not taking into account the *peculiar character* of the times in which the Fathers lived. This defect is the result of Barbeyrac not having carefully read the writings for himself and thereby 'not having possessed his mind thoroughly with a full and correct impression of those times'. He has merely been content to use passages supplied by others, passages detached from their contexts, on which he has hung his accusations.

Notes

1. J. Collinson, *A Key to the Writings of the Principal Fathers of the Christian Church who flourished during the first Three Centuries* (Bampton Lectures, Oxford, 1813).
2. *Ibid.* p. 13.
3. *Ibid.* pp. 13ff.
4. Collinson, citing Joseph Milner (1744–97), *History of the Church of Christ*, vol. iv, (completed by his brother Isaac after Joseph's death), p. 492. A new edition *History of the Church of Christ* (Cadell, 1834) in four volumes. Collinson citation is from an earlier edition of which he includes no details.
5. Cross, ed. *Oxford Dictionary of the Christian Church* 1st edn (OUP, 1957), p. 257.
6. J. J. Blunt, in *An Introduction to a Course of Lectures on the Early Fathers,* (Cambridge University Press, Cambridge, 1840).
7. William Palmer, citing Magee on *Atonement*, vol. ii, Appendix. p. 71; and Rose, *Protestantism in Germany,* pp. 145, 237–40, Appendix, pp. 34, 95, justly remark on the dishonesty of the Socinian and Rationalist infidels, in using the language of Christianity as if they believed its mysteries. *Treatise on the Church*, vol. ii (London, 1838), p. 49.
8. Richard Church, *History of the Oxford Movement* (Macmillan & Co, London, 1897), p. 264.
9. Collinson, *ibid.* pp. 19–20.
10. William Reeves, 'An Essay on the Right Use of the Fathers', in *The Apostolic Fathers of the Second Century,* ed. Wake and Burton (John Grant, Edinburgh, 1909), p. 231.
11. J. Daillé, *The Right Use of the Fathers,* (John Martin, London, 1651), Bk. I, i.
12. J. J. Blunt, *The Right Use of the Early Fathers* (John Murray, London, 1857), p. 27.
13. *Ibid.* p. 28.
14. *Ibid.* pp. 39–56.
15. Justin Martyr, *Apol.* 1. 34, 35. *ANF,* eds. Roberts and Donaldson (Wm. B. Eerdmans, Michigan, 1987), vol. i. p.174. The *Acts of Cyrenius* and the *Acts of Pilate* contain evidence of biographical facts about Jesus. In Luke 2 : 2 the KJV translators called the Roman Governor of Syria, Cyrenius instead of Quirinius. The Greek word used is Κυρηνίου. In the Vulgate the Latin translates 'Cyrino' so the AV translation is in keeping with the state of knowledge as it existed. Quirinius and Cyrenius are one and the same person. Is Cyrenius a Greek transliteration of a Roman name?
16. Justin, *Apol.* 1, 60, *ANF,* vol.i, p. 183.
17. Blunt, *ibid.* Lecture 3.
18. Daillé, *ibid.* p. 41.
19. *Ibid.* pp. 46–7.

20. Reeves, p. 235.
21. Joseph Priestley, *History of the Corruptions of Christianity* (1782), vol. i, p. 32.
22. Blunt, *ibid.* pp. 84ff.
23. Justin, *Dial.* 117, *ANF*, vol. i., p. 257.
24. *Ibid. Dial.* 47, *ANF*, vol. i. p. 218.
25. Blunt, *ibid.* p. 128.
26. Dodwell, *Dissert. in Irenaeum*, v, pp. 408–9.
27. Daillé, *ibid.* p. 69.
28. *Ibid.* p. 72.
29. George Bull, *Defence of Nicene Creed* (*LACT*, Parker, Oxford, 1852).
30. Daniel Waterland, 'On the Trinity', *Works*, vol. i (Clarendon Press, Oxford, 1823).
31. Justin, *Apol.* I, 65, 66, *ANF*, vol. i, p. 185.
32. Clement ofAlexandria, *Stromat.* I, i, *ANF*, vol. ii, p. 299.
33. Irenaeus, IV, xviii, 1, *ANF* vol. i, p. 484.
34. *Ibid.* I, xiii, 2, *ANF*, vol. i, p. 334.
35. *Ibid.* III, iii, 1. *ANF*, vol. i, p. 415.
36. Daillé, *ibid.* Bk. I, vi.
37. Reeves, *ibid.* p. 238.
38. Daillé, *ibid.* p. 112.
39. Reeves, *ibid.* p. 239.
40. Blunt, *ibid.* pp. 190–1.
41. Clement of Alexandria, *Stromat.* II, xx, *ANF*, vol. ii, p. 370
42. *Ibid.* I, vi. *ANF*, vol. ii, p. 307.
43. Eusebius, *Eccl. Hist.* V, xxiv, *NPNF*, Second Series, eds Schaff and Wace (Wm. B. Eerdmans, Michigan, 1976), vol. i, p. 242.
44. Tertullian, *De Praescr.* xiv, *ANF*, vol. iii, p. 249
45. Reeves, *ibid.* p. 243.
46. Eusebius, *Eccl. Hist.* III, xvi, *NPNF*, Second Series, vol. i, p. 147 ; III, xxxvi, p. 166 ; IV, xi, 182 ; VI, xiii, p. 258 ; IV, viii, p. 180.
47. Reeves, *ibid.* p. 247.
48. Jerome, Ep. lxi , *De Error*, *NPNF*, Second Series, vol. vi, p. 131.
49. John, Patriarch of Thessalonica, lived in the first half of the seventh century. As a defender of images he wrote about the subject in the form of a dialogue between a Jew and a Christian. An extract of it was read aloud at the Second Council of Nicaea. He claimed that angels have a body of a thin substance, but it was only a personal opinion and never became a belief of the Church. He was esteemed as a Father.
50. Daillé, *ibid.* Bk. II, p. 6.
51. Augustine,in his contest with Jerome aboutGal. 2 ; *Ep. ad Jerome quest. 19 T. 2. Fol. 14.* (Paris, 1579). *NPNF*, First Series, vol.i, ed. Schaff (T. & T. Clark, Edinburgh, Wm. Eerdmans, Michigan, 1988), Letter 40, p. 272.
52. Reeves, *ibid.* p, 249.
53. Jerome, Ep. cxxviii, *Ad Fabiola.*

54. *Ibid. Pref.* in Proverbs. *NPNF,* Second Series, vol. vi, eds. Schaff and Wace, p. 492.

55. Daillé, *ibid.* Bk. II, iii.

56. Justin, *Apol.* I, xlii, *ANF,* vol. i, p. 176

57. *Ibid.* I, xxxi. p. 173

58. Blunt, *ibid.* quoting Thirlby (one of Justin's editors), p. 207.

59. *Ibid.* p. 207.

60. Justin, *Dial,* ciii, *ANF,* vol. i, p. 255

61. Irenaeus, II, xxiv. 2. *ANF,* vol. i, p. 393.

62. Daillé, *ibid.* Bk. II, p. 50.

63. Blunt, p. 216.

64. Daniel Waterland, 'On the Use and Value of Ecclesiastical Antiquity', *Works,* vol. v, p. 312 (Oxford Edition).

65. Daillé, *ibid.* Bk. II, iv and v.

66. Irenaeus, II, xxii, *ANF,* vol. i, p. 390.

67. Clement of Alexandria, *Stromat.* I, xx, *ANF,* vol. i, p. 323

68. Waterland, *ibid.* p. 316.

69. J. W. Packer, *The Transformation of Anglicanism 1643–60* (Manchester University Press, 1969), p. 106.

70. J. B. Lightfoot, *Apostolic Fathers,* Pt. II. *S. Ignatius and S. Polycarp,* 2nd edn vol. i. (Macmillan, London and New York, 1889), p. 240.

71. *Ibid.* p. 243.

72. *Ibid.* p. 245.

73. Packer, *ibid.* p. 107.

74. John Pearson, *Vind. Ign.* p. 42.

75. D. Blondel, *Praef.* p. 39. sq.

76. Lightfoot, *Apostolic Fathers,* Pt. II, p. 331.

77. Eusebius, *Eccl. Hist.* III, xxxvi, *NPNF,* Second Series, vol. i, p. 166.

78. Blunt, *ibid.* p. 78. A comparison of comparable antithetical styles in Tertullian and Ignatius to substantiate Blunt's claim that Tertullian did read Ignatius.

79. George Bull, *De Fid.* sect. 4, iii, 6.

80. Irenaeus, IV, xxiv, 2 *ANF,* vol. i, p. 495 ; *Ignat. ad Polycarp,* iii, p. 13.

81. Polycarp, *Ad Philipp.* xiii, *ANF,* vol. i, p. 36

82. Polycarp, *Ad Philipp.* i.; *Ignat. ad Smyrna* xi; *Ad Ephes.* xi; Bishop Pearson's *Vind. Ignat.* Part I, v. See *ANF,* Vol. i,

83. Lightfoot, *Apostolic Fathers,* Pt. II, p. 331.

84. *Ibid.* p. 333.

85. *Ibid.*

86. Reeves, p. 256.

87. *Ibid.* p. 257.

88. Barbeyrac, *Preface,* sect. IX, p. 16.

89. A Believer, *The Spirit of Infidelity Detected,* (T. Payne, London 1723), p. 1.

90. Blunt, *ibid.* p. 24.

91. Blunt, *ibid.* p. 227.

12

Indirect Objections and Responses

The indirect objections to the Fathers came in the form of fashionable movements of thought that were critical and dismissive of the received patristic doctrine in the credal formularies. The doctrines of the Trinity and the Incarnation were the primary targets, with destructive consequences for Church and Sacraments. Three movements of thought with their indirect attack on the appeal to antiquity were *Deism,* a belief, arising from reason rather than revelation, in the existence of a non-interventionist Supreme Being. *Arianism,* which derived from the teaching of the priest Lucian and was developed by another priest, Arius, denied the divinity of Christ. *Socinianism* was a development of the Arian heresy and originated with two Italians named Socinus in the sixteenth century. Socinianism denied the real distinction of persons in the Godhead, the divinity of Christ and the divinity of the Holy Spirit. It gave birth to English Unitarianism.

Deism was more or less contemporaneous with the Revolution of 1688, and by 1790 Burke could speak of the Deistic writers as already forgotten. The pivot of the controversy with Deism is the disputed question of the sufficiency of natural reason to establish religion and enforce morality. The philosopher Hobbes, though utterly opposed to the kind of natural religion which formulated itself as Deism, was, as much as any single writer, responsible for giving the impulse to religious speculation, and helped to shake the old confidence in tradition, so that the influences of his writings were in the main negative, helping to sap the defences of authority. The influence of the Cambridge Platonists was a different element at work in the intellectual life of the nation, in their desire to establish a Christian philosophy on rational grounds. Hence their influence was more positive, accustoming the minds of men to the hope of finding in their own reason a judge capable of bringing to an end the weary series of doubtful disputations over matters of faith.

Locke (1632–1704), who was not a Deist, had an effect on the religious thought of his day which he neither intended nor approved, but without his influence Deism would not have become as fashionable as it did. His *Reasonableness of Christianity* (1695) laid down the lines along which the controversy was destined to move. It attempted to simplify the ancient faith, at first with an apologetic purpose, then with an increasing hostility, proposing a principle of discrimination between the supposedly valuable and the worthless elements of the Creed. The same pre-eminence is assigned to the ethical teaching of Christ, and the same conception is present of Christianity as a moral philosophy and code of precepts, rather than as a power enabling the enfeebled will. Miracles and prophecy are treated as external evidences of the truth of Christianity, and there is a conscious anxiety to discover a reconciliation between belief in the absolute impartiality of the Divine goodness and the position of privilege assigned to revealed religion. Such ideas, by no means new, are for the first time brought together in a combination that leads to a conclusion calling for the modification, and possibly the repudiation, of important elements in the hitherto accepted creed.

This thinking gave impetus to the deistic writers, among whom John Toland, Anthony Collins and Matthew Tindal are representative names. Toland published in 1696 his *Christianity not Mysterious*, maintaining that there is nothing in the gospel contrary to Reason nor above it, and that no Christian doctrine can properly be called a Mystery. Misinterpreting Locke, he equates reasonable with *not mysterious*. His concern is to enlarge the jurisdiction of reason and make it coextensive with the contents of revelation. His work had a critical influence on the comparative authority of reason and revelation, reason being arrogantly asserted as superior. In *Amyntor* (1699), he undermines the credit of Scripture by calling attention to a large mass of early Christian literature, and by suggesting surreptitiously that canonical and uncanonical writings alike were the offspring of superstition and credulity. Collins published his *Discourse of Free thinking occasioned by the Rise and Growth of a Sect called Freethinkers*, reiterating the claim of reason to pronounce upon the contents of revelation. He went further than Toland in attempting to provide a theoretic justification of the unlimited scope of reason over the whole field of moral and religious speculation, claiming an unconditional liberty to pursue investigation and upon a conviction of individual capacity to discover the truth. His *Discourse of the Grounds and Reasons of Christian Religion* (1724), discards the question of the relative reasonableness or unreasonableness of the contents of the Christian religion, turning to an enquiry into the credibility of prophecy and miracle. It was the beginning of the critical approach to the biblical documents, being a change of tack from inquiry into the fundamental truths of Christianity to disputation over the credibility or integrity of the New Testament writers themselves. Matthew Tindal's best known work, *Christianity as old as the Creation,* or *The Gospel a Republication of the Religion of Nature* (1730), brought to its logical conclusion the process initiated by Toland and Collins. His concern was to expound plain and simple rules by which anyone might distinguish between religion and superstition. Like his predecessors he repudiated mystery and mere deference to authority, and insisted on the duty of every man to fashion his own religious belief for himself. This is possible, he maintained, because the ultimate truth of religion is a common constituent in all creeds, and not the exclusive property of revelation.

The Context of George Bull's Response (1674–1710)

Robert Nelson, the biographer of George Bull, records that several Arian and Socinian pieces published in Holland were distributed in England.[1] The writers presumed themselves able to maintain these doctrines against 'the received Catholick Doctrine'. The controversy centred around the Godhead of the Son, and the Consubstantiality and Coeternity of the Son of God. Generally the Socinians saw the solution to the controversy residing in Scripture and Reason, rejecting the need for any patristic testimony. The Arians, however, disputed this omission of ancient patristic witness, boasting that the ancient Christian Fathers who lived before the Council of Nicaea were really on the side of Arius. The books of Sandius, who defended Arianism as 'the true Catholick Doctrine' on the testimony of the Ante-Nicene Fathers, were circulating among students of divinity without any antidote. The second edition of his *Kernel of Ecclesiastical History* was in circulation and was 'bent upon persuading such readers as are unlearned, and have very little acquaintance with the writings of the ancients, that the ante-Nicene Fathers, without exception, simply held the same doctrine as Arius'.[2] It was against the background of these controversies and the shallow Deism that was coming into fashion, that George Bull was persuaded to pen the much needed antidote in *Defensio Fidei Nicaenae (1685)*. In vindicating the Godhead of the Son Bull was also defending himself against the groundless charge of Socinianism, and demonstrating a consistency of belief in this doctrine among the Ante-Nicene Fathers and the Nicene Fathers that was derived from the Apostolical Age itself. A related concern was that if he could convince his readers of the divinity of the Son, then they might be brought to a right conviction concerning the divinity of the Spirit of God.

Impetus to Arian opinions was due partly to the arguments advanced by the Jesuit scholar Dionysius Petavius,[3] 'at whom I cannot sufficiently wonder', wrote Bull,[4] because of Petavius's claim that almost all the bishops and Fathers before Nicaea held precisely the same opinions as Arius. On the basis of this Sandius and others claimed Petavius was an Arian, and that their seventeenth-century Arianism could claim the support of the Ante-Nicene Fathers. Bull[5] claims that it is clear from the writings of Petavius himself that this conjecture by Sandius is entirely false. Petavius's aim was the promotion of the papal interest rather than the Arian, Bull's argument being that in convicting almost all the Ante-Nicene catholic doctors of Arian error, Petavius in the first instance is demeaning the authority of these Fathers of the first three centuries to whom Reformed Catholics appealed, 'as being persons to whom the principal articles of the Christian Faith were not as yet sufficiently understood and developed'.[6] Secondly, Petavius claimed that Ecumenical Councils have the power of settling and developing new articles of faith, a principle that gives credence to the additions which the Council of Trent 'patched on to the rule of faith', though in no way could Trent ever be defined as a general council.

> But so it is: the masters of that school have no scruples in building their pseudo-catholic faith on the ruins of the faith which is truly catholic. The divine oracles themselves, must, forsooth, be found guilty of so great obscurity, and the most holy doctors, bishops, and martyrs of the primitive Church be accused of heresy, in order that, by whatever means, the faith and authority of the degenerate Roman Church may be kept safe and sound. And yet these sophists (of all things) execrate us as if we were so many accursed Hams, and deriders and despisers of the venerable fathers of the Church; whilst they continually boast that they themselves religiously follow the faith of the ancient doctors, and reverence their writings to the utmost. That Petavius, however, wrote those writings with this wicked design, I would not venture to affirm for certain, leaving it to the judgement of that God who knoweth the hearts. At the same time, what the

Jesuit has written, as it is most pleasing to modern Arians, (who on this account with one consent look up to and salute him as their patron,) so we confidently pronounce it to be repugnant to the truth, and most unjust and insulting to the holy fathers, whether those of the Council of Nice, or those who preceded it.[7]

Not only did the Arians attempt to include Petavius among their number: they made a similar charge against Curcellaeus the Protestant writer because of his *Preface to the Works of Episcopius.*

Bull[8] describes Episcopius as 'a most learned theologian in all other respects but an utter stranger to ecclesiastical antiquity ', who though he affirmed the pre-existence of the Son in opposition to Socinianism, inveighs against the Nicene Creed, and Creeds composed after the third century which agreed with it.[9] Bull's anxiety is that students reading the description of the Nicene Creed and those who framed and composed after the third century, that it was 'precipitately framed from excitement, if not fury, and a maddened and unblessed party spirit, on the part of the bishops who were wrangling and contending with one another from excessive rivalry, rather than as what issued from composed minds',[10] might get a mean opinion of those venerable Fathers and those who preceded and followed them. His concern is to wipe out such disparagement of the Fathers by statements from Constantine and Eusebius. Constantine, in his *Epistle to the Churches,* had written, that in his presence as moderator of the Nicene Council, 'every point had there received due examination', and to the church of Alexandria he had written that points of ambiguity and differences of opinion were tested and accurately examined. Eusebius, 'an author of the utmost integrity', had also confirmed that the unanimous agreement to the Creed had not been drawn up hastily or inconsiderately but only after exact, deliberate, and careful investigation of each separate proposition.[11]

In *Irenicum Irenicorum,* the anonymous author proclaimed the Nicene Fathers as 'the framers of a new faith', and sought to prove this in his work by a collection of testimonies from the remains of the Ante-Nicene Fathers that appear to be inconsistent with the Nicene Creed. Curcellaeus described the book as containing 'irrefragable testimonies and arguments'. It was the identification of Curcellaeus with these writers in these particular sentiments that brought the charge of Arianism against him, being accused by Maresius, a hot Calvinist whom Nelson[12] describes as having a 'personal pique against him'. He accused him publicly of heresy in the Trinity and Incarnation, and in his *Anti-Tirinus* called him an anti-Trinitarian. Curcellaeus responded, claiming he was no anti-Trinitarian and challenging his adversary to prove where he had deviated from the Scriptural doctrine and the explication of it in the Fathers. He explained and defended himself by arguments and testimonies from Antiquity, 'to which he was not such a stranger as his master Episcopius'. Nevertheless, as Nelson goes on to point out, Curcellaeus was no less an enemy of the Council of Nicaea than Episcopius, for he asserted no more than a specified unity in the Divine Persons (that is, a unity with the Godhead limited because the Son is subordinate to the Father and, not being eternal, is of a different species). He defended the cause of Valentinus Gentilis, beheaded at Bern in Switzerland for Tritheism, and claimed particular support in Ignatius, Justin, Irenaeus, Athenagoras, Tertullian and Clement of Alexandria. Curcellaeus also accused what he called the modern and scholastical doctrine of the Trinity, of Sabellianism, as being inconsistent with Christ and the apostles, because it destroyed the notion of consubstantiality, as then currently understood in relation to the Father and the Son. Curcellaeus was, moreover, impatient with notions of divine relations within the Godhead, or of mutual consciousness, and with such terms as generation, procession, modes of subsistence or personalities. His concern was to discard all terms and phrases not legitimated by the scriptural writers. The Godhead of the Son and the Holy Spirit were subordinate to the Father and the Son, a subordination unquestionable and supported by the evidence of the primitive church. Petavius, and the author of the *Irenicum Irenicorum* were recommended as containing authentic testimonies from the patristic writings concerning these articles.

Bull sets out his purpose,

> ... to shew clearly that what the Nicene Fathers laid down concerning the divinity of the Son, in opposition to Arius and other heretics, was in substance (although perhaps sometimes in other words and in a different mode of expression) taught by all the approved Fathers and doctors of the Church without a single exception, who flourished before the council of Nice down from the very age of the Apostles.[13]

When Bull's work was published in 1685, his opponents in the main were not Englishmen; anti-Trinitarian opinions in Britain had as yet no prominent advocates, being, as Van Mildert[14] styles them in his *Life of Waterland*, 'importers of foreign novelties'. Nevertheless, his work anticipated theological trends that were to find expression in seventeenth century English theology through Dr Bury's *Naked Gospel* (Oxford, 1690) which advocated Arianism, and Dr Sherlock, the Dean of St Paul's, who published his *Vindication of the Doctrine of the Holy and Ever-Blessed Trinity* during that same year. Sherlock was influenced by the Cambridge Platonist Ralph Cudworth, an opponent of religious dogmatism, but the work was condemned by Robert South in *Animadversions* on Sherlock's *Vindication* (1690) and *Tritheism Charged* (1695), the latter title pinpointing the charge. The Vice-Chancellor and heads of Oxford houses condemned it as 'false, impious and heretical, contrary to the doctrine of the Catholic Church, and especially of the Church of England, to say "that there are three infinite, distinct minds and substances in the Trinity, or that the three Persons are three distinct infinite minds or spirits."'[15]

Bull's *Defensio* is a work in four books, the publication in the Library of Anglo-Catholic Theology being in two parts, each book expounding a principal pillar of the Catholic doctrine concerning Christ.

Book I *On the Pre-existence of the Son*

The pre-existence of Christ is maintained, against the Socinians, Arians, Sabellians and Tritheists, that as Son of God he pre-existed before his birth of the Virgin and before the world was. This is the unanimous doctrine of all the Fathers of the first three centuries and is not denied by the Arians. Against the Socinians he proves that all the divine apparitions in the Old Testament are explained concerning the Son of God in the testimonies of Justin, Irenaeus, Theophilus of Antioch, Clement of Alexandria, Tertullian, Origen, and Cyprian. This continued to be the Catholic doctrine after the Council of Nicaea as testified in Athanasius, Hilary, Philastrius, Chrysostom, Ambrose, Augustine, Leo the Great and Theodoret. Then he proves the existence of the divine Logos and his part in creation from the testimony of the Apostolic Fathers and others. He goes on to prove, against the Arians, that they betray their own cause by positing the Father to have created all things by his own Son out of nothing. It is impossible for a creature, which is itself made out of nothing, as they assert of the creation of God's Son, to have such a power communicated to it if it is less than infinite. The testimony of the primitive Fathers, even before Arius, is that God created the world by nothing that was without him, but by his Word only, which was with him and in him.

Book II *On the Consubstantiality of the Son*

His divine consubstantiality is defended against the Arians, that as Son of God he was not of any created or changeable essence, but of the very same nature as God his Father, being therefore rightly called, very God of very God, of one substance with the Father. In modern sociological jargon, consubstantiality would be described as a 'hinge issue', being that upon which the whole controversy between Nicaeans and Arians turns; interestingly enough, this is also Bull's way of describing it.[16] Before dealing with the patristic evidence he first turns to a vindication and expounding of the term ὁμοούσιος, 'of one substance', which was placed by the Nicene Fathers in their Creed.[17] In chapter 2,[18] beginning with the Apostolic Fathers, he expounds the understanding of consubstantiality in Barnabas, Hermas, and Ignatius, clearing Clement of Rome and Polycarp from the misrepresentations of Zwickerus, the author of the *Irenicum*, and Sandius.[19] He then begins his testimony from Justin,[20] with this Father's censure of those who deny 'that the Father of all things has a Son, who, being also the first-born Word of God, is also God'.[21] Irenaeus's testimony occupies the fifth chapter[22] and in chapter 6 Clement of Alexandria is defended against Petavius's accusations of Platonizing, against Peter Huet's of the making of the Son inferior to the Father[23] and against Sandius's of Arianism. Tertullian's doctrine is then shown to be coincident with the Nicaean[24] followed by that of the presbyter Caius and Hippolytus.[25] Origen, especially from his work against Celsus, is then woven into the argument[26] which is followed by the testimonies[27] of Cyprian, Novatian, and those of Theognostus, before citing the sentiments of Dionysius of Rome and Dionysius of Alexandria.[28] Gregory Thaumaturgus[29] further confirms Nicene doctrine, as also the letter of the six bishops who wrote to Paul of Samosata[30] when he denied the divinity of Christ, along with testimony from Pierius, Pamphilus, Lucian and Methodius, and some passages from Arnobius and Lactantius.

Book III *The Coeternity of the Son*

Book III, in Part II, takes up Bull's third thesis, the coeternity of the Son.

> For He who is truly and properly God, and is begotten of the substance of God, must necessarily possess all the peculiar attributes of God, infinity, immensity, eternity, omnipotence, the

being uncreated, and unchangeable, with those other properties without which true Godhead cannot subsist.[31]

The point is made that though the ancient writers expressed themselves differently on this matter, the greater part of them before Nicaea did teach his coeternal existence with the Father. Some writers antedating the Nicene Council give the impression of attributing a certain Nativity to the Son as God, preceding the creation of the world. As Bull points out, these writers speak not of a real Nativity, but of a figurative and metaphorical one and therefore in no way can they be accused of Arianism.[32] His next and third proposition is that certain Fathers who lived after the Arian controversy and were completely opposed to it, were consistent in holding the doctrine of the aforementioned Fathers or

> the mode in which they held their view. For they themselves also acknowledged that going forth of the Word, who existed always with God the Father, from the Father, (which some of them called his συνκατάβασις, that is, His condescension,) in order to create this universe; and confessed that, with respect to that going forth also, the Word Himself was, as it were, born of God the Father, and is in the Scriptures called the First-born of every creature.[33]

Bull, regarding their case to be peculiar, concludes his third book with a discussion of Tertullian and Lactantius,[34] concerning the charge that they had denied the coeternity of the Son. Tertullian lapsed into heresy, so there is a difficulty in establishing in what state he was when some of his works were written. Acknowledging Tertullian's express statement, 'that there was a time when the Son of God was not,' Bull claims that Tertullian used this statement problematically, in a characteristic way of argument peculiar to Tertullian and here by way of disputation with Hermogenes. As Nelson summarizes it,

> so as though he may seem absolutely to deny the Son's eternity, yet all the while he doth mean no more at the bottom, than those other Fathers, that have been before mentioned, namely, that that Divine Person who is called the Son of God, notwithstanding that he never but existed with the Father, was yet then first declared to be the Son, when he proceeded forth from the Father, in order to make or constitute the Universe, certain it is, that the same Tertullian elsewhere, in many places philosophizeth altogether as a good catholic, concerning the Son's co-eternity; the Supereminency of the Subject considered.[35]

Bull dismisses Lactantius as a rhetorician rather than a theologian, being little acquainted with the Holy Scriptures and the doctrine of the Church, who therefore fell into the most absurd errors, 'as would scarcely be excusable in a catechumen'.[36]

> But moreover we must necessarily conclude that those writings, that either those places in the writings of Lactantius, which seem to make against the Son's eternity, were corrupted by some Manichaean heretic, or else that Lactantius himself was certainly infected with the heresy of Manes. And after all, it must be owned, that even he too hath yet somewhere delivered a sounder opinion concerning the eternity of the Logos. All which particulars, our Author hath distinctly considered in the last chapter of this third section.[37]

Bull concludes that it is clearly true what Sissinius declared concerning the doctrine of the doctors of the Church who flourished before the Arian controversy, and is stated in Socrates.[38] 'The ancients studiously avoided attributing a beginning of existence to the Son of God; for they understood him to be co-eternal with the Father.'[39]

Book IV *On the Subordination of the Son to the Father*

In Book IV Bull takes up the thesis concerning the subordination of the Son in which he sets down three propositions. Chapter 1 states that the catholic doctors before and after Nicaea approved the decree of that Council that the Son of God is God of God, and that he has the same divine nature in common with the Father but subordinately, in that it is communicated from the Father, the Father alone having that divine nature from himself, thereby being the Original and Principle of divinity which is in the Son. The same Fathers unanimously declared[40] God the Father to be greater than the Son, not by nature or essential perfection, but only by Fatherhood, the Father being the Author. The third proposition, the doctrine of the subordination of the Son to the Father as to his 'Origination' and 'Principiation', was seen by the Fathers as safeguarding the Godhead of the Son, the unity of God and the preserving inviolate of the divine monarchy. The divine monarchy and subordination of the Son in the Blessed Trinity means that there is no lessening of the consubstantiality or coeternity of the Son and Spirit with the Father.

Bull's *Judicium Ecclesiae Catholicae*

A second work, *Judicium Ecclesiae Catholicae* (1694), was written against those who, professing themselves to believe the truth of the Nicene doctrine, argued that nevertheless after the example (as they alleged) of the ante-Nicene Church, an acceptance of that truth should not be made one of the terms of communion with the church; and that consequently the Nicene Council, though right as to the doctrine defined, was unjustified in adding an anathema to the decision. Again Bull conducts an elaborate examination of the ante-Nicene history and literature.

Bull's Distinctive Use of the Appeal to Antiquity

Bull quotes extensively from the sources because his opponents were also quoting from the Fathers as if they were on their side. In his thorough use of the sources his concern was to make clear the meaning and context of the passages to demonstrate their agreement with Scripture from the apostolical age to the time when the present creed was established. The main affirmation of his work is that the Nicene Fathers did not define or declare as an article of faith anything that was not there from the beginning, and that their doctrine is the true sense of Scripture. What distinguished Bull's application of the appeal to the Fathers was the way in which he applied it to counter Arianism and Socinianism, whose primary aim was to minimize the historic creeds. As McAdoo points out,

> For Bull orthodoxy was not so much a primal dogmatic formulation as the original deposit which was safeguarded and preserved by the form taken in the affirmation of the creeds ... the issue involved was not that 'the old is better,' but that the tendency of certain moderns was to whittle down what Bull and those who agreed with him regarded as irreducible.[41]

McAdoo goes on to say that it was not a simple matter of comparison of the Latitudinarians' welcoming attitude to modernity with that of Bull. What was in question were two different manifestations of modernity, one hostile and the other not apparently so.

> The one hinged on historical theology which was being called in question, and the other on reason which was being jubilantly heralded as the common ground of science and religion. In the one case a specifically theological situation had to be dealt with, while in the other, it was more a matter of preliminary adjustment and of preliminary soundings.

So Bull was

> ... tied to a specific situation, that of the defence of fundamen-
> tals in the terms of the Nicene faith. As he saw it the situation
> admitted of no relaxation of the argument and he pressed home
> the conclusions of his researches into the writings of the fathers
> as much against the moderate latitude of Episcopius as against
> the more radical interpretations of the evidence by other
> writers. Undeviating in his adherence to this line, Bull handles
> the opinions of others honestly and critically but always paying
> tribute to genuine learning wherever he meets it. His work
> remains an example of that exact use of sources and thorough-
> ness of investigation with which theology can never afford to
> dispense. Not only his own Church acknowledged a debt to a
> writer who described himself as an exile from the common-
> wealth of letters but whose careful scholarship informed his own
> judgement and set a standard for the work of others.[42]

Commenting on the translator F. Holland's introduction to the
1730 edition of *The Works of George Bull,* and his 'account of this way
in writing, of appeals to antiquity', McAdoo[43] sees something of
more significance than an eighteenth-century flavour and the later
Latitudinarian attitude which 'adds piquancy to his approval of the
appeal to antiquity'. This significance lies in the fact that

> ... Holland represents that solid Anglicanism of the times in
> that he grasps, as does Waterland, the importance of the rela-
> tionship between the three elements for theological method.
> Awareness of this essential proportion of theology persisted
> through the eighteenth century in spite of the growth of the
> partisan approach and in fact it never really disappeared.

After the Evangelical and Tractarian revivals it gradually re-
emerged, and

> ... began to clothe itself once more with life and with relevance
> as the increasing complexity of the human scene made ever-
> growing demands for a faith 'that was not afraid to reason nor
> ashamed to adore'. Firmly based on the primacy of Scripture
> and on the finality of fundamentals, reaching back to antiquity
> as to a living source of continuity of faith and order, it had and
> has a creed to offer and a liberality of outlook and a freedom of
> movement for the human spirit which is not only its attraction
> but its truth. The two great movements of the nineteenth
> century contributed much that was invaluable to Anglicanism,

and it is probably the case that those contributions could not have been made effectively, after the deadness of the late eighteenth century, without the aid of what may be called in rough terms party theology. But it also seems to be the case that in difficult times during the seventeenth century the spirit of Anglicanism was coping with a variety of equally pressing problems from a more stable centre when it held the three elements of theological method in proportion. Later history from the time of *Lux Mundi* onwards suggests that this is indeed its vocation, for nothing less answers the whole need or goes to meet the situation in anything like its entirety.[44]

Daniel Waterland's Response 1683–1740

In England the two divines identified as Arian were William Whiston, Professor of Mathematics at Cambridge, and his friend Dr Samuel Clarke, Rector of St James's Piccadilly. Whiston published his *Primitive Christianity Revived*, teaching what he described as 'Eusebian' doctrine, but choosing the less orthodox Eusebius of Nicomedia as the exponent of the true tradition of Christian doctrine rather than Eusebius of Caesarea. He also put out a revised form of the liturgy, from which he cut out all the 'Athanasian' doctrine, leaving only bare 'Unitarianism'. In 1712 Clarke, who was the real champion of sub-Trinitarian belief, published his *Scripture Doctrine of the Trinity*, citing 1251 texts, declaring the Father alone supreme, the Son divine only so far as divinity is communicable by the supreme God, and the Holy Spirit inferior to the Father and the Son, not in order only, but also in dominion and authority. Apparently of the fifty-five propositions advanced by Clarke there was only one to which an ancient Arian could not have subscribed. Their objections to the catholic doctrine of the Trinity were derived from certain texts which, isolated from the Bible as a whole, might be interpreted in an Arian way. For example a question raised was whether all power was given to Christ, (Matthew 28: 18), and whether all things were put in subjection under his feet after his Resurrection (Ephesians 1: 22.), if he were Lord long before? The book was long regarded as a kind of text-book of modern Arianism, and led to the same conclusion as Whiston: the Father alone is the one supreme God, the Son defined as being divine but only in so far as divinity is communicable by this supreme God, but the Holy Spirit is inferior to the Father and the Son, not only in order but in dominion and authority. Among the chief supporters of this new Arianism were Dr Whitby and the Revd John Jackson, Rector of Rossington and Vicar of Doncaster, and though Clarke's work was condemned by Convocation in 1714, the dispute was not silenced.

In his *Vindication* Waterland's response is to affirm that the Logos was from the beginning Lord over all, but the God-Man, (θεάνθρωπος), was not so until after the Resurrection. In that capacity as the God-Man, he received what he has always enjoyed in another, that is full power in both natures, which he had until this moment only received in one. The passage on which they tried to turn the whole argument was 1 Corinthians 8: 6. which in their interpretation expressly excluded the Son from being one with the Supreme God, and which, according to Clarke, is Pauline doctrine which the Trinitarians had falsified. Waterland's response is to turn the accusation of falsification on the Arians, pointing out that it is the orthodox who make the Son essentially the same God with the One, thereby preserving the oneness of divinity in the union of Persons. It is Dr Clarke's school who make two Gods, who corrupt St Paul's doctrine. For the orthodox there is a reason why the Son is included in the Godhead, because being essentially of the same divine nature he is intimately united to the Father. A series of sermons was published by Waterland, and these are in the second volume of his *Works,* where in the preface he states that they are a 'Supplement to my Vindication of Christ's divinity', in which his concern is not only to avoid repetition, but also for the most part to enlarge on what had been only briefly hinted. His concern is consistent with the *Vindication,* in being to 'justify our belief in *Christ Jesus* as a *Divine* Person, *coequal* and *coeternal* with God the Father', three points of which are concerned with St John's prologue.

To turn from Scripture to antiquity and to the opinion of the ante-Nicene Fathers, the preceding discussion has demonstrated how thorough was the work of George Bull in presenting this data, to which Waterland was the heir and successor. In the light of Bull's work, no Arian, ancient or modern, could claim the support of the Fathers. In claiming patristic support for their theory, the issue turns again on the *right use of the Fathers,* so that Waterland's task is to demonstrate how Dr Clarke's school of thought has deprecated the value of the patristic evidence to confirm their theory. Waterland therefore sets out to demonstrate what is and what is not the true character of the appeal to antiquity, how the Fathers are certain proofs in many cases of the Church's doctrine in that age, and probable proofs of what that doctrine was from the beginning, while setting the appeal to antiquity in its right relationship not only to Scripture but also to reason.

Waterland and The Use and Value of Ecclesiastical Antiquity

Though various opponents, including Dr Wells, attacked Clarke's book for its lack of any method of discerning the true sense of Scripture, as well as flying in the face of Creeds and patristic testimony, it was Daniel Waterland (1683–1740) who responded to the dispute as the champion of orthodoxy and with the most comprehensive of the whole question. In the image in which he is depicted in his portrait which hangs in Magdalene College, Cambridge, the former Master holds in his left hand a paper inscribed with the words, '*Vindication of Christ's Divinity*'; it is a graphic reminder of a divine whose life was devoted to the championing of orthodoxy. It was this work he published in answer to Jackson in 1719 when Waterland was Archdeacon of St Alban's and in the long battle of the pamphlets which followed, Waterland was conspicuous alike for basing his doctrine on Scripture alone and for the respect he showed for the Fathers. It has been said that if there had been no Bull there would have been no Waterland. The work of Bull was therefore essential in enabling Waterland to make his own distinctive contribution, but it was a dispute which marks the close of the age when the Fathers were confidently appealed to in theological disputes.

> ... It was not an age in which the authority of the Fathers was much considered. There was a strong tendency to assume that all the Church History that mattered began with the Reformation, or even 1688. The Patristic and Middle Ages were dismissed as 'Popery' and the Arians claimed that they were returning to a pure and primitive belief.[45]

Such a disregard for the Fathers was by no means lacking in the theological method of Waterland. Van Mildert pointed out that the principles of Waterland's use of ecclesiastical antiquity with respect to controversies of faith, 'are laid down with great precision: the extremes of irreverent disregard, on the one hand, and of undue confidence on the other, being carefully avoided'.[46] As Waterland himself points out,

> There is no occasion for magnifying antiquity at the expense of Scripture; neither is that the way to do real honour to either, but

to expose both; as it is sacrificing their reputation to serve the
end of novelty and error. Antiquity ought to attend as an handmaid to Scripture, to wait upon her as her mistress, and to
observe her; to keep off intruders from making bold with her,
and to discourage strangers from misrepresenting her. Antiquity
in this ministerial view, is of great use.[47]

The point he makes, against those whose concern is for a modern
corrupt church rather than for the pure and ancient faith, is, that
for Anglicanism it is antiquity superadded to Scripture that we
sincerely value and pay a great regard to, for this is the way of St
Athanasius and St Basil. They appealed to Scripture first, speaking
for itself, and proving its own sense to the common reason of
mankind, according to the just rules of grammar and criticism.
Then they referred to the well-known faith of all the ancient
churches, as 'superabundantly confirming the same rational and
natural construction'.[48] Waterland is arguing against a certain
gentleman, Dr Clarke, who insinuates that the sense which the
Trinitarians affix to Scripture is not natural, but made to appear
so, and pleads for imposing a sense upon Scripture instead of
taking one from the natural force of the words. Waterland insists
that the manner of scriptural interpretation by the Trinitarians is
just and natural, and that one great use of antiquity is to guard the
natural construction against unnatural distortions. His point is that
to do violence to Scripture in order to bring it to speak what we
have a mind to, or what we have preconceived, is making Scripture
insignificant, and setting up a new rule of faith.

He then makes eight points concerning this use of ecclesiastical
antiquity. First, *the ancients*, who lived nearest to the apostolic age
are useful to moderns as writers contemporary with it, because they
can illuminate the true import of *Scriptural words and phrases*.
Secondly, they shed light on *ancient rites and customs* upon which
true Scriptural interpretation may depend. Thirdly, through the
ancient Fathers we gain an insight into the *history of the age* in which
the New Testament was written. Fourthly, their authority derives
from authentic testimony, and living in the apostolic age they may
well retain some *memory* of what the Apostles themselves or their
immediate successors thought and said, and so enable the contemporary church to fix the *sense of Scripture* in controverted texts.
Taken together these can operate as 'an useful check upon any
new interpretations of Scripture affecting the main doctrines'.
Equally, they may be extended to establish what doctrines are
really *necessary and true*. His fifth point is the argument from tradi-

tion. The *Public Acts* of the ancient Church, in *Creeds used in Baptism, censures* passed upon heretics, and the observable *harmony* and *unanimity* of the several churches in such acts adds force to the argument. It would be unreasonable to assume that several churches would all unite in the same errors to corrupt the doctrine of Christ and deviate uniformly from the rule of faith. The charismata of the early Church are stressed as a sixth point, citing Irenaeus, Justin,[49] St Paul,[50] and Tertullian,[51] the visible presence of the Spirit residing in the Church being further proof of the doctrine then generally held. His seventh point claims that the sense of the ancients once known is a useful check upon any new interpretations of Scripture affecting the *main* doctrines. Waterland[52] sees this as having a *negative* voice and being sufficient reason for rejecting *novel* expositions the *ancients* universally rejected or never admitted. His eighth and final point is that what the *ancients* allowed as *necessary* must be safe doctrine, because if they fell into *fundamental* errors it would be failing in *necessaries.*

These considerations taken together Waterland sees as a *positive* argument to prove that what the ancients held as true and important, (Scripture in its easy natural sense being in agreement), should be accepted by us as Scriptural doctrines. This use of *ecclesiastical antiquity* was, with Scripture and Reason, an essential ingredient in Waterland's theological approach, enabling him to take such a comprehensive view of the whole Trinitarian controversy, and to respond not only to Dr Clarke, but also to Dr Whitby, Mr Arthur Sykes and the Revd John Jackson, who had involved themselves on the side of Arianism. J. H. Overton describes Waterland's response as 'a masterly and luminous exposition, the equal to which it would be difficult to find in any other author, ancient or modern'.[53] It will be sufficient to indicate the main points at issue in the dispute.

Dr Clarke's School of Thought

The issues of the debate as already stated are in Clarke's *Scripture Doctrine* and Waterland's *Vindication of Christ's Divinity.*[54] Dr Clarke's school of thought, being concerned with what they describe as *Scripture doctrine*, claimed that in the Bible the worship of God is appointed to one being, that is, to the Father *personally.* Worship to Christ is of a different kind, to that of a mediator, and as such can in no way possibly be paid to the one supreme God. The New Testament's ascription of titles and powers to the Son is consistent with this reservation of the supremacy of absolute and independent dominion to the Father alone. Neither the Son nor the Spirit ever have attributed to them the highest titles of God. Therefore the subordination of the Son is real, in terms of authority and dominion over the universe. The use of the Nicene Fathers' term *homoousios* did not mean one identical substance binding three intelligent agents in the same individual. Scripture does not express the doctrine in these words, accordingly, the difficulty of understanding a Scripture doctrine should not rest wholly upon non-Scriptural words. So the question is not how three persons can be one God, but how and in what sense, consistently with everything that Scripture affirms in Scripture about Father, Son and Holy Spirit, it can be claimed as true and certain that there is but 'one God the Father'. One of the outstanding features of this controversy is that members of this eighteenth-century Arian school of thought believed they were Bible Christians, and regarded the orthodox formulation of the doctrine of the Trinity as the result of the incursion of Greek metaphysics, but Clarke avoided the extremes of this position because he thought most of the Ante-Nicene authors were on his side in the matter of the Son's subordination to the Father.

For Waterland the real question at issue was the explicit tritheism in Clarke's exposition of the Trinity. To explain Christ's divinity as analogous to the royalty of a petty prince in subordination to a supreme monarch makes not only two kings, but two Gods, a superior and an inferior. Furthermore, to allow him a relative omniscience only is saying that while he knows all things he is ignorant of many things, and the ascription to him of what Waterland terms a 'negative eternity', because we know of no time when he was not, is no eternity at all, and might equally be said of angels. To deny consubstantiality and coeternity makes one an Arian. Clarke's school of thought then drew a distinction between the supreme sovereign worship due to the Father alone, and a relative, inferior worship which was due to the Son and the Spirit. Waterland points out that Scripture knows of no such distinction and that all religious worship is determined by Scripture and antiquity to be what is called absolute and sovereign.

> ... in some sense everything must be referred to the Father, as the first Person, the head and fountain of all. But this does not make two worships, supreme and inferior; being all but one acknowledgement of one and the same essential excellency and perfection, considered primarily to the Father, and derivatively

in the Son; who though personally distinguished, are in substance undivided, and essentially one.[55]

He then points out that Scripture and antiquity generally say nothing of a supreme God, because they acknowledge no inferior God. This was the language used by pagans and borrowed and used by Christian writers, as was the whole notion of 'mediatorial worship' which the Arians borrowed from the pagans and handed on. To Waterland's accusation of Arianism they protested with the point that they were not making Christ a creature, which in a direct sense may well be so. However, the consequences of reducing Christ to a dependence on the Father in existence and power, neither perfect in nature nor exalted in privileges, with the Father having a power to create another equal or superior, means that 'He who was in the beginning with God and through whom all things were made', cannot be anything more than a creature. When the *consubstantiality, the proper divinity* and the *coeternity* are denied, there is no middle ground between Arianism and Orthodoxy. Waterland remarked that even 'sober Arians' would condemn Clarke, because while they justified the worship of Christ from reasons antecedent to his Incarnation, his being God before the world, and Creator of the world in his own power, Clarke's school justified it on certain powers being given to Christ after his Resurrection. He saw in Clarke a confusion of thought, his use of *substance of the Father*, when he really meant *hypostasis*, or *person*. Hypostasis is incommunicable, and there is no need for his argument to prove what no one had denied, a subordination in some sense of the Son to the Father, a subordination of Person, not of nature.[56] Here in Waterland is an excellent exposition of patristic doctrine.

Clarke's emphasis was on *Scripture doctrine*, grounding his objections against the Catholic doctrine of the Trinity in certain texts, which taken by themselves might seem to favour the Arian view. Waterland rested his case on Scripture as he interpreted it, on the patristic understanding of Scripture and on the weakness of Clarke's argument in 'putting an Arian construction upon Catholic expressions',[57] or 'giving an uncatholic meaning to Catholic expressions'.[58] The opinion of the Ante-Nicene Fathers had been adequately handled by Bull, and though members of the Clarke school of thought, like their Continental counterparts, might see some confirmation of their views in these early Fathers, Bull has made clear their depreciation of such patristic evidence to reach these conclusions. Therefore Waterland's concern is to establish, in relation to the doctrine of the Trinity, what is and what is not the true character of the appeal to antiquity. In relation to Scripture the Fathers are to be confirmatory of scriptural doctrine rather than additional to it, having no authority in themselves but only as testimony to such doctrine.

> The Fathers are certain proofs in many cases of the Church's doctrine in that age, and probable proofs when compared with plain Scripture proof; of no moment if Scripture is plainly contrary, but of great moment when Scripture looks the same way, because they help to fix the true interpretation in disputed texts. Waterland, however, would build no article of faith on the Fathers, but on Scripture alone. If the sense of Scripture be disputed, the concurring sentiments of the Fathers in any doctrine will be generally the best and safest comments on Scripture, just as the practice of courts and the decisions of eminent lawyers are the best comments on an Act of Parliament made in or near their own times, though the obedience of subjects rests solely on the laws of the land as its rule and measure.[59]

Therefore he justifies against his opponents the necessity of unscriptural words, pointing out that

> The most useful words for fixing the notion of distinction, are person, hypostasis, subsistence, and the like: for the divinity of each Person, ὁμοούσιος, ἀγένητος, eternal, uncreated, immutable, etc. For their union, περιχώρησις, interior generation, procession, or the like. The design of these terms is not to enlarge our views, or to add anything to our stock of ideas; but to secure the plain fundamental truth, that Father, Son, and Holy Ghost are all strictly divine and uncreated; and yet are not three Gods, but one God. He that believes this simply, and in the general, as laid down in Scriptures, believes enough.[60]

At the same time, as R. T. Holtby[61] points out in his study of *Daniel Waterland*, his view was that Clarke had not only confused 'being' and 'person' but had also taken away the issue of Christ's divinity from Scripture and made it a matter of natural reason, whereas in truth it was to be settled *a posteriori* on the ground of Divine revelation. Nevertheless, 'this respect for the opinion of antiquity in no way involved any compromise with the leading idea of all eighteenth-century theology, that it should follow the guidance of reason. Reason was by no means to be sacrificed to the authority of the fathers'.[62]

An integrated theological method

Let Waterland's[63] own words sum up his integrated theological method.

> ... as to authority, in the strict and proper sense I do not know that the Fathers have any over us; they are all dead men; therefore we urge not their authority but their testimony, their suffrage, their judgement, as carrying great force of reason. Taking them in here as lights or helps is doing what is reasonable and using our own understandings in the best way.

'I follow the Fathers as far as reason requires and no further; therefore, this is following our own reason.'[64] He maintained that antiquity means the first three or a little more centuries,[65] and the Church is under the direction of Scripture and antiquity taken together, one as the rule and the other as the pattern or interpreter.[66] This is consistent with Article VI, for 'We allege not Fathers as *grounds, or principles,* or *foundations* of our faith, but as witnesses, and as interpreters, and faithful conveyers'.[67]

The central issues, writes Holtby,[68] were 'wholly a matter of Biblical scholarship'. He points out that Clarke's exegesis was better than Waterland's and his comments on the texts more convincing, both maintaining 'Scripture-doctrine' to be sufficient, as well as the theory of plenary inspiration.

> The strength of Waterland's position, however, and the reason for its ultimately more satisfactory character, was its greater theological insight. In stressing the importance of the writings of Antiquity as witnesses to 'Scripture-doctrine' (though no doubt he exaggerated the unanimity of the Fathers and under-estimated the flexibility of expressions of Christian doctrine in their age), he safeguarded the fundamentals of orthodox teaching on the Trinity, for the patristic writers had formulated 'truths of Revelation' systematically and clarified the implications of New Testament doctrine. Waterland indeed had a much livelier sense than Clarke of the Church, not only as the community which had given birth to the New Testament but also as the divinely appointed society in which the truths of 'Scripture-doctrine' were apprehended. He was wrong to see a fully developed Trinitarianism in the New Testament: he was right to see in Clarke's scheme a threat to the religion of the New Testament.[69]

His estimate of the value of Antiquity guarded his position, and at the same time left untouched the fundamental presupposition that the Biblical data constitute the ground of all doctrine. As Overton commented, 'Among the many merits of Waterland's treatment of the subject, this is by no means the least-that he pins down his adversary and all who hold the same views in any age to the real question at issue'.[70]

In being a true successor to George Bull, Waterland stands in that great tradition of Anglican divines that link him with Hooker and Andrewes, and his reverence for Antiquity is more character-istic of the seventeenth than of the eighteenth century. For the last twenty-five years of his life he was the only outstanding Anglican theologian to cite the Fathers as authoritative witnesses to the sense of Scripture. Weaknesses there were in his theology, not so much in the limitations implicit in his biblical literalism, but in his lack of any effective understanding of doctrinal development, stemming from his unsatisfactory understanding of Revelation as something given in propositional form. However,

> The most fitting final comment on Waterland is that he was through and through a Church of England man and that he stands in a line of distinguished Anglican theologians. His lasting contribution to the corpus of Church of England theol-ogy are his works on the Sacraments and on the Athanasian Creed, but in all his work, including that which most patently bears the mark of contemporary controversy, he writes in a spirit which is recognisably Anglican, and with the presuppositions which create that spirit. 'The case depends upon Scripture, antiquity and reason', is a statement which in some measure exemplifies this distinctive spirit, but the Anglican ethos does not easily admit of precise definition. Sufficient is it to suggest that Waterland may worthily claim an honoured place between such distinguished representatives of the Anglican tradition as Hooker and Westcott. [71]

Like them his zeal for the primitive faith and doctrine not openly epitomises his work but informs the ardour of his faith and his sense of divine grace.

Notes

1. Robert Nelson, *The Life of George Bull* (London, 1713).
2. George Bull, *Defensio Fidei Nicaenae*, pp. 8–9. Part I (*LACT*, Parker, Oxford, 1851).
3. Dionysius Petavius, *Of the Trinity*, i. 5, 7.
4. Bull, *Defensio*, p. 9.

5. *Ibid.* p. 11.
6. *Ibid.* p. 12.
7. *Ibid.* p. 12.
8. *Ibid.* p. 6.
9. *Ibid.* p. 6. citing Episcopius, *Institutiones Theologicae,* iv, 34 (sect. 2).
10. *Ibid.* p. 7, citing Eusebius, *Life of Constantine,* iii. 17. *NPNF,* Second Series, eds. Schaff and Wace, (Wm Eerdmans, Michigan 1976), vol. i, p. 524.
11. *Ibid.* p. 8, citing Eusebius, 'Letter', to his own diocese in *Socrates Eccles. Hist.* i, 8. *NPNF,* Second Series, vol. ii, p. 10.
12. Nelson, *Life,* p. 288.
13. Bull, p. 12.
14. W. Van Mildert, 'A Review of the Author's Life and writings', in *The Works of Daniel Waterland* (Clarendon Press, Oxford, 1823), p. 37.
15. F. J. Foakes-Jackson, cited in 'Arianism ', in *Encyclopaedia of Religion and Ethics,* vol. i, p. 785.
16. Bull, *ibid.* Pt. I, p. 55.
17. *Ibid.* pp. 55ff.
18. *Ibid.* pp. 86ff.
19. *Ibid.* pp. 104f. ch. 3.
20. *Ibid.* p. 135, ch. 4.
21. Justin, *Apol.* I, lxiii, *ANF,* vol. i, p. 184.
22. Bull, *ibid.* p. 160.
23. P. Huet, *Origeniana,* ii, 2, *Quaest.* 2, n. 10, p. 122.
24. Bull, ch. 7, p. 193.
25. *Ibid.* ch. 8, p. 206.
26. *Ibid.* ch. 9, p. 217.
27. *Ibid.* ch. 10, p. 285.
28. *Ibid.* ch. 11, p. 302.
29. *Ibid.,* ch. 12, p. 322.
30. *Ibid.* ch. 13, p. 336.
31. Bull, *Defensio,* Pt. II, bk. iii, ch. 1, p. 369.
32. *Ibid.* Pt. II, bk. iii, ch. 5, pp. 433ff.
33. *Ibid.* Pt. II, bk. iii, ch. 9, p. 484.
34. *Ibid.* Pt. II, bk. iii, ch. 10, p. 508.
35. Nelson, *Life,* p. 311.
36. Bull, Pt. II, bk. iii, ch. 10, p. 545.
37. Nelson, p. 312.
38. Socrates, *Eccl. Hist.* V, x. *NPNF,* Second Series, vol. ii, p. 122
39. Bull, Pt. II, bk. iii, ch. 10, p. 554.
40. *Ibid.* Pt. II, bk. iv, ch. 2, p. 571.
41. H. R. McAdoo, *The Spirit of Anglicanism* (A & C Black, London, 1965), p. 409.
42. *Ibid,* pp. 409–10.
43. *Ibid.* pp. 401–2.
44. *Ibid.* p. 402.

45. S. C. Carpenter, *Eighteenth Century Church and People* (John Murray, London, 1959), pp. 140–1.
46. Van Mildert, in D. Waterland, *Works,* vol. i, p. 121.
47. Waterland, 'The Use and Value of Ecclesiastical Antiquity', p. 257.
48. *Ibid.* p. 255.
49. *Ibid.* p. 273, citing Justin, *Dial.* p. 308, edit Par. alias 315, 329; p. 308, *ANF,* vol. i, eds. Roberts and Donaldson (T. & T. Clark, Edinburgh, Wm Eerdmans, Michigan), p. 243; p. 315, *ANF,* vol. i, p. 246.
50. *Ibid.* Galatians 3: 2.
51. *Ibid.* citing Tertullian, *Praescrip.* xxviii, xxix. *ANF,* vol. iii, p. 256
52. *Ibid.* p. 275.
53. C. J. Abbey and J. H. Overton, *The English Church in the 18th Century,* (Longmans, Green & Co, London, 1887), p. 205.
54. Waterland, 'Vindication of Christ's Divinity', *Works,* vol. i.
55. *Ibid.* p. 427.
56. *Ibid.* p. 535.
57. *Ibid.* p. 395.
58. *Ibid.* p. 461.
59. Abbey and Overton, *ibid.* pp. 210–11.
60. Waterland, *ibid.* p. 461.
61. R. T. Holtby, *Daniel Waterland 1683–1740, A Study in Eighteenth-Century Orthodoxy* (Charles Thurnam & Sons Ltd, Carlisle, 1966), p. 26.
62. Abbey and Overton, *ibid.* p. 211.
63. Waterland, 'Use and Value', p. 330,
64. *Ibid.* p. 330.
65. Waterland, ' The Importance of the Doctrine of the Trinity ', *Works,* vol. i (Clarendon Press, Oxford, 1823), p. 639.
66. *Ibid.* p. 654.
67. *Ibid.* pp. 652–3.
68. Holtby, *ibid.* p. 44.
69. *Ibid.* p. 44.
70. Abbey and Overton, *ibid.* p. 206.
71. Holtby, *ibid.* pp. 210–11.

Part Four:

Rediscovering the Fathers

13

Fathers and Tractarians

Antecedents

Michael Ramsey claimed that 'Next to the Caroline divines in the seventeenth century it was the Tractarians who specially cherished the appeal to the ancient Fathers'.[1] This gives the impression, though it is unlikely to have been in the mind of Bishop Michael, that the appeal to the Fathers died among English theologians after the Caroline divines. As stated earlier, after Waterland there followed a decline in a dominance of the appeal to antiquity, though not a complete absence. Less well-known men continued to defend the Anglican appeal to the Fathers and attempted to limit the damage to the reputation of the Fathers that resulted from the writings of Daillé and others. Note has been taken of the Bampton lectures of 1786 in which the Revd George Croft, Vicar of Arncliffe, applauds Joseph Bingham for vindicating Anglican doctrine and discipline 'from the practice of the primitive churches'.[2] Croft's third sermon examines the authority of the ancient Fathers. Henry Kett's Bampton lectures for 1790[3] have also been mentioned regarding his concern to vindicate the writings of the Fathers of the Church in general, and to recommend the works of the earliest Fathers in particular. His object is to rectify some misrepresentations of the historian Gibbon in the fifteenth and sixteenth chapters of *The Decline and Fall of the Roman Empire,* and those of Dr Priestley, who was originally a Presbyterian minister and scientist and became a Socinian. Priestley published in 1782 his *History of the Corruptions of Christianity* and in 1786, *History of the Early Opinions concerning Jesus Christ,* that outraged the orthodox. The Revd John Collinson, mentioned in chapter 11, delivered his Bampton Lectures in 1813 when he was Rector of Gateshead. His theme was *A Key to the Writings of the Principal Fathers of the Christian Church (during the first three centuries).* In his first sermon he deals with objections and responses to the appeal to antiquity, in the use of the Fathers in the Roman Catholic Church and among continental Protestants, and claims for the Anglican appeal to them that it is a check to the 'restless and inordinate spirit' on both sides. 'Divines in England endeavoured to restore a due and proper estimation to the primitive writings: and of these none occupy a more distinguished place than Bishop Bull and Dr. Cave'.

John Kaye[4] (1783-1853), on his election as Regius Professor of Divinity in Cambridge in 1816, revived the public lectures that had been suspended for a hundred years. He became the first to recall theological students to the study of the Fathers. He gave courses of lectures on *The Ecclesiastical History of the Second and Third Centuries, illustrated from the writings of Tertullian* (first published in 1825 and reaching five editions by 1845), on *Justin Martyr* (published 1829, 1836, 1853), on Clement of Alexandria (published 1835). Two series of lectures were published posthumously, *The Council of Nicaea in connection with the Life of Athanasius* (in 1853), and *The Ecclesiastical History of Eusebius* in 1855. Despite encouraging a zeal for patristic study he regarded the Oxford Movement with suspicion but no doubt had an indirect influence at this level. It is not surprising that a consciousness of the value of the Fathers was present in certain church circles at the beginning of the 19th century. W. J. Sparrow Simpson's observation of the number of books concerned with the teaching of the Fathers that appeared at the beginning of the nineteenth century has already been noted in chapter 1.[5]

The appeal to the Fathers among the Tractarians was a living heritage despite a decline in the appeal to antiquity among eighteenth-century divines. Latitudinarian divines may well have shifted the emphasis away from their seventeenth-century predecessors' appeal to antiquity in their interpretation of the Scriptures.

> Nevertheless Georgian Anglicanism continued to value the Fathers. The Roman Catholic controversialist, John Milner, at the turn of the century, insisted that what he called 'Hoadlyism' was not representative of the Church of England which 'so far from undervaluing the ancient Fathers, requires her clergy to consult their interpretation of the Scriptures in preaching to the people under pain of excommunication.'[6]

The Tractarian appeal to the ancient Fathers was not the rediscovery that some have tended to assume. There is before them a line of eminent men of learning, and what happened in 1833 had been smouldering in what Dean Burgon described as the 'residuum of the altar-fires of a long succession of holy and earnest men'.[7] Burgon lists some of these men who had 'retained their hold on Catholic Truth amid every discouragement'. The list includes, Thomas Randolph (1701–83), William Jones of Nayland (1726–1800), Samuel Horsley (1733–1806), William Cleaver (1742–1815), John Bowdler (1754–1823), Charles Daubeny (1744–1827), Reginald Heber (1783–1826), Charles Lloyd (1784–1829), Alexander Knox (1758–1831), John Jebb (1775–1833), Thomas Sikes (1766–1834), William Van Mildert (1765–1836), Christopher Wordsworth (1774–1846), Martin J. Routh (1755–1854), John Kaye (1783–1853), Joshua Watson (1771–1855), and Hugh James Rose (1795–1838). Such men would not have regarded themselves as Tractarians and like Martin Routh would have been averse to labels and parties; nevertheless, they were the precursors of the Tractarians, and it was from these men that the Tractarians inherited what has been described truly as English Church theology.

Martin Routh is without doubt one of the most interesting and remarkable figures that has ever appeared in Oxford. Thomas Mozley spoke of him as 'the greatest name in patristic theology at Oxford – indeed a name in Europe'.[8] Dean Church said that he 'stood alone among his brother Heads in his knowledge of what English theology was'.[9] Church was describing the reaction of the authorities who attacked and condemned Tractarian teaching in violence and ignorance.

> But Oxford was not only a city of libraries, it was the home of what was especially accounted Church theology; and the Tractarian teaching, in its foundation and main outlines, had little but what ought to have been perfectly familiar to any one who had taken the trouble to study the great Church of England writers. To one who, like Dr. Routh of Magdalen, had gone below the surface, and was acquainted with the questions debated by those divines, there was nothing startling in what so alarmed his brethren, whether he agreed or not; and to him the indiscriminate charge of Popery meant nothing. But Dr. Routh stood alone among his brother Heads in his knowledge of what English theology was. To most of them it was an unexplored and misty region; some of the ablest under the influence of Dr. Whateley's vigorous and scornful discipline, had learned to slight it. But there it was.

Routh was born in 1755 and died in his one hundredth year having retired as President of Magdalen at ninety-four after sixty-three

years. In 1788 he produced a prospectus of his *magnum opus,*
Reliquiae Sacra, the first two volumes of which appeared in 1814. In
1848, sixty years after the appearance of the prospectus, the fifth
and last volume was published when their author was ninety-four.
His aim was to bring together and to edit the remains of the
Fathers of the second and third centuries of whose works only fragments survive. In his preface he explained that he took as his 'limit
the epoch of the first Nicene Council. He fixed on that limit,
because as he said the period is so illustrious in the annals of the
Church, and because, in matters of controversy, those Fathers are
chiefly appealed to who preceded that epoch'. He was twenty-eight
when he advised the envoys of the Anglican Church in America not
to accept episcopal orders from the Danish Church because of
their irregularity as an invalid succession. He saved them from
taking a step which would have been fatal to the catholicity of their
church and directed them to the Scottish Episcopal Church for the
creation of an American episcopate.

Routh had a great personal regard for Newman and they would
often meet for extended discussion of theological matters. He
spoke of Newman as that 'clever young gentleman of Oriel, Mr.
Newman', and later as 'the great Newman'. What Newman thought
of Routh may be seen in his dedication to him in 1837 of his
volume of Lectures. To 'MARTIN JOSEPH ROUTH, D.D.,
President of Magdalen College, who has been reserved to report to
a Forgetful Generation what was the Theology of their Fathers,
This Volume Is Inscribed.' Routh's evaluation of the Oxford
Movement can be given in his own words.

> Having been prevented by circumstances unnecessary to
> mention from reading any of the lately published tracts with the
> exception of No. 90, I am consequently not prepared to give an
> opinion of them. But a perusal of many of the acknowledged
> writings of Dr. Pusey and Mr. Newman enables me to express my
> admiration of the ardent piety, holy views, and scrupulous
> adherence to the ancient summaries of Catholic belief displayed
> in them. I likewise state my persuasion that these, in conjunction
> with other estimable works, have contributed to correct many
> erroneous notions too long prevalent amongst us, and subvert-
> ing the unity and authority of the National Church.[10]

What alarmed many minds in the teaching of the Tractarians was
perfectly natural to Routh with his solid patristic learning and wide
knowledge of English theology since the Reformation. Their
appeal to antiquity he did not find disturbing. He alone of the

Heads of Oxford Colleges, with the exception of Dr Richards, the Rector of Exeter College, stood by them in the conflict, and he followed the course of the Movement with sympathy and understanding, counting among his friends some of its strongest supporters. Routh was a devoted member of the Church of England with a great reverence for Catholic tradition. He was, to put it in his own words, 'attached to the Catholic Faith taught in the Church of England, and averse from all papal and sectarian innovations'. 'He represents the permanence of the Catholic tradition in the English Church, linking the theology of' the Nonjurors and the Caroline Divines with the Oxford Movement'.[11] Routh's greatest sympathy with the Tractarians lay in those expressions of' Christian doctrine which they held in common with the Elizabethan divines. But, while he held tenaciously to his opinions, there was no narrowness of outlook. He never gave the cold shoulder to his friends who went over to Rome, but treated them with a generosity quite uncommon in 'his time, and especially to Newman when he retired to Littlemore and found himself snubbed and bullied by everybody in authority'.

Before and after 1833 there was a consistency in the tenaciously-held principles of the orthodox, the difference being in their methods, their tempers, and their tones of mind. So John Keble would often comment after hearing a theological statement: 'It seems to me just what my father taught me'. As Churton pointed out in his *Memoir of Joshua Watson*, Pusey rejoiced at the measure of agreement between himself and Watson, the leading layman of the Clapton Sect.

I cannot say [he writes], how cheering it was to be recognised by you as carrying on the same torch which we had received from you and those of your generation, who had remained faithful to the old teaching. We seemed no longer separated by a chasm from the old times and old paths, to which we wished to lead people back; the links which united us to those of old seemed to be restored.

Henry Cary in the Preface to his book[12] quotes from John Jebb the Bishop of Limerick:

A principle which especially characterises the Church of England and distinguishes her from every other reformed communion, is her marked and avowed adherence to the catholic faith as received in the primitive and purest ages of Christianity. She has acted on this universally acknowledged truth that whatsoever is new in the fundamentals of religion, must be false. On this ground, and believing that in the earliest ages the great truths of Christianity were known to, and plainly professed by the Church, she [and here he quotes from *The Peculiar Character of the Church of England* by Dr. Jebb, the Bishop of Limerick] 'in the first instance, and as her grand foundation, derives all obligatory matter of faith, that is, to use her own expression, all "that is to be believed for necessity of salvation," from the Scripture alone: and herein she differs from the Church of Rome. But she systematically resorts to the concurrent sense of the Church catholic, both for assistance in the interpretation of the sacred text, and for guidance in those matters of religion, which the text has left at large: and herein she differs from every reformed communion.'

John Jebb, Bishop of Limerick, and Alexander Knox, his guide, philosopher, and friend, were pioneers and anticipators of the movement in several important points that include the unbroken continuity of the Church and the *via media* character of the Church of England. He was a great advocate of Vincentius's rule, that

has been *received, extolled* and *acted* upon by such men as Ridley, Jewel, Grotius, Overal, Hammond, Beveridge, Bull, Hickes, Bramhall, Grabe, Cave, and our own Archbishop King, ... even Chillingworth ... and Jeremy Taylor ... I cannot at present feel any difficulty in applying Vincentius' rule. If a doctrine is propounded to me, as vitally essential, that is, to speak technically, as matter of faith, before I can receive it as such, I must go to the catholic succession, and ascertain, whether that doctrine has been held *semper, ubique, ab omnibus:* convinced that if it has not been so held, my assent is not due to it as a *matter of faith.* If, again, a doctrine which I hold, is impugned as heretical, next to the Scripture, and as interpretative of Scripture, I must go to the catholic succession; and, if I find this doctrine universally asserted, I cannot believe that it is any other, than the sincere truth of the Gospel.[13]

The famous 'Appendix' to Bishop Jebb's sermons, of which Knox was virtually the author, might well have been one of the *Tracts for the Times,* while many of Knox's letters could have been the letters of a tract-writer. What he wrote about the character of the Church of England motivated the correspondence between Newman and the Abbé Jager that influenced Newman's *Lectures on the Prophetical Office of the Church.*

Nearer to the actual movement is the great work done by Hugh

James Rose who is described as the 'restorer of the old paths', and restoration was the aim of the whole movement. Rose was, in T. Mozley's view, 'the one commanding figure, and very lovable man, that the frightened and discomfited church-people were now (1833) rallying round. Few people have left so distinct an impression of themselves as this gentleman'.[14] In the opinion of Sir W. Palmer, he was

> in his time a bright and shining light of the Church of England. He had been Christian Advocate of the University of Cambridge. He was the most powerful and most followed preacher there; a profound scholar, an eloquent orator, a deep thinker, and an admirable theologian ... Had this noble man lived, he would have been the greatest ornament and the most trusted leader of the church.[15]

In words which now have become classical, he was the man 'who, when hearts were failing, bade us stir up the gift that was in us, and betake ourselves to our true mother'.[16] Rose bore faithful witness to the same divine truths as Routh. He had already fully established his reputation as an able maintainer of apostolic order and vindicator of half-forgotten church principles by his Four Sermons preached at Cambridge in April 1826 'On the Commission and consequent Duties of the Clergy'. These sermons, more than anything else which proceeded from this faithful priest, served to stir up people's minds and were an effectual reminder to the clergy of those ancient truths which the clergy least of all can afford to forget. Never at any time has the Church of God been bereft of faithful men so to witness to a forgetful and a careless generation, and the first thirty years of the nineteenth century is no exception. Rose was constant in his teaching about the need for the maintenance of principles in their integrity, against the temptations to be a church expedient that played to the gallery of an ungodly age by surrendering what is unpopular. The constant keynote of his discourses was his pleading for some half-forgotten but vital ancient verity; or vindicating some neglected fundamental of the faith. Newman wrote to Rose on 1 January 1834 about the need for the bishops to come forward and stop those clergy who were throwing away so much in the name of innovation. Rose started, and ably edited, the *British Magazine*, the first number of which appeared in March 1832. The leaders of the movement accepted it as the organ of the party, and both Newman and Keble expressed their determination to support it and not allow the *Tracts for the Times* to interfere with it. It was at Rose's parsonage in Hadleigh that the first meeting was held which led immediately and directly to the Oxford movement.

Rose was an authoritative voice and a commanding figure. He became editor of *The Theological Library*, a series of manual volumes on various subjects, and he invited Newman to contribute a History of the Principal Councils. The volume appeared in 1833 under the title *The Arians of the Fourth Century*, and proved to be Newman's greatest work, that Rose claimed would 'take its permanent stand in our literature'. When Chaplain to the Archbishop of Canterbury, Rose wrote to Pusey after the Archbishop had accepted dedication of the *Library of the Fathers*: 'The more I think of it the more I am pleased. For the ordinary men to read the large and Christian views of the Gospel they will find in the Fathers, will be of great consequence. The only objection I have is that it will be a *coup-de-grace* to all Greek among divinity students'.[17] An interesting series of papers appeared in 1833 in successive numbers of the *British Magazine* and were eventually (viz. 1840) collected into a volume entitled *The Church of the Fathers*. The first series appeared in October 1833.[18] Rose thought very highly of them and wrote to tell Newman in April 1835.

When he wrote to Newman from Lambeth in May 1836 Rose expressed concern at the English being an anti-reading nation, including the clergy, the larger majority of whom would not be students. He felt they could not be left to their own guidance but would need direction and authority and therefore, those who teach ought to be of a different *genus* and for a very long period at least, should be.

> The Homilies of the Fathers may be studied with the greatest advantage by those who can exercise their judgment; but to attempt to address audiences *now* in such or such a manner, *because* it was done by this or that Father, (and only and simply because it happened to be the style of his day in all public speaking), in the 4th or the 5th century, cannot, I think, lead to good, and *may* lead to a good deal of evil ... I wish, in a word, considering what English readers commonly are, that Antiquity should be studied by them only with full, clear and explicit directions how to derive from it that good which *is* to be derived from it; and to avoid the sort of quackery of *affecting* Antiquity, which is very likely to lay hold of quick, but not very comprehensive, minds. ... if such minds are led to search out all the opinions and practices of Antiquity as of great value, *because* they are derived from Antiquity, where they and we shall get to, it seems

hard to tell. It is an expedition in which I most earnestly desiderate good guides and experienced drivers; and then, we shall return from it rich; in *health* and in *knowledge.*

To conclude *my* homily. It seems to me that if you will have the patience to go on teaching the younger Clergy *what* the Church is: what are the true notions of the *Sacraments* and the *Ministry:* and how entirely what we teach has ever been taught by the Catholic Church; if you will give its full colouring and relief to all those parts of our system, about the actual existence of which no one can doubt, (Commemorations of Saints and Martyrs, Fasting, &c.), but which have been thrown into the shade, by pouring in the light of Antiquity through *your own windows;* – you will do the greatest service. But for *the mass,* I am persuaded you must confine yourself to that; and to giving them specimens of the pure moral and doctrinal *tone* (not manner) of teaching in the early Church.

For the next class, you will do the greatest service if you will direct and closely confine them *in* their study of Antiquity, as well as warmly exhort them to it; teaching them especially, I think, to study the wholesome tone of doctrine contained in the writings of the great Lights of the Church, rather than to look for supplements and corrections of any defects of our own.[19]

In spite of his reservations the *Library of the Fathers* was an undertaking which lay very near to Rose's heart. The first volume (a translation of Augustine's *Confessions*) was not published until November 1838. Rose did not live therefore to see the first of those 39 volumes that gave so important an impulse to the study of the patristic writings, and were not discontinued until January 1858. Rose's prime aim was to induce the clergy to acquaint themselves with the Greek and Latin Fathers in the original idiom and persuade those who do read such texts, that 'the Gospel is something larger than *Justification* or the *Quintoquarticular Controversy*'. Rose died too early to see the final issue of that movement, though he lived long enough to find that there was much in its methods of which he disapproved. On the whole, therefore, he must be regarded as by far the most prominent and effective of the precursors of the revival, rather than its actual originator.

In Oxford Dr Charles Lloyd, the Regius Professor of Divinity, in his lectures on the Book of Common Prayer gave quite a new view to many of his hearers. Some young hearers afterwards became very prominent in the movement and included Newman, Pusey, Hurrell Froude, Isaac Williams, and Frederick Oakeley. Lloyd's

teaching affected the movement deeply. As an independent
thinker Lloyd was considerably in advance of the high churchmen
of his time, and through association in his youth with French
emigrant clergy, to whom he was indebted, he absorbed truer views
of the Catholic religion than were generally current in this
country. He gave to his hearers very definite ideas of Catholics and
Catholic doctrine. His Lectures on the Prayer Book informed his
students, first with the Missal and then the Breviary, as sources
from which all that is best and noblest in the English liturgy is
derived. Pusey was a thorough disciple and on his premature death
he mourned for him as 'a second father', 'the guardian friend,
with whose guidance I had hoped to steer securely amid all the
difficult shoals through which the course of a theologian must in
these days probably be held'.[20]

The publication of William Palmer's *Origines Liturgicae or Antiquities of the English Ritual with a Dissertation on Primitive Liturgies*,
published in 1832, anticipated Professor Lloyd's work and was
partly a result of his researches. Palmer had begun his researches
in Ireland but moved from Trinity College, Dublin, to Worcester
College, Oxford to benefit from the Oxford libraries. Bishop Lloyd
died in 1829 with his work unfinished, and Palmer was persuaded
to resume his researches, and to incorporate with it the results of
Bishop Lloyd's work. The *Origines* helped to remind those who had
heard Lloyd's lectures of what they had heard and to inform others
on this important subject. Hence the book is a chief factor in the
preparation for the movement which was fast approaching. Palmer
was 'insisting upon the almost forgotten fact that the Prayer Book
is mainly a translation from earlier office-books, and so represents
the descent of the Reformed Church of England from the church
of earlier days, and this book powerfully contributed to increase
that devotion to the traditions of the church which characterised
the Tracts'.[21]

Going public

What had been fomenting suddenly went public on 14 July 1833
and marked in Newman's mind the beginning of the Oxford
Movement. In John Keble's famous Assize Sermon on that date the
thoughts that had been gestating in the minds of this long line of
High Churchmen found public expression. Keble identified and
defined what he saw as an apostate mind. He feared that the nation
was deliberately rejecting her ancient belief that 'as a Christian

nation she is also a part of the Christian Church, and in all her legislation and policy bound by the fundamental rules of that Church'.[22] The signs were present not only in the Erastianism of the Irish Bishoprics Bill but also in a prevalence of religious indifference and the liberalism that tolerated every religious belief. Added to this was 'a notable increase in perjury and disregard for the sanctity of an oath' and a disrespect for 'the successors of the apostles', the bishops. Bishops themselves were partly to blame, in those who undervalued the sacred nature of their office and those who were not sure whether they believed in Apostolic Succession. In face of such episcopal scepticism Keble's anxiety was for 'those members of the Church who still believe her authority to be divine and the oaths and obligations by which they are bound undissolved and indissoluble by the calculations of human expediency'.[23] Keble's use of the term Erastian is in the strict sense of a church subjected to the State, and his concern is how to avoid becoming tainted with Erastian principles while remaining in communion with the Church of England. With the government's declaration of Catholic Emancipation he claimed that a secular authority had 'virtually usurped the commission of those whom our Saviour entrusted with at least one voice in making ecclesiastical law in matters wholly or partly spiritual...' Also, they had 'ratified this principle; that the Apostolic Church is only to stand, in the eyes of the State, as one sect among many', her pre-eminence depending upon 'the accident of having a strong party in the country'.[24]

Battiscombe, in her study of Keble, points out how his foresight led him to visualize the Church without the Establishment and thereby ceasing to be co-extensive with the nation. Church and State would become separate and despite any opposition between them, in their manner of working, this is to be 'regarded as the pursuit of one great aim pursued by contrasting means'.[25] In this new relationship the Church of England would remain what it had always been, the representative in England of the whole Church Catholic and Apostolic 'built upon the apostles and prophets, Jesus Christ Himself being the chief corner-stone.' As such her authority was the authority of Christ handed on in apostolic succession, and even if she disappeared, the Catholic and Apostolic Church would live on, assured of a complete, universal and eternal victory, even in the face of the gates of Hell. It may sound a novel idea to the mind of the troubled church in pre-Victorian England, and even to Froude and Newman, but for Keble it was a conviction inherited from the Caroline Divines. On 25 July 1833 at Hadleigh Rectory, Hugh James Rose, the rector, Hurrell Froude, William Palmer and

Arthur Perceval met to discuss anxieties and thoughts that had brought them together and had been made public by Keble's sermon.

It was natural that the Tractarians in claiming continuity with the undivided Church should then look to the church of the Fathers as possessing the tradition whereby Scripture is to be interpreted. These preoccupations gave great impetus to patristic study in the Church of England. *Tracts for the Times* were published to popularize Tractarian teaching, as also *catenae* of patristic passages. English translations of selected patristic works appeared in the *Library of the Fathers*.

Tracts for the Times

Tracts had normally been the method whereby Evangelicals communicated their teaching. Perhaps it was the presence of an Evangelical pedigree in some of the early Tractarians that influenced the adoption of this kind of publication to promote their cause, but as Dean Church[26] pointed out 'these early tracts were something different from anything of the kind yet known in England'. Newman, who started life as an Evangelical, wrote the first Tract and described how he felt about this momentous task.

> I had supreme confidence in our cause; we were upholding that primitive Christianity which was delivered for all time by the early teachers of the Church, and which was registered and attested in the Anglican Formularies and by the Anglican divines. That ancient religion had well-nigh faded out of the land through the political changes of the last 150 years, and it must be restored. It would be, in fact, a second Reformation – a better Reformation, for it would return, not to the sixteenth century, but to the seventeenth.[27]

The Tract was entitled *Thoughts on the Ministerial Commission, respectfully addressed to the Clergy* and with Tracts 2 and 3 is dated 9 September 1833. The first two Tracts contain the essential principle of the Oxford Movement, the appeal to apostolic authority and to the doctrine of apostolic succession against the Erastianism of the supporters of the Establishment and the Liberalism of the opponents of the doctrine. Ministerial authority is derived not from the State, but from 'the apostolic rock on which our authority is built and the gift of the apostolic spirit conferred in ordination'.[28] Clergy were to stir up this gift that was in them and exalt their bishops, the successors of the apostles. The first forty-six of these Tracts were brought together into a single volume. They were prefaced by an 'Advertisement', that explained their nature and object as a contribution,

> towards the practical revival of doctrines, which, although held by the great divines of our Church, at present have become obsolete with the majority of her members, and are withdrawn from public view even by the more learned and orthodox few who still adhere to them. The Apostolic Succession, the Holy Catholic Church, were principles of action in the minds of our predecessors of the 17th century; but, in proportion as the maintenance of the Church has been secured by law, her ministers have been under the temptation of leaning on the arm of flesh instead of her own divinely-provided discipline, a temptation increased by political events and arrangements which need not here be more than alluded to.[29]

Topics included the true and essential nature of the Church and its relation to the primitive church, its authority, polity and government, and objections to its claims in England then current. Liturgy and Discipline, 'the sins and corruptions of each branch of Christendom' were also discussed. There were extracts from seventeenth-century Anglican divines, Beveridge, Wilson and Cosin, among others. Under the title *Records of the Church*, texts or passages from early Ante-Nicene writers were printed in the Tracts. Epistles of Ignatius, accounts of the Martyrs of Lyons and Vienne, the Martyrdom of Polycarp, Justin Martyr on Primitive Christian Worship, Tertullian on Baptism, with Tertullian and Irenaeus on the Rule of Faith, found their way into these Tracts. Others writers included Cyprian on Church Unity, and the later writer Vincent of Lérins on the Tests of Heresy and Error. There was nothing in their teaching that was not sanctioned by the Prayer Book or the authoritative teaching of Anglican divines. Nevertheless, an ignorance of church history and church principles, alongside a paucity in the kind of theological knowledge and learning necessary for discerning the difference between what is Catholic and what is specifically Roman, determined an emotional reaction from those who perceived these doctrines as novelty when they should have known better. When Edward Pusey joined the Tract writers, he brought not only a name as a Professor and Canon of Christ Church, but also a massive learning that changed the character of the Tracts into longer and more weightier treatises.

The Library of the Fathers

As a boy Pusey had a certain familiarity with the Fathers, though in those early years in his estimation he placed them below modern divines. What changed his mind he explains in a letter[30] that was a response to a request from Dr. Arnold for help with two sermons. Dr. Arnold, known for his antipathy towards the Tractarians needed Pusey's advice about which books to consult on the patristic view of Prophecy. Pusey makes plain the true claims of the Fathers as interpreters of Holy Scripture, and admits that like Dr. Arnold he once measured Christian antiquity by a modern standard before discovering that the two systems are entirely different and at variance. He describes how he was led back to the ancients. First, he found that the majority of Old Testament quotations in the New created difficulties in the modern system, that were absent in the ancient; so that the ancient system was more like that of inspired Scripture. Secondly, most ancient Jewish interpretations, in general principles, harmonized with the ancient Christian, but the modern interpretations derived from a modern philosophical-grammatical Jewish school. This school was an unbelieving one since it arose in opposition to the Gospel. Calvin's interpretative system, the basis of most modern, is from the later Jews, as are early Protestant Old Testament commentators. Thirdly, Pusey found the same interpretations in different parts of the Church therefore independent of each other and deriving from a common source. Fourthly, he was struck with the Fathers' great combination of Scripture and the beauty and truth of things he had rejected earlier as fanciful. Fifthly, the Father's views seemed to Pusey to be possessed with greater consciousness of the mysterious depth of every work and way of God. The fundamental principle of the patristic mind is that nothing in God's creation is accidental, everything has a meaning if we would find how to read it. 'All things are made double one against another, and he hath made nothing imperfect'.[31] Pusey admitted that it had taken him some time to arrive at this view and that he is,

> not looking at the modern view as untrue, but as a small portion of the truth only, and wrong when it assumes to be all, and for the most part miserably shallow. At the same time, neither do I see my way through all the *details* of ancient interpretation; I have not studied enough for it; I am only satisfied that the principles of their system are right, and that much which one should reject at first sight as fanciful, is true.[32]

He did suggest a number of texts but he strongly cautioned Arnold against 'any attempt to engraft the Fathers into a modern system,' as this would only end in 'disappointment and disgust.' He ended with a strong dissuasive that anyone imbued with modern principles should not attempt such a study as it might do more harm than good.

Pusey did progress from his early familiarity with the Fathers through extracts, to a deeper engagement in the reading of a succession of treatises, and at one time 'lived in St. Augustine'. This engagement imparted to him a mystical quality that derived from a deepening immersion in that patristic understanding of the participation of the Christian in the divinity of Christ that he found in the Greek Fathers and their Christian Platonism. Within Pusey, Keble, Newman and Marriott, a conviction was growing in 1835–36, that the Church of England was impoverished in having lost sight of the Fathers who had so enriched the theology of the Caroline divines. If English theology was to be recalled to the teaching and principles of the primitive church then the texts of these patristic writers must be made accessible. There was also the mistaken notion that the Fathers belonged to Roman Catholics and that Anglicans only used them to build arguments against the Church of Rome. Therefore it would be better for people to have access to the larger works of the Fathers themselves rather than learning from mere extracts. Some of the reasons for thinking of a *Library of the Fathers* are given by Pusey in the Prospectus of that work:

> the circumstance that the Anglican branch of the Church Catholic is founded upon Holy Scripture and the agreement of the Universal Church, and that therefore the knowledge of Christian antiquity is necessary in order to understand and maintain her doctrines and especially, her creeds and her liturgy. [He pleads] the importance at the present crisis of exhibiting the real practical value of Catholic antiquity, which is disparaged by Romanists in order to make way for the later Councils, and by others, in behalf of modern and private interpretations of Holy Scripture ... Romanists [he says] are in great danger of lapsing into secret infidelity, not seeing how to escape from the palpable errors of their own Church without falling into the opposite errors of Ultra-Protestants. [And thus] it appeared an act of special charity to point out to such of them as are dissatisfied with the state of their own Church a body of ancient Catholic truth, free from the errors alike of modern Rome and of Ultra-Protestantism.[33]

It was more than an exercise in polemics. Other reasons motivated this publication venture, not least the substantive value of these texts themselves as being sacred reading, as being a corrective to narrowness and as bringing the thought of particular churches into communion with the thought of the Universal Church when outwardly united. In their engagement with errors in their original form these texts are a safeguard against modern errors. The Tractarian distrust of originality and novelty served to intensify their desire to stand only in the ancient ways and communicate information about these ways. There are significant commentaries on the New Testament from Fathers with a representative position in the primitive church 'especially because the language of the New Testament was to them a living language'.

> But more especially do the Fathers attest the existence of Catholic agreement in a great body of truth in days when the Church of Christ was still visibly one, and still spoke one language; and thus they all bear witness against the fundamentally erroneous assumptions of modern times, that truth is only that which each man troweth, and that the divisions of Christendom are unavoidable and without remedy.[34]

On the publication of the first volume, the Archbishop of Canterbury advised Pusey to prefix some observations to meet popular misapprehensions, as those in the *Sola Scriptura* School might think that Scripture is being usurped or another authority added to it. Pusey appeals to the 1571 Canon to support the Anglican appeal to the Fathers, that what clergy preach must be consistent with Scriptural doctrine and 'collected out of that same doctrine by the Catholic Fathers and ancient Bishops'. The Convocation which made this Canon also enforced subscription to the Thirty-Nine Articles. 'The contrast then in point of authority is not between Holy Scripture and the Fathers, but between the Fathers and *us* [Pusey's italics]; not between the book interpreted and the interpreters, but between one class of interpreters and another; between ancient Catholic truth and modern private opinions'.[35] The principle of the appeal to antiquity, is not to individual Fathers but to the *consensus patrum*. Their authority is authentic when their teaching, in the spirit of the Vincentian Canon, witnesses to that which has been received by all the Churches in all places and at all times. To the critic who sees the authority of the Fathers superseding that of the Church of England,

Pusey maintains that there is no more of antagonism between the Fathers and the Church of England than between the Fathers and Holy Scripture. The Fathers interpret the true mind of the Church of England by the light which they throw upon its formularies, which in many cases belong to the ages in which they themselves lived and taught.[36]

There is much doctrine in the prayers and liturgies of the Book of Common Prayer that derives from the primitive church and it cannot be understood except within that context of antiquity. This exercise was not a search for anything new, but was in order to appreciate better the doctrine and devotion of the Church of England. It was too easy for those who had never read the Fathers to deprecate them, but if they were to be brought within general reach the need was to translate them into English editions. Newman and Pusey at first differed about the nature of the translations, the former preferring the free and idiomatic, and the latter, exact and literal translations. Pusey's intention is expressed in his preface to the *Confessions of St Augustine*. As a translator, he wants 'to preserve as much as possible of the condensed style of St. Augustine, and to make the translation as little as might be of a commentary, that so the reader might be put as far as possible in the position of a student of the Fathers, unmodified and undiluted by the intervention of any foreign notions'. This would procure for the reader a greater insight into Augustine's uncommented meaning and so let the author speak for himself without interference from the translator.

There was no shortage of able contributors who gathered around Keble, Newman and Pusey in this great literary venture. Oakeley translated Augustine's Anti-Pelagian treatises, and Church's translation of the Catechetical Lectures of St Cyril of Jerusalem was the second volume published. Pusey claimed Keble and Newman knew 'ten times more' about the Fathers than he, but at Newman's insistence he reluctantly wrote the preface to the *Library*. After early anxieties the sales increased and in 1853 topped 3,700, and extended over forty-seven years from Pusey's first volume in 1838 until 1885 when the latter part of St Cyril on St John appeared. Its influence on the Oxford Movement goes without saying.

It was at once an encouraging and steadying influence: it made thoughtful adherents of the Movement feel that the Fathers were behind them, and with the Fathers that ancient undivided Church whom the Fathers represented. But it also kept before their minds the fact that the Fathers were, in several respects, unlike the moderns, not only in the English Church, but also in the Church of Rome. And, above all, it reminded men of a type of life and thought which all good men, in their best moments, would have been glad to make their own.[37]

There were Evangelicals who welcomed the *Library* as representing the best of what an Evangelical professed, and this might have been a place of co-operation between Tractarians and Evangelicals but their different agenda meant that they failed to appreciate and act on it. Edward Bickersteth, a leading Evangelical, wrote to Pusey expressing his 'sincere pleasure' with the *Library,* as a venture that would be more seasonable and more beneficial to the Church of England than most things. To be united in a common mind in those days of disunity he found a great privilege. He suggested that there might be an introductory address to challenge the damage done to the Fathers by such people as Osborne, Whitby, Edwards, Barbeyrac, and Daillé, 'candidly admitting what truth requires, yet showing the real value of their writings'.[38]

Through the *Library of the Fathers,* these Tractarians were responsible for a revival of interest in the Fathers even though the works of only thirteen Fathers and ancient writers were offered. This was due to Pusey's sense of the superior value of the fourth-century writers who spoke consciously in the name of the Universal Church. It came to form the basis for a more familiar and still widely used work, the *Ante-Nicene Christian Library* and the *Library of Nicene and Post-Nicene Fathers.* Texts for English readers became available as never before, continuing in our own day with the latter being available now on compact discs. For these Tractarians the renewal of the English Church was a search for the 'Church of the Fathers'. For Newman in particular, as a result of his search, he discovered the great theologians of seventeenth-century Anglicanism. From English theologians deeply saturated in the theology of the Fathers, such as Hooker, Andrewes, Laud, Hammond, Pearson, Jeremy Taylor and George Bull, Newman drank deeply.[39] In his *Apologia,* he claims that it was in August 1831 while reading George Bull's works in preparation for his book on the Arians, that he became convinced of his belief that 'Antiquity was the true exponent of the doctrines of Christianity and the basis of the Church of England'. It was not unnatural that another project should emerge in the *Library of Anglo-Catholic Theology* comprising texts of Caroline divinity. The two libraries witnessed to the concern of the Tractarians with the importance of order, continuity and sacraments, in their clarifying of Anglican identity. They had found this affirmed by the Caroline divines, who had identified the Church of England with the primitive church and her doctrine as that expressed by the catholic consent of Christian antiquity.

John Keble

Fundamental to all that Keble believed and wrote about is the sacramental character of the Church as the living Body of Christ and its catholicity that is firmly rooted in the Vincentian Canon, what has been believed everywhere, always and by all. This theme, the Church's catholicity, permeates his sermons, the poetry of *The Christian Year, The Tracts,* the preface to his edition of Hooker's *Laws of Ecclesiastical Polity* (1836) and his sermon at the Archdeacon's Visitation in Winchester Cathedral. This sermon in Winchester was described by Newman as a 'masterly exposition of the meaning of Tradition'. Here his concern is with the limits of the civil power in ecclesiastical matters, the vindication of the Anglican Church in relation to the claims of Rome and the authority of the episcopal succession. Scripture and Tradition are coinherent and this coinherence is responsible for the systematic arrangement of the Articles of the Faith in the Creed, the interpretation of Holy Scripture, the episcopal government of our church, guaranteed by the apostolical succession, sacramental life and practical matters of church discipline. All these tenets of apostolic and catholic doctrine, patristic and Anglican, were implicit in Keble's religious thought. Though he admitted in 1845, that when he wrote *The Christian Year* he did not fully understand the doctrine of the Holy Eucharist, so that it did not adequately represent Keble's later thinking, nevertheless, Pusey always claimed that the real source of the Oxford Movement was to be found in it. It does set the tone of Tractarianism and the truths for which it stood can be found there when read in the light of later events. The doctrine of Apostolical Succession is there in the poem for St. Matthias' Day,

> Who then, uncalled by Thee,
> Dare touch Thy Spouse, Thy very self below?
> Or who dare count him summon'd worthily,
> Except Thine hand and seal he show?
> Where can Thy seal be found,

> But on the chosen seed, from age to age
> By Thine anointed heralds duly crown'd,
> As kings and priests Thy war to wage?

The Tractarians' use of the Fathers

The Tractarians eventually came to the point where they found it impossible to use their inheritance in the same way as their predecessors. The difference was one of attitude rather than theory. For their predecessors the theory of tradition was to be 'corroborative' of the doctrine of the Church of England and thereby 'preservative or conservative'.

> Keble's theory is also, in a manner, preservative – keep the deposit of faith which you inherit. But it is not only preservative. He has begun to compare the teaching and practice, common or popular in the present Church of England, with the teaching or practice of antiquity, and to find the present Church wanting. Therefore the idea of primitive tradition is not only a preservative idea, but a quest for reform. It is a demand for the restoration of, or re-emphasis upon, those beliefs and practices approved or authorised by antiquity but wanting or fragmentary in the present age. [40]

As Keble pointed out, while it was in no way a search for novelty, because antiquity will disclose truths that have been 'mislaid' or 'forgotten' it will give the impression of being new.

As Peter Nockles notes in his book *The Oxford Movement in Context*, the seeds of this divergence of approach to antiquity in Newman are traceable to the source of his introduction to the Fathers in Joseph Milner's *History of the Church of Christ*. 'As Stephen Thomas argues, like Milner, but unlike his Caroline mentors such as Bishop Bull, Newman responded to antiquity, "not by the attempted extinguishment of his personal perspective, but existentially, imaginatively, and polemically"'.[41] Nockles goes on to point out that Newman's portrayal of the church of Ambrosian Milan had a polemical purpose.

> He appealed to antiquity not primarily for testimony to a particular disputed doctrine as had Mant, Kaye or Burton, 'as if the Church were some fossil remains of antediluvian era', but in order to provide the model of a living church that could be reproduced in the nineteenth century. Yet there was a tension in

Newman between on the one hand the need to prove himself a sound Anglican, and on the other hand his growing conviction that the Fathers went beyond Anglican teaching.

Newman's criticism of the old High Churchmen was that their patristic learning tended to be primarily a factual and historical knowledge of the early church, and its defect lay in the absence of any appreciation of its moral and spiritual character. These Tractarian predecessors valued patristic witness because its nearness to apostolic times made it a more reliable interpreter of scriptural truth than modern commentators. Therefore it was valuable as a weapon for the vindication of orthodoxy in authenticating the truth of Anglican formularies and the teaching of Reformers and Carolines for whom it was the interpreter of scriptural truth. Newman came to view this methodology as a forcing of patristic witness into an arbitrary conformity with modern notions of scriptural truth enshrined in Anglican formularies. In his catholic interpretation of the Thirty-Nine Articles his approach was the very antithesis of this.

> Whatever ... be the true way of interpreting the Fathers, if a man begins by summoning them before him, instead of betaking himself to them, by seeking to make them evidence for modern dogmas, instead of throwing his mind upon the text ... he will certainly miss their sense.[42]

In these old High Churchmen the appeal to antiquity was always in a restrictive mode in not being able to trespass beyond what Reformers and Carolines had enshrined in Anglican formularies, and was grounded on the inherited principle of distinguishing between fundamentals and non-fundamentals in doctrine and worship. In practice, this placed Scripture as the only Rule of Faith in a primary role and assigned to other writings a secondary role as illustrative of doctrine and worship, giving them a subsidiary place as not essential to our Creed. Fundamentals were restricted to apostolic ministry and the Church's credal definitions, and non-fundamentals to other doctrines of lesser importance. The Tractarians were impatient with these limitations of what they described as the 'Waterland School' and what was described by Liddon[43] as Waterland's 'timid and apologetic tone when discussing the use and value of ecclesiastical antiquity', in an age when English divines were more influenced by Mosheim and Daillé. Initially, Newman adhered to the principle of fundamentals.

Yet as he expounded the *via media* in those *Lectures* [*on the Prophetical Office*], he appears to have reacted against the static version of fundamentals being restricted to a few credal articles, and came to invest a whole range of doctrines and practices with a degree of dogmatic authority that ignored the distinctions on which old High Churchmen and he himself had earlier insisted. For Newman's introduction of the concept of a 'Prophetical Tradition' encompassing the doctrine of the first five centuries of the undivided church, in effect vastly widened the scope of what he regarded as matters 'of faith' and blurred any antithesis between essentials and non-essentials.[44]

Hugh James Rose was disturbed by Newman's divergence from the old High Church use of antiquity and what he feared as the raising up of the primitive church that in many minds would be identified as the Church of Rome. In a letter to Newman (May 1836) he expressed his hesitations about

> the effects of turning ... readers ..., out to grass in the spacious pastures of Antiquity without very strict tether. All that is in Antiquity is not good; ... without strict and authoritative guidance ... they are just as likely to get harm as good: to deduce very false and partial conclusions from very insufficient premises; and to set up as objects for *imitation* what may catch the fancy and strike the imagination, but what is utterly unfit for our present condition.[45]

For Rose and his school the 'strict and authoritative guidance' they brought to their reading of the Fathers was that of Reformers and Carolines. He re-emphasized this point to Newman that unlike the Reformers the appeal to antiquity is not an uncharted journey, 'a journey of discovery'. 'We know exactly what the Truth is...' That 'Truth' was the Anglican Tradition enshrined in these divines and the purpose of the appeal to antiquity was to defend it. Therefore it is futile to think that the journey is the search for 'a new Atlantis'.[46] Among the Tractarians, almost from the beginning there was a growing antipathy towards this approach. For them this inheritance needed to be supplemented and a new patristic norm for orthodoxy was emerging in them as they sought to find the sense of the Fathers by throwing their mind upon the text rather than making the Fathers evidence for modern dogmas. At the same time, 'they believed that the Bible could only be approached with the proper spirit of reverence when it was approached not with the fallen, objective, detached, intellectualist mind of the individual, but with the eyes of the ancient and undivided Church for which the Biblical texts were in fact written, and selected some to be biblical and others not'.[47] This was the reason for making these patristic texts available to the English reader 'with something of the same religious spirit in which the Reformers had sought to make the Bible available in the language of the people'. To Keble, Newman and Pusey, this appeal to antiquity was no theological device as it had sometimes seemed to be in the 'high and dry' High Church School.

> It is not a negative, nor is it a mere form. It is (if the expression be allowed, for they would not have used it) a sacrament. The Church is seen to be like a living being, with its breath, and its limbs, and its head. And tradition is not like certain sentences spoken from the mouth, though the words of the mouth are part of tradition. It is more like the beating of the heart or the breathing of the lungs, or the character of the man, which is part hidden, part reflected in his appearance, part issuing in his conduct, part appearing in his words. 'Prophets or Doctors', wrote Newman, 'are the interpreters of the revelation ... Their teaching is a vast system, ... pervading the Church like an atmosphere, irregular in its shape, from its very profusion and exuberance ... This, I call Prophetical Tradition, existing primarily in the bosom of the Church itself, and recorded in such measure as Providence has determined, in the writings of eminent men.' This atmosphere is best expounded by Newman, because he possessed the most acute and sensitive mind among the leaders, and above all because he possessed by nature and by musical ear and had developed by practice, a gift of writing good prose. He was incapable of representing tradition as an ecclesiastical device. It was sacramental of the life of heaven, the Church visible as a sign of the invisible. It was an earthly story of the communion of the saints in heaven. His feeling for historical continuity, his affection for the past, his reverence for an other worldly sanctity, his love of 'orthodoxy' not as orthodoxy or rigidity but as faithfulness to every truth revealed, his sense of the richness and exuberance of the Christian tradition – all these enabled him to set forth tradition as a kind of sacrament ... Tradition is the life of the Church, which, though visible, is more invisible than visible. Tradition, apostolic succession, ministry, episcopate – despite the strength of his language against dissent, he seldom sees these as engines against dissent. He sees them as rungs in Jacob's ladder, where the angels ascend and descend.[48]

The critics accused Newman and his circle of devising a new form of private judgement. They responded by claiming the authority of Canon 1571 that what is to be preached must be in accordance with Scripture and antiquity as defined by Vincentius of Lérins and the threefold test of catholicity in his *Commonitorium*, 'what has been believed everywhere, always, and by all'. The accusation against this was that the Tractarians had departed from the Waterland–Van Mildert line that carefully defined this Canon as *antiquity consistent with Anglican formularies,* on the principle that our formularies are prior to antiquity and that a proper use of antiquity is the vindicating of them. Furthermore, the appeal was to living authority in the episcopate, so that 'access to the ancient Church must be through the channel of our own English Church, and under the control of living rulers',[49] as well as to the authority of written Canons. In appealing directly to antiquity as an absolute standard by which to judge the Church of England, the consequence for the Tractarians was the abandonment of the principle of fundamentals. Such fundamentals were not confined to explicitly Scriptural or credal doctrines, but to such doctrines as were authoritative, as being confirmed by 'genuine apostolical tradition and a catholic consent of the Fathers'. In consequence the Tractarians conflated with doctrines that had always been considered binding and *de fide,* other not so ancient doctrines and practices that had not appeared in the church's formularies or been uniformly taught, though some divines may have recommended them.

> This class of doctrine and practice included: the alleged necessity of turning to the east in prayer; the ideal and superiority of the celibate state; the absolute duty of fasting; the necessity of prayers for the dead; the concept of purification and growth in grace of souls in an intermediate state; notions of post-baptismal sin; reserve in communicating religious knowledge and the *disciplina arcani*; and theories of the mystical or allegorical scriptural interpretations of the Fathers. Perceval believed that it was the Tractarian 'attempt to propagate this latter class (of doctrine) by the same medium, apparently on the same ground, with the same force, and from the same quarter as the former, that gave rise to all the confusion, awakened suspicion, and destroyed confidence'.[50]

This issue had been a cause of division among the Non jurors, splitting them into 'Usagers' and 'non-Usagers'. The older High Churchmen were not averse to obsolete primitive customs as such but insistent on the authoritative right of the church to abolish them. Palmer claimed '... those apostolical customs which are not necessary to salvation, may be suspended or abrogated by the successors of the apostles, if there are good reasons for doing so'.[51] But as Chadwick said of the 'high and dry',

> They were shallow; their theory attempted to rest upon the reasoning of its propositions and took no account of the force of personality; they were far too concerned with defending the Church, maintaining the privileges of the establishment; they were sober, sensible men, suspicious of extremism or (in its eighteenth-century sense) enthusiasm. And by contrast, Newman thought of the Oxford men as men of personal influence and enthusiasm, suspicious of sobriety and common sense, anxious to strive after depth and to penetrate mystery even at the expense of clarity, content to be less coherent so long as they were not shallow, using propositions as means rather than ends, more concerned with truth than with the defence of the Establishment, more content even to let the Establishment go so long as truth prevailed.[52]

Yet it was precisely this divergence from the old High Churchmen in their approach to antiquity, that created in the Tractarians an antipathy towards the Reformers and the dismissal of their claim by the High Church Party to be the lineal successors of Caroline divinity or successors to the Laudians. Deference to antiquity therefore meant that the primitive church rather than the Reformers became the ultimate reference point by which to expound the meaning of the Church of England. Keble and Newman make a claim for such a precedence in their preface to Froude's *Remains*, a viewpoint Pusey eventually embraces even though he had defended *Tract 90* by deference to the use of antiquity in Ridley and Cranmer. In this they differ from the old High Churchmen who always had to check the Fathers by the Reformers. Disillusionment with the seventeenth-century divines followed, and a loss of enthusiasm with the *Library of Anglo-Catholic Theology* when Copeland resigned the editorship because the Caroline divines did not go far enough and when judged by antiquity were found wanting. The patristic learning of these Tractarians was massive but their use of it sometimes lacked historical discrimination, and their use of the Carolines was at times a too narrowly selective approach in the interests of attempting to produce a theologically coherent system. Charles Wordsworth, whose *Theophilus Anglicanus* was an attempt to respond to this Tractarian stance, claimed that the Tractarians had not sufficiently understood the mind of the Carolines. Though these seventeenth-century divines were lumped together under the name 'Caroline' they had never been a 'school' that spoke with one voice, and Newman's attempt to systematize Caroline divinity and build a coherent dogmatic edifice on it was misconceived since it was not designed to support such a structure. Therein lies the clue to his disillusionment and ultimate loss of faith in the *via media*.

> For Newman wished the Church of England literally to represent the church of antiquity in doctrinal fullness if she was to compete with the Church of Rome. Yet, Newman was seeking the impossible. Caroline divinity, however blended, harmonised and supplemented, could never have fulfilled his expectation.[53]

While Newman and his colleagues 'enhanced the importance of history for the Church, their own lack of historical scientific method could lead them to conclusions which later called for modification'.[54] Ramsey cites one example:

> In the first of the *Tracts for the Times* J. H. Newman used the concept of apostolic succession in a manner which confused together the succession of bishop to bishop in their Sees, the succession of consecrators to consecrated, succession in the conveying of grace and succession in the handing down of true doctrine. This confusion continued in some of the Tractarian writers. Subsequently a more discriminating study of ancient literature has brought about a far more careful distinction of facts and concepts, as is found (to give one example) in the essay on 'Apostolic Succession in the volume *Essays on the Early History of the Church and the Ministry* edited by H. B. Swete (1917).

Tract 90

The strong Romanizing tendencies that began to develop among a group of the younger Tractarians became a threat to the integrity of the Movement and a danger to the church. Newman says of this new party that it 'cut into the original Movement at an angle, fell across its line of thought, and then set about turning that line [of thought] in its own direction'.[55] W. G. Ward was a dominant member in this party and Newman speaks of such people who came to him to 'pump' him as to how he got over this or that difficulty in the Anglican position. He admitted that he did not share in the apprehensions implied in the question, 'What will you make of the Articles?'[56] Newman's response was to publish *Tract 90*, 'Remarks on Certain Passages in the Thirty-Nine Articles', to demonstrate that these Articles were capable of a catholic interpretation. What caused him to write it he explains in this same passage of the *Apologia*, 'was the restlessness actual and prospective, of those who neither liked the *Via Media*, nor my strong judgement against Rome. I had been enjoined, I think by my Bishop, to keep these men straight, and I wished so to do: but their tangible difficulty was subscription to the Articles; and thus the question of the Articles came before me'. The allegation of this party that was shared also by their opponents was, that the Thirty-Nine Articles were irreconcilable with the Catholic teaching that Newman had defended on the authority of the great Anglican divines and that both parties identified with the Roman Catholic Church. With his faith and confidence in *Ecclesia Anglicana* in a state of doubtful transition from 1839, Newman continues to use Caroline divinity in 1841 for his apologetic purposes in *Tract 90*, even though as Dean Church[57] recognizes it is somewhat one-sided and selective.

> ... in the heyday of the *via media*, Newman selected 'here a teacher, there an authority' but accepted 'them no further than they fell in with his views'. She felt that he snatched at 'every chance saying of any of our Divines', even though 'the whole tenor of the work has no weight with him'.[58]

The Tract was intended to strengthen those of Romanist sympathies in their allegiance to Anglicanism. It was never intended for those who expressed their outrage towards it. These sympathizers felt deeply that while the Creeds and the Prayer Book were capable of interpretation in a Catholic sense, the Thirty-Nine Articles expressed a decidedly Protestant outlook. Newman claimed that the Articles may well be 'the offspring of an uncatholic age' but they 'are through God's good providence, at least not uncatholic and may be subscribed to by those who aim to be Catholic in heart and doctrine'. They could be taken in their plain, literal sense rather than be interpreted according to the opinion of those who compiled them. It was another phase in that larger quest to prove the Church of England's literal identity with the primitive church. His concern was to interpret the Articles in the light of antiquity to demonstrate that they are not 'uncatholic'.

> ... Newman in no way intended Tract 90 to be a reconciliation with Rome; and the fact that some still believe he intended this

cannot be based on a reasoned study of the documents, but can only be an inference from what happened subsequently, in 1845, or from the joyous deductions based on the Tract by extremists like Ward.[59]

Newman's was not the first attempt at such a venture. Christopher Davenport (1595–1680), an English convert who became a Roman Catholic Franciscan, had published his *Paraphrastica Expositio Articulorum Confessionis Anglicanae* (published separately in 1634, afterwards as an appendix to his *Deus, natura, gratia*). He ventured to illustrate that the Thirty-Nine Articles could be interpreted in harmony with Catholic tradition.[60] Henry Cary's work, *Testimonies of the Fathers of the First four Centuries To the Doctrine and Discipline of the Church of England as set forth in the Thirty-Nine Articles,* is a similar exercise published in 1835. Other such publications are Bishop Burnet's *Exposition of the Thirty-Nine Articles* (1699), William Beveridge's *The Doctrine of the Church of England* consonant *to Scripture, Reason, and Fathers in A Discourse on the Thirty-Nine Articles* (1710), and Edmund Welchman's *Exposition of the Thirty-Nine Articles in Scripture and the Fathers* (1790). Over twenty-five years after Newman's *Tract 90* Bishop Forbes, 'the Pusey of Scotland', wrote, 'I venture in the following work to assume, – that the position of the Anglican Church requires that the Articles shall be interpreted in the Catholic Sense; that this sense exposes us to fewer difficulties than any other canon of explanation; and, that historically there is support for this theory'.[61] The point at issue among Newman's critics was not so much the argument for a catholic interpretation of the Articles on the basis of primitive models of faith and order. It was his failure to require, as previous writing on this issue had presupposed, that Roman Catholic doctrine, and in particular the Conciliar definitions of the Council of Trent, be tested and readjusted at the same bar of antiquity.

Newman explains[62] that the Articles were drawn up against the *political* supremacy of the Pope more than against the doctrines of the Church of Rome. He himself was not in favour of papal supremacy. The framers were also concerned to win over the moderate Romanists, therefore the Articles were intentionally so drawn up that 'their bark should prove worse than their bite'. In recognizing the doctrine of the Homilies as 'godly and wholesome' and insisting on subscription to that proposition in Article 35, they were being tolerant of 'Catholic teaching' and of much that was 'Roman'. Such 'Catholic teaching' included acceptance as authoritative several Apocryphal books, the primitive church of the first seven hundred years as pure, the recognition of six councils, acceptance of the bishops of the first eight centuries and many of the Fathers as endowed with the Holy Spirit. They quote from the Fathers on the Eucharist or Lord's Supper as 'the salve of immortality, the sovereign preservative against death', the meat received in the Sacrament as the 'invisible meat and ghostly substance'. Matrimony and Ordination are defined as Sacraments, and in addition to Baptism and the Lord's Supper there are other Sacraments. In the Articles 'alms-deeds' is stated as purging the soul from sin and fasting used with prayer has great efficacy with God. Such doctrine to be found in The Homilies is regarded as 'godly and wholesome' and the best comment upon the Articles. This indicates, Newman claims, that their intention is not to effect a complete break with what he called the 'Catholic teaching,' of the first centuries, nor the dogmas of Rome. Such Catholic teaching that can also be found in the Roman Church is contained 'in no small portion' in the Homilies. Furthermore, because the Articles were drawn up before the end of the Council of Trent and the promulgation of its Decrees they must be aimed at something else. That 'something else' is the dominant errors and popular corruptions and abuses 'authorised and suffered by the high name of Rome'. Newman regarded the writers of the Articles as witnesses not authorities, and the Convocation of 1571 as the authority imposing them. This same Convocation that confirmed the Thirty-Nine Articles prescribed the Canon that required preachers to '... be *careful* that they should *never* teach aught in a sermon, to be religiously held and believed by the people, except that which is agreeable to the doctrine of the Old and New Testament, and *which the Catholic Fathers and ancient Bishops have collected* from that very doctrine' [Newman's italics].[63]

Old High Churchmen were critical of an ambiguity in his meaning; others of his inconsistency since, in *Tract 15* and Froude's *Remains*, Trent had been accused of error. Also there was that degree of historical inaccuracy in distinguishing between the versions of doctrine condemned, Romanist and not Tridentine.[64] The old high churchmen also claimed that *Tract* 90 enshrined a 'dangerous misapplication of a legitimate principle', in that the Church's formularies 'were being tried by a merely private judgement as to what was and was not antiquity'. Newman's use of canon 1571 to support his central thesis was irreconcilable with the application of that principle, claimed Bishop Phillpotts.[65]

It was left to Edward Churton to reassert what old High Churchmen insisted was the true 'catholic' principle on interpreting the Articles as 'articles of peace' in the manner upheld by Laud, Taylor and Bramhall. For Churton, this Laudian interpretation was opposed alike to the rival theories of Tractarian, Evangelical and latitudinarian subscription ... In short, the Articles meant both more than latitudinarians allowed, and less than Evangelicals maintained, but also represented 'catholic' principles in a sense different from that advocated by the Tractarians.[66]

Patristic, Catholic, Ecumenical

Owen Chadwick[67] describes the Oxford Movement as 'a movement of the heart than of the head ... primarily concerned with the law of prayer, and only secondarily with the law of belief "thought"... it was earnestly dogmatic'.

> It always saw dogma in relation to worship, to the numinous, to the movement of the heart, to the conscience and the moral need, to the immediate experience of the hidden hand of God – so that without this attention to worship or the moral need, dogma could not be apprehended rightly. The Creed was creed – the truth; not a noise of words to evoke prayer. But it roused the mind to prayer, and only through prayer and life was it known to be truth.

Chadwick attempts an approximate evaluation of respective individual contributions. He sees Pusey as representative of the moral and mystical, Keble of the moral and pastoral, and Newman of the moral and intellectual.[68] As in the early Fathers of the Church whose teaching they so revered, it is impossible to separate these Tractarians from their work or the work from their actual history and life with which it is so entwined, and the two are never confounded. Their search is for a wholeness of life, the catholicity in which their own church claims to be rooted, and being in relationship with the whole they seek to grow and develop within it. As Chadwick noted, to them 'the church is seen to be like a living being, with its breath, and its limbs, and its head, and tradition more like the beating of the heart or the breathing of the lungs'. Rooted in this life, the mystery of Christ present in the history of mankind and the Eucharist is where catholic truth is found and in which the mystery of Creation and Redemption is revealed. Here is their *Sitz-im-Leben*, the life of grace, where as catholic persons they seek to grow ecclesially as well as theologically and within the full potential of their humanity. Salvation then becomes, not the return journey of the individual soul to its Maker, but the catholic process, the gradual unfolding of a universal transfiguration in which people are saved, not from the world, but with the world through the church. Theirs is an ideal of theology not divorced from prayer and liturgy but a way of life structured by theological vision.

> The growth of the person in grace is something different from simple individualism. It is as we are being freed from our individual restrictions that we begin to taste the liberty of persons, the freedom of the sons of God. This involves a religion which is neither that of heart and mind, of feeling or intellect, but which is characterised by the mad fervour of the great theologians and spiritual writers of East and West alike, who have discovered the secret of 'putting the mind in the heart'.[69]

Catholicity is like a compass that reveals the true orientation of their lives and it is a patristic catholicity that is their compass, which they must follow if they are to grow into catholic truth. It teaches them to read the Bible differently, in the catholic way, and to find that the Bible and Apostolic Tradition cannot be properly understood outside their proper patristic *Sitz-im-Leben*. This is antipathetic to the modern liberal approach. What they rejected as Liberalism, as Pusey's letter to Arnold, cited on page 280, illustrates, was the exclusive application of an approach that disregards church history and ignores the 'proper' setting or context of the Bible, the living and apostolic community, the catholic church of the Fathers within which the Bible emerged. Newman[70] makes this point, and that this has been the practice of our divines since the Reformation. They

> have betaken themselves to the extant documents of the early Church, in order to determine thereby what the system of primitive Christianty was; and so to elicit from Scripture more completely and accurately that revealed truth, which, though revealed there, is not on its surface, but needs to be *deduced* and *developed* from it.

This same expectation lay behind the publication of the *Library of the Fathers,* that the 'study of the writings of the Fathers will enable us to determine morally, to make up our minds for practical purposes, what the doctrines of the Apostles were'. The undivided

Church of the Fathers is what ensures authoritatively, normatively and critically, the historic continuity of the apostolic community and her apostolic faith and order. Only within this context will the Scriptures disclose their meaning but outside this context their meaning will be altered.

One hundred and seventy years ago the Oxford Fathers returned to prescriptive sources, such as Bennett, Schmemann and Florovsky have called for in our own day, that our outlook and mentality might be realigned and reformed by them. The 'church theology' that took seriously the ecclesiastical mind had been supplanted by a historicism in which the spirit of polemicism and antagonism dominated and served to obscure the catholic truth of the Fathers and the Bible in a general historical relativism and reductionism.

> But Newman had seen the Patristic and Apostolic truth from the original sources, from what to his opponents seemed to have been 'the subjectivism, fixed or inside stance'. He knew in the personal depths of his own being that the Fathers of the Catholic Church and their catholic dogmas were in touch with the catholic truth both personal and natural, which is the one and only truth for the world and for its history. So, he sought through writing and action to restate the Patristic truth of catholicity in his own times and in the modern linguistic and cultural idiom. I am convinced that no work of Newman is deprived of this Patristic quality, and I believe that its particular value lies in the fact that the Patristic catholic heritage of the truth of the Gospel comes to us through Newman in the language of our modern world. Newmanists have stressed this modernity of Newman.[71]

Fr Dragas makes a number of points. First, Newman's modernity is not modernism, because it is neo-patristic. Secondly, the *return to the Fathers* and the primitive church cannot ignore the history of division that has gripped humanity not only in a formal institutional way, but also in a living way that affects us psychologically and personally. As the Fathers 'met and overcame historically the pluralistic and totalitarian challenges of the general history of their time', so today's historical division will have to be overcome historically through responsible dialogue and action. Thirdly, Newman insists that the Fathers must be our guides in contemporary ecumenism, 'because they taught and applied the principles governing the catholic response to the challenge of discord and division presented to them by the old hellenistic pluralist culture'. Fourthly, the great difficulty in overcoming the contemporary cultural challenge to Christianity is its post-Christian stance. Fifthly, the possibility of ecumenical dialogue between Roman Catholic, Anglican, Orthodox and Reformed is made possible by Newman, in the way in which he has sown afresh the Christian seed in the modern world. Sixthly, the catholicity of the Fathers is crucial for understanding Newman fully and assessing his significance for the 'contemporary historical manifestation of the *Una Sancta*'.

> ... in the context of schism and division, Newman had at first to state catholicity in a dogmatical and apologetic manner. But the more he examined the Fathers, the more he came to realize that catholicity is primarily an existential, historical, theological reality which embraces the whole man, individually and socially, and has world-wide ecumenical dimensions. It was in the Fathers acting concretely in history as catholic persons that Newman met the force of catholic reality. The Fathers were concrete manifestations, embodiments, witnesses to the living pattern of the truth which undercuts the roots of the divisions sown by human failure and sin. They were imbued with the life-giving power of God who in Christ has taken up our human weakness, redeemed it and perfected it for ever. Newman saw in the Fathers the primordial realities of human existence, which are connected with God's dealings with men, the economies of creation and redemption. He found in the Fathers the Christ of the Apostles as the life-giving Spirit active in the history of mankind and leading it to conformity with his spiritual and perfect form. It is in the mystery of Christ's presence in the history of the world, as it is always consummated in the eucharistic presence in order to press forward to the future, that the heart of Newman's catholic truth should be found and not in the particular incidents of his life. He saw this mystery through the Fathers and sought to affirm it existentially and historically in his own particular time and historical contexts.[72]

Dragas sees Newman as a gift of the Fathers of the Church to the Roman Church with that apostolic and patristic catholicity that it is impossible to restrict within human boundaries, not even the Roman ones. It becomes the litmus test for all catholicity and the world-wide Church must be apostolically and patristically evaluated by it. Such catholicity can never be restricted when 'functioning critically within the general history of the world nor when challenging the restrictions of heresy'. Dragas goes on to say that too often because of its historical roots the danger is to perpetuate

schism by a defence mechanism that tries to find solutions to 'the
situation by restricting the restrictions'. The Fathers refused to
operate in this way because it would only lead them into a cul-de-
sac of 'deadly dialecticism'. Their avoidance of this restrictive way
meant that

> ... the Fathers were able to manifest the catholic truth in a history
> which has acquired normative status for all history, including our
> own. Newman saw and sought to appropriate this patristic stance.
> Again and again Newman realized and stressed that faith
> precedes law and order and therefore, orthodoxy does not
> discuss with heresy using equal terms. Even when orthodoxy
> employs heretical terms she employs them negatively and differ-
> entially because she ultimately remains all-embracing and
> ecumenical, rather than restrictive and particularist. It always
> views the whole and argues with catholic terms and statements,
> because God views it all and because the range of God's incor-
> ruptible grace, established in Christ and the foundation of the
> Church in the world, is and remains all-embracing and catholic.[73]

We need to reaffirm this patristic theological perspective, the
catholic truth of the Fathers that Newman rediscovered and
restated for the contemporary church. It is the *esse* of Newman's
theological vision that the Roman Church should be affirming
rather than constraining it within a restrictive context, ecclesiastical or cultural. Dragas points out that in the light of this vision
Newman's 'antipathies, Roman, Anglican, and Protestant are not
ends' and cannot be regarded as such. A proper reading of the
Fathers requires taking note of their proper catholic context, their
own *Sitz-im-leben*. This is the life of grace, which is never 'restrictive,
antithetical, polemical, or dialectical, but holistic, constructive,
creative and liberating, because it is imbued with the virtue and
humility and free submission to the power and grace of God, which
constitutes the unfailing foundation of man and his world'.

> Newman developed catholically and believed in catholic devel-
> opment. He was concerned with human development in God's
> grace, rather than development of abstract forms. The essence
> of the Church, the Atonement, established in Christ and given
> to humanity through the ministrations of the visible apostolic
> Church could not change. The resurrection, the fundamental
> locus of the new Creation, the catholic Church, is an established
> and perfect reality, the catholic truth. But mankind is given in
> the Pentecostal gift the ability to participate in it and taste its

power so that it may transform the old history and proceed through death to the *pleroma* of the Resurrection. Christians are catholics *in via* in development and growth ... they know that he is constantly coming to make them whole in his wholeness and integrate the world with catholicity. This is what Newman has bequeathed to the modern Roman Church and through her to all the Christian Churches everywhere – the catholic truth of the Risen Lord with all its implications for Christian life and growth in history.[74]

The structures of the church are the mere externals of history and do not constitute the essence of what the church is. Life is the essence of the church for Newman as for the Fathers, and what constitutes that life in the church is her catholicity which is nothing less than the life-giving presence and act of God in history, that is the *sui generis* experience of the church. This means, that 'The Church of Christ is not an institution; it is a new life with Christ and in Christ, guided by the Holy Spirit. Christ the Son of God came to earth, was made man, uniting his divine life with that of humanity'.[75] So the aim of its mission is not to convey certain convictions and ideas. It is to introduce people '... into the New Reality, to convert them, to bring them through by their faith and repentance to Christ Himself, that they should be born anew in Him and into Him by water and the Spirit'.[76] Hence, the Roman Church is not catholic because Roman, but catholic as Roman, and the critical question this raises, claims Dragas, is whether the same affirmation can be made about other churches. If what constitutes catholicity is 'the life-giving presence and act of God in history', are the Orthodox Church and the Anglican Church catholic in the same sense as the Roman? The Fathers would affirm this, and Newman who learned from them that catholicity rests on the Mystery of God's free presence and act in human history, affirmed it as an Anglo-Catholic. The Orthodox too, believe in the reality of a non-Roman catholicity.

This does not mean that we can continue living in a 'local catholicism' for it is a contradiction of what being catholic means. A catholic is required to make the attempt to overcome schism by reintegrating with other catholics, in a word to be ecumenical and this is always the outcome of following the Fathers, of being patris-tic. As the Fathers have taught us, catholicity can never be a ghetto, for then it is a dead traditionalism and not dynamic, nor is it living and growing horizontally in a catholic community in history, seeking in ecumenical activity the reintegration of the world in the

grace of its Creator and Redeemer. With Newman individual
Tractarians were moving in this direction, but in Newman's judgement *Ecclesia Anglicana* was not, and at that moment in time could
not. It was inhibited by the principle of comprehensiveness that
locked together in compromise Protestants and Catholics. The
weakness in Evangelical ecclesiology arose from separating Christ
and the Church and thereby apostolicity and catholicity. For
Hooker and the Carolines, as for the Tractarians, and surely too in
Anglican formularies, Christ and the Church are inseparable, but
being locked into the compromise created by the principle of
Anglican comprehensiveness any development of their catholicism
ecumenically was limited.

Newman's disillusionment with Anglicanism arose because he
felt that the quest for catholicity rooted in the appeal to antiquity
in Reformers and Caroline divines had become restrictive. It had
become a mere theoretical and confessional device in Anglican
polemic with Roman Catholics and a theological device to justify a
via media. Hence it could be no more than a self-indulgent
catholicity rather than ecumenical activity and with the Protestant–
Catholic structure of *Ecclesia Anglicana,* Anglo-Catholics would not
be able to affirm catholicity ecumenically and thereby overcome
the problem of schism and division. The theory was there but the
practice was inhibited. Nevertheless, their engagement with the
undivided primitive church gave to them a vision of the One, Holy,
Catholic and Apostolic Church that sowed the seeds of a desire and
quest for unity in catholic truth and holiness. The fact that
Newman travelled a different road to realize his vision does not
mean that his fellow Tractarians

> were less zealous for the truth and less ready to appropriate it
> existentially and to suffer the practical consequences. But
> because they conducted their catholic quest in the context of a
> historically established ecclesiastical schism, they were faced
> with an inescapable and terrible dilemma, namely, whether to
> proceed individually or ecclesiastically. Having appropriated
> catholicity as individuals and as a Church group, they found that
> they could not act ecumenically towards Rome without risking
> their relationship with the *Ecclesia Anglicana,* which as a whole
> was not ready for such action and activity. So they concentrated
> their efforts within the Anglican Communion until catholicity
> would be fully integrated and restored from the inside and the
> whole *Ecclesia* would be able to engage in ecumenical action.
> The hard fact remained that the schism had run its historical

course and could only be overcome by a counter anti-schismatic history. Newman's Anglo-Catholic friends followed the second option, remaining faithful to the original aspiration of the Tractarian movement. Newman, however, chose the first alternative, i.e. he chose to meet the ecumenical implications of his personal appropriation of catholic truth with personal action. There is no clear answer to the critical question which history poses here. Who would not find it difficult to arbitrate between Newman and Pusey? Who would not acknowledge the catholicity of both, the personal ecumenism of the catholic Newman demonstrated in his conversion to Rome, and also the restrained ecumenism of catholic Pusey demonstrated in his catholic activity with the *Ecclesia Anglicana*?[75]

This is not to diminish the gravity of schism nor to justify a parochial catholic activity, but to recognise that catholicity cannot be obliterated by schism, though it may be covered or masked by the consequences of schism. Newman's conversion did not betray Anglicanism or the Tractarians and their principles, nor did it wipe out catholicity within Anglicanism. With his Tractarian friends Newman was part of a single-minded movement within Anglicanism that aimed to uncover the historically-established catholicity of the English Church in theory, practice and life. The Fathers of the undivided and primitive church gave them a vision of catholic truth that was life rather than mere theory. As a result they found that no longer could they read the Fathers obliquely through the restrictive parameters of the Reformers and Caroline divines to defend the Anglican formularies against Rome. They discovered the true way of interpreting the Fathers by summoning them before themselves and listening, instead of approaching them in order to make the Fathers evidence for modern dogmas. Unless one throws one's mind upon the text without restrictive parameters their sense will be missed. Reading the Fathers properly means to read them in their proper catholic context, their own *Sitz-im-Leben*, the life of grace where one is to grow ecclesially and humanly. This can never be 'restrictive, antithetical, polemical, or dialectical, but holistic, constructive, creative and liberating, because it is imbued with the virtue and humility and free submission to the power and grace of God, which constitutes the unfailing foundation of man and his world'.[76] This may well be a departure from the old High Churchmen's way, but here among the Tractarians may be the starting point for rediscovering the catholicity of the Fathers in this new age of *ARCIC*, where in the ecumenism of today we may well see, in the face of the Roman Catholic Newman, certain Anglican features that have never been erased because they belong to the *Una Sancta*.

Notes

1. A. M. Ramsey, 'The Ancient Fathers and Modern Anglican Theology', in *Sobornost*, Series 4: no. 6 (Winter–Spring 1962, pp. 289–94.
2. G. Croft, Sermon I, 'The Use and Abuse of Reason', *Vindication of the Church of England against the Objections of the Principal Sects* (Clarendon Press, Oxford, 1786), p. 2.
3. Henry Kett, The Bampton Lectures 1790, *A Representation of the Conduct and Opinions of the Primitive Christian, with Remarks on Certain Assertions of Mr. Gibbon and Dr. Priestley* (Clarendon Press, Oxford, 1790).
4. E.V. *Article* in *DNB*.
5. W. J. Sparrow-Simpson, 'The Study of the Fathers', in *The Priest as Student*, ed. H. S. Box (SPCK, London, 1939), p. 97.
6. J. Milner, 'Letters to a Prebendary ... With remarks on the Opposition of Hoadlyism to the Doctrines of the Church of England (London, 1802), p. 385', cited by Peter B. Nockles, *The Oxford Movement in Context, Anglican High Churchmanship 1760–1857*, (Cambridge University Press, 1994), p. 105.
7. J. W. Burgon, *Lives of Twelve Good Men* (John Murray, London 1891), p. 81.
8. T. Mozley, *Reminiscences*, 1882, vol. i. p. 318
9. R. W. Church, *The Oxford Movement, Twelve Years 1833–1845* (MacMillan & Co Ltd, London, 1897), p. 304.
10. J. R. Bloxham, ' The Magadalen College Register: the demies', vol. iv. p.35, cited by R. D. Middleton, *Magdalen Studies* (SPCK, London, 1936), p. 22.
11. S. L. Ollard, 'Martin Joseph Routh', *Dictionary of English Church History* (A. R. Mowbray & Co Ltd, London and Oxford, 1912), p. 526.
12. Henry Cary, *Testimonies of the Fathers of the First Four Centuries to the Doctrine and Discipline of the Church of England as Set Forth in the Thirty-Nine Articles* (D. A. Talboys, Oxford, 1835), p. i.
13. John Jebb, 'Letter to the Rev Dr Nash', in *Life of John Jebb DD FRS, with a Selection of his Letters* (James Duncan, London, 1837), Charles Forster, p. 532.
14. T. Mozley, *Remininsces chiefly of Oriel College and the Oxford Movement*, vol. i. p. 308
15. W. Palmer, Article in *The Contemporary Review*, May 1883, p. 644, cited by Burgon, *ibid.* p. 85.
16. J. H. Newman, 'Dedication', *Parochial and Plain Sermons*, vol. iv (Rivingtons, London, 1882).

17. H. J. Rose, cited in Burgon, *ibid.* p.100
18. *British Magazine*, October 1833, vol. iv. p. 421.
19. H. J. Rose, cited by Burgon *ibid.* pp. 109–11
20. H. P. Liddon, *Life of Edward Bouverie Pusey,* in 4 vols (Longmans, Green & Co, London, 1893–7), vol. i. p. 202.
21. Liddon, *ibid.,* p. 264.
22. J. Keble, 'Assize Sermon', *John Keble, A Study in Limitations* by G. Battiscombe (Constable, London, 1963), p. 152.
23. J. Keble, cited by Battiscombe, *ibid.* p. 154.
24. J. Keble, *ibid.* p. 154.
25. See Battiscombe, *ibid.* p. 155.
26. R. W. Church, *ibid.* p. 110.
27. J. H. Newman, in Froude's *Remains,* i. p. 265, cited by Church, *ibid.* p. 111.
28. Newman, *Tract* 1.
29. 'Advertisement', *Tracts for the Times,* by Members of the University of Oxford, vol. i. For 1833–4 (Rivington, London & Parker, Oxford, 1834).
30. H. P. Liddon, *ibid.* vol. i. p. 410.
31. Ecclesiasticus 42: 24.
32. H. P. Liddon, *ibid.* pp. 411–12.
33. H. P. Liddon, cited, *ibid.* p. 416
34. H. P. Liddon, *ibid.* p. 417.
35. H. P. Liddon, cited *ibid.* p. 418.
36. H. P. Liddon, *ibid.* p. 419.
37. H. P. Liddon, *ibid.* p. 434.
38. H. P. Liddon, *ibid.* p. 435.
39. T. M. Parker, 'The Rediscovery of the Fathers in the seventeenth-century Anglican Tradition', in *The Rediscovery of Newman.* eds. J. Coulson and A. M. Allchin (Sheed & Ward and SPCK, London, 1967), pp. 31–49.
40. O. Chadwick, *The Mind and Spirit of the Oxford Movement, Tractarian Essays* (CUP, 1990), p. 29.
41. P. B. Nockles, *The Oxford Movement in Context, Anglican High Churchmanship, 1760–1857* (CUP, 1994), p. 112.
42. J. H. Newman, 'British Critic', 25 (January, 1839), 54, cited by Nockles *ibid.* p. 114.
43. H. P. Liddon, *ibid.* p. 414.
44. P. B. Nockles, *ibid.* p. 116.
45. H. J. Rose, 'Letter', 9 May 1836, cited by Burgon, *ibid.* pp. 109–11.
46. H. J. Rose, 'Letter', 13 May, 1836 cited by Burgon, *ibid.* p. 114.
47. O. Chadwick, *ibid.* p. 30.
48. O. Chadwick, *ibid.* p. 31–32.
49. William Sewell, cited by P. B. Nockles, *ibid.* p. 118.
50. P. B. Nockles, *ibid.* pp. 119–120.
51. W. Palmer, *Origines Liturgicae or Antiquities of the English Ritual,* 2 vols. (London, 1832), vol. ii, p. 15; J. H. Pott, 'The Rule of Faith

Considered', in a Charge Delivered to the Clergy of the Archdeaconry of London (London, 1839), pp. 36–7, cited by P. B. Nockles, *ibid.* p. 122.

52. O. Chadwick, *ibid.* pp. 20–1.
53. P. B. Nockles, *ibid.* p. 130.
54. A. M. Ramsey, 'The Ancient Fathers and Modern Anglican Theology', in *Sobornost,* Winter-Spring 1962, Series 4: No.6, p. 291.
55. J. H. Newman, *Apologia,* (Fount Paperback, William Collins Sons & Co Ltd, 1977), pp. 221–2.
56. *Ibid.* p. 154.
57. R. W. Church, *ibid,* pp. 286–7. See pp. 281–4 on Newman's transitional state of mind.
58. Anne Mozley, cited by P. B. Nockles, *ibid.* p. 133.
59. Chadwick, *ibid.* p. 45.
60. Christopher Davenport, *The Oxford Dictionary of the Christian Church,* eds. F. L. Cross and E. A. Livingstone (3rd Edition, OUP 1997), p. 451.
61. A. P. Forbes, *An Explanation of the Thirty-Nine Articles* (James Parker & Co., Oxford and London 1871), p. xxxix.
62. *Apologia,* pp. 157ff.
63. cited in the *Apologia,* p. 160.
64. P. B. Nockles, see discussion *ibid.* pp. 138–9.
65. P. B. Nockles, *ibid.* p. 140.
66. P. B. Nockles, *ibid.* p. 142.
67. O. Chadwick, *ibid.* p. 1.
68. O. Chadwick, *ibid.* p. 38
69. A. M. Allchin, *Christian,* Autumn 1976 (All Saints Margaret Street Institute of Christian Studies).
70. J. H. Newman, in Cyril of Jerusalem, *The Catechetical Lectures,* (John Henry Parker; Rivington, London, 1839), Preface p. xv and xvi.
71. G. D. Dragas, 'John Henry Newman as a Starting Point for Rediscovering the Catholicity of the Fathers Today', a lecture given in Rome, 1979, during the celebrations of the centenary of Newman's cardinalate. It became the basis of an article 'Newman's Greek Orthodox Sense of Catholicity', published in *One in Christ,* 17 (1981), pp. 46–8. It is reprinted in *Ecclesiasticus, Orthodox Church Perspectives Models and Eikons* (Printed at Darlington Carmel 1984, pp. 97–128), p. 103. I am indebted to this article for the insights and thoughts which follow.
72. G. D. Dragas, *ibid.* pp. 105–6.
73. G. D. Dragas, *ibid.* pp. 107–8.
74. G. D. Dragas, *ibid.* p. 109.
75. S. Bulgakov, *The Orthodox Church* (SVS Press, New York 1988), p. 1.
76. G. Florovsky, *Bible, Church, Tradition: An Eastern Orthodox perspective* (Nordland, Massachusetts, 1972), p. 69.
75. G. D. Dragas, *ibid.* pp. 118–19.
76. G. D. Dragas, *ibid.* p. 109.

14

Redeeming the Present

This book is more than a mere catalogue of controversies that happened at a particular time in the history of Anglicanism within the wider context of the western church, for while the material is in one sense historical, in another sense it is of more than historical significance. In the divines of sixteenth- and seventeenth-century England, in Reformer and Caroline, in the old High Church School and the Tractarians, what is being made present in England is the spirit and the substance of that catholic vision of the mystery of Christ which characterizes those early centuries of the primitive church in East and West. This enables us to understand more fully the particular characteristics which mark the Anglican tradition we have received. Despite the discontinuities of the time there is an awareness of the continuity and wholeness of the Church's tradition in which these divines lived and for which they worked. Their aim and purpose was to be representatives of the Christian tradition in all its fullness, organic wholeness and unbroken unity. Hence what we find in their understanding of continuity is no mere mechanical concept, no theological device, but continuity as a dynamic transmission of certain living qualities of faith and order.

Therefore the principle upon which the English Reformation proceeded was by appealing against Rome to Holy Scripture as interpreted by the primitive church, so that in its intentions and first issues it was neither Lutheran nor Calvinist, but a return to primitive ancient Catholic Christianity. The Book of Common Prayer was an embodiment of the desire of the English church to restore ancient and primitive doctrine and worship. If the note of controversy seems to creep in too often, it is because the immediate cause of most of the writings of this era of Anglicanism's history was the need to clarify its beliefs in the face of opposition. For example, Hooker, in his *Laws of Ecclesiastical Polity,* and Laud, in his

Conference with Fisher the Jesuit, had the same fundamental aim, to make plain the position of the Church of England as contrasted with Papists on the one hand and the Continental Reformers on the other. Their theory of the position of the English church was a restatement of the doctrine of the original Reformers that there had been no break in the continuity of the church, so that she was still the same ancient catholic but reformed church of these islands.

The Fathers were held in esteem not only as witnesses to the content of the primitive faith but as a guide to the right interpretation of Holy Scripture. Throughout, in Reformer, Caroline and Tractarian, the same fundamental principle is present, that while Scripture is the supreme standard of faith, the Fathers represented the tradition of the Church by which Scripture was rightly interpreted. While initially the Reformers used the Fathers chiefly as a means of proving what was and what was not primitive doctrine and practice, the Carolines built on this principle and developed this use of the Fathers by making patristic thought and piety a vehicle in which to structure their own theological vision. In neither is there any transformation of the Fathers into a formal and infallible authority, nor the degeneration of their theology into a patristic scholasticism. For their concern is not merely to return to texts, abstract tradition, formulas and propositions, but to recover the true spirit of the Fathers, the secret inspiration that made them true witnesses of the Church. Their appeal to the Fathers is much more than a historical reference to the past: it is an appeal to the *mind of the Fathers,* and to follow them means to acquire their mind. This is what saves their use of the Fathers from a mere appeal to authority as such, rigid masters from whom no appeal is possible, and issues in an approach that is critical and reasonable. This saved them from becoming preoccupied with the controversies of their time in the doctrines of justification and predestination, as they set out to restore the grandeur of Christian truth by following the Nicene Fathers in making the Incarnation the central doctrine of the faith. It placed them beyond their age and culture and empowered them to transcend the limitations of nationalism as well as enabling them to avoid the temptation of building a scientific theology on the plan of Calvin. This patristic basis is what makes their theology something quite different from Tridentinism or Continental Protestantism. Furthermore, it was an ideal of theology that was not divorced from prayer and liturgy, for it provided a way of life and worship informed and structured by theological vision.

In the objections and objectors that this appeal to antiquity produced, there was lacking the catholicity, widemindedness, suppleness, sanity and contemporaneity of the Fathers. As objections were motivated by the controversies of the sixteenth- and seventeenth-century western church, the appeal was to texts, formulas and propositions, a mere historical reference to the past, rather than to the *mind of the Fathers*. There is no attempt to read the Fathers in their proper *Sitz-im-Leben*, the life of grace, nor is there any ecclesiological understanding of the context in which they speak. As Blunt points out against Daillé, it is the incidental nature of patristic testimony that is relevant to the issues with which he is concerned rather than direct and prescriptive testimony, and the *consensus patrum* rather than individual statements or isolated texts. For Barbeyrac, whose knowledge of the Fathers was from extracts rather than the texts, it is his unfamiliarity with the wholeness of patristic testimony and the nuances of their thought and strictures on moral issues that demolishes his objections. So it is the Fathers who speak in their own defence. George Bull's thorough grasp of the Ante-Nicene Faith, like Hooker's before him, enabled him to discern in the attacks on traditional apostolic and catholic doctrine, the resurgence of an *Arianism* that in no way could be justified by an appeal to the Fathers.

Thus did Anglican theology rediscover its roots, build and maintain its foundation in the study of the Fathers, and through that redemptive understanding of the centrality of the Incarnation learn to see the Christian Faith as an integral whole. It also found the gateway to what was scriptural and primitive, and a living tradition which guided the interpretation of Holy Scripture. This is what gave to Anglicanism that clue to the Catholic Church of the past and future, eastern and western, and its own identity within it. This influence of the Fathers continued, in the Tractarians whose concern was for a Catholic interpretation of the Church of England, amidst Evangelical, liberal and Erastian interpretations. However, we have seen how the Tractarians wanted to depart from the approach of the old High Churchmen who came to the Fathers and read them through the restrictive parameters of the Anglican formularies. For them, this inheritance of Anglicanism needed to be supplemented and a new patristic norm for orthodoxy was emerging in them as they sought to find the sense of the Fathers by throwing their mind upon the text rather than making the Fathers evidence for modern dogmas. The appeal to antiquity continues also in the modern phase of Anglican theology with the centrality of the Incarnation in such theologians as Westcott, Gore and the

Lux Mundi school, and William Temple and in such patristic scholars as H. B. Swete, Maurice Relton, Darwell Stone and F. L Cross,
to name a few.

Michael Ramsey[1] enumerates three ways in which, in the
modern phase, patristic influence has been apparent. First, in the
frequent use of the doctrine of the Logos, reflecting Irenaeus or
Clement of Alexandria, and demonstrating the unique revelation
of God in Christ as the central tower of a continuous divine activity in creation, nature, history, culture and civilization. Secondly,
there has been the constant influence of the Chalcedonian
doctrine of the One Person and Two Natures of Christ. Thirdly,
there has been an emphasis on the negative and protective aspects
of the ancient Christological definitions. In this way, says Ramsey,
Anglicanism 'has preferred the Fathers, who use dogma as a
pointer to the scriptural facts, rather than the Schoolmen, who
have seemed to use dogma as the starting point for deductive
doctrinal formulations'. The Fathers have left their mark on other
matters of doctrine, not least in Eucharistic sacrifice, Real Presence
and teaching about the Communion of Saints to encourage the
belief that the living and departed are one in a fellowship of
common prayer and praise rather than in terms of mediation.

These same Fathers who spoke to Cranmer and Jewel, and the
Reformers, to Hooker, Andrewes, Laud, and the Carolines, to
Keble, Newman and Pusey, can speak to us today with that same
sharpness and contemporaneity, for their writings are timeless,
dynamic and always contemporary. A conviction regarding this
possibility in relation to seventeenth century Anglican theological
method is expressed by McAdoo, who rightly states,

> Having listened to these voices from our past I venture to think
> that it is a fair assessment to judge that seventeenth century
> Anglican theologians did not use the threefold appeal like the
> Stamp Act of 1765 to guarantee by a cursory reference to origins
> the authenticity of this or that article of belief or doctrinal
> formulation. Rather, within the given limitations of the scholar-
> ship and the knowledge of their times, did they apply the criteria
> with sensitivity, honesty, and freedom, and in some cases, with a
> surprising modernity. No review of how they went about it could
> fairly describe their procedure as simplistic. Is it possible for us
> in our situation to do the same, given a changed perspective in
> society and in scholarship?[2]

In the Preface to his book *From Gore to Temple*, the Hale Memorial
Lectures of Seabury–Western Theological Seminary delivered in

1959, Michael Ramsey expressed the same conviction when he said,

> ... the times call urgently for the Anglican witness to Scripture, tradition and reason – alike for meeting the problems which Biblical theology is creating, for serving the reintegration of the Church, and for presenting the faith as at once supernatural and related to contemporary man.[3]

He reiterated this same conviction in lectures[4] given in Nashotah House in 1979, stressing the importance of the threefold appeal not only in relation to Anglican identity but also in its ecumenical implications for the reintegration and unity of the whole Church. Such a conviction has been conceived and born in both these contemporary theologians through their living engagement with Fathers, Reformers, Carolines, Tractarians, as they continue to speak to the contemporary church.

The solitary confinement of the present

A point of connection with our own age and the seventeenth century finds expression in some words of Bishop Beveridge describing his 'senseless age', where 'there is scarcely anything in Christianity itself which is not either called in doubt in private, or made a matter of controversy in public ... and what is most absurd, nothing is esteemed of before novelty itself, but the newer anything is, so much the greater number and the more does it please, and the more anxiously it is defended'.[5] His response lies in his seven points about the nature of catholicity enumerated in chapter 10. Bishop Knapp-Fisher made the same criticism of people in our own age in their 'frenetic preoccupation with the present. Life is nothing but today. They pay little or no attention to the past, of which we can know something, or to the future, of which we can know nothing'.[6] Like the Athenians in St Paul's time, they are obsessed with anything new, precisely because it *is* new. This cult of the new, which leads to a solitary confinement of everyone and everything in the present, can be clearly discerned in the *new theology*. The Bishop goes on to point out that today's theologians have misunderstood the vocation of the Christian theologian which is that of 'relating the revealed datum of Christian truth, final, absolute, and fundamentally permanent ... to the essentially changing intellectual framework of the world in which he lives'. This solitary confinement in the here and now

ignores God's involvement in the past and his purposes for the
future, and is the consequence of an accommodation to the
contemporary world's diminished awareness of the dimension of
eternity and the significance of time. It leads to an over eager identification of the spirit of the age with the Holy Spirit of God. Its
ultimate conclusion is innovation rather than renovation.

> In consequence they draw a false distinction between experi-
> ence and history. They do not recognize that history represents
> the accumulated experience of past generations confronted by
> situations which are often in their essential features very similar
> to those which face us today. The traditions we inherit, if we will
> heed them, can assist us in solving problems which are not pecu-
> liarly our own; and we cannot afford to dismiss as irrelevant the
> lessons of the past. The present is but a fragment of history, and
> our contemporary experience can only be understood and eval-
> uated in the light of that, of those who have lived before us.[7]

In the madness of the sixties, when 'the baby was being thrown
out with the bathwater', Professor Eric Mascall in October 1962
delivered his Inaugural Lecture as Professor of Historical Theology
in the University of London. His theme was 'Theology and
History'. Mascall was concerned that theologians cannot seek
objectivity by pursuing it as a deliberate ideal, looking over their
shoulder for the 'approbation of the secular scholar', 'or at any
rate that if it is so achieved it will be only at the cost of triviality,
irrelevance and dullness'.[8]

> What is needed rather is an intense conviction of the truth and
> vitality of the Christian religion, a confidence in the relevance of
> theology to matters outside the academic sphere, and a combi-
> nation of humility with intellectual integrity. This last, for the
> theologian as for other scholars is primarily a matter of
> ingrained attitude rather than of self-conscious and anxious
> striving; it is a *habitus,* in the traditional sense, a matter of
> connaturality, of *bent.* For fruitful scholarship depends not only
> on a pose of disinterested detachment – it is possible to be so
> disinterested and detached that one never does anything of
> importance at all – but also upon the precise nature of one's
> subject-matter and a sense of relevance and proportion, and
> these are much less easy to achieve.[9]

Mascall's next point is supported by reference to two recent (to
the 1960s) publications by scientists of distinction. Dr Michael
Polanyi's *Personal Knowledge* and Dr William Pollard's *Physicist and*

Christian. Both authors are making the point that in order to become a scientist, it is not sufficient merely to become tutored in scientific method and then start applying it to the science of one's choice. One has to enter into the community of scientists, 'live with them, think with them, argue with them, and one's expertise and originality will be developed in the process'.

> Now if this is true of the scientist it is, I believe, even truer of the theologian, but in his case the matter is vastly more complex. For, if the theologian believes that Christianity is true and is himself a practising Christian, he is not only a member of the community of theologians but also a member of the Christian Church; he will be theologizing not from outside but from inside the revelation, the Church and the faith.[10]

Within this context as a theologian claims Mascall, he will need, as Gilson has said that Thomas Aquinas possessed, a perfect intellectual modesty and an almost reckless intellectual audacity. But he will make no advancement to our knowledge of the Christian religion unless 'his theologizing is a function of his membership of the Christian Church and takes place under the illumination of the Christian revelation'. Certain theologians ignore this fundamental of their existence as Christian theologians to plan reconstructions of Christian theology and morals in their own heads. It is a bid to make it relevant and acceptable to people in the twenty-first century, but it may well end up being totally irrelevant and unacceptable to the people of the twenty-second century. Even the most original thinkers have to depend upon a body of corporate knowledge, much of which has to be taken on trust, and a 'fiduciary framework' (Polanyi) of fundamental attitudes which shape the way we test and acquire knowledge.[11] A corporate framework of belief does not negate reason but is its very condition and this rooting of reason in the particularity of a cultural tradition does not imply absolute relativism.

> To see the world from a particular standpoint which our tradition has given us is the condition of creaturely knowledge. To trust a tradition for the insight and knowledge it has given us, to go on to appropriate more of what it has to offer, is not irrational, nor is it necessarily conservative. Even the revolutionary, whatever his destination, can see only from where he is. [12]

What we have in the resources of the patristic tradition that has been appropriated into Anglicanism by the Reformers, Carolines, Tractarians and others, is a tradition that was outside the parameters of their particular time and thought, the solitary confinement of the 'present'. It offered to them alternatives that were not available to the historically-limited world of their time and enabled them to escape from the imprisoning effects of their contemporary religious controversies by bringing a productive past that still lived in the Church. It brought a critical stance to those controversies of their time and enabled them to render the more recent answers of their time questionable and not to be accepted simply as given. As this book has demonstrated, the appropriation of the *ekklesiastikon phronema,* the ecclesiastical mind, enhanced the life of Anglicanism beyond the increasingly closed options of the sixteenth, seventeenth and nineteenth centuries. This was by no means regression into conservatism, a simple conservation of the past. These theologians were concerned with the future, to find in the past the way into the future by reading and listening attentively to the Fathers in order to find where they dissented from the Reformation controversies, and what they offered as constructive solutions, for therein may lie their relevance.

What results, particularly so in the Carolines and the Tractarians, is a contextualization of the patristic mind within the parameters of an English theology, as they used the thought and piety of the Fathers within the structure of their own theological vision. This brought the resources of the past into a positive and critical relationship with their own particular historical context for the sake of the future, but allowed that historical context to be critical of these same resources from the past. In their *return to the Fathers,* they demonstrated how the theology of their day could overcome its inner weakness and deficiencies. This was not done by a mere repetition of the Fathers or the transforming of them into a purely formal and infallible authority, and their theology into a patristic scholasticism, which Schmemann warns against in the introduction to this book. What we find in this Anglican appropriation is the recovery of the spirit of the Fathers, of the secret inspiration that made them true witnesses of the Church, and the acquiring of their mind. They recovered and made their own the experience of the Church not as mere 'Institution, doctrine or system', but as the all-transforming *life,* the passage into the reality of redemption and transfiguration. They saw that you cannot enter into the truth of Christianity apart from its history, and that the historical *condition* of Christian truth is not something that starts in Bethlehem and ends on Calvary. It applies equally to the Church, the Body of Christ, 'which he launched into history no less unreservedly than the Body of his flesh'.[13] It placed them in the larger room of the Christian centuries and freed them from the solitary confinement of the present.

As a result they avoided what has become the defect of so much theology today, the division between theology and spirituality. It is a dissociation between the mind and the heart, between thought and feeling, that has its roots in what T. S. Eliot described as 'a dissociation of sensibility', and is damaging to theology, as Andrew Louth writes,

> ... for it threatens in a fundamental way the whole fabric of theology in both its spiritual and intellectual aspects. Cut off from the movement of the heart towards God, theology finds itself in a void – for where is its object? Where is the God with whom it concerns itself? Even if God can be reached by reason, even if natural theology is possible, real theology could never be confined within such narrow limits. For theology (as opposed to religious studies) concerns itself with the Scriptures, with tradition, with the development of dogma, with the history of the Church, all of which is natural enough to the Christian, to one who *believes*. But belief, faith, is not a purely rational exercise; it involves, as an indispensable element, the response of the will or the heart to the One in whom we believe. Cut off from this, theology has to justify itself, not directly, but indirectly, as an indispensable part of European culture.[14]

Louth goes on to say that such a division undermines Christian prayer too, in its movement of the heart towards God's love revealed in Jesus Christ, because in being severed from theology prayer loses its objectivity, its concern with reality. 'Prayer is engagement with the object of our faith, an object which is in some way apprehended or known; and in such cognitive engagement the *mind* is involved. Faith is, to use the traditional phrase, *cum assensione cogitare, to think* with assent. We do not just feel something in prayer, we know something.'

Being steeped in patristic divinity, our divines avoided this contemporary phenomenon of a dissociation between thought and feeling. In the characteristic phrase of Michael Ramsey they 'did their theology to the sound of church bells' because they understood the issue of theology to be, 'not only one of intellectual clarity but of a union of human lives with God in the way of holiness'. It was in the many-sided thought and sanctified divinity of the undivided Church that they found a theology that knew of no such dissociation between thought and feeling, between theology and spirituality. There they discovered that *theologia,* in its strictest sense is discourse about God, in his being and relations, the doctrine of the Trinity. In a wider sense it means also contemplation of the Trinity, because, as Evagrius claimed, the one who prays is a theologian and the theologian is one who prays, or in the words of John Klimakos, 'the climax of purity is the beginning of theology'. The theologian lives in the Trinity. For '*theologia* is the apprehension of God by a man restored to the image and likeness of God, and within this apprehension there can be discovered two sides (though there is something artificial about such discrimination): what *we* call the intellectual and the affective.'[15]

Returning to prescriptive sources

As Gareth Bennett told us in the *Crockford Preface* for 1989, it is the deliberate rejection of this balanced synthesis, the distancing of the modern church from what had been regarded as its prescriptive sources and the rejection of 'living in a tradition', that has produced the crisis within Anglicanism. So we are told that 'we must live amid the ruins of past doctrinal and ecclesiastical systems, looking to the Scriptures only for themes and apprehensions which may inform our own individual exploration of the mystery of God'. In consequence God and his Church become imprisoned within the relativism of the present and accommodated to the transitory fashion of the political correctness of the age. An American theologian comments, 'Any consensus in theology today begins with the rejections of the classical Christian tradition as this is generally known in Western Culture', so that it has a strongly reductionist flavour that is consequent upon modern theologians making the 'canons of science' and 'critical history' normative criteria.[16] If revelation, worship and tradition are the 'fundamental womb' in which theology is conceived and developed, and where it flourishes, then the modern theologian needs to be reminded that

> A true and truly Christian theology will surely be deeply rooted in revelation and tradition, in worship and prayer in the Christian community, in compassion and service in the world, in fear and trembling before the wonder of the Christian gospel, and in humble dependence on the grace and agency of the Holy Spirit. Yet precisely these notes are the ones missing from the prevailing canons of theological discourse.[17]

Modern theology's extreme this-worldliness with its self-imposed parameters, shifts human life away from its context in God's purposes into the meaninglessness of nothing more ultimate than the ever-changing and relative arrangements of the human enterprise itself. The legacy of the Enlightenment, that naïve confidence in the autonomy of human reason that can operate independently of the effects of personal disposition, social context, cultural background and religious community, is challenged not only by post-modern philosophy and hermeneutics but also by classical Christianity.[18] Robert L. Wilken writes

> In many fields of creative work, immersion in tradition is the presupposition for excellence and originality. Think, for example of music ... I am regularly struck how they [musicians] speak with such respect of their teachers and masters, and how to a person they learned to play the piano by first playing in someone else's style or learned to blow the trumpet by imitating Louis Armstrong or someone else. Similarly, one is impressed with how often a folk singer like Jean Redpath speaks about tradition as a necessary condition for making and singing folk music. How often we are admonished not to let the old traditions be forgotten. Why? Surely not for historical or archaeological reasons, but because musicians, like painters and writers and sculptors, know in their fingertips or vocal chords or ears that imitation is the way to excellence and originality.[19]

The same must be true of theology. As Thomas Oden playfully puts it, watching the Church Fathers 'play theology is like watching Willie Mays play center field or Duke Ellington play "Sophisticated Lady"'.[20] Wilken is convinced that the way we learn to think is by reading good thinkers and letting their thoughts form our thoughts. This means submitting ourselves to learn from writers who have demonstrated their trustworthiness over decades and centuries as reliable interpreters of God in Christ's mysterious presence in the history of the world.

> Christians, Wilken insists, will find their identity only by recalling an unimagined world, a world that pursued truth "with the mind in the heart" – a community that insisted that how and what one thinks, who one is, and how one lives are an inseparable whole – facilitating a holistic reading of reality frequently reflected in the writings of the Church Fathers.[21]

Only a return to prescriptive sources in the *mind of the Fathers* will lift us into a larger room and raise us, like Hooker and Andrewes, above the controversies and theological fashions of our age. Here in the larger room of the Christian centuries in which the Holy Catholic

Church lives, we will find what will enrich, invigorate, give beauty, proportion, and force to our theology. Our vision will portray the Christian faith as an integral whole with its centre in the Incarnation, the Church as an organism where dogma, prayer and life are one whole, and where, in the words of Michael Ramsey 'the issue of theology is not only one of intellectual clarity but a union of human lives with God in the way of holiness'. Renewal in catholic truth will only come from a reconstruction of the *One Holy Catholic and Apostolic Church,* not through the construction of some external religious or cultural form, or ideology. It can come only when the living pattern of catholic truth is embodied in people imbued with the life-giving power of God, who in Christ has taken our human nature, redeemed it and perfected it for ever. The *lex credendi,* tradition, catholic dogma and doctrine, is not a backcloth of abstract theory to be adapted according to the fashions of the Age. This is the *reality* in which we live, *the union of human lives with God in the way of holiness.* Through it we see refracted the meaning of all human existence, the economies of creation and redemption, and hence the need to know this truth in the personal depth of our being, for it is the Christ of the apostles as the life-giving Spirit, active in the history of humankind and leading it to conformity with his spiritual and perfect form. Here in the Mystery of Christ, present in the history of humankind and the Eucharist, is where catholic truth is found, so that our proper *Sitz-im-Leben* is the life of grace in which we as catholic persons need to grow and develop to the full potential of our humanity. This is saving life, the catholic process, in which men and women are gradually transfigured and saved, not from the world, but in and with the world through the Church. It is walking in the way of holiness as we live in and serve the catholicity of the Church.

If the achievements of autonomous reason have produced a sense of meaninglessness and hopelessness, then we need to look beyond the plausibility structure of modern thought and find a new starting point which begins as an act of trust in divine grace. In this classical model for understanding is the basis for the renewal of our secularized culture, a way of understanding that does not claim to be demonstrable in terms of 'modern' thought and is not 'scientific' in the popular sense of that word. Rather is it centred in that divine revelation of God in Christ to which scripture witnesses and which the Fathers have interpreted that surely is the starting point for the exploration of the mystery of human life.

An appeal to the first six centuries

What this book has tried to demonstrate is that there can be no question that, subject always to the supreme authority of Scripture, our church appeals in defence of her doctrines and ceremonies to the ancient Fathers and to catholic antiquity. In the first public order on the subject issued after Elizabeth I's accession, the first six centuries are expressly mentioned as giving the standard to be kept in view, and Bishop Jewel and other authoritative writers adopted the appeal to that period. Admittedly, Andrewes appealed to four centuries, but this does not dismiss the larger limit as having authoritative recognition. This means that nothing can be accepted as truly Catholic which does not have the assent and observance of the Christian Church before the end of the sixth century. The crucial issue facing Anglicanism today is an arbitrary liberalism that exalts into traits of virtue the modern notions of 'inclusivity', 'plurality' and 'diversity' which are respectable terms for 'anything goes'. In a time such as this, when our church, in the words of one of our bishops to the author, 'has fallen captive to a hermeneutic of sociological reductionism', it becomes imperative to consider the fact that there are errors of doctrine, no less than faults of conduct, which no church can safely allow in its priests and members. The crucial question is, what are the limits beyond which toleration of such reductionism cannot be extended? On the basis of what has always been true liberality, a generosity of spirit, our church has always been emphatic about what was deemed essential, alongside leaving as open questions many matters on which there was no conciliar decision of the universal Church requiring acceptance of a particular belief under pain of anathema. At the same time, while condemning certain extreme positions, it allowed widely differing opinions which came between them as lawful.

This is the spirit of a true catholicism, a spirit our Reformers embodied in the canon of 1571, which required its priests to teach nothing but what is agreeable to Holy Scripture and what the catholic Fathers and ancient bishops have collected out of that said doctrine. Herein is an expression of true catholicism, the catholicism of the primitive church owned by the Church of England and in which is delineated the limits of toleration in doctrine and manners. Those limits are bound by the Creeds sanctioned by the Ecumenical Councils, and we have no right to deviate from the sense intended by their authors. Nor must we be undermined by a cultural determinism that clamours for what is insidiously described as a 'restatement' of truth, or the emasculating of truth to accommodate political correctness. An essential ingredient of our claim to be catholic requires an obedience to something much larger than ourselves, what may be described as our ancient catholic Mother, while at the same time Reformation rather than innovation emancipates us from any narrower obligations. Our formularies encapsulate for us those great outlines of Scriptural and catholic truth and within those outlines our church abstains from exercising authority over us. While the canon of 1571 speaks of this, a canon of 1603 cautions us not to depart from the churches of Italy, France, Spain and Germany, except in those particulars 'wherein they were fallen, both from themselves in their ancient integrity and from the Apostolic Churches which were their first founders'. Our catholicity is indissolubly bound up with the *phronema* or *mind* of the Fathers, which in essence was a scriptural mind, and, as stated in the first chapter, it was this ecclesiastical mind that was appropriated by Anglicanism and made the basis of Christian living and the context of Christian thinking.

There are clues to what we mean by 'ancient' and its limits. As already stated, John Jewel defined these limits as the first six hundred years, and Hooker was in agreement. Andrewes fixed the limit of antiquity to four Councils and the first five hundred years, or maybe the limit can be extended to the breach between East and West. This appeal to the rock whence we were hewn is part of our origin and of which we have no reason to be ashamed. It is not an appeal to flawless centuries of church history, for there is no such age. As we have seen in previous chapters, the appeal was by no means to a mere formal principle mechanically applied. It embodied a critical discrimination and discernment, and the same goes for such an appeal in this present age, where we can no longer use the Bible precisely in the way Reformers, Carolines and Tractarians used it. What is most needed in our fragmented communion and disunited church is a principle that will be rallying and uniting. It was mentioned in Chapter 1 that every four years in Oxford, patristic scholars of many communions co-operate happily in conferences organized by Anglican scholars for international and ecumenical participants. Again, the presence of the Orthodox Church that has become a feature of life in the western world can help to balance and correct the western bias in Roman and Protestant theology.

We can never devote too careful study to the age of the giants of the Church, as we may call the great Fathers without exaggeration; to the great formative period of the Church's life; to the age in which Christian theology was only by degrees becoming stereotyped; to the age, above all, which brings us back, both in time and thought and language, nearest to the primitive source of our faith. Here, if anywhere, we may expect to discern principles of general application; here, if anywhere, we shall be able to test later developments, and to find guidance in later difficulties.

And yet even here we must be on our guard ... we are bound to follow out such rules of practice and to apply such principles as we discover, not as they were applied and followed out under the circumstances of those days, but as they ought to be applied and followed out under the altogether different circumstances of our own day. To apply them just as they stand would be in reality just as absurd as to adopt for present-day use the polity, or the food, or the dress of our Anglo-Saxon forbears.[22]

Bishop Collins goes on to point out that in engagement with the first six centuries we may not follow them in all points without hesitation, and that in some respects their best lesson for us is that of solemn warning. There are features of church life in the first six centuries that require study only so that we may avoid them as we listen to the warnings of ecclesiastical history. In this spirit let our method be to explore the Tradition and to bring back things old and new, things which have been lost or become obscured. The Fathers remain an authoritative reference point for the Church, even though today they may be ignored or despised. While recognizing that they require interpretation and need to be brought into a dialectic with modern thought, our concern should be the recovery of *the patristic mind,* the *ekklesiastikon phronema,* a neo-patristic synthesis rooted in that central vision of Christian faith, Jesus Christ, Incarnate, Crucified, Risen and Glorified. This will enable the recovery of what was always regarded as integral within Anglican theological method, a concern for church history and the 'proper', historical setting or context of the Bible, the living apostolic community, and will ensure, authoritatively, normatively and critically, the historic continuity of the apostolic community and her apostolic faith and praxis. Making this ecclesial dimension the basis of Christian living, and the context of Christian thinking, will not add anything to Scripture, but it is the only means to ascertain and to disclose more fully the true meaning of Scripture. Herein lay the seeds of reformation for our Reformers when in the face of a medieval scholasticism over-dependent on Aristotle, in which philosophical concepts were being used to interpret the Bible, they found that the Fathers breathed the very spirit of the Bible in a manner that was historical and exegetical and not systematic. In the face of the liberal scholasticism of today, where the concepts of secular philosophies are being used to interpret the Bible in order to harmonize it with the political correctness of the age, the Fathers can help us find the seeds of a new reformation and to beware of the dangers of a too-facile syncretism. Our hermeneutic must also include taking note of Anglican and other modern prophets, alongside the theologians of Orthodoxy in the West and the contribution of the Second Vatican Council on the role of the Church in the modern world.

Rediscovering the Fathers

When Thomas Oden came under the influence of patristic thought it dawned on him that theology must be done in the context of the worshipping community. In the Church's life and reflection he discovered certain constant themes and practices, 'a central "consensual" understanding of God's entry into history in Jesus Christ'. The history and tradition of the Church became a corrective to his tendency to idealize the innovative and the new.

> Then while reading Nemesius something clicked. I realised that I must listen intently, actively, without reservation. Listen in such a way that my whole life depended upon hearing. Listen in such a way that I could see telescopically beyond my modern myopia, to break through the walls of my modern prison, and actually hear voices from the past with different assumptions entirely about the world and time and human culture. Only then in my forties did I begin to become a theologian. Up to that time I had been teaching theology without having sufficiently met the patristic mentors who could teach me theology.[23]

Oden had experienced a 'redirection', 'a hermeneutical reversal' in which he 'learned to listen to pre-modern texts.' From the Fathers he learned that hermeneutics could not be severed from character, disposition and obedience, a patristic emphasis essential for the theologian. Listening to a text and obedience to a text became for Oden 'the most important single lesson I have learned hermeneutically ... Carl Rogers taught me to trust my experience. The ancient Christian writers taught me to trust that Scripture and tradition would transmute my experience'.[24]

As a result Oden realized that Jewish and Christian believers have been through many modernities, and the present is not the first or the only one. 'Human beings see the river of time from a particular vantage point on the bank, but God, as if from above, sees the entire river in its whole extent, at every point, and simultaneously' (Hilary, *On the Trinity*, 12).

> The central feature of Jewish and Christian consciousness in the postmodern situation is the profound rediscovery of the texts of long-ignored classical Jewish and Christian traditions, rabbinic and patristic. For Christians, this means especially the eastern church Fathers of the first five Christian centuries. The methodological fulcrum that began changing this trajectory is attentiveness to the written Word, and its most widely received early expositors.
>
> What is happening amid this historical situation is a return to the sacred texts of the early Christian Scripture and the exegetical guides of the formative period of its canonization and interpretation. Post-modern Christians are those who, having entered in good faith into the disciplines of modernity, and having become disillusioned with the illusions of modernity, are again studying the Word of God made known in history. It is attested by prophets and apostolic witnesses whose testimonies, letters and gospels have become canonical texts for the world-wide, multicultural, multigenerational remembering and celebrating community. Those who gave definitive form to the ecumenical interpretation of these texts are the patristic writers, four in the East (Athanasius, Basil, Gregory Nazianzen, and John Chrysostom), and four in the West (Ambrose, Augustine, Jerome, and Gregory the Great).[25]

Oden goes on to say that it is possible within the premises of post-modern consciousness to approach all this testimony and experience in a scientific way that is an objective, fair-minded enquiry. To be scientific and objective does not imply leaving out the object of the inquiry, God. This is Polanyi's point, that there is a personal participation of the knower in the act of knowing which does not make our understanding subjective, because this fusion of the personal and the objective demonstrates that all knowing of any kind involves personal commitment and the acceptance of personal responsibility for one's beliefs. Hence, the best way to take God seriously is to take seriously the historical concretions of consciousness – prayers, texts, liturgies, spiritual disciplines – which have emerged out of the worship of God.

Many would agree that the present is the threshold of a new era but, as Oden points out, disagreement will come when trying to define precisely what is passing away, what is emerging and how Christian orthodoxy and catholicity relate to both. What he describes as a world that is passing away 'is the world dominated by the failed ideas of autonomous individualism, narcissistic hedonism, reductive naturalism, and absolute moral relativism.'[26] It has been a world dominated by 'Nietzschean relativistic nihilism, Marxist social planning, Freudian therapy, and Bultmannian historicism'.[27] The children of the world they spawned struggle to survive in single-parent hovels with latchkey kids shaped morally by television,[28] while others die on the streets of San Francisco. Russia and America may differ in many ways but in his book, *Two Worlds, Notes on the Death of Modernity in America and Russia,* Oden defines *The Mod Rot* as the unhappy aroma of dying modernity. He dates the modern period from the French Revolution in 1789, to the Fall of the Berlin Wall in 1989. His thesis is that in both societies Enlightenment optimism, scientism and hedonism are decaying, and this finds expression in a *mod rot* penetrating all political barriers and economic histories. He was invited to Russia by the Department for the Comparative Study of Religion, the former Department for Atheism at Moscow State University, to lecture on Christianity. This experience stimulated these reflections. Like America, Russia suffers from the rapidly deteriorating assumptions of modernity and no longer actively resists religion but is looking for ways 'to incorporate the vitality of religious understandings and communities and sacramental life into its common ethos'. They found Oden's description of modernity, the emergence of post-modern consciousness and the vitality of Orthodox Christianity within the post-modern consciousness, a plausible and accurate reflection of many analogous aspects of their own experience. What he sees in these two worlds, is a perishing modernity and an emerging post-modernity and his concern is to demonstrate how classical Christianity can endure and maintain its perennial appeal.

He believes in the rediscovery of ancient ecumenical Christianity as a new possibility for dialogue between Russian and American university studies in religion, because underneath the substratum of Russian social consciousness lies a deep and secret formation of one thousand years by the patristic writers of the first five centuries that is only now beginning to be rediscovered west of Geneva and Rome. Oden provides bibliographical evidence for this rediscovery of the ancient Christian writers, especially Eastern Church Fathers, which is emerging within contemporary Christian scholarship including that of evangelical Protestantism.[28]

> The renewal of the study of patristic sources brings the American tradition suddenly closer to the Eastern tradition, and thus inevitably closer to the Russian tradition and its related Slavic variations. This long-postponed inquiry is as inviting to post-liberal Americans as it is to post-atheistic Soviets. It offers a trans-Protestant and postmodern basis upon which the future of religious dialogue might proceed in our two diverse societies. This opens up a new avenue of dialogue reaching across the gutted barriers of what used to be called the cold war.
>
> I do not wish to idealize the Eastern patristic tradition, but simply to recognize it as the base layer of all subsequent Christian exegesis and moral reflection. The major doctors of the West from Jerome to Gregory the Great followed after and gratefully received the major orthodox formularies of the East. Remember that all of the ecumenical councils occurred east of Athens. Later writers looked east to reform the West. So it happened repeatedly with the Renaissance and Anglican forms of patristic renewal. It continues to happen today.[29]

Oden goes on to point out that what is being rediscovered in these patristic writers is a 'well-formed and exquisitely nuanced hermeneutic'. What they have to say is clear and well-grounded textually in the biblical tradition, while they themselves are philosophically sophisticated. At the same time they are not afraid to dialogue with culture and accept responsibility for cultural formation and nation-building. 'And they take us much more substantively into ecumenical dialogue than current dickerings of ecumenical bureaucrats'. It was Léon Bloy who believed that the Church in the West will be renewed by the Russian Church that has suffered in *fire and water*. Now we have substantial new common ground for what Oden describes as 'the dialogue of the Paleo-ecumenism' that can become our future. All the Oecumenical Councils took place east of Athens but the major doctors of the West from Jerome to Gregory the Great received and handed on the *paradosis*, the major orthodox formularies of the East. Later writers looked east to reform the West. It happened repeatedly with the Renaissance and we have seen in the Anglican Church that these same patristic writers have provided a way of theology in which she was rooted that has been a constant inspiration and guide to renewal.

We need to let these Fathers speak again, Ignatius, Irenaeus,

Athanasius, the Cappadocians, Ambrose and Augustine, Anselm
and Aquinas, the Reformers, Jewel and Hooker, Andrewes and
Laud, John Keble and the Tractarians. They can speak to us today
with that same sharpness and contemporaneity, for their writings
are timeless, dynamic and always contemporary. Let us invite the
piety and thought of these Fathers into the structure of our own
theological vision and exposition by emulating the Carolines and
Tractarians whose theological procedure could not be described as
simplistic, and see what happens in the different perspective of
today's society and scholarship.

> In our approach another principle of our hermeneutic should
> be to avoid rushing in with the question of relevance, but instead
> to gain a strong or significant irrelevance, since relevance and
> significance are not the same. Relevance here means relevance
> to modern questions. The questions emerge from the modern
> discussion, and so they exist as *a priori* guides in the historical
> search, telling us beforehand what to see. How can we judge
> whether these questions are good guides? Are they well-formu-
> lated? Are there deeper questions?

These questions are raised by the authors of *The Pastor, Readings
from the Patristic Period.*[30] The authors are concerned with the ' how-
to' of pastoral care and the component elements in the process of
clergy character formation. What is taught is either from a strictly
scriptural base, or 'from a base of modern psychological and sociological theory as it has been appropriated by the Church, or
through a combination of scripture and modern scientific insight'.
Their regret is that rarely in the teaching of pastoral formation is
there direct reference to 'the fascinating history and tradition of
the early church'. What is sadly missing is 'the traditional balance
of the trialogue of revelation among Scripture *and* reason *and*
tradition ... Tradition is the bridge that spans Scripture and
contemporary scientific insight, and pastoral theory and praxis are
impoverished by having lost touch with the Church's valuable
heritage of tradition and time-hallowed practical experience'.[31]

> A historical approach that patiently attends to the thick descrip-
> tion of the individuality of a subject will let its questions emerge
> naturally from the data observed. Since our texts were written
> fifteen hundred years ago, and over 5,000 miles away, the emer-
> gent questions may well be irrelevant. But for this very reason
> they will also be independent of the modern discussion. As inde-
> pendent voices they can cross-examine and critique the

presuppositions of our modern concerns. The historian's task in this programme is to establish a strong independent voice and, as far as possible, to keep it true to itself so that it can speak not only to our questions but also against them. Such a programme is more difficult, more dangerous, and more interesting.[32]

This was the conclusion to which Keble, Newman, and Pusey came in their approach to the Fathers. They found that they could no longer read the Fathers obliquely through the restrictive parameters of the Reformers and Caroline divines, to defend the Anglican formularies against Rome, as had traditionally been the Anglican way of reading the Fathers. They discovered that the true way of interpreting the Fathers is to summon them before themselves instead of approaching them in order to make them evidence for modern dogmas. Unless one throws one's mind upon the text without restrictive parameters their sense will be missed. Reading the Fathers properly means to read them in their proper catholic context, their own *Sitz-im-Leben*, the life of grace. This can never be 'restrictive, antithetical, polemical, or dialectical, but holistic, constructive, creative and liberating, because it is imbued with the virtue and humility and free submission to the power and grace of God, which constitutes the unfailing foundation of man and his world'.[33]

The Fathers will speak to an issue facing us that is far bigger than the saving of the Church of England. In the face of today's arbitrary liberalism, what we are being called upon to save is the Apostolic Faith and Order of the Church for which Ignatius died. It will challenge the uncritical assumptions of much contemporary ecumenism and not be instantly popular, but in its appeal to Scripture and antiquity it will face it with something deeper. At the same time it will show us how theology can, and cannot, be influenced by the culture of the age. In other parts of the world there are other Christians facing this same liberalism in their own churches, who share our concern. Is God leading us into a new kind of unity with such Christians? Will this be a faithful remnant in which the world will see what it desires to see, a reintegrated and holy Church which reflects the oneness and unity of the Blessed Trinity, because it is rooted in the Apostolic Faith and Order? If this Third Millennium is going to be a time of transformation, then the reintegration of the Church should be our priority, and individual churches should resolve to avoid doctrinal 'space-flights' and unilateral decisions that erect further obstacles to unity. Such unilateral action by individual churches only betrays the fact that unity is not their priority. For the sake of unity John Bramhall was prepared to accept the reducing of the papacy to the primitive form, and the papal court to be regulated by the Canons of the Fathers, which was the sense of the Councils of Constance and Basle: then the reduction of the Creed or necessary points of faith to what they were in the first four Ecumenical Councils, admitting no additional articles but only necessary explications and all things that cause offence to be removed. In such a disposition of humility lies a willingness to admit that our own self-estimation is often inflated and exaggerated. To betake ourselves to the Fathers to listen in humility rather than look through the restrictive parameters of the Roman Church, the Greek Church, the Anglican Church, Protestantism, or a myopic modernism, can instantly alter the scene.

> We see that the diversities of doctrine and organisation, which seem at first sight to enrich our western life, are really an impoverishment. For each sect or confessional group has a partial view of the truth and owes its distinctiveness to the fact that others also have partial views. Each is right when it points out what the others lack; but each is open to a similar criticism from the others. And where each has some things and is wanting in others, no one has the fullness of Christian faith and life. That is the true meaning of the fragmentation of the West.[34]

Despite this fragmentation of the West, and the indigenous loyalties to what has been received in *Ecclesia Graeca, Ecclesia Romana, Ecclesia Anglicana* and Western Protestantism, this being granted,

> ... the truly 'loyal' member will be just that one who is striving to see beyond the present state of his Church to something richer and truer. Such a Church in effect appeals from itself as at present informed to itself as better informed, in the future, and must be constantly consulting those sources from which that better information may be expected to come. The official formularies of the Church of England and its tradition of theological method are in accord with this requirement; for the appeal to Scripture and the appeal to the Fathers both leave room for reinterpretation and adjustment as the Bible and the Fathers come to be better understood.[35]

Derwas Chitty writes:

> I must content myself now with urging the Orthodox to realize to the full their vocation – that in their tradition they have the

answer to modern science and social theory, the way of union for the Church, and the key to the world's salvation: and with urging my brother English, of whatever party or denomination they may now be, to use this light to rediscover the same treasure hidden in our own past, in the days when the One Christ first came to our forefathers. I am *not* urging this as a means to outward unity. That would be a joy and a strong weapon: but even when we have attained explicit unity of Faith sufficient for it, it is not unlikely that international politics would still, in one way or another, long hinder its attainment. No – it is simply for the conversion of ourselves, of our country, and of the world that we must act upon what we have discovered.

Here I must bring you to earth. For such action must, among other things, involve our seriously considering a revision, in several respects, of our teaching, and our liturgical and devotional practice. In some cases, this may mean a return from modern 'Anglo-catholic' practice to something more like the older ways of the Church of England. In others, points may need to be stressed which have been much longer forgotten.[36]

Surely this was the primary concern of the Tractarians, so that despite their mistakes they may well be at least the starting point for rediscovering the significance of the Fathers today. Herein lies a way towards that authentic note of a western Orthodoxy, catholic Christianity, with a western patriarchate in Rome, alongside others, or a Primacy, and all for the sake of unity. For the content and significance of the Christian experience preserved in this Apostolic Faith and Order transcends all individual perceptions and defies all final rational analysis. For it contains within itself a truth more adequate than the world's own and therein lies its authority and influence. It comes in all its saving power to identify with the world, but as soon as the world attempts to accommodate and trim that Apostolic Faith and Order to its own limited insights, it is lost, and the Church with the world ends up like a ship aground on rocks. The Fathers in every age have been aware of this and that the only way of salvation for a shipwrecked Church and world is to be conformed to the Eucharistic self-giving of God. Let this be our ministry of reconciliation, the way for people of the tradition today, living and working for the reintegration of the whole Church 'Eastern, Western, our own'. In this Third Millennium we will need to hear less of individual denominations and more of the *Una Sancta*, the *One, Holy, Catholic and Apostolic Church,* in whose catholicity all our fragmentation can be made whole.

The only reality that can illuminate our troubled times and give meaning and reality to the irrationality of our confused age is the *One Holy Catholic and Apostolic Church,* the *'little leaven'.*

Today more than at any other time our personal existence must be anchored in the local parish. The truth of the Church, the reality of salvation, the abolishment of sin and death, the victory over the irrational in life and history, all these for Orthodox derive from the local parish, the actualization of the Body of Christ and the Kingdom of the Father, the Son and the Holy Spirit. The liturgical unity of the faithful has to be the starting point of all things for which we hope: the transformation of the impersonal life of the masses into a communion of persons, the authentic and genuine (rather than the merely theoretical and legal) observance of social justice and the deliverance of work from the bondage of mere need and its transformation into an engagement of personal involvement and fellowship. Only the life of the parish can give a priestly dimension to politics, a prophetic spirit to science, a philanthropic concern to economics, a sacramental character to love. Apart from the local parish all these are but an abstraction, naïve idealism, sentimental utopianism. But within the parish there is historical actualization, realistic hope, dynamic manifestation.[37]

Notes

1. A. M. Ramsey, 'The Ancient Fathers and Modern Anglican Theology', *Sobornost,* Series 4: No. 6, Winter–Spring 1962, pp. 292–3.
2. H. R. McAdoo, *Anglican Heritage: Theology and Spirituality* (Canterbury Press, Norwich, 1991), pp. 101–2.
3. A. M. Ramsey, *From Gore to Temple* (Longmans, London, 1960), p. ix.
4. A. M. Ramsey, *The Anglican Spirit,* ed. Dale Coleman (SPCK, London, 1991).
5. William Beveridge, translated from the Preface to *Codex Canonum Ecclesiae Primitivae vindicatus ac illustratus, Autore Gulielmo Beveregio, Ecclesiae Anglicanae presbytero* (London, 1678). Published as an Introduction in the Latin/English edition of Vincentius Lirinensis, *For the Antiquity and Universality of the Catholic Faith against the Profane Novelties of All heretics,* p. ix.
6. E. G. Knapp-Fisher, *Where the Truth is Found* (Collins /Fontana, Glasgow, 1975), p. 13.
7. *Ibid.* p. 19.
8. E. L. Mascall, *Theology and History,* (Faith Press, London, 1962), p.5.
9. *Ibid.* p. 5.
10. *Ibid.* p. 6.

11. R. J. Bauckham, 'Tradition in Relation to Scripture and Reason' in *Scripture, Tradition and Reason, A Study in the Criteria of Christian Doctrine*, eds. B. Drewery and R. J. Bauckham (T. & T. Clark, Edinburgh, 1988), p. 133.
12. *Ibid.* p. 134.
13. Mascall, *ibid.* p. 7.
14. A. Louth, *Discerning the Mystery* (Clarendon Press, Oxford, 1983), pp. 2–3.
15. *Ibid.* p. 4.
16. William J. Abraham, 'Oh God, Poor God – The State of Contemporary Theology', *The Reformed Journal* 40, no. 2 (February 1990), p. 19. Cited by Christopher A. Hall, *Reading Scripture with the Church Fathers* (IVP, Illinois, 1998), p. 19.
17. *Ibid.* p. 20
18. *Ibid.* p. 24
19. Robert L. Wilken, 'Remembering the Christian Past' (Grand Rapids, Michigan, Eerdmans, 1995), p. 171, cited by Hall, *ibid.* p. 28.
20. *Ibid.* p. 28
21. cited by Hall, *ibid.* p. 28.
22. W. E. Collins, 'Sermon by the Bishop of Gibraltar', in *The Conditions of Church Life in the First Six Centuries* (SPCK, London, 1905), pp. 48–9.
23. Thomas Oden, 'Word of Life', pp. 219–20, cited by Hall, *ibid.* p. 18.
24. *Ibid.* p. 18.
25. Thomas C. Oden, *Two Worlds, Notes on the death of Modernity in America and Russia* (IVP, Illinois, 1992), pp. 53–4.
26. *Ibid.* pp. 54–5.
27. *Ibid.* pp. 36–7.
28. *Ibid.* p. 58.
28. *Ibid.* p. 173–5.
29. *Ibid,* pp. 59–60.
30. P. L. Cuthbertson and A. B. Shippee, *The Pastor, Readings from the Patristic Period* (Fortress Press, Minneapolis, 1990), p. 3.
31. *Ibid,* Preface, pp. xi–xii.
32. *Ibid,* p. 3.
33. Dragas, *ibid,* p. 109.
34. H. A. Hodges, *Anglicanism and Orthodoxy, A Study in Dialectical Churchmanship* (SCM Press, London 1957), pp. 50–1.
35. *Ibid,* p. 41.
36. Derwas J. Chitty, 'Orthodoxy and the Conversion of England', published by the Anglo-Orthodox Society (Colchester, 1990), p. 1.
37. C. Yannaras, 'Orthodoxy and the West', in *Orthodoxy Life and Freedom, Essays in Honour of Archbishop Iakovos* ed. A. J. Philippou (Studion Publications, Oxford, 1973), p. 145.

Bibliography

Abbreviations

ANF   *Ante-Nicene Fathers.*
NPNF   *The Nicene and Post-Nicene Fathers.*
LACT   *The Library of Anglo-Catholic Theology* (1841).
SPCK   Society for Promoting Christian Knowledge.
DNB   *Dictionary of National Biography* .

The Books of Common Prayer 1549–1662.
C. J. Abbey and J. H. Overton, *The English Church in the Eighteenth Century* (Longmans, Green & Co, London, 1887).
G. W. O. Addleshaw, *The High Church Tradition* (Faber & Faber Ltd, London, 1941).
A. M. Allchin, *Participation in God* (DLT, London, 1988).
Lancelot Andrewes, *Works* (*LACT*, Parker, Oxford, 1870).
Lancelot Andrewes, *The Devotions of Bishop Andrewes,* translated by J. H. Newman (Parker & Co, Oxford, 1886).
John Baines, *The Life of William Laud, Archbishop of Canterbury* (Joseph Masters, London, 1855).
John Barbeyrac, 'The Preface', *The Law of Nature and Nations in Eight Books,* by Baron Pufendorf, translated from the Latin by Basil Kennett DD, Sometime President Corpus Christi College Oxford. 'The Preface' contains *An Historical and critical Account of the Science of Morality and the Progress it has made in the world, from the earliest times down to the publication of this work,* translated from the Latin by Mr Carew of Lincoln's Inn (fifth edition, London, 1769).
G. Battiscombe, *John Keble, A Study in Limitations* (Constable, London, 1963).
A. Believer, *The Spirit of Infidelity Detected* (T. Payne, London, 1723).
William Beveridge, *Works* (*LACT*, Parker, Oxford, 1842–6), 12 vols.
Joseph Bingham, *The Antiquities of the Christian Church,* vols. i and ii

(Chatto & Windus, London, 1875). Other editions were published and are listed in his entry in the *DNB*.

J. H. Blunt, ed., *Annotated Book of Common Prayer* (Rivingtons, London, 1884).

J. J. Blunt, *An Introduction to a Course of Lectures on the Early Fathers* (Cambridge University Press, Cambridge, 1840).

J. J. Blunt, *On the Right Use of the Early Fathers* (John Murray, London, 1857).

J. E. Booty, *John Jewel as Apologist of the Church of England* (SPCK, London, 1963).

J. E. Booty, 'Richard Hooker', in *The Spirit of Anglicanism*, ed. W. J. Wolf (T. & T. Clark Ltd, Edinburgh, 1979).

E. C. E. Bourne, *The Anglicanism of William Laud* (SPCK, London, 1947).

John Bramhall, *Works* (*LACT*, Parker, Oxford, 1842–5), 5 vols.

A. G., 'John Bramhall', *DNB*, vol. ii (Oxford University Press, Oxford, 1917), p. 1111.

W. J. Brown, *Jeremy Taylor* (SPCK, London, 1925).

George Bull, *Defence of the Nicene Creed*, vols. i and ii (*LACT*, Parker, Oxford, 1851).

J. W. Burgon, *Lives of Twelve Good Men*, (John Murray, London, 1891).

J. Byrom, *The Glowing Mind* (SLG Press, Oxford, 1991).

A. C. Capey, ed. *Thomas Cranmer: Two Studies* (first published SPCK, London, 1956), with a new Preface by A. C. Capey (The Brynmill Press, Doncaster, 1989).

S. C. Carpenter, *Eighteenth Century Church and People* (John Murray, London, 1959).

Henry Cary, *Testimonies of the Fathers of the First Four Centuries to the Doctrine and Discipline of the Church of England as Set Forth in the Thirty-Nine Articles* (D. A. Talboys, Oxford, 1835).

William Cave, *The Lives of the Apostles and the Two Evangelists St. Mark and St. Luke*, revised by Henry Cary (J. Vincent, Oxford, 1840).

William Cave, *The Lives of the Most Eminent Fathers of the Church that flourished in the first Four Centuries*, vols i and ii, revised by Henry Cary (J. Vincent, Oxford, 1840).

J. H. O., 'William Cave', *DNB*, vol. iii, p. 1250.

Owen Chadwick, *The Spirit of the Oxford Movement Tractarian Essays* (Cambridge University Press 1990).

Derwas J. Chitty, 'Orthodoxy and the Conversion of England', published by the Anglo-Orthodox Society (Colchester, 1990).

R. W. Church, 'Bishop Andrewes', *Pascal and Other Sermons* (Macmillan & Co, London, 1895).

R. W. Church, *The Oxford Movement, Twelve Years 1833–1845* (Macmillan & Co Ltd, London, 1897).

John Collinson, *A Key to the Writings of the Principal Fathers of the Christian Church who flourished during the First Three Centuries* (Bampton Lectures, 1813).

J. Coulson and A. M. Allchin, eds. *The Rediscovery of Newman.* (Sheed & Ward and SPCK, London, 1967).

Thomas Cranmer, *Works*, vol. ii, ed. J. E. Cox (Parker Society, Cambridge, 1846).

Works, On the Lord's Supper, ed. J. E. Cox (Parker Society, Cambridge, 1844).

F. L. Cross and E. A. Livingstone, eds. *The Oxford Dictionary of the Christian Church* 1st edn (Oxford University Press, London, 1957) and 3rd edn (Oxford University Press, 1997),

G. Cuming, *The Anglicanism of John Cosin* (Durham Cathedral Lecture, City Printing Works, Chester-le-Street, 1975).

P. L. Cuthbertson and A. B. Shippee, *The Pastor, Readings from the Patristic Period* (Fortress Press, Minneapolis, 1990).

John Daillé, *The Right Use of the Fathers* (John Martin, London, 1651).

Evan Daniel, *The Prayer Book , Its History, Language and Contents* (Gardner, Darton & Co, London, 1901).

G. D. Dragas, *Ecclesiasticus* (Darlington Carmel, Darlington, 1984).

G. E. Duffield, ed. *Scripture Tradition and Reason, A Study in the Criteria of Christian Doctrine*, (T. & T. Clark, Edinburgh, 1988).

G. E. Duffield, ed., *The Work of Thomas Cranmer*, Introduction by J. I. Packer (Courtenay Library of Reformation Classics, Sutton Courtenay Press, 1964).

A. S. Duncan-Jones, *Archbishop Laud* (Macmillan, London, 1923).

Richard Field, *Of the Church*, 3rd edn (Cambridge University Press, Oxford, 1835).

R. H., 'Richard Field', *DNB*, vol. vi, p. 1274.

G. Florovsky, *Bible, Church, Tradition: An Eastern Orthodox Perspective* (Nordland, Massachusetts, 1972).

W. H. Frere, *A History of the English Church in the Reigns of Elizabeth and James I.* 1558–1625 (Macmillan & Co, London, 1904).

W. H. Frere, *Bishop Lancelot Andrewes, as a Representative of Anglican Principles* (SPCK, London, 1897).

Henry Gee and W. J. Hardy, *Documents Illustrative of English Church History* (Macmillan & Co, London, 1896).

S. L. Greenslade, *The English Reformers and the Fathers of the Church*, An Inaugural Lecture as Regius Professor of Ecclesiastical History (Oxford, 1960).

John Griffiths, ed. *The Homilies*, (SPCK, 1908 edition, based on Clarendon Press, 1864).

Henry Hammond, *Works* (*LACT*, Oxford, 1847–50), 4 vols.

W. A. Hammond, *The Definitions of Faith and Canons of Discipline of the Six Oecumenical Councils, with the Remaining Canons of the Code of the Universal Church* (Parker, Rivingtons, London, 1843).

R. P. C. Hanson, The Bible as a Norm of Faith: An Inaugural Lecture as Lightfoot Professor of Divinity' (University of Durham, Titus Wilson & Son, Kendal, 1963).

H. A. Hodges, *Anglicanism and Orthodoxy, A Study in Dialectical Churchmanship* (SCM Press, London 1957.

R. T. Holtby, *Daniel Waterland* (C. Turnham & Sons, Carlisle, 1966).

Richard Hooker, *The Works of that Learned and Judicious Divine, Mr. Richard Hooker, with an Account of his Life and Death by Isaac Walton*, vols. i & ii (Oxford University Press, Oxford, 1850). The basis of this edition is the text of 1836.

Sir Edwyn Hoskyns, 'The Importance of the Parker Manuscripts', *Cambridge Sermons* (SPCK, London, 1938).

John Jewel, *Works*, The First Portion, ed. J. Ayre, (Parker Society, Cambridge, 1845). *Works*, The Third Portion, ed. J. Ayre (Parker Society, Cambridge, 1848).

B. J. Kidd, *The Thirty-Nine Articles* (Rivingtons, London, 1911).

E. G. Knapp-Fisher, *Where the Truth is Found* (Collins/Fontana, Glasgow, 1975).

William Laud, *Works* (*LACT*, Parker, Oxford, 1847–60), 8 vols.

H. P. Liddon, *Life of Edward Bouverie Pusey*, in 4 vols (Longmans, Green & Co, London, 1893–7).

J. B. Lightfoot, *Apostolic Fathers, Part II. S. Ignatius and S. Polycarp* 2nd edition, vol. i (Macmillan, London and New York, 1889).

N. Lossky, *Lancelot Andrewes the Preacher (1655–1626). The Origins of the Mystical Theology of the Church of England*, translated by Andrew Louth (Clarendon Press, Oxford, 1991).

N. Lossky, 'La Patristique dans la Predication Anglaise du debut du xxviie Siècle; Un Exemple, Lancelot Andrewes', *Extrait du Messager de L'Exarchat du Patriarche Russen en Europe Occidentale*. No. 105–8, janvier–décembre 1980–1981.

A. Louth, *Discerning the Mystery* (Clarendon Press, Oxford, 1983).

H. R. McAdoo, *The Spirit of Anglicanism* (A. & C. Black, London, 1965).

Douglas Macleane, *Lancelot Andrewes and the Reaction* (George Allen & Sons, London, 1910).

D. MacCulloch, *Thomas Cranmer* (Yale University Press, New Haven and London, 1996).

E. L. Mascall, 'Theology and History: An Inaugural Lecture as Professor of Historical Theology' (Faith Press, London, 1962)

A. J. Mason, *Thomas Cranmer* (Methuen, London, 1898).

E. C. Miller, Jr, *Toward a Fuller Vision* (Morehouse Barlow, Connecticut, 1984).

P. E. More and F. L. Cross, eds, *Anglicanism : The Thought and Practice of the Church of England, Illustrated from the Religious Literature of the Seventeenth Century* (SPCK, London, 1951).

J. B. Mozley, 'Archbishop Laud', in *Essays Historical and Theological* vol. i (Rivingtons, London, 1878), p. 106.

R. Nelson, *Life of George Bull* (London, 1713).

J. H. Newman, *Apologia Pro Vita Sua,*(Fount Paperback, William Collins Sons & Co Ltd,1977).

P. B. Nockles, *The Oxford Movement in Context.Anglican High Churchmanship 1760–1857* (Cambridge University Press, 1984).

Thomas Oden, *Two Worlds, Notes on the Death of Modernity in America and Russia* (IVP, Illinois, 1992).

S. L. Ollard and G. Crosse, eds. *Dictionary of English Church History* (Mowbrays, London, 1912).

R. L. Ottley, *Lancelot Andrewes* (Methuen & Co, London, 1905).

J. W. Packer, *The Transformation of Anglicanism 1643–1660* (Manchester University Press, 1969)

Thomas M. Parker, 'The Rediscovery of the Fathers in the 17th Century Anglican Tradition', J. Coulson and A. M. Allchin, eds. *The Rediscovery of Newman* (London, 1967).

John Pearson, *An Exposition of the Creed,* revised and corrected by E. Burton, sixth edition (Clarendon Press, Oxford, 1877).

F. S., ' John Pearson', *DNB*, vol. xv, p. 613.

John Pearson, *Vindiciae Epistolarum S. Ignatii* (*LACT*, Parker, Oxford, 1849).

A. M. Ramsey, 'The Ancient Fathers and Modern Anglican Theology', in *Sobornost*, Series 4: 6 (1962), pp. 289–94.

A. M. Ramsey, *The Gospel and the Catholic Church* (Longmans, London, 1959).

A. M. Ramsey, *From Gore to Temple* (Longmans, London, 1960).

A. M. Ramsey, *The Anglican Spirit,* ed. Dale Coleman (SPCK, London, 1991).

William Reeves, 'An Essay on the Right Use of the Fathers', in *Apostolic Fathers of the Second Century,* Wake and Burton, (John Grant, Edinburgh, 1909), p. 195.

J. Ridley, *Thomas Cranmer* (Clarendon Press, Oxford, 1962).

C. H. Sisson, ed., *Jeremy Taylor, Selected Writings* (Carcanet Press Ltd, Manchester, 1990).

J. C. Sladdon, *The Appeal to the Fathers in John Jewel, Bishop of Salisbury 1560–1571* (Texte u. Untersuchungen Studia Patristica vol. ix, p. 594 : Akademie-Verlac-Berlin, 1966).

W. M. Southgate, *John Jewel and the Problem of Doctrinal Authority* (Harvard University Press, 1962).

W. J. Sparrow-Simpson, 'The Study of the Fathers', in *The Priest as Student*, ed. H. S. Box, (SPCK, London, 1939).

Darwell Stone, *The Christian Church*, (Rivingtons, London, 1915).

Darwell Stone, *The Conditions of Church Life in the First Six Centuries* (SPCK, London, 1905).

S. Sykes and J. Booty, eds., *The Study of Anglicanism* (SPCK & Fortress Press, London, 1988). The Thirty-Nine Articles.

Herbert Thorndike, *Works* (*LACT*, Parker, Oxford, 1844–56), 6 vols.

J. B. M., ' Herbert Thorndike', *DNB*, vol. xix, p. 770.

L. S. Thornton, *Richard Hooker* (SPCK, London, 1924).

Daniel Waterland, 'The Use and Value of Ecclesiastical Antiquity', *Works,* vol.v (Clarendon Press, Oxford, 1823), *Works,* vols i and ii (Clarendon Press, Oxford 1823).

P. A. Welsby, *Lancelot Andrewes 1555–1626* (SPCK, London, 1958).

C. Wheatly, *A Rational Illustration of the Book of Common Prayer of the Church of England* (J. Bohn, London, 1898).

Chr. Wordsworth, *Theophilus Anglicanus* (Rivingtons, London, 1898).

Relevant Works of the Fathers have been consulted in the *ANF* and *NPNF* (Eerdmans Editions).

Index